09.

ONLINE SEARCHING:
Principles and Practice

ONLINE SEARCHING:
Principles and Practice

R. J. Hartley, E. M. Keen,
J. A. Large and L. A. Tedd

BOWKER
SAUR ●

London ● Melbourne ● Munich ● New Jersey

British Library Cataloguing in Publication Data

Online searching: principles and practice.
1. Libraries. On-line bibliographic information retrieval services.
I. Hartley, R. J.
025.5'24
ISBN 0-408-02290-6

Library of Congress Cataloging-in-Publication Data

Online searching: principles and practice / by R. J. Hartley . . . [et al.].
408 p.   21.5 cm.
Includes bibliographical references.
ISBN 0-408-02290-6
1. On-line bibliographic searching.   2. Data-base searching.
I. Hartley, R. J.
Z699.35.O55O54   1990
025.3'132—dc20   89-25275
                                                              CIP

Published by Bowker-Saur
60 Grosvenor Street, London W1X 9DA
Tel: +44(0)71 493 5841   Fax: +44(0)71 580 4089
Bowker-Saur is a division of REED REFERENCE PUBLISHING

Typeset by Dataset Marlborough Design, Oxford
Cover design by Calverts Press
Printed on acid-free paper
Printed and bound in Great Britain by
Biddles Ltd, Guildford and King's Lynn

About the Authors

Dick Hartley is currently lecturer in the Department of Information and Library Studies, The University College of Wales, United Kingdom (formerly the College of Librarianship, Wales, CLW). He teaches in the areas of information retrieval and online searching and his current research interest is in the improvement of subject searching in online public access catalogues.

Prior to teaching, he worked for more than 12 years in academic, public and national libraries. He is currently Chairman of the Aberystwyth Online User Group and Treasurer of the UK Online User Group.

Michael Keen is currently Senior Lecturer in the Department of Information and Library Studies, The University College of Wales, United Kingdom. He has long experience of teaching information retrieval principles stemming from his research on the second Aslib-Cranfield and SMART projects. Later work on index evaluation was funded by the British Library Research and Development Department (BLR & DD). He has recently been made a Fellow of the Institute of Information Scientists. He has developed a number of computer-based training aids for online searching and has published a number of papers on information retrieval research and search strategies.

Andy Large is now the Director of the Graduate School of Library and Information Studies at McGill University in Montreal, Canada. He is joint editor of *A Manual of Online Searching* and has written many articles and conference papers on online themes. Whilst at CLW his online research projects, funded by the BLR & DD and the European Space Agency Information Retrieval Services, concentrated on training and information retrieval software. He is joint editor of the quarterly journal *Education for Information*.

Lucy Tedd works as a freelance consultant, writer and some-time lecturer, and since 1984 has been editor of Aslib's journal on library automation, *Program*. In the mid-1970s she became involved with various BLR & DD funded projects on the teaching of online searching at CLW. In the early 1980s she continued work for the BLR & DD in co-ordinating a series of projects on the introduction of online searching in public libraries in Britain. She was the author of *An Introduction to Computer-based Library Systems* and joint author of *Online Searching – an introduction.* She has also written many articles, research reports and conference papers related to online searching.

Preface

Online searching is an increasingly commonplace activity. It is no longer confined to libraries and librarians but is practised by a growing number of end-users – scientists, managers, doctors, lawyers, accountants and so on. The range of information now available online and the ease of retrieving discrete elements from even the largest of databases makes it an attractive competitor to print on paper. *Online Searching: Principles and Practice* introduces the reader to this online world; it describes how to find information online, what kinds of information can be found and also how to operate an online service. Its definition of online encompasses a variety of services including videotex, CD-ROM, in-house systems and online public access catalogues (OPACs), and practical examples are used throughout to illustrate points of principle.

The first chapter provides an overview of online searching and introduces the reader to the logical steps involved in conducting an online search. Chapter 2 looks at the historical development and current status of the online industry, including a brief description of some major search services. The following four chapters then examine the ways in which information can be retrieved from online systems. Chapter 3 looks at databases and records and describes the way in which data records are arranged so as to facilitate flexible and rapid location of information from even the largest of databases. Chapter 4 introduces the basic searching concepts – how to find, examine and output information – while Chapter 5 considers more sophisticated retrieval facilities which can further benefit the searcher. The sixth chapter discusses search strategies – how to construct them and how to modify them in the light of search results.

Searching skills are to no avail if the online searcher does not know where to search. Chapter 7 therefore provides a survey of important databases in a variety of subject areas. The searcher – both professional intermediary and end-user – is the topic of Chapter 8: the search process is outlined and different kinds of software package intended to simplify online searching are evaluated. Chapter 9 looks at the management and training implications of introducing and operating an online information service.

Technological developments are making it more difficult to define online services as sharply as was once the case, and any consideration of online systems today must take account of a variety of services. Accordingly, Chapter 10 looks at in-house search systems, including CD-ROMs, Chapter 11 surveys videotex systems (viewdata and teletext) and Chapter 12 is concerned with OPACs.

Most commercially-available online systems are based upon boolean matching algorithms, but other matching mechanisms are available, some of which are examined in Chapter 13.

Online services operate in a wide variety of environments and an appendix presents a number of case studies from public, academic and special libraries and information units.

Online searching has generated a vast literature over the past 20 years and certainly too much for the newcomer readily to assimilate. The references and further readings at the end of each chapter have been selected to provide the reader with an introduction to this material.

The range of search services and databases now available throughout the world makes it impossible to provide examples from them all. Nevertheless, the book does include search examples from many of the major European and North American services and from a wide variety of databases including full-text, numeric and bibliographic. Wherever possible points are explained with reference to examples drawn from real searches.

Online Searching: Principles and Practice seeks, then, to offer a broad introduction to online searching and is aimed at anyone who wants to learn about online services and how to use them. It should be valuable to teachers, students and practitioners in the library and information fields, but equally it is intended for the growing numbers of end-users who wish to explore the possibilities which online searching affords them. A study of this book should equip the reader with the necessary background and confidence to take up searching, although practice will be needed to improve proficiency.

The authors would like to acknowledge the cooperation of the search services and database producers in allowing them to reproduce searching extracts. They would also like to thank the staff of the libraries and information units who agreed to be interviewed for the case studies and commented on draft versions,

although the responsibility for any misunderstandings or misinter-
pretations remains with the authors. Finally, they wish to register
thanks to their families for tolerating any domestic shortcomings
to which authors are all too prone, and to each other for working
as a team and remaining as firm friends at the end of this venture
as they were at its outset.

Aberystwyth
March 1989

Contents

Figures

Search Examples

Tables

Chapter 1

General Introduction

What is Online Searching?

The phrase 'online searching' is used in this book to describe the process of directly interrogating computer systems to resolve particular requests for information; the search will usually be conducted by means of a keyboard and screen, that communicate with a computer system, possibly remote, which contains files of data. The search process is dynamic and interactive: results are made available almost immediately to the searcher who can then, according to the usefulness or otherwise of the information retrieved, refine the original request and continue the interaction until the best result possible is obtained. Some searches may only take a few minutes: others may last half an hour or more. Some requests may be for one precise piece of information: others may seek a lot of relevant information or might need to browse through the stored data.

The last 30 years have not only seen computers replace manual methods of information retrieval but the introduction of many kinds of computer retrieval system. For example, some systems are located remotely from the users but can still be interrogated rapidly, even by many hundreds of users simultaneously, whereas others are installed locally in a library, office or workplace. The main types of online search system can be grouped and categorized in several ways, but this book distinguishes four main types: external search services, Compact Disc Read Only Memory (CD-ROMs) search systems, search systems in which the databases are stored locally, such as Online Public Access Catalogues, and videotex/teletext systems.

External search services

There are four components in a remote or external online search service:

1. Information providers (or database producers) who have supplied their data to a search service usually in the form of discrete records ready for computer processing.
2. A search service (or host) which has mounted these records as one or more databases on a large computer and supplied search software so that many users can access the records in the database at the same time.
3. Communications links which are available using both special networks and ordinary telephone lines.
4. A suitable computer terminal or workstation with the necessary communication facilities in order to provide access to the service.

The growth of these external search systems is described in Chapter 2 and the range of databases available for searching is discussed in Chapter 7. One of the most used services is Dialog Information Services, based in California but used throughout the world. It provides access to about 320 databases which, by early 1989, contained over 175 million records. Dialog provides a common way for searching any of these diverse databases by means of its own proprietary software. The telecommunications links are available for access to the search service from many countries. An example of a search on the SPORT database on Dialog is given later in this chapter. Other examples of external search services are BLAISE, the British Library Automated Information Service in London, ESA-IRS, the European Space Agency Information Retrieval Service in Frascati, Italy, and the ORBIT Search Service in McLean, Virginia.

In library and information units the activity known as online searching has conventionally meant searching external databases containing bibliographic records in the manner just outlined. A typical bibliographic database contains records describing published material, predominantly articles from journals, and often including a summary or abstract of the article's contents (as do the items retrieved from the search on the SPORT database). A more recent development is the provision of databases covering 'source' information such as data on chemical substances, companies or financial matters. These source databases may be available on general external services, such as Dialog, or more specialized services such as Pergamon Financial Data Service (PFDS), Telerate, Quotron, Dow Jones or Reuters. Some databases are very small and specialized, containing a few thousand records: others are large and general, with several million records. Some go back 25 years or more in coverage; others cover only more recent information.

CD-ROMs

Some databases are now becoming available on small very high density optical discs known as CD-ROMs: Compact Disc–Read Only Memory. Physically similar to the compact audio disc they are particularly appropriate for storing information that is not updated very frequently, such as dictionary and encyclopaedia entries, and retrospective files of bibliographic descriptions. The searching of the CD-ROM discs is carried out locally using special players that are linked to standard microcomputers, or using specially designed CD-ROM workstations. The supplier provides the search software to use on the microcomputer as well as the information on the CD-ROM. Thus no external search service has to be accessed and paid for, and no communication links are needed.

Each CD-ROM can store many thousands of short records, up to a quarter of a million per disc, and by early 1989 there were almost 400 commercially available CD-ROM databases. The Library Association in the UK is an example of an early information provider on this medium, with its LISA (Library and Information Science Abstracts) on CD-ROM distributed as one disc with software by Silver Platter Information. This means that LISA is now available in three media: in print form, in database form through external services (Dialog and ORBIT), and as a database on CD-ROM. More details about CD-ROMs will be found in later chapters and especially in Chapter 10.

Locally stored databases

In addition to searching publicly available databases either remotely or on CD-ROM, many libraries and information units are creating their own locally stored databases which are then searched online, usually via a local computer. A large number of software packages such as ASSASSIN, CAIRS, POLYDOC and STATUS have been developed for this purpose and microcomputer versions of these (ASSASSIN-PC, Micro-CAIRS, Mikro-POLYDOC and Micro-STATUS) have also appeared. Chapter 10 looks in more depth at online searching of locally stored databases.

One particular type of in-house database is the library catalogue. Online public access catalogues (known as OPACs) provide facilities for library users to carry out online catalogue searches and then to check the availability of the item required; such systems are being implemented in libraries in different parts of the world. Many of the large library automation systems (for example, ALS, CLSI, DOBIS/LIBIS, Geac and URICA) have OPAC modules whereas online access to the catalogue database is the norm in the automation packages for smaller libraries (for example, CALM, PC-PALS and TINlib) Online searching aspects of OPACs are described in Chapter 12.

Videotex/teletext systems

The final category of online search system covered in this book is videotex and teletext; this covers a range of systems which use a modified television set or appropriate workstation to display computer-based information using a mixture of text, graphics and colour in a visually very different way to other online search services. A teletext service, such as CEEFAX or ORACLE in Britain, involves the information being broadcast by television authorities using spare lines in the television signal, whereas videotex systems, such as CAPTAIN in Japan, Telidon in Canada or PRESTEL in Britain, use telephone lines to provide a two-way interactive link between the searcher and the system. More details on searching videotex and teletext systems are given in Chapter 11.

Basic Elements of an Online Search

An online search can be split into the following nine basic elements: Searcher, search formulation, input search formulation, workstation, link to computer system, search software, store of information, retrieved items and printer (see Figure 1.1 and below).

Searcher

The person who actually carries out the search may be the person with the information need (often referred to as the end-user) or it may be an intermediary. An intermediary is usually a librarian or information scientist who interprets the request for information

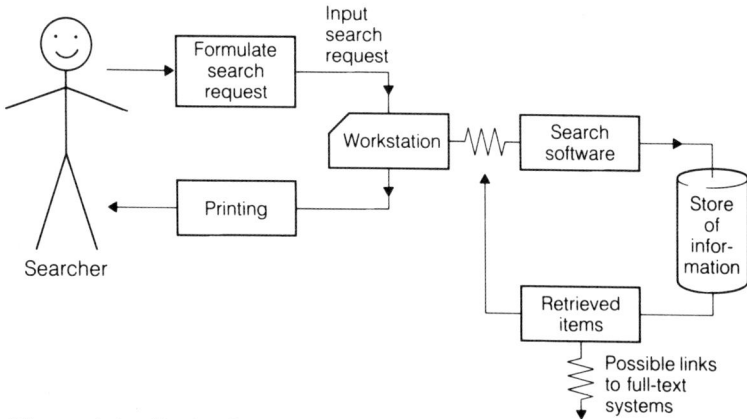

Figure 1.1   *Basic elements of an online search*

from the user and 'translates' it into the necessary language of the search system. Increasingly there are search systems being developed which are aimed directly at end-users. In Chapter 8 the searcher and the whole search process is discussed in more depth.

Search formulation

The search request may be formulated in various ways. Some online search systems expect the searcher to input commands, usually via a keyboard. For example:

FIND SWIMMING

might be used to command the computer to search for items containing the term 'swimming'. Terms may then be linked together using special operators, known as boolean operators; these are AND, OR, NOT. So:

FIND WOMEN OR FEMALE

would be used to link synonymous terms, whilst

FIND WOMEN AND SWIMMING

would be used to link different concepts and:

FIND SWIMMING NOT DIVING

would be used to exclude a concept

such as looking for items that include 'swimming' but which don't refer to 'diving'. As well as command-based systems there are menu-based systems which offer the searcher a *menu* or list of options; menu-based searching is often easier for the novice searcher. A more detailed discussion of formulating search requests is provided in Chapter 4.

Input search formulation

The formulated search is usually input using a keyboard. A character typed on the keyboard is translated into the appropriate code, transmitted to the computer's central processor and then echoed on to a visual display screen or VDU. Edstrom (1987) describes different types of visual display screens used for online searching and also summarizes the knowledge of their possible health hazards. Currently there are many variations of VDU screen; the original 12-inch or 14-inch amber, green or white on black/grey backgrounds type of screen has developed into larger more colourful screens capable of supporting more graphics.

Function keys can be used to carry out a specific sequence of commands. Also there are keys to control (move left, right, up, down) the cursor on the VDU, the cursor being a symbol (such as a square, triangle or underline) used to identify visually the position on the screen.

Workstation

In the early days of online searching (that is, early to mid-1970s) searches were usually carried out from a *dumb* terminal linked to a remote computer system. By the late 1980s most online searches are carried out via a microcomputer *workstation* with either twin floppy discs or a hard disc. The search may be carried out on the workstation itself (with the information being stored on CD-ROM or disc) or the workstation can be made to operate as a terminal for linking to a remote computer system. Figure 1.2 shows in diagrammatic form a typical workstation. A printer is required if some *hard copy* of the search is to be retained.

When a workstation is used to connect to remote computer systems special software is required to make the workstation act as a terminal (this is called terminal emulation) so that it will send and receive data appropriately. Also software may be used to dial automatically the telephone number for the remote computer and

Screen/Monitor

System box which
might include
CD-ROM drive, hard disc
or floppy disc.

Printer   Keyboard

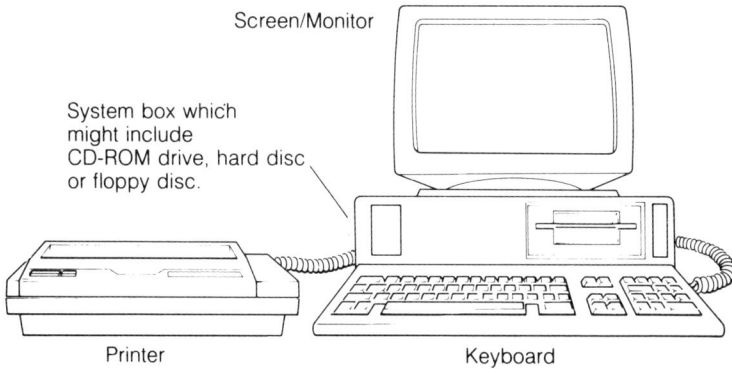

Figure 1.2   *Typical components of a workstation*

then to enter the appropriate *logging-in* passwords and codes; this may be referred to as communications software. This software enables searches or files of data to be prepared locally and then sent *down the line* to the remote computer – this is referred to as uploading. The reverse process, that of downloading is frequently practised as it enables information retrieved in the search to be transferred directly from the remote computer to a local computer for further processing before being output. Further details of workstations and terminal emulation software are given in Chapter 9.

Link to computer system

A remote computer system (sometimes referred to as a *host*) can be accessed by directly dialling that computer's telephone number. This can prove expensive as ordinary telephone charges are incurred. To reduce these costs special telecommunications networks designed for transmitting digital information (that is, information to or from computer systems) may be used. Details of some such networks are given in Chapter 2.

To access such a network (or networks) a telephone call using the public switched telephone network (PSTN) may be required. In such circumstances a modem (short for modulator/demodulator) is required to convert the digital information (used by the computer equipment) to analogue information (sound waves) for which most PSTNs are currently designed. Many modems include some *intelligence* to carry out the necessary *hand shaking* so that the remote computer and the workstation can communicate with each other. The speed at which data are transmitted is an important characteristic of the link to the computer system. Speed is measured in baud which normally equates to bits (binary digits '0' or '1') per second (bps). The common speed for receiving data from remote computer systems over the PSTN is 1200 baud (120 characters per second). However 2400 bps modems are beginning to be used, as described by Miller (1987). Transmission can be made at the same speed (for instance, 300 or 1200 baud) in both directions or alternatively split speed working is possible where the computer sends data at 1200 baud and the user sends data at 75 baud such as in the Prestel videotex service. More details on modems and standards are given in Chapter 9.

Another characteristic of the link is the mode of transmission. Full duplex transmission enables data to be transmitted in both directions along the line at the same time whereas half duplex allows transmission in only one direction at a time. The mode of transmission is determined by the remote computer service. It is necessary to ensure that the workstation is set to receive/transmit data in the appropriate mode before the link is made.

Linking workstations and computers within a given local area (such as an office building or a university campus) can be accomplished using a local area network (LAN) which enables data to be transmitted at high speeds. The case study on Unilever Research Port Sunlight Laboratory in the Appendix describes how searches are carried out on microcomputers which are linked via a LAN to a centralized mainframe computer which coordinates printing and telecommunications.

Search software

The program, or set of programs, which processes a search request carries out a search of the stored data and reports on information found is known as the search software. Much of the software used for online searching is of the free-text retrieval (FTX) type. This means that search terms from say a title or abstract (in a bibliographic retrieval system) are formed into an index (or inverted file) and the search is carried out on this index (this is described in more depth in Chapter 3). FTX software (for example, Quest, Questel Plus and Dialog) is used for searching remote computer systems (ESA-IRS, Télésystèmes-QUESTEL and Dialog, respectively), while packages such as CAIRS, STAIRS and STATUS are used for searching in-house databases, as described in Chapter 10. In the case of CD-ROM databases the search software is supplied with the disc. Thus Dialog Ondisc MEDLINE is a CD-ROM product that includes the Dialog search software and the bibliographic database on medicine – MEDLINE. The facilities and functions offered by the search software are described in more depth in Chapters 4 and 5.

Software for searching *source* databases of financial or statistical information usually includes facilities for manipulating the data into a suitable form such as graphs or tables.

Store of information

The store of information which may be searched online is usually structured into collections (known as databases) of individual items (known as records) which are made up of different parts (known as fields), such as author, title, publisher and date of publication for a bibliographical record. At the start of the search one or more databases may be chosen; the search is carried out on search terms derived from the fields and the retrieved records are displayed.

The information may be physically stored on different types of media. Floppy discs, or diskettes, which are thin plastic discs coated with a magnetic material, may be use for some smallish (perhaps a few hundred records) personal databases on micro-computers. Their capacity ranges from about 70 kilobytes (Kb) to 1 megabyte (Mb) (the byte is the unit of information, usually 8 bits, used to represent a character). Hard discs (sometimes known as Winchester discs or fixed discs) are single discs which are contained in a sealed (that is, dust free) unit along with the *heads* which are needed to write information to and read information from the discs. The capacity of such discs ranges from 5 to 300 Mb. On the bigger (often called mainframe) computers which may be accessed remotely there are likely to be large numbers of disc drives onto which are loaded exchangeable packs of perhaps 10 hard discs loaded on to a spindle. The Dialog Service, for instance, has over 380 000 Mb of online disc storage.

Optical discs, which include CD-ROMs, store information by using a laser to burn minute pits in the disc. The disc is then protected by laminates on either side and is read by another laser in a special player. The capacity of a CD-ROM is currently about 550 Mb. Optical discs can be used to store graphic and audio images as well as numbers or text.

For the vast majority of databases that are searched online, the data cannot be changed or corrupted by the searcher.

Retrieved items

When the search software has retrieved some items it is necessary for the searcher to look at them. In bibliographic retrieval systems the 'item' stored, searched and retrieved is a bibliographic citation consisting of various fields such as author, title, journal, descriptors (terms to describe the item), abstract, language, year of publication, accession number and so on. When a record has been retrieved all, or part of it, may be displayed on the screen and then perhaps printed. If a remote computer system is used, records may be printed 'offline' at the remote site and then mailed to the searcher. Alternatively retrieved records may be downloaded to some local store and then printed after the link to the remote computer has been broken. The rights and wrongs of downloading (with its possible copyright implications) have been the subject of many papers in the online searching literature during the 1980s. Jameson (1987) provides an overview of this area and describes how some search services have attempted to cope (for example, ESA-IRS developed a new command DOWNLOAD). Remote online search services may have links to document supply services for the provision of the full-text of the item. The British Library's Automated Information Service (BLAISE), for instance, has a link to the British Library Document Supply Centre (BLDSC) at Boston Spa. However, a current trend is to have more full-text source documents available online. Dialog, as Summit (1987) reported, has found that when both citation and source databases are offered for the same publication the citation database is used for searching and the source database for retrieving relevant items; he foresees that, because of the high cost of inputting source documents, a possible development would be to store the full-text in image (rather than magnetic) form for retrieval purposes. A further development is that of electronic publishing where the source document exists primarily in electronic form; Jaynes and others (1988) describe such developments.

Printer

Any workstation used for online searching usually has a printer linked to it so that a *hard-copy* of the search can be obtained. Printers vary in quality, speed and cost. The cheapest are *dot-matrix* printers in which characters are formed by a matrix of dots in the printhead. *Daisy-wheel* printers are based on a device (looking like a daisy) incorporating pre-formed characters at the end of each *petal*. The highest quality is achieved by using a laser printer. Although laser printers are more expensive than other kinds of printer, their consistent high quality, low noise and ease of use and maintenance has resulted in their being increasingly used. Kelly (1988) provides a general overview of laser printing and its use for various library applications.

Sample Searches of External Services

Search one

Search Example 1.1 shows the results of a search of the SPORT database on the Dialog search service for items on women and swimming. The SPORT database is international in scope and is produced by the Sport Information Resource Centre in Ottawa, Canada. It covers theses and monographs (published since 1949) and journal articles (published since 1975) on all aspects of sport, fitness and recreation; it corresponds to the printed *Sport Bibliography*.

```
DIALOG INFORMATION SERVICES
PLEASE LOGON:
********
ENTER PASSWORD:
********

Welcome to DIALOG
Dialog level 18.5.6A

Last logoff 13oct88 06:58:56
Logon file 001 13oct88 07:33:14
***File 555 is not working***

File 1:ERIC – 66–88/OCT.

    Set Items Description
    ___  _____  _____
```

?begin 48
  13oct88 07:52:18 User   Session
   $0.05 0.003 Hrs File1
  $0.05 Estimated cost File1
  $0.01 Telenet
  $0.06 Estimated cost this search
  $5.44 Estimated total session cost 0.318 Hrs.

File 48:SPORT DATABASE 1977–Sep 88
  (COPR.SIRC 1988)

  Set Items Description
  ――― ―――― ――――――――

?select swimming
  S1 7532 SWIMMING
?select women or female
  6160 WOMEN
  2104 FEMALE
  S2 7643 WOMEN OR FEMALE
?select s1 and s2
  7532 S1
  7643 S2
  S3 318 S1 AND S2
?type 3/6/1–3

3/6/1
0225935
Sleeker, stronger: sports – both traditional and, like women's
  bodybuilding, daringly new – are changing in China's cities.

3/6/2
0222544
Estudo comparativo do tempo de reacao visuo-manual simples em
  praticantes de esportes.
Comparative study of simple visuo-hand reaction time in athletes of
  various sports.

3/6/3
0220125
Approche du coefficient hydrodynamique du nageur tracte.
Evaluating the hydrodynamic coefficient of the towed swimmer.

?select fit?
  S4 17034 FIT?
?select s3 and s4
  318 S3
  17034 S4
  S5 29 S3 AND S4
?type 5/5/1–2

5/5/1
0210880
Submaksimalniat test PWC170.
The submaximum test PWC170.
Panayotova, S.
Vaprosi na fiziceskata kultura (Sofia), 9, 1987, 31–36
LANGUAGE(S): Bulgarian DOCUMENT TYPE: Journal article
LEVEL: Advanced
SECTION HEADING: 408310 Aquatic sports – Swimming – Testing and
    evaluation
The author presents the application of the abovementioned test to
    Bulgarian elite female swimmers. The test has been experimentally
    applied in its original version in 1976, then in 1981 it has been applied
    in a simplified version, with two 150 m-loads. The present article
    compares the validity of the results from the two test variants on the
    basis of the actual achievements of the swimmers. The positive sides
    and drawbacks of both variants are given concisely at the end of the
    article, together with suggestions for the appropriateness of the one
    or the other under different training conditions.
KEYWORDS: swimming; physical fitness; testing; method; PWC170;
    comparative study; Bulgaria; woman; elite athlete

5/5/2
0205792
Physical fitness of young Belgian swimmers.
Francaux, M.; Ramyead, R.; Sturbois, X.
Journal of sports medicine and physical fitness (Torino, It.), 27, 2, June
    1987, 197–204.
NO. REFERENCES: 13
LANGUAGE(S): English DOCUMENT TYPE: Journal article
COUNTRY OF PUBL.: Italy
LEVEL: Advanced
SUBFILE: v.16
SECTION HEADING: 408123 Aquatic sports – Swimming – Physical
    fitness
The young swimmers were rarely investigated in Belgium in spite of the
    growing importance for this sport. At high level, the training includes a
    daily physical practice as far as 25 km/week. The aim of this study is to
    analyse the physiologic response obtained during bicycle ergometer
    tests from 130 boys and 98 girls engaged in swimming at the rate of
    8–14 hours/week and between the ages of 10–15 (male) and 10–18
    (female). The results show a progressive and important adaptation of
    heart rate for a given work load, aerobic capacity and mechanical
    power output. Multiple regression equations are proposed in order to
    enable simple submaximal tests to be carried out for routine
    examination. If the literature is in accordance with these results, we
    must remember that the physical condition of these swimmers is the

result of their growth, of their training and of the selection process.
KEYWORDS: swimming; physical fitness; elite athlete; adolescent;
  Belgium; evaluation
?select lv=advanced
  S6 50914 LV=ADVANCED
?select s5 not s6
      29 S5
      50914 S6
  S7   8 S5 NOT S6
?type 7/5/1–3

7/5/1
0149032
Swimming through your pregnancy. 1st ed.
Katz, J.
Garden City, N.Y.: Dolphin Books/Doubleday & Co., 1983
  xvi, 260 p. :ill.
LANGUAGE(S): English DOCUMENT TYPE: Monographic
COUNTRY OF PUBL.: United States
ISBN: 0–385–18059–4 LC CARD NO: 82–45296
CLASSIFICATION NO.: GV837.5 SIRC BOOK NO.: 18188
LEVEL: Basic
SUBFILE: v.11, 12 and 13
SECTION HEADING: 408398 Aquatic sports – Swimming – Women;
  975900 Physical fitness – Programs and activities – Women-
  pregnancy exercises
KEYWORDS: swimming; woman; pregnancy; child; exercise; infant;
  program

7/5/2
0122867
Swimming and physical fitness during pregnancy.
Sibley, L.; Christensen, C.; Rubling, R.O.; Bolen, T.; Cameron-Foster, J.
Journal of nurs-midwifery 26(6), Nov/Dec 1981, 3–12.
LANGUAGE(S): English DOCUMENT TYPE: Journal article
LEVEL: Intermediate
SUBFILE: v.11, 12 and 13
SECTION HEADING: 408398 Aquatic sports – Swimming – Women;
  975900 Physical fitness – Programs and activities – Women-
  pregnancy exercises
KEYWORDS: woman; physical fitness; swimming; pregnancy – heart
  rate; blood pressure

7/5/3
0113169
Notre beau bebe: la culture physique de la femme enceinte, l'education
  physique du tout-petit, l'initiation a la natation, la gymnastique pre-
  corrective.

Faurobert, L.
Paris: Ed. ouvrieres, 1954
　184 p. :ill.
LANGUAGE(S): French DOCUMENT TYPE: Monographic
CLASSIFICATION NO.: RJ61 SIRC BOOK NO.: F38N 1954
LEVEL: Basic
SECTION HEADING: 975900 Physical fitness – Programs and activities –
　Women-pregnancy exercises; 972200 Physical fitness – Children and
　adolescents
KEYWORDS: Gymnastics; swimming; pregnancy; woman; infant
?**logoff**
　13oct88 07:56:01 User007244 Session A25.9
　　$4.34 0.062 Hrs File48
　　$1.25 5 Types in Format 5
　　$0.75 3 Types in Format 6
　　$2.00 8 Types
　$6.34 Estimated cost File48

Search Example 1.1　*The SPORT database on Dialog*

　In this example a communications software package was used to
set up the connection between the searcher's workstation in
Aberystwyth, Wales, and the remote search service in Palo Alto,
California. The relevant passwords and codes had previously been
stored in the software package and the searcher merely had to
choose the Dialog option from the list of available search services.
　To enter the SPORT database (File 48) on Dialog the command
BEGIN is used followed by the file number:

　　BEGIN 48

The search terms *swimming* and *women* with the synonym *female*
are entered using Dialog's SELECT command.

　　– SELECT SWIMMING
　　　results in a set (referred to as set 1) of 7532 items
　　– SELECT WOMEN OR FEMALE
　　　results in a set (set 2) of 7643 items.

The SELECT command is also used to link the two concepts of the
search with the boolean AND operator; this results in set 3 with
318 items. The titles of the first three documents are displayed
using the TYPE command and the international aspects of this
database can be seen with one article on China, one in Spanish and

another in French. To reduce the number of retrieved items another concept FIT? (to match with fit, fitness, etc.) is introduced and this results in a set of 29 items; the full details, including abstracts, of the first two items are printed. The articles all look to be related to advanced swimming and so it is decided that the boolean operator NOT be used to exclude items that are at the advanced level; this results in eight items being retrieved, the first three of which are displayed online and look to be relevant. The cost (not including telecommunications costs) of carrying out the search which took around four minutes was about $6.

Search two

The second search, for the financial details of companies in Oxford involved in publishing books, was carried out using the JORDANWATCH database on the PFDS (Pergamon Financial Data Services) search service in Britain. Jordans is a firm which has been serving the legal and accountancy profession with details of company information since the 1860s. Its online database contains information on all registered companies in the United Kingdom together with detailed financial data on selected companies. The PFDS service specializes in business and financial databases and uses search software, known as BASIS, which includes a menu option.

In Search Example 1.2 the full logging-in procedure is shown. To access any of the remote search services a fairly complex logging-in procedure is necessary. This involves:

1. Telephoning the nearest node of a telecommunications network which is to be used to access the search service; in this case the British national packet switched service – the Public Data Network (PDN) (formerly known as PSS).
2. Identifying the location of the workstation to the network by inputting what is referred to as the Network User Identifier (NUI).
3. Identifying the location of the search service (in this case a284400162); this is sometimes known as the network user address (NUA).
4. Identifying the type of workstation.

NUI?

ADD?
a284400162

234284400162+COM

Welcome to Pergamon Financial Data Services

Username:

Password:

Version 4 of the PFDS System Reference Manual is now available. The cost is thirty pounds for the manual and binder. To place an order, please call the Help Desk.

File PLANEX will no longer be available after 30th September 1989. For further enquiries please contact Alexandra Mackenzie on 041 332 8541.

For a copy of the training schedule for September 1989 to February 1990, please call the Help Desk.

HELP DESK 01 993–7333

17 AUG 1989   16:15 (LONDON TIME)

InfoLine Version 4.1

Please enter a file name or MENU

/MENU

FILE SELECTION
Please enter a number from 1 to 9,   H (Help) or L (Logout)
Or U (Terminals Menu)

1 : Finance and Credit	6 : CROSS FILE SEARCHING
2 : Marketing and Sales	7 : Gateway to ESAIRS Files
3 : Business News	8 : Gateway to OAG
4 : UK Trademarks	9 : Command Usage
5 : Other Files	

>**1**

Finance and Credit Databases

Company and Financial Information

The help on this menu explains the coverage of the Finance and Credit databases

Please enter a number from 1 to   H (Help) or L (Logout)
6, Or U (File Selection Menu)
  1: BROKER   3: FTA   5: JSS
  2: CHECK   4: JORDANS   6: CROSS FILE

>4

```
* * * * * * * * * * * * * * * * * * * * * * * * * * * * *
*                                                       *
*      JORDANWATCH VERSION 2      *
* * * * * * * * * * * * * * * * * * * * * * * * * * * * *
```

Select option
  1 – Jordanwatch Company Information
  2 – Order / Monitoring
  3 – PFDS Searching
  4 – Logoff

Enter option number

/3

You are now in the PFDS Search System
Please enter a Command, type MENU to return

/S SI=47531 AND AD=OXFORD

Set 1: 259   SI=47531
Set 2: 5400   AD=OXFORD
Set 3: 16   SI=47531 AND AD=OXFORD
/D F1/1

Item 1
  Name and Registered Number
  PERGAMON HOLDINGS LIMITED   01982083
                                      NAME CHANGE
                                    JORDANWATCH

/D F4/1

Item 1
PERGAMON HOLDINGS LIMITED   01982083
  Name and Registered Office   – Name change –

    Full Name   PERGAMON HOLDINGS LIMITED

    R/O   HEADINGTON HILL HALE
                    OXFORD
                    OX3 0BT

Dates Made Up To	Filed	JORDANWATCH
Accounts	31/12/87	12/87
Annual Return	02/08/88	02/08/88

```
         Year End   31/12
     Incorporated   24/01/86
      Last Update   8929
```

Changes of Name
    Date   Previous Name/New Name
    17/03/86   FILITO LIMITED/PERGAMON HOLDINGS LIMITED
Document Filing Dates

Document Type	Latest Filing Date	Document Type	Latest Filing Date
Cert. of Incorporation	24/01/86	Petitions for Winding-up	
Change of Name	17/03/86	Meeting of Creditors	
Change in R/O	10/03/86	Scottish winding-up Docs.	
Change in M & A	12/01/87	Liquidation Document Lodged	
Change in Share Capital		Receivership Document Lodged	
Change of Directors	08/05/89	Public Co. Trading Cert.	
Charge Lodged	04/07/89		
Mem. of Satisfaction Lodged	18/07/89		

```
Accounts               31/12/87
Annual Return          02/08/88
```

?DATES for further details

Balance Sheet	8712	8612
	(£000's)	(£000's)
Fixed Assets	651,800	288,462
Current Assets	614,900	276,969
Current Liabilities	(538,500)	(319,743)
Net Current Assets/(Liabilities)	76,400	(42,774)
Tot. Assets Less Current Liabilities	728,200	245,688
Long Term Debt	(489,800)	
Other Non-Current Liabilities	(5,000)	(1,748)
Minority Interests	(12,300)	
TOTAL	221,100	243,940
Share Capital	1,000	1,000
Reserves	220,100	242,940
TOTAL	221,100	243,940

Details of Assets		8712	8612
–Consolidated–		(£000's)	(£000's)
Fixed	– Tangible	196,100	60,756
Assets	– Intangible	6,700	
	– Investments & Other	449,000	227,706
	TOTAL	651,800	288,462

Current Assets			
	– Stock/W.I.P.	167,400	57,780
	– Debtors	60,900	5,740
	– Investments		55,071
	– Bank & Deposits	49,600	532
	– Other	337,000	157,846
	TOTAL	614,900	276,969

Current Liabilities			
	– Creditors	(138,900)	(18,121)
	– Loan/Overdraft	(373,000)	(299,738)
	– Other	(26,600)	(1,884)
	TOTAL	(538,500)	(319,743)

Profit & Loss Account	8712	8612
–Consolidated–	(£000's)	(£000's)
Turnover	1,009,900	208,349
Profit/(Loss) Before Interest	73,100	17,555
Interest Paid	(57,100)	(7,627)
Profit/(Loss) Before Taxation	16,000	9,928
Taxation (Charge)/Credit	(7,800)	(4,778)
Profit/(Loss) After Taxation	8,200	5,150
Minority Interests	(2,800)	(647)
Extraordinary Items	19,800	(1,360)
Profit/(Loss) For Period	25,200	3,143
(Dividends)		
(Other Appropriations)		70
Retained Profit/(Loss)	25,200	3,213

Other Information	8712	8612
	(£000's)	(£000's)
Authorised Capital	20	1,000
Issued Capital	1,000	1,000
Total Remuneration	57,000	26,857
Number of Employees	5,900	3,679

Secured Indebtedness				
	(£'s)	0	as at	02/08/88
	(£'s)	0	as at	06/08/87

Trade Description
  ELECTRONIC PUBLISHING, ONLINE INFORMATION SERVICE,

Auditors
  COOPERS & LYBRAND

Industry Classification
  47531 PUBLISHERS OF BOOKS
  47545 ANCILLARY PRINTING SERVICES
  34100 INSULATED WIRES AND CABLES
  34430 RADIO AND ELECTRONIC CAPITAL GOODS
  83600 ACCOUNTANTS, AUDITORS, TAX EXPERTS
  83702 TECHNICAL SERVICES

Directors as given in the last Annual Return

1   Mr I.R. Maxwell
    Headington Hill Hall, Oxford

2   CSS Financial Services Ltd
    2nd Floor Hamilton House, Marlowes, Hemel
    Hempstead, Herts

Financial Ratios	8712	8612
Current Ratio	1.14	0.87
Liquidity Ratio	0.83	0.69
Shareholder Liquidity Ratio	0.44	139.55
Solvency Ratio (%)	17.45	43.14
Gearing (%)	398.06	123.59
Share Funds/Employee (£'s)	37,475	66,306
Working Capital/Employee (£'s)	15,153	12,340
Total Assets/Employee (£'s)	214,695	153,691

Financial Changes & Trends	8712 TO (£000's %)	8612
Fixed Assets	363,338	125.96
Current Assets	337,931	122.01
Stock	109,620	189.72
Debtors	55,160	960.98
Total Assets	701,269	124.02
Current Liabilities	218,757	68.42
Creditors	120,779	666.51
Bank Overdraft	73,262	24.44
Long Term Liabilities	505,352	28910.3

Profitability Ratios	8712	8612
Profit Margin (%)	1.58	4.77
Return on Shareholders Funds (%)	7.24	4.07
Return on Net Assets (%)	2.20	4.04
Return on Total Assets (%)	1.26	1.76

Stock Turnover	6.03	3.61
Debtors Turnover	16.58	36.30
Net Assets Turnover	1.39	0.85
Turnover/Employee (£'s)	171,170	56,632
Remuneration/Employee (£'s)	9,661	7,300

Profitability Changes & Trends	8712	TO	8612
	(£000's		%)
Turnover	801,551		384.72
Profit before Tax	6,072		61.16
Interest Paid	49,473		648.66
Number of Employees	2221		60.37

Subsidiary Company

BUMPUS, HALDANE & MAXWELL LIMITED	00037060
PERGAMON AGB PLC	00115634
RINGMAG LIMITED	00195721
NUFFIELD PRESS LIMITED	00208024
MAXWELL COMMUNICATION CORPORATION PLC	00298463
NEWPORT & ROBINSON LIMITED	00840665
ALLCENTRE PROPERTIES LIMITED	00892284
ADVERTISING MANAGEMENT LIMITED	00918078
BRASSEY'S DEFENCE PUBLISHERS LIMITED	01309191
MAXWELL BUSINESS INFORMATION SERVICES LIMITED	01533513
METROMODE LIMITED	01858496

Search Example 1.2   *JORDANWATCH on PFDS*

After this process connection to the PFDS computer is made and it is then necessary to input the appropriate user name and password for the search service so that bills can be eventually prepared and sent to the user.

The welcome message gives details of new manuals, database changes and the time in London. The option is then given of choosing a file or the menu; in this example the menu approach is chosen. The first option (Finance and Credit) of this first menu is selected, followed by the fourth option on the second menu to ensure that the JORDANWATCH database is selected. There is a further menu within the database; if information on a particular known company were required, then the first option would be selected. In the example the third option is chosen so that the BASIS command language can be used to link items that have been indexed with the Standard Industrial Code (SIC) number 47531 (which is applied to companies that are publishers of books) and those companies with an Oxford address. Thus the command

/select si = 47531 and ad = oxford

generates sets (in a similar way to the previous search example). The first set contains 259 items and refers to companies that are book publishers, the second set contains 5400 and refers to companies with an Oxford address, and the third set contains the 16 items that refer to book publishers in Oxford. The name and registered number of one of these companies is displayed using the basic format (F1) for which no charge is made. The full details (using format F4) of this company are then displayed to show the range of information contained in a record of this type; records such as this cost £9.75 each to display.

General Aspects of Online Searching

Use and users

Most of the information in this section deals with the general aspects related to the use of external search services and CD-ROMs; the other online search systems are dealt with in the relevant chapters.

Williams (1987) provides some interesting statistics on the growth of online searching generally in the early 1980s; these include:

1. The number of databases available publicly for online searching grew from 600 in 1980 to 3000 by 1985.
2. The number of records in those databases grew from 190 million in 1980 to 1680 million in 1985.
3. The number of searches of the word-oriented, full-text, bibliographic, directory and related databases grew from 6 million in 1980 to 18 million in 1985.

The fact that the records and databases available for searching grew more quickly than the actual use made of the services accounts for some of the volatility in the online marketplace that is described in more detail in Chapter 2. Williams concludes by stating that:

> Information is certainly the most important product in the US industry but it is expensive and can not be mass-produced.

Online searching of bibliographic information was initially carried out in the industrial and commercial sector by information scientists or librarians. However, with many organizations (for example, the large chemical companies) now providing a well-established system for online searching, quite a lot of searching is being carried out by end-users. Academic, government and public libraries also provide access to remote online search services. The use of such services by public libraries in Britain developed from initial funding by the British Library Research and Development Department (BLR&DD) in the late 1970s. By 1987, 85 of the 167 public library authorities in Britain provided access to remote online search services (Batt, 1988). East and Forrest (1988) analysed the use of such services by 19 public libraries over a six-month period and found that the most used search services were Dialog (32 per cent), PFDS (26 per cent), BLAISE (12 per cent) and ESA-IRS (10 per cent) and that the most used databases were in business and industry (41.9 per cent, particularly JORDANWATCH and ICC UK companies), general reference (15.9 per cent, Textline, BNBMARC and WHITAKER'S) and science and technology (12.9 per cent). East and Forrest also analysed the use of remote search services by nine British polytechnic libraries and found that the most used services were Dialog (40 per cent), ESA-IRS (24 per cent) and Mead Data Central (16 per cent). The most used databases were in science and technology (46.7 per cent, particularly INSPEC, CA SEARCH and COMPENDEX), legal (20.4 per cent, LEXIS) and business and industry (10.9 per cent, particularly ABI/INFORM and MANAGEMENT CONTENTS). Batt also reported that 84 public library authorities in Britain provided access to videotex services and 67 had local databases of community information available for searching online.

In the Federal Republic of Germany (FRG) the number of online search service users increased from 400 in 1982 to 1200 in 1986 generating a turnover of 34.7 million deutschemarks. The most used search services were Dialog, DIMDI and STN.

Henty (1987) reports on a survey made of the use of online

bibliographic services in Australian academic libraries. Dialog proved to be the most used service (used by all 26 reporting institutions). The average number of search services used was eight and the maximum was 16. One university reported carrying out about 4500 searches during 1986 but 50 per cent reported carrying out fewer than 400 searches per year.

Another report – *Key Note Report, (1987)*, published by the ICC Information Group – looked in more depth at the structure, market size, recent developments and future trends of the online database industry in Europe. General points that emerged were:

1. Britain is the largest market in Europe for online databases.
2. There is a trend towards end-user searching with several online search services marketing their products to doctors, solicitors, stockbrokers, market researchers, managers and so on (of the new users signed by Dialog in 1986, 80 per cent were claimed to be end-users).
3. The growth of the financial services sector and the advent of 24-hour trading on the international stock markets have given a massive boost to the demand for stockmarket data.
4. The West European market for online database searching (including videotex) was estimated at $600m–$700m in 1986. This is likely to expand to about $2000m. in 1990 given recent growth rates of 28–32 per cent.
5. Text databases (either bibliographic or full-text) account for a very small proportion of the market, the major share going to source (particularly financial) databases.

Collier (1988) provides an estimate of $49 million for the turnover in Europe of searches for textual and bibliographic information, (with Dialog at $12m, Data-Star and Télésystèmes-QUESTEL at $8m each and STN at $7m). The equivalent figure for the United States is estimated at around $300m. Collier (1988) highlights, however, the problems of compiling such statistics and allocating the turnover to any particular country when searches may originate in one country, be carried out on a computer in another country using data collected in a third country from information originally published in a fourth country. This international aspect of online searching of remote services was exemplified in Search Example 1.1 and also in a videotape *The Invisible Ingredient* produced by Euronet-Diane; this shows a

Danish development manager in a food processing firm who needs to be absolutely certain that the oil used in producing the firm's margarine contains no pork fat as the margarine is to be sold in the Middle East. A search is carried out (in Denmark) on the FOOD SCIENCE AND TECHNOLOGY ABSTRACTS database (produced in Britain) using the ESA-IRS search service (in Italy) which results in a reference to relevant work being carried out in the Netherlands.

There are various user groups that have been set up with the aim of bringing together those involved in online searching and related topics either in a geographic region, for example, Aber OLUG (Aberystwyth Online User Group), UKOLUG (UK Online User Group) and Manitoba Online User Group, or in a particular subject area or using a particular product or service (for example, STATUS Users' Group, Prestel Users' Group). There are also groups of information providers, for example, Groupement Français des Fourmisseurs d'Information en Ligne (the French Association of Online Information Providers) and EUSIDIC (the European Association of Information Services).

In some organizations or small companies it may not be cost-effective to set up access to, and train people to use, the remote online search services. Especially in such cases searches may be carried out by other organizations such as public libraries, academic libraries, national libraries, database producers or online brokerage firms (such firms exist mainly to carry out online searches for others). Turpie (1987), for instance, lists 126 organizations in Britain that carry out searches for others.

The advent of databases on CD-ROM means that some users may have an option of carrying out a search on CD-ROM or via a remote online search service. This is the case at Texas A&M University where, through generous funding, about 20 CD-ROM players were acquired. Texas A&M library has used remote online search services since 1976 and its use has grown from about 464 hours searching per year in 1982/3 to about 1700 hours per year in 1986/7, of which about 75 per cent was by end-users. The impact of four CD-ROM databases – ERIC (education), DISSERTATION ABSTRACTS, PSYCLIT (psychology) and AGRICOLA (agriculture) – on online searching of remote services has been analysed by Anders and Jackson (1988). They found that by using CD-ROM far more users could be introduced to the concepts of computerized literature searching (100 users a day) in a fairly stress-free environment than would be the case with remote online searching; such users often wish to complement their CD-ROM search with a search for more up-to-date information on a remote search service.

Costs

As in other areas the costs of using remote online search services can be split into setting up and running costs.

Setting up costs would include purchase of equipment (that is, microcomputer with suitable interface, communications software, printer and modem), training of suitable staff, acquisition of necessary manuals and setting up the necessary telecommunications links. The total cost of all this can vary greatly; the ICC Information Group report (1987) estimates that most users will spend about £1000–£2500 on equipment.

Payment for using remote services can take various forms. For many years a number of services have operated a 'pay as you use' scheme where charges are normally a combination of the length of time spent online and the number of items retrieved; these charges are usually database dependent. A comparison of the database charges made by different remote services is provided by Woodrow (1988). On top of the database/service charge there will be a charge for the telecommunications system used to access the remote service. In the early days of online searching in the mid-1970s, a figure of £1/minute was often quoted as a rough and ready guide for the total cost of a search; this rule was still valid in the mid-1980s for academic and public libraries where typical searches last between 10 and 20 minutes.

During the 1980s technical advances have increased the efficiency of searching and there are now moves by various search services to alter the basis for charging. ESA-IRS has adopted (from January 1989) a policy involving a very low connect time charge combined with a much higher royalty charge for each item retrieved and a small charge for each selection of a new database. O'Leary (1988) reports that charging algorithms are likely to become more complex during the 1990s and might take account of:

1. Connect time.
2. Baud rate differentials.
3. Field(s) searched, that is, fields added by a database producer (abstract, descriptor, classification codes) may cost more to search than fields such as author and title.
4. Online and offline displays.

The general problems of pricing in the online industry reflect the links between the searchers, the database producers and the search services; Hawkins (1989) describes some of the factors affecting this pricing. Some remote services offer 'discount prices' depending on the amount of searching carried out by a user on the service during the year. Others operate a subscription system in which an annual payment of hundreds or perhaps thousands of pounds allows unlimited access during the year. CD-ROM databases are made available on an annual subscription basis with prices typically being between £500 and £2000 per year. Some, however, are very much more: a CD-ROM containing data on Europe's top 25 000 companies from Extel Financial and the ICC Information Group is available from Clarinet Business Publications for an annual subscription of £18 000. CD-ROM players currently cost between £500 and £1000.

The literature

The year 1977 was important in the history of online searching. The technique of carrying out online searches on remote services was becoming more widespread and the literature on the subject burgeoned with the birth in January of that year of two journals, *Online* and *Online Review*. Between them these two publications contain many important papers. Prior to 1977 papers on online searching appeared in a variety of journals as evidenced in two bibliographies: Hall (1977) and Hawkins (1977). Hawkins has continued to produce updates to his bibliography as annual supplements to *Online Review*. Another important event in 1977 was an international meeting on online information held in London. This has become an annual event attracting many thousands of European (and other) attendees. The proceedings of these conferences provide a good source of material on online searching; so too do the proceedings of the two major American conferences, the Online Meeting and the National Online Meeting, as well as national user group meetings.

Journals such as *Database* and *Database Searcher* concentrate on practical aspects of searching with papers often including valuable hints on searching techniques on particular databases; *Online Notes* and *Information World Review* cover the current news regarding the online industry. Some subject-oriented journals exist, for example, *Online Business Information*, *Online Sci-Tech*

Information and *Inside Business*, which is aimed at users of Dialog's business information sources. Other journals which may contain relevant material include *Electronic Library, Information Technology and Libraries, Journal of the American Society for Information Science, Journal of Information Science, Microcomputers for Information Management, Monitor* and *Program.* Raitt (1984) provides a collection of significant papers on online searching published prior to 1983.

The day-to-day details of searching a particular database or search service may be given in a specific newsletter, for example, *Chronolog* and *News and Views* are the newsletters for Dialog and ESA-IRS, respectively, whilst *INSPEC Matters* and *BIOSIS Newsletter* are examples of newsletters available from database producers. The newsletters of various user groups can also provide useful overviews of developments in specific areas; the *UKOLUG Newsletter*, for instance, has sections covering CD-ROM and telecommunications developments. CD-ROM developments generally are covered in publications such as Silver Platter's *Silver Platter Exchange* (which gives news of users of Silver Platter's CD-ROMs), *CD-ROM Librarian, CD-ROM Review* and *Electronic and Optical Publishing Review.* There are now also several regular conferences on optical publishing such as Optical Info in the Netherlands and Optical Information Systems International in London.

General textbooks on online searching began to appear during the early 1980s (for example, Henry *et al.*, 1980; Meadow and Cochrane, 1981). Some more recent textbooks have concentrated on specific areas; for example, Walsh, Butcher and Freund (1987) provide a good overview of developments in business information.

References

Anders, V. and Jackson, K.M. (1988) Online vs. CD-ROM – impact of CD-ROM databases upon a large online searching program. *Online*, **12** (6), 24–32
Batt, C. (1988) *Information Technologies in Public Libraries 1987.* Winchester: Public Libraries Research Group
Collier, H.R. (1988) What actually is the online universe. In *Online Information 88: 12th International Online Information Meeting Proceedings*, pp. 723–732. Oxford: Learned Information

East, H. and Forrest, V. (1988) Indicators of online use. In *Online Information 88: 12th International Online Information Meeting Proceedings*, pp. 91–102. Oxford: Learned Information

Hall, J.L. (1977) *Online Information Retrieval 1965–76 Bibliography*. London: Aslib

Hawkins, D.T. (1977) Online information retrieval bibliography 1965–76. *Online Review*, 1 (Supplement)

Hawkins, D.T. (1989) In search of ideal information pricing. *Online*, 13 (2), 15–30

Henry, W.M. and others (1980) *Online Searching: An Introduction*. London: Butterworths

Henty, M. (1987) Survey of Australian academic libraries' online bibliographic retrieval systems. *Australian Academic and Research Libraries*, 18 (4), 187–200

Jameson, A. (1987) *Downloading and Uploading in Online Information Retrieval*. Bradford: MCB University Press

Jaynes, J.T. and others (1988) Publishing books electronically in the networks of tomorrow: a vision of the present. In *Online Information 88: 12th International Online Information Meeting Proceedings*, pp. 359–372. Oxford: Learned Information

Kelly, C.J. (1988) Laser printing for a variety of library applications. *Information Technology and Libraries*, 7 (1), 41–50

Key Note Report (1987) *On-line Databases: An Industry Sector Overview* 3rd edn. London: Keynote Publications

Meadow, C.T. and Cochrane, P.A. (1981) *Basics of Online Searching*. New York: Wiley

Miller, R. (1987) 2400bps – is it the wave of the future. *Online*, 11 (4), 26–32

O'Leary, M. (1988) Price versus value for online data. *Online*, 12 (2), 26–30

Online Searching in Science and Technology (1989). London: British Library, Online Search Centre

Raitt, D.I. (1984) *Introduction to Online Information Systems*. Oxford: Learned Information

Summit, R.K. (1987) Online information: a ten-year perspective and outlook. *Online*, 11 (1), 61–64

Turpie, G. (1987) Editor. *UK Online Search Services*, 3rd edn. London: Aslib

Walsh, B.P., Butcher, H. and Freund, A. (1987) *Online Information: A Comprehensive Business User's Guide*. Oxford: Basil Blackwell

Williams, M.E. (1987) Highlights of the online database industry: assessing the status of the online industry. In *Proceedings of the National Online Meeting*, pp. 1–4. Medford, New Jersey: Learned Information

Woodrow, M. (1988) *Comparative Cost Chart of Online Files*. Biggleswade, Bedfordshire: Clover Publications

Chapter 2

History and Development of
the Online Industry

Introduction

The techniques of storing and retrieving bibliographic data on computer systems were developed during the 1960s. By 1969 various database producers were creating magnetic tapes containing bibliographic records (that could be searched) as 'by-products' of the production of their printed indexing and abstracting journals. Many of these magnetic tapes were acquired by large organizations, such as Shell Research Ltd and ICI, and used to run in-house information retrieval services such as the production of indexes, a selective dissemination of information (SDI) service and retrospective searching (which was in batch mode in the early days).

Batch mode searching involved a search request being linked with other search requests and input to the computer system (in a batch). The searches were processed and the resulting retrieved items printed. Batch searching involved some delay, often of the order of days or weeks, between the receipt of a search request and the dispatch of the output. Also there was no interaction possible between the searcher and the system. Nevertheless, in many cases it was still preferable to searching the printed indexes.

Software used for batch mode searching was then usually written in-house but some general packages such as ASSASSIN and POLYDOC started to appear in the late 1960s and early 1970s. The first major retrospective search service to become available to the general public was that offered by the US National Library of Medicine (NLM) in 1966. In 1964 the NLM started to produce its *Index Medicus*, an index to the world's biomedical literature, by computer. The linked magnetic tape service was known as MEDLARS – Medical Literature Analysis and Retrieval System.

Bourne (1980) cites the first investigation of online bibliographic searching as that done by Bagley in 1951 at the Massachusetts Institute of Technology (MIT). He attempted to program an early computer to search encoded abstracts and found that although it might be technically possible it was not feasible due to problems with the then existing equipment and the cost. In 1960 the System Development Corporation (SDC) publicly demonstrated an interactive system known as Protosynthex which searched the entries of an encyclopaedia and used many of the techniques now available to current online searchers.

Several other organizations in the United States also began to be involved in this area. In 1964 the Lockheed Missiles Corporation demonstrated an online system, known as CONVERSE, to search its in-house library database. In 1965 the Technical Information project (TIP) at MIT made use of the Project MAC (Multi-Access Computer) to search 35 000 citations to the physics literature. The aim of this project was to provide a test-bed for evaluating search strategies and to learn how the then modern technology could aid scientific information interchange. This system formed the basis of several subsequent online systems. Also in 1965 SDC, in a project funded by the Advanced Research Projects Agency (ARPA) of the US Department of Defense, was involved in developing a system which allowed 13 government and private organizations access, via a telephone, to a file of 200 000 bibliographic records on foreign technology. The software for this system was developed and became known as ORBIT (Online Retrieval of Bibliographic Information Time-Shared). Following the development of its in-house system Lockheed was awarded a contract (also in 1965) to develop an online retrieval system for some 200 000 document citations at the US National Aeronautics and Space Administration (NASA). This software was known as RECON (Remote Console) and was based on Lockheed's own software which had been renamed Dialog. IBM also started to become involved in this area and by 1966 was developing an online bibliographic retrieval system – the forerunner of its STAIRS (Storage and Information Retrieval System) – for in-house purposes.

By 1969 some of the experimental online systems were being translated into working systems. The Space Documentation Centre of the European Space Agency (ESA) acquired RECON from its American counterpart and began to offer an online information service covering several databases to 10 terminals in seven European countries. At the NLM the Abridged Index Medicus by Teletypewriter Exchange Network (AIM/TWX) provided access, via SDC and the telephone network, to 100 journals in clinical medicine. The system was well received by medical librarians and within six months some 90 institutions were using it. In 1971 the full MEDLARS online, or Medline service became operational from the NLM which used the ELHILL (named after the Lister Hill National Centre for Biomedical Communications) software, a modification of SDC's ORBIT.

During 1971–72 the online services began to extend access to their systems. The Lockheed Dialog system began as a commercial search service in 1972 with databases from the US Office of Education (ERIC), the US National Technical Information Service (NTIS) and the National Agricultural Library (AGRICOLA).

Another major impetus to the world-wide use of these online services came during the 1970s with advances in telecommunications and the establishment of networks such as Tymnet and Telenet in the United States. *Nodes* to these networks began to appear in Europe from about 1974 and subsequently in the rest of the world thus providing comparatively cheap and easy access to remote stores of information. More details of these developments are given later in the chapter.

Developments in telecommunications, online processing systems, suitable search software and the ability to store large quantities of data which could be quickly accessed as well as the availability of appropriate people to harness the technology have therefore created the current online industry. An account of the leading lights in the American online information industry during 1976–86 is given by Provenzano (1987a), who provides an insight into the rapid development of the industry. Meadow (1988) gives a chronological account of some of these major developments, starting with Vannevar Bush's postulation in 1945 of an online interactive information retrieval system and ending with the sale of the Dialog Information Services by Lockheed to Knight-Ridder for $353 million in 1988.

Growth of Databases and Database Producers

The term *database* was defined by Williams (1974) as an "organized set of machine-readable records containing bibliographic or document-related data". Collections of machine-readable records which contained other than bibliographic data were generally referred to as non-bibliographic databases or databanks during the 1970s. However, both sets of collections are now referred to as databases but often are classified, as by Cuadra (1988), as follows:

1. *Reference* databases. These refer or point the user to another source (for example, document, organization or individual) for additional information or the full-text. They include bibliographic databases which contain citations and often abstracts of the printed literature (for example, journal articles, reports, patents, dissertations, conference proceedings, books or newspaper items) as well as referral databases which contain references to information such as organizations' names and addresses.

2. *Source* databases. These contain the original source data such as numeric information (original survey data or statistically manipulated representations of data), textual-numeric information (such as company annual reports, handbook-type data or chemical and physical properties), full-text (for example, a full newspaper item, a technical specification, or a court decision) and software which can be downloaded for use on a local computer.

The rapid rate of growth of databases, database producers and search services can be seen in Table 2.1 (extracted from Cuadra, 1988).

	No. of databases	*Database producers*	*Search services*
1979/80	400	221	59
1980/81	600	340	93
1982/83	1350	718	213
1983/84	1878	927	272
1984/85	2453	1189	362
1986	2901	1379	454
1987	3369	1568	528
1988	3893	1723	576

Table 2.1   *Growth of online databases*

More details on the current range of databases in particular subject areas are given in Chapter 7.

Access to the growing scientific literature of the late 19th century and early 20th century was improved by various learned societies and institutions producing printed indexing and abstracting publications in specific subject fields. In 1898, for instance, the Physical Society and the Institution of Electrical Engineers (IEE) in Britain started a joint publication of abstracts of all appropriate papers in physics and electrical engineering; this was known as *Science Abstracts*. INSPEC (Information Services in Physics, Electrotechnology, Computers and Control) as part of the IEE now carries on this work and produces three abstracts journals: *Physics Abstracts*, *Electrical and Electronic Abstracts* and *Computer and Control Abstracts*. In 1965 preliminary studies were made into the feasibility of using computer techniques in the publication of these abstracting journals. The computer-based system began operating in 1969 on a self-supporting basis and the resulting INSPEC database (of about 3 million records in 1988) is now available on many online search services. Aitchison (1988) describes the role of database producers with particular reference to the INSPEC database. In the United States *Index Medicus* was first published by the National Library of Medicine in 1879 with the linked MEDLARS database being available since 1966. *Chemical Abstracts Issues and Indexes* appeared in printed form in 1907 and the Chemical Abstracts Service (CAS) has been producing the linked database since 1967.

Hall (1986), in the fourth edition of his directory of online bibliographic databases, states that by the end of 1972 there were about six bibliographic databases available for public searching; this compares with 75 in 1976 and 250 by 1986. The actual numbers of citations in these databases range from about 3 million in 1972 to 139 million at the end of 1986. Although there is inevitably some overlap by the various database producers it is reckoned that there were about 100 million unique references by 1986. Hall concentrates on bibliographic databases and the difference in numbers between him and Cuadra indicates the large number of non-bibliographic or source databases that are available.

Examples of the types of organization which produce bibliographic databases are given in Table 2.2. Although some organizations are involved in producing very large databases, that is, several million references (for example, BIOSIS, COMPENDEX, CAS, INSPEC, MEDLINE, SCISEARCH), Hall estimates that 40 per cent of the databases he covered were small (less than 100 000 references).

Type of organization	Example(s)	Database name	Subject
Academic	London Business School	SCIMP	European management
	University of North Carolina	POPULATION BIBLIOGRAPHY	Demographics and population
	University of Sydney	BIBLIOGRAPHIC INFORMATION ON SOUTH EAST ASIA	South East Asia
Commercial	Derwent Publications Ltd	WPI	Patents
	Institute for Scientific Information	SCISEARCH	Science
International	Food and Agriculture Organization of the United Nations	AGRIS	Agriculture
	International Nuclear Information Service	INIS	Peaceful applications of nuclear energy
Learned/ professional society	Royal Society of Chemistry	CHEMICAL HAZARDS IN INDUSTRY	Chemical hazards
	Library Association	LISA	Librarianship
National organization	Centre National de Recherche Scientifique	FRANCIS	Social and human sciences
	US National Center on Child Abuse and Neglect	CHILD ABUSE AND NEGLECT	Child abuse
National library	British Library	UKMARC	General
	Library of Congress	LCMARC	General
Research associations	Institut Textil de France	TITUS	Textiles
	Water Research Centre	AQUALINE	Hydrology

Table 2.2 *Some types of reference database producers*

Some of these databases have been made available online following the setting up of an in-house information retrieval service. The Rubber and Plastics Research Association (RAPRA Technology), for instance, since 1919 has collected relevant information which it recorded in the form of classified abstracts on cards. Since 1971 it has used the ASSASSIN software package to manage this in-house. The RAPRA database is now available for searching on the ORBIT search service.

A major development in bibliographic databases over recent years has been the broadening in scope of subject coverage. Initially most databases covered the scientific or technical literature but now most areas of knowledge are covered by various databases as described in Chapter 7.

The type of information included in reference databases has also developed. Various organizations involved in book production or producing bibliographies now make their databases available for online searching. The publisher John Wiley, for instance, produces the WILEY CATALOG/ONLINE database (the online version of its printed *General Catalog*) which contains details of all items published, distributed or sold by the company since 1940. Also many national libraries some of which have been using computer systems to produce their national bibliographies since the early 1970s now have online versions of their databases. The Deutsche Bibliothek in the Federal Republic of Germany (FRG), for instance, produces BIBLIO-DATA, a database of books published in the FRG since 1966; this is available for searching on the STN International search service. The US Library of Congress' MARC records (LCMARC) database, covering books published in the US since 1968, is available on various search services such as Dialog, the large shared cataloguing service of OCLC (Online Computer Library Center), BLAISE and the University of Tsu Kuba in Japan. During the 1980s reference databases containing 'directory' information became available. Examples include Bowker's MICROCOMPUTER SOFTWARE AND HARD-WARE GUIDE (computer products), MARQUIS WHO'S WHO (biographical details of about 100 000 people) and the CUADRA DIRECTORY OF DATABASES. The majority of these reference databases have developed as by-products of printed publications and are made available for online searching via a remote search service.

The development of source databases for online searching began during the 1970s and by 1977 a chapter on numeric databases and systems appeared in the *Annual Review of Information Science and Technology* (Luedke, Kovacs and Fried, 1977). Source database producers cover subjects which include company information, financial information, news and current affairs, legal information and chemical information. More details of some of these source databases are given in Chapter 7.

Some of the producers of source databases and services have been providing information services for many years. Jordans, for instance, was formed in 1863 to provide company information (that is, details of products, annual reports, directors and finances) to the legal and accountancy professions in Britain; the JORDAN-WATCH database (available on PFDS or directly) provides information on 900 000 limited companies in the UK. Reuters, too, originated in the 19th century with Baron Julius de Reuter setting up a small business in Aachen, FRG, which relied on pigeons to convey commercial intelligence. Reuters has always used current technology to transmit information around the world and is now a major producer of source databases on financial matters such as foreign exchange rates and stock market details. Many such organizations are used to providing their services directly to the end-users and this has happened too with the online search services; unlike the reference databases which are often accessed by librarians or information specialists, the source databases are searched by end-users.

Many producers of financial source databases only make their information available through their own remote search services. Data Resources (DRI), for instance, produces a wide range of databases such as DRI AGRICULTURE DATABANK, DRI EUROPE DATABANK, DRI CURRENT ECONOMIC INDICATORS DATABANK and DRI NATURAL GAS DATABANK (to name but a few) that are available for searching on their own service. Information provided by DRI and other similar economic forecasting firms such as Chase Econometrics and Wharton Econometric Forecasting Associates was originally processed using the computing facilities of the database producers; however, with the growth of microcomputer-based workstations some of the data can be downloaded and 'manipulated' locally to produce the necessary graphs and tables.

The 1980s saw a great rise in the number of source databases available for online searching, particularly in the commercial information area. Dialog developed its services to assist end-users in searching its business source databases by setting up the Dialog

Business Connection (O'Leary, 1986) which provides a menu-driven interface to five applications areas:

1. Corporate intelligence.
2. Financial screening.
3. Products and markets.
4. Sales prospecting.
5. Travel planning by linking in to the Official Airline Guide Electronic Edition.

Another major development during the 1980s with respect to source databases has been the rapid increase in the number of full-text databases available for searching. Several newspaper publishers (for example, The Financial Times) now make full-text versions of their papers available for searching. More details of these types of news database are given in Chapter 7. Tenopir (1988) describes users and uses of full-text databases and highlights the different search strategies required when searching such databases.

Growth of Online Search Services

Cuadra (1978) identified some 15 online search services of international scope in 1977; these included BRS (Bibliographic Retrieval Services), Lockheed Dialog, Mead Corporation, OCLC and SDC. As can be seen in Table 2.1, by 1988 Cuadra had identified 576 search services; many of these are firms which provide access primarily to source databases.

The online industry is a volatile one and by late 1988 there had been some major births, deaths and adoptions of search services. SDC, one of the first organizations involved in the online searching field, was acquired by the Burroughs Corporation in the early 1980s. Also in the early 1980s SDC formed a link with Derwent Publications, producers of patent databases such as the WORLD PATENTS INDEX (WPI), to set up the Derwent SDC Search Service; this was responsible for SDC's European work through a host computer in England. In 1986 SDC was purchased by Pergamon Press which had previously, in mid-1980, taken over an existing, but not very successful British online search service known as InfoLine, and formed Pergamon InfoLine. The new merged company is known as Pergamon ORBIT InfoLine. In late 1988 Pergamon also bought other companies involved with the online information industry; these included the Official Airlines Guide from Dun and Bradstreet, Macmillan's (a large US publisher) and BRS Information Technologies, an American online search service.

The New York Times Information Bank was an early news-based search service that started to operate in 1973, and ceased operating in the late 1970s. A more recent news-based service is Textline. This British service was set up by Finsbury Data Service in 1980 and was acquired by Reuters in 1986. Reuters is an important financial online search service (Oppenheim, 1987, quotes its 1986 profits as $193 million), which in 1987 took over the Canadian firm of Sharp Associates, producers of financial databases. Other major financial online search services include the American firms ADP, Data Resources (DRI), Telerate and Quotron Systems. The sale of Dialog to Knight-Ridder during 1988 is yet another example of a take-over in this volatile market. Knight-Ridder is a large American newspaper and communication company which operates VU-TEXT a search service that specializes in news databases.

In parallel with the work undertaken in the 1970s to develop the telecommunications network, Euronet, the Commission of the European Communities (CEC), and in particular the Directorate General for Telecommunications, Information Industries and Innovation (DGXIII) encouraged organizations to make scientific, technical, economic or social databases available on Euronet. The term DIANE-Direct Access Network for Europe was used to describe these information services. Mahon (1980) gives a good account of the development of Euronet-Diane which by 1983 had grown to provide access to 370 databases available on 40 search services to 2500 users undertaking about 35 000 searches a year.

The European Host Operators Group (EHOG) was set up with funding from the CEC as a forum in which the information providers could discuss matters of common policy with the CEC, the PTTs or others. Current details of European online search services are available on the DIANE GUIDE database on the CEC's search service ECHO (European Commission Host Organization). There are now over 90 European search services and these vary greatly in size, number of users and number of databases. Table 2.3 gives an idea of the range of services and subjects covered.

In order to overcome the problems for the searcher in using a wide variety of command languages on the various search services, the CEC funded work on the development of a common command language (CCL) in the late 1970s; Negus (1979) provides a description of this language. The CEC continues to fund projects

Service	Country	Subjects
BELINDIS	Belgium	Belgian databases as well as INIS
CED (Centro Elettronico di Documentazione Giuridica)	Italy	Italian Law
CIDC (Consorcio de Informacion i Documentacion de Catalunya)	Spain	Catalan economic and statistical data
Datacentralen	Denmark	Various – including literature on energy published in Nordic countries
Fiz-Technik	FRG	Engineering and industrial management information
G.CAM	France	News, business and financial data
Helecon	Finland	Business and management
INPADOC	Austria	Patents
MIC-KIBIC (Karolinska Institute Library and Information Centre)	Sweden	Swedish biomedicine and Medline
Meridian Systems Management	Britain	Various – including House of Commons database POLIS
Time-sharing	Portugal	Portuguese law and legislation
TNO	Netherlands	Shipping industry

Table 2.3   *Examples of European online search services*

to enhance information services in Europe; its priorities for 1989/90 are for work on:

1. Intelligent interfaces.
2. Tourism information.

3. Patents information.
4. Cooperation between libraries.
5. Image banks.
6. Road transport information.
7. Information on standards.

Some European search services (such as Data-Star) are now being actively marketed in the United States and Ojala (1988) describes this activity.

By 1992 Europe will become a 'single market' which will enable the free movement of goods, persons, services and capital between European countries. There are beginning to be, and no doubt will continue to be, many developments in the online search services in Europe related to this. The Spearhead database from the British Department of Trade and Industry on the Profile search service, for instance, provides details of measures agreed, being discussed and likely to be discussed by the CEC. It is thought that the single European market will have a great impact on the business community and therefore business information services. Holmes (1988) looks at the current state of these services and outlines some of the problems such as the variation in business activity codes (the Standard Industry Classification – SIC – codes are used in Britain whereas most other European countries use the less specific General Industrial Classification of Economic Activity – NACE codes), language, units of currency, national variations of the rules governing the disclosure of company information and so on.

Brief descriptions of some remote search services are now given to provide the reader with a feel for the wide variety of such services available. A fuller description of these services and some more specialized ones is given by Saffady (1988a). Up-to-date details of search facilities and database holdings are best obtained directly from the search service.

BLAISE

The British Library Automated Information Service (BLAISE) is the name given to a range of library and information retrieval services provided by the British Library in London. BLAISE was set up in 1977 and initially offered access to the US National Library of Medicine's MEDLINE range of databases and the UK MARC databases. By the late 1980s the BLAISE search service, known as BLAISE-LINE, had about 20 databases, all bibliographic; these include the UK MARC database (from 1950), the LC MARC database (from 1968), material published and distributed by Her Majesty's Stationery Office (HMSO), the British Library Catalogue (BLC), the union catalogue of the University of London, 18th century items and grey literature. The link to the NLM databases is provided through BLAISE by a service known as BLAISE-LINK; searching is carried out at NLM in Bethesda, Maryland. Apart from the main MEDLINE databases (from 1966) a variety of other medically-related databases – for example, BIOETHICSLINE (ethical questions), CANCERLINE (cancer), POPLINE (population and family planning) – are available for searching at NLM.

BRS Information Technologies

BRS Information Technologies of New York was established in the mid-1970s to provide innovative and cost effective online searching. The service provides online access to over 130 databases which cover both reference – for example, DISSERTATION ABSTRACTS ONLINE and EMBASE (Excerpta Medica) and source – for example, the full-text HBR ONLINE (*Harvard Business Review*) and the KIRK-OTHMER ONLINE (*Encyclopedia of Chemical Technology*) – databases. BRS has a particularly strong collection of medical databases including the AIDS Knowledge Base from San Francisco General Hospital. The search software, BRS/Search, is command-driven and is also available for searching in-house reference or source databases on a mainframe, mini or microcomputer. A menu approach to searching is available using the BRS/Brkthru service. BRS also operates a special evening service known as BRS/After Dark which offers subscribers access to many BRS databases at a very low hourly rate. A separate company, BRS/Europe, has developed the BRS/Search software by adding more features (including interfaces with full windowing facilities) for use with CD-ROM databases.

In late 1988 it was announced that the Maxwell Group had acquired BRS from its previous owners, the Thyssen-Bornemisza Group. BRS' databases will complement those available on other Pergamon ORBIT InfoLine search services.

Data-Star

Data-Star was set up by Radio Suisse, Switzerland in 1980 and has grown so that it now has a large collection of over 100 databases, many of which specialize in European data. The broad subjects covered include:

1. Biomedicine, with reference databases such as MEDLINE, EMBASE, AIDS, PSYCINFO (*Psychological Abstracts*) as well as full-text source databases such as MARTINDALE ONLINE which gives the uses of each drug and known problems and side effects.
2. Chemistry with reference databases such as CA SEARCH as well as source databases such as CHEM-INTELL (details of chemical trade and production statistics).
3. Science and technology with reference databases such as COMPENDEX, SCISEARCH, INSPEC, NTIS and POLLUTION ABSTRACTS.
4. Business with source databases on companies such as ICC (UK), HOPPENSTEDT (FRG, Netherlands and Austria), KYODO (Japan) and INVESTEXT (world), market information, industry information with databases such as TRADSTAT giving monthly import/export statistics from 14 trading countries, and reference databases such as ABI/INFORM, PREDICASTS and MANAGEMENT CONTENTS.
5. News with databases, such as DOW JONES TEXTSEARCH, as well as the news in specific areas, for example, PHIN (pharmaceutical industry) and CNEW (European Chemical industry).

Dialcom

Dialcom is the name used for a family of business information services provided by British Telecom (BT). BT set up the Prestel videotex service in the 1970s (as described in Chapter 11) and in the early 1980s an electronic mail service known as Telecom Gold was initiated by BT. In 1986 BT moved into the online business information field with a search service known as HOTLINE which provided access to a range of about 20 databases covering business news, company information and marketing data. In 1988 BT bought Dialcom Inc in the US.

Dialog

Dialog Information Services Inc was a wholly-owned subsidiary of the Lockheed Corporation of Palo Alto California until it was sold to Knight-Ridder in 1988. This online search service was one of the first to operate commercially when it began in 1972. In its 1986 and 1987 annual reports some of the basic statistics of the service given were:

1. There are more than 320 databases covering a wide subject area.
2. There are more than 80 000 customers of Dialog in 80 countries.
3. It includes references and abstracts from more than 100 000 publications.
4. It includes information on more than 12 million companies.
5. It contains the complete text of over 450 periodicals.
6. It contains data on six million patents in 26 countries.
7. It has data on nearly nine million chemical substances.

Dialog has been a market leader in online reference search services for many years. However, it has continued to enhance its search software (new commands such as OneSearch, which allows the searching of multiple databases as though they are one), to add more databases to its vast collection and to diversify into new markets. Examples of new services include:

1. Knowledge Index – a low-cost evening and weekend service for accessing about 50 of Dialog's databases.
2. Dialog Business Connection – an easy-to-use, menu-driven service aimed at business professionals.
3. Dialog Medical Connection – an easy-to-use, menu-driven service aimed at biomedical researchers, physicians and health professionals.
4. Dialmail – an electronic mail service for the online community.
5. Dialog onDisc – a service that provides various databases (for example, ERIC, NTIS, CANADIAN BUSINESS AND CURRENT AFFAIRS and MEDLINE) on CD-ROM with the Dialog search software.

DIMDI

The Deutsches Institut für Medizinische, Dokumentation und Information (DIMDI) is based in Köln (FRG) and started to offer an online search service, initially via a special telecommunications network (DIMDINET) to medical databases, such as MEDLINE, in the early 1970s. DIMDI has developed a general relational-based information processing system known as GRIPS to search its databases stored on Siemens computers. DIMDI is an important European online search service providing access to over 50 reference and source databases (containing about 40 million records) many of which are in the biomedical area; examples include AGRIS (from the Food and Agriculture Organisation), ASYLDOC (legal aspects relating to asylums), CAB ABSTRACTS (from the Commonwealth Agricultural Bureau International), Excerpta Medica's EMBASE, and HSDB, a toxicological database. DIMDI also has a number of German language databases such as ELFIS (information on food, agriculture and forestry), DEG-WEINE-LISTE (data on wine analyses) and BIFOS (court decisions on the Narcotics Act of the FRG). A menu-driven approach (in either English or German) is a recent addition to the GRIPS software. DIMDI continues to add databases to its collection especially in the psycho-social aspects of biomedicine. DIMDI is also accessible via the German videotex service Bildschirmtext.

Dow Jones News/Retrieval

Dow Jones & Company Inc set up its Dow Jones News/Retrieval (DJNR) information service for American stockbrokers in 1974. It is now a large online search service in America which specializes in business and investment support information; Dow Jones publishes the *Wall Street Journal* and this is available in full-text on the service. Databases include DISCLOSURE/ONLINE, JAPAN ECONOMIC DAILY, INVESTEXT and various news databases (for example, NEWS/RETRIEVAL WORLD REPORT and NEWS/RETRIEVAL SPORTS REPORT). The service is aimed at end-users and the software incorporates features to enable business people to manipulate the information retrieved.

ECHO

ECHO, the European Commission Host Organization, was set up in 1980 by the CEC to contribute actively to, and encourage and support the use of, online information in Europe. Unlike other search services it is a non-commercial organization and it offers access to unique databases (either wholly or partly supported by the CEC) which are not available on any other online search service. These databases may be multilingual; eight languages in total are covered – English, French, German, Italian, Spanish, Portuguese, Danish and Dutch. Some databases are aimed at providing the user with guides to the online information sources available in Europe such as DIANE GUIDE, which gives details of funded work in the CEC, and EABS, which contains references to CEC-funded scientific and technical research. EURODICAUTOM is an online terminological database which contains scientific and technical terms, contextual phrases and abbreviations in the official European community languages (with the exception of Greek).

ECHO also acts as a test-bed for some new databases which are loaded at a pre-commercial stage so that database producers can test out the market and gain customer reaction. The number of ECHO's clients rose from 1200 in 1985 to 4500 in 1988.

ESA-IRS

The Information Retrieval Service of the European Space Agency (ESA-IRS) of Frascati, Italy, started to offer an online search service in the early 1970s using a special telecommunications network known as ESANET. The search software used now, ESA-QUEST, evolved from the original RECON software developed for the equivalent American organization NASA. Originally its databases were space-oriented but over the years the scope has widened considerably to cover a variety of subject areas. There are now over 130 databases, mainly bibliographic, containing more than 40 million references. Apart from core databases in science and technology other areas covered include:

1. Business and finance (ABI/INFORM, INFOCHECK, BUSI-NESS SOFTWARE).
2. Corporate intelligence management (CHEM-INTELL, JORDANWATCH, NTIS).
3. Health and safety (CHEMICAL HAZARDS IN INDUSTRY, HSELINE, NIOSH).
4. Patents (COMPUTERPAT, PATSEARCH).
5. News (BIS INFOMAT, MIDEAST).

ESA-IRS has continued to develop its software with commands

such as DOWNLOAD (to enable downloading of data for local later reuse), ZOOM (for analysing terms in retrieved sets) and QUESTCLUSTERS (for searching on multiple databases). ESA-IRS also offers a communications software package, Mikrotel, for users with microcomputers to link in with the system, an electronic mail service and the opportunity for users to create their own menus. ESA-IRS is one of the most used online search services in Europe and there is a network of national centres in various European countries such as Belgium, Denmark, Ireland, Netherlands, Spain, Sweden and Britain which provide local support and training as well as the main offices in Frascati and Paris. In Britain this centre is at the Department of Trade and Industry and in the early years the service was marketed under the name of Dialtech.

JOIS

The Japan Information Centre of Science and Technology (JICST) Online Information System (JOIS) was set up in 1976. Initially it was used within Japan but in 1985 overseas searchers were able to gain access to this service. JICST's main work is in preparing abstracts in Japanese (using Kanji characters) of scientific, technological and medical articles published in Japan; this forms the main JICST database on JOIS. English abstracts of these articles are converted automatically from indexed Japanese keywords using a special JICST thesaurus; this database JICST-E is also available for searching on JOIS. Some source databases are also becoming available on JOIS. JICST also imports some major western databases (including BIOSIS, CAB, FSTA, INSPEC, MEDLINE and EMBASE) which are also available for searching in Japan on JOIS. The original command language on JOIS is being developed to include features such as multifile searching, proximity searching and downloading.

Kompass Online

This online service started in 1985 and provides access to many of the company directories, such as *Kompass*, *Kellys*, *Directory of Directors* and *UK Trade Names*, published by Reed International. The main file contains details of about 160 000 UK companies with information on their products grouped into one or more of Kompass' 45 000 categories. Details of 270 000 European companies in 11 European countries are available on a separate database, EKOL (European Kompass Online).

Mead Data Central

Mead Data Central (MDC) is part of the American Mead Corporation, an international forest products and electronic publishing company. In 1973 MDC introduced LEXIS, a full-text online database aimed directly at lawyers, that has become well used in both America and Europe. In 1980 MDC set up NEXIS, a full-text business and news oriented database, which contains over 350 publications, some 40 of which are specifically aimed at international information. Examples of publications covered include the *Financial Times*, *TASS*, *Japan Economic Journal* and the *Xinhua* (New China) News Agency. Other services available on MDC include:

1. EXCHANGE, which contains analyses from leading banking, brokerage and research firms on financial and economic matters.
2. MEDIS, which contains various medical publications and details of new medical and surgical devices and treatments.
3. NAARS, which contains the annual reports from more than 4200 companies.

ORBIT Search Service

The ORBIT Search Service, now a division of Pergamon ORBIT InfoLine (as outlined earlier in the chapter), concentrates on scientific, technical and patent information. The service, based in McLean, Virginia, US, is a host to some 100 databases covering more than 75 million references. ORBIT is particularly strong on patent information with databases such as:

1. INPADOC, from the International Patent Documentation Center.
2. WPI, from Derwent Publications.
3. CLAIMS, from the IFI Plenum Data Company.
4. JAPIO, from the Japan Patent Information Organization.
5. USPATENTS from Derwent Publications.

Several databases produced by various British research associations which were previously available on the British Pergamon

InfoLine service have been switched over to ORBIT; these include:

1. AQUALINE, from the Water Research Centre.
2. PIRA, from the Paper and Board, Printing and Packaging Industries Research Association.
3. RAPRA ABSTRACTS, covering commercial and technical information on plastics and rubber.
4. WORLD SURFACE COATING ABSTRACTS, from the Paint Research Association.

A special telecommunication link, known as ORBITNET, enables European users to access the ORBIT computers directly.

PFDS

PFDS (Pergamon Financial Data Services) is also a division of Pergamon ORBIT InfoLine. This British-based service was renamed (from Pergamon InfoLine) in early 1988 and aims to provide information services to the European business community. PFDS includes databases in the following areas:

1. Marketing and sales prospecting, with databases such as DUN AND BRADSTREETS, KBE (Key British Enterprises), DMI (Duns Market Identifiers), INDUSTRIAL MARKET LOCATIONS, NATIONAL COMPUTER INDEX and IRISH COMPANY PROFILES.
2. Finance and credit checking, with databases such as JORDAN-WATCH and INFOCHECK.
3. Corporate intelligence and news, with databases such as BIS INFOMAT, NEWSFILE, WHO OWNS WHOM, DIRECTORY OF AMERICAN RESEARCH AND TECHNOLOGY, MID-EAST and CHEMICAL AGE PROJECT FILE.

PFDS provides a range of output options for information retrieved from its databases using the BASIS software. A front-end menu option as shown in Search Example 1.2 is available which can be used to assist searching, particularly by end-users.

Other Pergamon companies are involved in the online industry too: Pergabase produces the system CHEMQUEST for locating suppliers of commercially available chemicals, and Pergamon Compact Solution is the European licensee for the KRS (Knowledge Retrieval System) – a software package designed to integrate text retrieval and graphics on CD-ROM databases.

Profile Information

Profile Information is the name given in 1987 to the former Datasolve Information Online service when that service was acquired by FT Information Online, part of the Financial Times group of companies. Profile now specializes in the provision of full-text online information tailored to meet the requirements of specific business sectors. Among Profile's 1000 plus information sources are:

1. Major newspapers such as the *Financial Times*, *The Guardian*, *The Independent*, *The Washington Post* and *The Wall Street Journal*.
2. Other international news services such as the Associated Press, TASS newswires and Asahi News Service.
3. International business magazines such as *The Economist* and *Business Week*.
4. Specialist publications and services for specific business sectors, particularly marketing and finance.

The McCARTHY ONLINE database (produced by McCarthy Information, a wholly owned subsidiary of the Financial Times), which provides articles from a broad range of English and foreign language publications as well as key facts on selected companies, is also available. The search software is designed to be easy to use and the service is aimed at end-users as well as intermediaries. Searchers can acquire an integrated package consisting of a workstation, laser printer and suitable software to analyse the company reports retrieved from the database.

STN International

STN (Scientific and Technical Information Network) International is the name given to a service operated cooperatively by three organizations (one in Japan, one in FRG and one in the USA) for the international scientific community. The Japanese partner is the Japan Association for International Chemical Information, in Tokyo. The German partner is FIZ-Karlsruhe (Fachinformations Zentrum Energie, Physik, Mathematik); this service was founded in 1977 with the aim of providing and disseminating information in energy, physics, mathematics and related areas. The American partner is the Chemical Abstracts Service, a division of the American Chemical Society, and producer of the CAS Online database, which is available on STN with abstracts. About 70 databases are available for searching on STN using the commands of the Messenger software. Structure searching is also available to provide the capability for searching chemical structure diagrams; the construction of such searches may also be done offline using the STN Express software package.

Télésystèmes-QUESTEL

Télésystèmes-QUESTEL is a French online search service which started to operate during the 1970s. It provides access to about 60 databases which include the following subjects:

1. Patents with a strong collection of databases such as Derwent's WPI, the European Patent Office's documentation databases and the French patent database (FPAT).
2. Chemistry, including CAS, JANSSEN (a catalogue of chemical products), MERCK INDEX (bibliographic, chemical, physical and toxicity data).
3. Trademarks, both French and international from the World Intellectual Property Organization.
4. Medicine, including MEDLINE and BIOETHICSLINE.
5. Science and technology including PASCAL, produced by the Centre de Documentation Scientifique et Technique, and other French-produced databases in gas research, geology, energy, agriculture, telecommunications, as well as BIBLAT, a multi-disciplinary database on Latin America from the Universidad Nacional Autonoma de Mexico.
6. Business, including Dun & Bradstreets and several French-produced databases.
7. News, including AFP (news dispatches from Agence France-Presse) and QUESTA (questions addressed to cabinet ministers by members of the French parliament).

The Questel software is designed to be adaptable for various types of end-user from medical professionals to stock brokers. A more powerful search package, Questel Plus, is available for specialists in online information retrieval. In 1979 Télésystèmes-QUESTEL introduced DARC, a chemical substructure searching system developed at the University of Paris. DARC is designed for use by chemists with both graphic and text input devices, and can be used for both in-house and external searching. In particular, the MARKUSH-DARC system is used for the input, storage and retrieval of compounds included in the definition of generic structure representations commonly used in patents.

Télésystèmes-QUESTEL is a subsidiary of the COGECOM Group which specializes in telecommunications, engineering, data processing and office automation. The online search service has 7000 customers world-wide. In 1981 a subsidiary, Questel Inc, was founded in the US and there are representatives of the service in various other countries, including IST-Informatheque in Canada, Fraser Williams (Scientific Systems Ltd) in Britain and Maruzen Co Ltd and Kinokunyia Ltd in Japan. Fraser Williams has produced a microcomputer software package, CHEMLINK, for building chemical structure queries for processing on Télésystèmes-QUESTEL.

Textline/Newsline/Dataline

These online business search services were set up in 1980 by a British firm, Finsbury Data Services; in 1986 they became part of Reuters. Textline provides facts, figures and comments on a wide range of topics covering banking and finance, computing and electronics, property and construction, marketing, insurance and investment, chemicals, accountancy, travel, and aerospace and defence in many countries. Newsline is a daily current awareness news service whilst Dataline provides company financial data and forecasts.

Developments in Telecommunications Technology

During the 1960s work was in progress in America on developing techniques to enable physically remote computer systems to talk to each other. The result of this work was a prototype network developed by ARPA (Advanced Research Projects Agency) and known as ARPANET. ARPANET was a collection of leased lines dedicated to the transmission of digital (computer) signals. A unique feature of ARPANET was that it used a technique known as *packet switching*. In a packet switching system small defined blocks of data (called packets) are independently transmitted from point to point between the source and the destination and then reassembled into proper sequence at the destination. The advantages of packet switching (as opposed to circuit switching in which a single path through the network linking the source to the destination is set up) are that it maximizes network use (and therefore is cost-effective); it enables different routes to be explored in the case of failure or congestion; and it enables better error control. During the late 1970s and 1980s this technique was employed by most national data networks. The devices for assembling and disassembling the packets of data are known as PADs (Packet Assembler/Disassembler). When using a packet switched network the computer (or terminal) is connected to the local 'node' or packet switching exchange (PSE). These PSEs are linked by high speed transmission lines to form the network.

ARPANET started to operate experimentally in America in the early 1970s linking computer systems in academic and research establishments. There was also a link to University College, London, which enabled early British online searchers to access MEDLINE at the National Library of Medicine. The experience and expertise gained from ARPANET was used in the design of the Tymnet and Telenet data networks that started to operate in America in 1971 and 1975, respectively. These are both known as value-added networks (VANs) because their owners lease transmission lines from AT&T (American Telephone and Telegraph) and add their own switching and communications facilities. Tymnet and Telenet now have nodes in many other parts of the world (for example, in Japan, Australia, New Zealand, France, Spain, Sweden, the UK, Canada and Mexico) thus enabling online searchers in those countries access to the remote services in America.

In the 1970s several national Postal, Telegraph and Telecommunications (PTT) authorities began to explore the possibilities of setting up national data networks for transmitting digital data that could be grafted on to the existing analogue network without fundamental engineering changes. Examples of such networks include IBERPAC (Spain), Transpac (France), Datex-P (FRG), DDX-P (Japan), Austpac (Australia), Helpac (Greece), SKDP (Indonesia) and Datapak (Sweden). A major impetus for this expansion was the adoption in 1976, by the CCITT (Comité Consultatif International Télégraphique et Téléphonique) of a connection standard known as X.25 for public packet switched data networks. In Britain an Experimental Packet Switched Service (EPSS) was set up in 1977 and this was followed by the full operational service, known as Packet Switch Stream (PSS) in 1981; during 1988 PSS became known as PDN (Public Data Network).

IPSS – the international packet switching service – enables links from PDN to 56 other data networks in 40 countries. Casey (1982) provides a good overview of international developments in these networks up to the early 1980s.

A further impetus to the growth of the European online industry was the approval in 1971 by the Council of Ministers of the CEC of a series of resolutions to create a network for the collection and dissemination of scientific and technical information within the community. The first phase (1975–77) involved detailed negotiations between the national PTTs for the development of a data network to provide distance-independent access to a number of online search services in Europe. The resulting network had nodes (or PSEs) in Frankfurt, London, Paris and Rome and remote concentrators in Amsterdam, Brussels, Copenhagen, Dublin and Luxembourg; thus it provided the then nine member countries of the CEC with a national access point. During the second phase (1978–80), this network was implemented and became known as Euronet-Diane.

By 1984 this telecommunications network had disappeared as each of the countries involved had developed its own data network and arrangements were made between all the PTTs for transmission of data across national borders. However, the CEC is still very involved in this area and the newsletter *Information Market* keeps readers informed of European developments. There are currently plans to set up a European-managed data network involving 18 PTTs. All developments in telecommunications are generally aimed at providing more reliability for the online searcher of remote services. However EUSIDIC (the European Association of Information Services) found, in its 1988 Survey (Eusidic, 1988) of some 5669 calls originating in Europe to European search services, that almost a quarter failed.

A particular telecommunications network that is used to link British universities, polytechnics, research establishments and the British Library is JANET (the Joint Academic Network). Buxton (1988) describes how JANET is used to search other libraries' catalogues, to search BLAISE-LINE and other remote search services.

Most of the telecommunications networks used to access remote online search services are known as wide area networks (or WANs). The term is used to differentiate such networks from local area networks (LANs) which may be used to link workstations in a particular building or restricted geographic area (not exceeding about 10 km). Since the mid-1970s WANs have relied on ordinary analogue telephone lines to link the user's workstation to the network. However, in the future ISDN (the Integrated Services Digital Network) will provide a fully digital network in which both voice and data can be transmitted in a digital manner from point to point. Tuck (1988) describes the existing WAN technology and outlines the developments of ISDN. The concept of ISDN was proposed by the CCITT in 1984, and the aim is that any communications device (for example, telephone, fax machine, terminal, computer) can, via a standard wall socket and without the use of a modem, transmit information to another device attached to a similar socket. Such a development will encourage the use of full-text databases and enhance the delivery of source documents with the higher speed access.

Further developments in telecommunications involve the use of fibre optics, where information is transmitted down thin flexible fibres of glass as a digital series of light pulses. This technology enables large volumes of data to be transmitted at very high speeds.

Growth of Databases on CD-ROM

CD-ROM databases started to appear in the mid-1980s and by late 1988 there were 390 products (*CD-ROM Directory*). The capacity of a CD-ROM disc is currently about 550 Mb but work on higher density discs is in progress. This means that the ERIC database of 600 000 or so records on education published since 1966 currently requires three CD-ROM discs. Hatvany (1987) of Silver Platter Information, a firm producing many databases on CD-ROM, states that a prototype CD-ROM containing the equivalent of four gigabytes (4000 Mb) has been produced using sophisticated data compression techniques. As with microfiche, the 'mastering' process of producing a CD-ROM is expensive, whilst copies can be produced at a relatively low cost. One of the factors affecting the growth of databases on CD-ROM has been the setting up of an international standard ISO 9660 (sometimes referred to as the High Sierra standard), for storing information on CD-ROM discs and the quick acceptance of this standard by database producers. Roth (1988) provides more details on the development of CD-ROM and its applications.

Many organizations in the online industry, including online search services (such as BRS and Dialog), database producers (like the Library Association and CAB International) and software producers (such as STATUS and BRS/Search) have entered the CD-ROM market. There are also some examples of database producers coming together to merge databases on a similar subject into a CD-ROM product. PERINORM, for instance, is a CD-ROM database containing information on standards from STANDARD-LINE (British Standards Institution), NORIANE (Association Française de Normalisation, AFNOR) and DTR (Deutsches Institut für Normung, DIN). PERINORM contains bibliographic entries for current and draft, European and international standards; it can be searched using English, French or German. A CD-ROM of British companies has been produced by Jordans in conjunction with the Belgian firm, Bureau Marcel van Dijk; this is known as FAME (Financial Analysis Made Easy) and incorporates software to analyse the company information retrieved.

Many in the publishing world see CD-ROM technology as being revolutionary especially when CD-ROM and CD-audio/video players are combined to provide a reference source including the written word, the spoken word, music and pictures.

Originally databases on CD-ROM could only be searched by a single user at a time. Using a workstation similar to that shown in Figure 1.2, a single CD-ROM disc would be inserted into a CD-ROM player which would then be searched by a single user. Cambridge Scientific Abstracts, publisher of medical and scientific information developed, in late 1988, a multi-platter facility that enables four CD-ROM disc drives to be linked for simultaneous searching, and an American company, Meridian Data, has developed CD-ROM disc drives built especially for use with local area networks.

In a study of the market opportunities for CD-ROM in Europe (Daum, 1988), it was forecast that CD-ROM's "main database distribution will be complementary to online's, delivering value-added subsets of single or multiple databases to niche markets". A view of the marketing opportunities from an American perspective is provided by Arnold (1988). He includes estimates of sales of CD-ROM products in America during 1988; Bowker's BOOKS IN PRINT PLUS (250–400), Lotus' CD/Corporate (200–400), Silver Platter's ERIC (100–200), and foresees that the newer optical disc technologies open up facilities for publishers to create a tailored optical information project which may only sell to a handful of customers. CD-ROM databases are, and will be, very useful tools in developing countries which typically do not have the necessary telecommunication facilities to link with the remote online search services.

CD-ROM discs are one example of optical discs. Saffady (1988b) provides a general overview of the whole spectrum of optical storage technology. Other types of optical discs include CD-I (Compact Disc-Interactive), WORM (Write Once Read Many times) and multiple write discs. WORMs come in two sizes 5¼ inches and 12 inches. The 5¼-inch WORM discs are capable of storing 100–400 Mb on each side and are designed for microcomputers whilst several 12-inch WORMs may be placed in a jukebox-like device to provide a large storage capacity.

A number of projects involving CD-ROM technology are currently being funded by the CEC. These include:

1. The ADONIS project (Stern and Campbell, 1988), which involves links between publishers and librarians particularly with regard to the supply of copies of previously published articles that are protected by copyright. During 1987–90 a trial is taking place which will deliver the text and graphics from over 200 medical journals on weekly editions of CD-ROM to selected document fulfilment centres such as the British Library Document Supply Centre, Medical Library in Köln (FRG), the Royal Academy of Science in Amsterdam and the Centre de Documentation Scientifique et Technique in Paris.
2. The production of a CD-ROM database containing monthly updates of three medical databases: MEDLINE, EMBASE and PASCAL. This project, known as Medata-ROM, involves Télésystèmes, CNRS and Inserm (France) and Excerpta Medica (Netherlands). The database will be accessible in French and English and will be searched using the Questel-Plus software.
3. The Bio-ROM project (led by Derwent Publications), which will offer biotechnology patents abstracts and journal literature on CD-ROM with Questel software being used to handle the graphics.
4. An encyclopaedic work on chemistry, which will be available on CD-ROM with access menus in either French, German or English and facilities for full-text searching and for chemical sub-structure searching.

When online searching of the remote search services started in the mid-1970s medical librarians were amongst the first to make use of the new information source. Similarly, by the late 1980s, it appears that many users of CD-ROMs are in the medical field.

Growth of Gateways

Gateways of various types appeared during the 1980s, with the aim of making the search process easier and more attractive to the end-user. Unruh (1987) of the National Federation of Abstracting and Information Services (NFAIS), an organization which has developed a code of practice for gateways, identifies three types of gateway:

1. Front end to host system. In this case special software located at the user's site or at the remote computer is used to enhance the search process (for example, Tome Searcher as described in Chapter 8).
2. Front end to front end to host system. In this case the front end accessed by the user links to another front end which then accesses the remote online search service (such as Easynet, as described in Chapter 8).
3. Host system to host system. In this case the gateway arrangement allows users of one search service to be linked to another search service (as in the link between ESA-IRS and PFDS).

Easynet is a system aimed at end-users which was set up in the USA in the mid-1980s. Using a menu-based approach it switches searchers automatically to a suitable database on a particular host service in order to retrieve information to solve their query. About 13 remote search services (including Dialog, Profile and Télé-systèmes-QUESTEL) can be accessed via Easynet. More information on searching using Easynet is given in Chapter 8. European access to Easynet is available through various sponsors or 're-marketers', many of whom incorporate the Easynet service with their own telecommunications network. In Britain, for instance, Istel launched its INFOSEARCH service in 1987; this makes use of a national private network INFOTRAC to link to Easynet, as well as to other British and European databases. Thus users of INFOSEARCH do not have to pay separate bills to cover database use but a fixed charge each month, independent of how much searching has been undertaken. Other such sponsors include Italcable in Italy, Teldan in Israel and Sanoma and the Finnish PTT in Finland. Another example of this type of gateway is Citicorp's Global Reporter, which integrates data from financial information services such as Dow Jones, Financial Times Business Information, Knight-Ridder and Standard & Poor's to provide a single easy-to-use system.

Unruh (1987) identifies some of the advantages of gateways:

1. Users have a wider array of databases available.
2. Users do not have to sign multiple contracts, learn multiple system protocols and command languages, receive bills from multiple organizations.
3. Users may be able to take advantage of automatic database selection or selection assistance in subject areas with which they are not very familiar.
4. Database producers may find that gateways expand market penetration.
5. Host systems may experience increased usage.

Inevitably, however, there are some disadvantages, including possibly an increase in cost, possible copyright problems and a reliance by the user on the efficiency of the gateway.

In summary it can be seen that the online industry has developed greatly in the past 20 years and each year sees more tools and technology available to assist in the search for relevant information.

References

Aitchison, T.M. (1988) The database producer in the information chain. *Journal of Information Science*, **14** (6), 319–327

Arnold, S.E. (1988) Marketing CD-ROM information products: the international opportunities and challenges. In *Online Information 88: 12th International Online Information Meeting Proceedings*, pp. 517–523. Oxford: Learned Information

Bourne, C.P. (1980) Online systems history, technology and economics. *Journal of the American Society for Information Science*, **31** (3), 155–60

Buffet, P. (1987) Questel and Minitel: a suitable marriage. In *Online Information 87: 11th International Online Information Meeting Proceedings*, pp. 1–7. Oxford: Learned Information

Buxton, A. (1988) JANET and the librarian. *Electronic Library*, **6** (4), 250–263

Casey, M. (1982) Packet switched networks – an international review. *Information Technology: Research and Development*, **1** (3), 217–244

CD-ROM Directory 1989: An International Directory of Information Products on CD-ROM (1988). London: TFPL

Cuadra, C. (1978) Commercially funded online retrieval services – past, present and future. *Aslib Proceedings*, **30** (1), 2–15

Cuadra, C. (1988) Editor. *Directory of Online Databases*, **9** (3). New York: Cuadra/Elsevier

Daum, A. (1988) *CD-ROM in Europe*. London: KR Publishing

Eusidic (1988) *European Telecommunications: The Information Industry Perspective*. London: Eusidic

Hall, J.L. (1986) *Online Bibliographic Databases: A Directory and Source Book*, 4th edn. London: Aslib

Holmes, P. (1988) Prospects for European business information in the free market in 1992. In *Online Information 88: 12th International Online Information Meeting Proceedings*, pp. 749–760. Oxford: Learned Information

Luedke, J.A., Kovacs, G.J. and Fried, J.B. (1977) Numeric databases and systems. In *Annual Review of Information Science and Technology*, vol. 12, edited by M. Williams, pp. 119–181. White Plains, New York: Knowledge Industry Publications

Mahon, B. (1980) Euronet-Diane: the European online information network. *Program*, **14** (2), 69–75

Meadow, C. (1988) Online database industry timeline. *Database*, **11** (5), 23–31

Miller, R. (1987) Integrated Services Digital Network (ISDN): telecommunications of the future. *Online*, **11** (2), 27–38

Negus, A.E. (1979) Development of the Euronet-Diane Common Command Language. In *Proceedings of the 3rd International Online Information Meeting*, pp. 95–98. Oxford: Learned Information

Nicholls, P.T. (1988) Laser/optical database products: evaluation and selection. *Canadian Library Journal*, **55** (5), 296–300

O'Leary, M. (1986) Dialog Business Connection: Dialog for the end-user. *Online*, **10** (5), 15–24

Ojala, M. (1988) Best of British information online. *Database*, **11** (6), 15–27

Oppenheim, C. (1987) The importance of online financial information. In *Online Information 87: 11th International Online Information Meeting Proceedings*, pp. 323–333. Oxford: Learned Information

Provenzano, D. (1987a) Where are they now? *Online*, **11** (1), 25–44

Provenzano, D. (1987b) European databanks on the march. *Online*, **11** (5), 17–40

Roth, J.P. (1988) Editor. *CD-ROM Applications and Markets*. Westport, Connecticut: Meckler

Saffady, W. (1988a) The availability and cost of online search services. *Library Technology Reports*, **24** (3), 293–502
Saffady, W. (1988b) *Optical Storage Technology 1988: A State of the Art Review*. Westport, Connecticut: Meckler
Stern, B.T. and Campbell, R. (1988) ADONIS: the story so far. In *CD-ROM: Fundamentals to Applications*, edited by C. Oppenheim, pp. 181–219. London: Butterworths
Tenopir, C. (1988) Users and uses of full-text databases. In *Online Information 88: 12th International Online Information Meeting Proceedings*, pp. 263–270. Oxford: Learned Information
Tuck, B. (1988) Wide area networks: review and update. In *Telecommunications for Information Management and Transfer*, edited by M. Collier, pp. 17–32. Aldershot: Gower
Unruh, E.L. (1987) Gateways: rights, responsibilities and rewards. In *Online Information 87: 11th International Online Information Meeting Proceedings*, pp. 187–195. Oxford: Learned Information
Williams, M.E. (1974) Use of machine-readable databases. In *Annual Review of Information Science and Technology*, vol. 9, edited by C. Cuadra, pp. 221–284. Washington: American Society for Information Science

Chapter 3

Database Structures

The organization of data in a database affects the ways in which information can be retrieved, and therefore it is useful if users of online search services know something about database structures.

Records

Chapter 7 considers the wide variety of databases currently available from online search services. Information can be bibliographic, numeric or full-text, and within these broad categories there are many differences between information stored on, say, a patent database and a dissertations database, although both are bibliographic, or an encyclopaedia database and a legal documents database, although each is full-text. Nevertheless, the basic structure of the databases in all these cases will be similar. These databases are collections of information stored in machine-readable form which have been organized in such a way that discrete items can be retrieved when needed. Each database is made up of many records (containing the information) and rather complicated indexes (which ensure that the information can quickly be located).

Records are the basic units in a database. Each item on the database constitutes one record, so that each patent would be represented by one record, just as would each article from an online encyclopaedia. Every record, therefore, contains a different set of data. The structure of all the records on a database, however, is the same, although that structure will almost certainly differ from the record structure on a different database – the differences might be small or they might be very considerable. It is important to remember that database structures can be quite different even though the databases are available on the same search service. These structural differences are most marked between different types of database; a record in a bibliographic database, for example, will look quite different from a record in a numeric or

full-text database. This can be clearly seen in Figures 3.1, 3.2 and
3.3 where three databases are all available on the same service,
Dialog, but their record structure is very different.

EJ355132   UD512902
  Southeast Asian Curriculum Developers: A Link between Teachers,
Staff, and Students.
    Ferguson, Laura
    Equity and Choice, v3 n2 p34–36 Win   1987
    Language: English
    Document Type: JOURNAL ARTICLE (080); GENERAL REPORT (140)
    Journal Announcement: CIJSEP87
    Three Southeast Asian teachers, one from Vietnam, one from
Cambodia, and one from Thailand, develop curriculum materials for
native language instruction for students in Project LOWELL, the Lowell
(MA) Public Schools transitional program for limited English speaking
Asian refugee children. Their duties and the importance of them are
discussed. (PS)
    Descriptors: *Asian Americans; Bilingual Education Programs;
*Cambodian; Curriculum Development; *Elementary Education; Limited
English Speaking; Native Language Instruction; Program Descriptions;
Refugees; *Thai; Transitional Programs; *Vietnamese
    Identifiers: Asians; *Lowell Public Schools MA

Figure 3.1   *Bibliographic record from the ERIC database*

The record in Figure 3.1, taken from ERIC, a bibliographic
database of educational materials collected by the Educational
Resources Information Center of the United States Department of
Education, describes an article from the journal *Equity and Choice*.
The record contains the author's name, title, abstract, journal
name, language, document type, and a number of descriptors and
identifiers. In the case of ERIC, descriptors are subject terms
assigned by indexers from a published *Thesaurus of ERIC
Descriptors* to represent the content of the original document. This
Thesaurus is updated from time to time to take account of
developments in educational and related subjects covered by the
ERIC database. Identifiers are terms assigned to provide additional
indexing beyond descriptor terms. They are semi-controlled free-
language terms which tend to be more specific than descriptors
(project names, institutions, geographic or geopolitical names,
personal names, etc.) or which have not yet been added to the list
of descriptors. These elements within the ERIC record will not
necessarily be the same ones as are found in records from other

bibliographic databases. The use of descriptors and identifiers in particular is related to the specific policy of the individual database producer. For example, in BIOSIS PREVIEWS, another biblio-graphic database, there are no identifiers, but descriptor/keywords are included. These are natural language terms based on the author's terminology and the article content which are assigned to indicate such things as methodology and instrumentation used, specific drugs, diseases, enzymes and organs, or scientific and common names of organisms (see also Figure 3.4). Garman (1988) describes the processes involved in developing and incorporating a controlled vocabulary into a database.

The numerical record in Figure 3.2 is taken from ECONBASE: TIME SERIES & FORECASTS database and shows the hourly earnings of mining machinery in the U.S. month by month over a series of years. A glance at its structure reveals that it is quite different from the ERIC record.

```
0011235
AVERAGE HOURLY EARNINGS, MINING MACHINERY, UNITED STATES
    Series Code:    WRHP3532U
    Corp Source:    BLS; EMPLOYMENT AND EARNINGS
    SIC Code:       3532 (MINING MACHINERY)
    Start Date:     JANUARY, 1972 (7201)
    Frequency:      MONTHLY
    Units:          US DOLLARS, NOT SEASONALLY ADJUSTED
```

1989	JAN	11.3500	FEB	11.2800	MAR	11.3500
	APR	11.2100	MAY	11.2500	JUN	11.2300
	JUL	11.200				
1988	JAN	11.3200	FEB	11.3300	MAR	11.5300
	APR	11.4200	MAY	11.3800	JUN	11.4000
	JUL	11.4300	AUG	11.4700	SEP	11.4400
	OCT	11.3100	NOV	11.2200	DEC	11.4200
1987	JAN	11.1100	FEB	11.3500	MAR	11.3900
	APR	11.2000	MAY	11.3400	JUN	11.3900
	JUL	11.6100	AUG	11.2700	SEP	11.3400
	OCT	11.5100	NOV	11.3800	DEC	11.4000
1986	JAN	11.3300	FEB	11.3800	MAR	11.4300
	APR	11.2400	MAY	11.3500	JUN	11.4100
	JUL	11.5700	AUG	11.4200	SEP	11.4200
	OCT	11.2800	NOV	11.3000	DEC	11.3200
1985	JAN	11.3900	FEB	11.3900	MAR	11.4200
	APR	11.2500	MAY	11.4100	JUN	11.4000
	JUL	11.5400	AUG	11.3000	SEP	11.5500
	OCT	11.5100	NOV	11.4500	DEC	11.7300
1984	JAN	11.1000	FEB	11.2100	MAR	11.1800
	APR	11.2300	MAY	11.4400	JUN	11.5000
	JUL	11.7300	AUG	11.1700	SEP	11.3000
	OCT	11.2800	NOV	11.2200	DEC	11.5300

1983	JAN	10.5100	FEB	10.8400	MAR	10.8700
	APR	10.8500	MAY	10.8700	JUN	10.9800
	JUL	11.1200	AUG	10.8300	SEP	10.9900
	OCT	11	NOV	10.9900	DEC	11.1400
1982	JAN	10.0700	FEB	10.1800	MAR	10.2400
	APR	10.1300	MAY	10.2300	JUN	10.3400
	JUL	10.3500	AUG	10.3800	SEP	10.5300
	OCT	10.4900	NOV	10.7500	DEC	10.8100
1981	JAN	9.0400	FEB	9.1500	MAR	9.2700
	APR	9.2400	MAY	9.5500	JUN	9.5900
	JUL	9.6700	AUG	9.6600	SEP	9.8100
	OCT	10	NOV	10.0200	DEC	10.2100
1980	JAN	8.1800	FEB	8.2300	MAR	8.3600
	APR	8.2900	MAY	8.3500	JUN	8.3600
	JUL	8.4800	AUG	8.5800	SEP	8.6600
	OCT	8.6800	NOV	8.9100	DEC	9.1000
1979	JAN	7.4800	FEB	7.6200	MAR	7.6000
	APR	7.6800	MAY	7.7300	JUN	7.7700
	JUL	8.1100	AUG	7.9200	SEP	7.9400
	OCT	8.0200	NOV	8.0800	DEC	8.2200
1978	JAN	6.7700	FEB	6.8500	MAR	6.9300
	APR	6.9400	MAY	7.0200	JUN	6.9800
	JUL	7.0500	AUG	7.0100	SEP	7.1300
1977	JAN	6.1000	FEB	6.1800	MAR	6.2300
	APR	6.2900	MAY	6.4500	JUN	6.4600
	JUL	6.5000	AUG	6.4500	SEP	6.4700
	OCT	6.5700	NOV	6.5800	DEC	6.7500
1976	JAN	5.7000	FEB	5.6700	MAR	5.6900
	APR	5.7300	MAY	5.7700	JUN	5.8300
	JUL	5.8700	AUG	5.9300	SEP	5.9700
	OCT	6.0600	NOV	6	DEC	6.1400
1975	JAN	5.2600	FEB	5.2300	MAR	5.3200
	APR	5.3600	MAY	5.3700	JUN	5.3800
	JUL	5.5100	AUG	5.5700	SEP	5.5300
	OCT	5.5900	NOV	5.6000	DEC	5.7000
1974	JAN	4.7500	FEB	4.7300	MAR	4.7800
	APR	4.7900	MAY	4.8400	JUN	4.9200
	JUL	5	AUG	4.9300	SEP	5.0500
	OCT	5.0300	NOV	5.1300	DEC	5.2300
1973	JAN	4.4200	FEB	4.4100	MAR	4.4000
	APR	4.4400	MAY	4.4800	JUN	4.5500
	JUL	4.6200	AUG	4.6500	SEP	4.6800
	OCT	4.6900	NOV	4.7100	DEC	4.6900
1972	JAN	4.0900	FEB	4.1000	MAR	4.1200
	APR	4.1400	MAY	4.1500	JUN	4.2000
	JUL	4.3100	AUG	4.2900	SEP	4.2800
	OCT	4.2900	NOV	4.3100	DEC	4.3900

Figure 3.2 *Numeric record from the ECONBASE: TIME SERIES AND FORECASTS database (excerpt)*

Figure 3.3 is a record from the full-text database which includes the complete text of the 1769 edition of the BIBLE (KING JAMES VERSION). It is quite unlike either the bibliographic or the numeric records, including, for example, information on book (Genesis), chapter (1) and verses (1–29).

Genesis 001

001 In the beginning God created the heaven and the earth.

002 And the earth was without form, and void; and darkness was upon the face of the deep. And the Spirit of God moved upon the face of the waters.

003 And God said, Let there be light: and there was light.

004 And God saw the light, that it was good: and God divided the light from the darkness.

005 And God called the light Day, and the darkness he called Night. And the evening and the morning were the first day.

006 And God said, Let there be a firmament in the midst of the waters, and let it divide the waters from the waters.

007 And God made the firmament, and divided the waters which were under the firmament from the waters which were above the firmament: and it was so.

008 And God called the firmament Heaven. And the evening and the morning were the second day.

009 And God said, Let the waters under the heaven be gathered together unto one place, and let the dry land appear: and it was so.

010 And God called the dry land Earth; and the gathering together of the waters he called the Seas: and God saw that it was good.

011 And God said, Let the earth bring forth grass, the herb yielding seed, and the fruit tree yielding fruit after his kind, whose seed is in itself, upon the earth: and it was so.

012 And the earth brought forth grass, and the herb yielding seed after his kind, and the tree yielding fruit, whose seed was in itself, after his kind: and God saw that it was good.

013 And the evening and the morning were the third day.

014 And God said, Let there be lights in the firmament of the heaven to divide the day from the night; and let them be for signs, and for seasons, and for days, and years:

015 And let them be for lights in the firmament of heaven to give light upon the earth: and it was so.

016 And God made two great lights; the greater light to rule the day, and the lesser light to rule the night: he made the stars also.

017 And God set them in the firmament of the heaven to give light upon the earth,

018 And to rule over the day and over the night, and to divide the light from the darkness: and God saw that it was good.

019 And the evening and the morning were the fourth day.

020 And God said, Let the waters bring forth abundantly the moving creature that hath life, and fowl that may fly above the earth in the open firmament of heaven.

021 And God created great whales, and every living creature that moveth, which the waters brought forth abundantly, after their kind, and every winged fowl after his kind: and God saw that it was good.

022 And God blessed them, saying, Be fruitful, and multiply, and fill the waters in the seas, and let fowl multiply in the earth.

023 And the evening and the morning were the fifth day.

024 And God said, Let the earth bring forth the living creature after his kind, cattle, and creeping thing, and beast of the earth after his kind: and it was so.

025 And God made the beast of the earth after his kind, and cattle after their kind, and every thing that creepeth upon the earth after his kind: and God saw that it was good.

026 And God said, Let us make man in our image, after our likeness: and let them have dominion over the fish of the sea, and over the fowl of the air, and over the cattle, and over all the earth, and over every creeping thing that creepeth upon the earth.

027 So God created man in his own image, in the image of God created he him; male and female created he them.

028 And God blessed them, and God said unto them, Be fruitful, and multiply, and replenish the earth, and subdue it: and have dominion over the fish of the sea, and over the fowl of the air, and over every living thing that moveth upon the earth.

029 And God said, Behold, I have given you every herb bearing seed, which is upon the face of all the earth, and every tree, in the which is the fruit of a tree yielding seed; to you it shall be for meat.

Figure 3.3   *Full-text record from the BIBLE (King James Version) database*

Not only do the various databases differ in record structure, but the same database may have different record structures according to the search service on which it is mounted. Figures 3.4 and 3.5 show a record from the same database, BIOSIS PREVIEWS®, on Dialog and ESA-IRS respectively. The title of the article, its authors' names, the abstract and the assigned index terms are the same in both records, of course, as this information is supplied by BioSciences Information Service, the producer of BIOSIS PREVIEWS. (Note that the index terms are called *Descriptors/ Keywords* on Dialog and *Terms* on ESA-IRS.) A careful examination of these two records, however, reveals a considerable number of differences. To start with, the records actually look quite different despite the fact that much of the information is common to both. There are also a number of divergencies in content. On Dialog, for example, the Journal title is abbreviated while on ESA-IRS the full title is used. Dialog indicates more clearly the language of the article and also provides a description of the Concept Codes and the Biosystematic Code as well as providing four Super Taxa.

    0017557918   BIOSIS Number: 84024453
    GLUTAMINE SYNTHETASE IN LIVER OF THE AMERICAN
ALLIGATOR ALLIGATOR-MISSISSIPPIENSIS
    SMITH D D JR; CAMPBELL J W
    DEP. BIOL., RICE UNIV., P.O. BOX 1892, HOUSTON, TEX. 77251,
USA.
    COMP BIOCHEM PHYSIOL B COMP BIOCHEM   86 (4). 1987.
755–762. CODEN: CBPBB
    Language: ENGLISH
    Subfile: BA (Biological Abstracts)
    1. Glutamine synthetase was shown to be localized in liver
mitochondria of the American alligator, Alligator mississippiensis, by
immunofluorescent staining of frozen liver sections and by the detection
of enzymatic activity and immunoreactive protein in the mitochondrial
fraction following subcellular fractionation of liver tissue by differential
centrifugation. 2. The primary translation product of alligator liver
glutamine synthetase mRNA was shown to have an Mr = 45,000 which
is similar if not identical in size to that of the mature subunit. This mRNA
was found to be heterogeneous in size with a major form corresponding
to 2.8–3.0 kb and a lesser form corresponding to around 2 kb. Both are in
excess of the size required to code for the glutamine synthetase subunit.
The synthesis and presumably the mitochondrial import of glutamine
synthetase in alligator liver are thus very similar to the same processes in
avian liver. 3. Despite the excretion of a high percentage of nitrogen as
ammonia, the demonstration of a mitochondrial glutamine synthetase
indicates the alligator has the typical avian-type uricotelic ammonia-
detoxification system in liver. This suggests that the transition to
uricotelism occurred in the sauropsid line of evolution and has persisted
through both the lepidosaurian (snakes, lizards) and archosaurian
(dinosaurs, crocodilians, birds) lines.

Descriptors/Keywords: LEPIDOSAURIA ARCHOSAURIA BIRD
    MESSENGER RNA TRANSLATION MITOCHONDRIA
    DETOXIFICATION URICOTELIC EVOLUTION
    IMMUNOFLUORESCENT STAINING
Concept Codes:
    *01500 Evolution

*02506 Cytology and Cytochemistry-Animal
*10010 Comparative Biochemistry, General
*10062 Biochemical Studies-Nucleic Acids, Purines and Pyrimidines
*10806 Enzymes-Chemical and Physical
*10808 Enzymes-Physiological Studies
*13012 Metabolism-Proteins, Peptides and Amino Acids
*14004 Digestive System-Physiology and Biochemistry
*15504 Urinary System and External Secretions-Physiology and
        Biochemistry
 01054 Microscopy Techniques-Cytology and Cytochemistry
 10064 Biochemical Studies-Proteins, Peptides and Amino Acids
 10300 Replication, Transcription, Translation
 10804 Enzymes-Methods
 22501 Toxicology-General; Methods and Experimental
 23004 Temperature: Its Measurement, Effects and Regulation-
        Cryobiology
 34502 Immunology and Immunochemistry-General; Methods
        Biosystematic Codes:
 85404 Crocodilia
Super Taxa:
  Animals; Vertebrates; Nonhuman Vertebrates; Reptiles

Figure 3.4 *Record from BIOSIS PREVIEWS on Dialog*

84024453   Biological Abstracts
  GLUTAMINE SYNTHETASE IN LIVER OF THE AMERICAN
ALLIGATOR ALLIGATOR-MISSISSIPPIENSIS
  SMITH D D JR; CAMPBELL J W
  DEP. BIOL., RICE UNIV., P.O. BOX 1892, HOUSTON, TEX. 77251,
USA.
  COMPARATIVE BIOCHEMISTRY AND PHYSIOLOGY B
COMPARATIVE BIOCHEMISTRY(ENGLAND) 1987. Vol. 86, no 4 p755-
762, English Coden: CBPBB

  1. Glutamine synthetase was shown to be localized in liver
mitochondria of the American alligator, Alligator mississippiensis, by
immunofluorescent staining of frozen liver sections and by the detection
of enzymatic activity and immunoreactive protein in the mitochondrial
fraction following subcellular fractionation of liver tissue by differential
centrifugation. 2. The primary translation product of alligator liver
glutamine synthetase mRNA was shown to have an Mr = 45,000 which
is similar if not identical in size to that of the mature subunit. This mRNA
was found to be heterogeneous in size with a major form corresponding
to 2.8–3.0 kb and a lesser form corresponding to around 2 kb. Both are in

excess of the size required to code for the glutamine synthetase subunit. The synthesis and presumably the mitochondrial import of glutamine synthetase in alligator liver are thus very similar to the same processes in avian liver. 3. Despite the excretion of a high percentage of nitrogen as ammonia, the demonstration of a mitochondrial glutamine synthetase indicates the alligator has the typical avian-type uricotelic ammonia-detoxification system in liver. This suggests that the transition to uricotelism occurred in the sauropsid line of evolution and has persisted through both the lepidosaurian (snakes, lizards) and archosaurian (dinosaurs, crocodilians, birds) lines.

Concept Codes: 01054/ 01500–/ 02506–/ 10010–/ 10062–/ 10064/ 10300/ 10804/ 10806–/ 10808*/ 13012–/ 14004–/ 15504–/ 22501/ 23004/ 34502
Biosystematic Codes: 85404
Terms: LEPIDOSAURIA ARCHOSAURIA BIRD MESSENGER RNA TRANSLATION MITOCHONDRIA DETOXIFICATION URICOTELIC EVOLUTION IMMUNOFLUORESCENT STAINING

Figure 3.5 *Record from BIOSIS PREVIEWS on ESA-IRS*

The way in which information is stored in a database – the record structure and the associated indexes – affects the ways in which the searcher can locate that information. It is therefore essential that the searcher should be familiar with the structure of any database used on any particular search system. If in doubt, the searcher should consult relevant documentation, including the database and search system manuals, before commencing the search (for a further discussion of pre-search planning, see Chapter 8). Failure to take this elementary step could seriously jeopardize results.

Fields

Records are divided into a number of separate fields, each field containing one element of information in the record. The significance of fields in online searching can best be illustrated by taking a record from an imaginary database (see Figure 3.6). This record contains bibliographic information about a journal article. It is divided into nine fields: accession number, title, author, journal, year, pagination, language, abstract and descriptor (index terms).

The information contained in this sample record can be indexed in several ways. Firstly, a decision might have been made by the database producer that certain fields would not be indexed at all because no-one is likely to want to search in them. In this case it

```
an:      1233
ti:      Market planning in the software industry
au:      French, John
jn:      Planning Quarterly
yr:      1987
pg:      vol 17, pp.162–175
la:      English
ab:      A study of market forces and marketing in the French software
         industry. Includes forecasts of market growth and industry
         profitability
de:      France, Market Planning, Marketing, Software
```

Figure 3.6   *Sample bibliographic record*

has been decided that the pagination (pg) field will not be indexed; all other fields will be indexed and therefore searchable. Secondly, it is possible to index each term in a searchable field rather than the entire field or only the first term in the field. In practice, search systems usually do not bother to index a small number of very common words which occur very frequently and which are of little value as search terms. These non-indexed terms are called stop words and might, for example, exclude the following words from the index of the sample record: in, the, a, of, and. All other terms in the eight searchable fields will be included in the database index, and this indexing is carried out by the computer. Whenever new records are added to the database, the computer updates the indexes to that database. Thirdly, terms can be defined in several ways to meet the requirements of the database. A term might be defined as one word, as a phrase, or as both. This will become clearer by looking at the index terms which might be generated from the sample record (see Figure 3.7).

English (la)   Market Planning (de)
Forces (ab)   Marketing (ab, de)
Forecasts (ab)   Planning (ti, de)
France (de)   Planning Quarterly (jn)
French (ab)   Profitability (ab)
French, John (au)   Software (ti, ab, de)
Growth (ab)   Study (ab)
Includes (ab)   1987 (yr)
Industry (ti, ab)   1233 (an)
Market (ti, ab, de)

Figure 3.7   *Index terms generated from sample record*

The fields have been indexed as follows:

word only – an, ti, yr, la, ab
phrase only – au, jn
word and phrase – de
not indexed – pg

Most fields have been indexed word by word. This allows searching to take place on individual words in the title and abstract fields as well as by language, year of publication and accession number. Such a capability provides a very powerful retrieval mechanism. Subject searching is not solely reliant on use of assigned index terms in the descriptor field but can draw upon the words that the author has used in the title and the abstract of the article; this is called 'free-text' searching.

Two fields – journal name and author – can only be searched as phrases and not as individual words. A search on the word 'quarterly' would not retrieve the sample record because this word is not entered in the index; only the phrase 'Planning Quarterly' is to be found. It is often useful to keep proper names grouped together as phrases rather than dealing with them as individual words.

Finally, the descriptor field has been indexed both by single words and by phrases. That is to say, the individual words 'Market' and 'Planning' are each entered in the index (and therefore are searchable) as well as the phrase 'Market Planning'. One point to note about all the index terms – words or phrases – is that upper and lower case letters are treated as being identical; although 'market' occurs with a lower case 'm' in the abstract field and an upper case 'M' in the title and descriptor fields it is only entered once in the index.

Indexing procedures are not determined by the searcher but by the database producer and the online search system. The searcher cannot alter the ways in which a database record is structured or indexed but must become familiar with the individual characteristics of any database which is to be used and the searching facilities available on the particular search system.

Many databases and search systems allow the user to look for occurrences of individual words or phrases not only in the record as a whole but within specific fields. Thus, the user might restrict a search on the word 'French' to the language field only. This strategy would then avoid retrieval of records discussing, for example, the French software industry (and therefore containing the word French in, say, the abstract field) but which refer to

English-language documents, not French-language ones (see the record in Figure 3.6). A further refinement offered by some search systems is the provision not of just one index to each database but of several indexes. One index (often called the Basic Index) may be intended for subject searching and in a bibliographic record contain search terms from, say, the title, abstract and descriptor fields. Separate indexes could then be provided for such fields as language, author, publication year, and so on; records on the ERIC database include almost 20 of these additional indexes. In the case of a numerical database like CHASE ECONOMETRICS on Dialog, the Basic Index contains terms from just two fields (title and descriptor) but five additional indexes are provided (corporate source, frequency, Standard Industrial Classification, etc). The use of additional indexes is discussed further in Chapter 5.

File Structure

A user can retrieve records from an online database very quickly – ten seconds would normally be considered a long time to wait for a response – even though the database might contain, as does BIOSIS PREVIEWS, over five million records. This impressive perform-ance is partly accounted for by the hardware and search software, but an important contributory factor is the file organization of the database.

Records are held on disc, usually in order of accession number (in fact this is a rather simplified description but the details of record arrangement on discs are not germane to this discussion). Even high speed computers, however, would take some time to search sequentially through all the records every time a term was sought in the database. Instead, an inverted file structure is usually employed to accelerate search times. The online searcher need not be familiar with the intricacies of actual inverted file structures, but an understanding of the principles behind them sheds light on how the search software works during an online search. More detail can be found in Levine (1981) and in Salton and McGill (1983).

A simple model of an inverted file approach is shown in Figure 3.8. It contains three separate files: the print file, the postings file (also called the inverted file by some writers) and the index file (also called the dictionary file or even, confusingly, the postings file by some commentators – terminology is inconsistent). The

actual records are stored in the print file by accession number.
Figure 3.8 shows just one of the records in the print file, record
1233 (the imaginary record from Figure 3.6). The other two files
provide access to the print file. The first of these is the index file; it
contains all the indexed terms from all the records on the database
arranged in alphabetical sequence. Whenever new records are
added to the print file of the database, the indexable terms are
added to the index file. If the term is not already in this file, it is
added in its alphabetical sequence and a posting number of '1' is
added against it; that is to say, the term occurs in one record on the
database. An example of this in Figure 3.8 is the term 'industry'. If
the term already exists in the index file then the postings number is
simply increased by one. The addition of the term 'Market' would
cause the postings number to increase from 1028 to 1029; there are
now 1029 records containing that term. Should a term occur more
than once in a record (as the term 'Market' does in Figure 3.6) the
postings number is still only increased by one as the index file lists
the number of individual records in which each term is found, not
the total number of occurrences of that term throughout the
database. It must be emphasized that this indexing process is
implemented by the search system at every database update and
does not require the attentions of a human indexer.

Index file

Postings	Term	Postings file location
: :	: :	: :
27	Foam	8935
6	Force	1690
103	Forces	0881
21	Forecasts	6522
759	Foreign	2941
48	France	0757
56	French	1289
2	French, John	7269
141	Growth	0184
3	Hierarchical	9668
112	Includes	2100
1287	Industrial	3109
1	Industry	9573
1029	Market	1177
84	Market Planning	7131
62	Market Strategy	9503
184	Marketing	6109

2043	Markets	6932
649	Move	2373
172	Moving	4142
487	Planning	1999
11	Planning Quarterly	4231
108	Profitability	2548
388	Software	7282
155	Study	0980
: :	: :	: :
: :	: :	: :
: :	: :	: :

Postings File
Location Record numbers
1177	7, 68, 781 . . . 1017
	1233 . . . 2394 . . .
7282	68, 104, 166, 891 . . .
	1233 . . . 1988 . . .

Print File
1232	. . . .
1233	Market planning in the
	software industry.
	French, John
	Planning Quarterly
	1987
	Vol 17,pp.162–175
	English
	A study of market forces
	and marketing in the
	French software industry.
	Includes forecasts of
	market growth and
	industry profitability.
	France, Market Planning,
	Marketing, Software.
1234	. . . .

Figure 3.8 *File structure*

The index file includes one other important element – the postings file location. This location number acts as the link between the index file and the postings file; it points to the place in the postings file where more information is stored about each term listed in the index file. More information about the term 'market' (in the index file with 1029 postings) can be found by checking its postings file location (1177) and then finding this location in the postings file.

The postings file has a location number for every term in the index file. Linked to this number are the record numbers of all the records on the database which include that term. The postings file, then, links the index file with the print file. The term 'market' can be found in records 7, 68, 781, 1017, 1233 and so on.

The print file contains all the records on the database stored in sequential order, usually by record number. It is the textual part of the database and holds the information which the users are actually looking for in a search. In Figure 3.8 just one record is shown (record 1233 from Figure 3.6).

It is now time to see exactly how this inverted file structure enables information to be found on a database. The user might be interested in finding records containing the term 'market'. When this term has been entered at the keyboard, the index file is first checked by the search software to see if 'market' exists on the database. If it cannot be found then the computer responds to the user by indicating that there are no postings for that term. Alternatively, if the term is found then the user is told the number of postings for that term – in the case of 'market', 1029 records contain the term. If the user now wants to look at some of these records, the postings file location for 'market' leads to location 1177 in the postings file where a list of relevant record numbers are stored. These in turn lead to the actual records in the print file, and as many as the user requests can be displayed.

The postings file plays a more crucial intermediary role if the search is slightly more complex than in the last example. Suppose that the user wants to find records about the software market. In this case records are required which contain not only 'market' but also 'software'. Once again, the index file would first be consulted to establish whether the two terms exist and if so, how many records contain each of these terms. 'Market' is to be found in 1029 records and 'software' in 388 records. The user has asked, however, for records containing both these terms; that is to say, only records which are listed at both the relevant locations in the postings file are required. The computer examines the postings file at location 1177 (market) and 7282 (software) and compares the record numbers at 1177 with the record numbers at 7282. Every time a record number is found at both locations (numbers 68, 1233) then a record has been identified that contains both 'market' and 'software'. The user is told how many such matching records have been found – these are called the *hits* – the records which match the search request. The computer can carry out such matches, even when very many record numbers are involved at each location and more than two terms are involved, at very high speeds. If the user wants to look at some or all of the hits, these can then be found by finding the record numbers in the print file. A similar three-stage process involving an initial check in the index file, a matching algorithm in the postings file and a final retrieval from the print file is employed when users want all records containing either one term or else a second term (either 'market' or 'markets' where all record numbers at postings file locations 1177 and 6932 are collectively found) or one term but not another ('software' except where 'market planning' is discussed, that is, all records at postings file location 7282 except those also listed at location 7131).

The actual file structures used by online systems are often a little more complicated than these examples indicate. For example, if searches can be made for terms in particular fields within the record ('market' as long as it is in the title field) then the index file must include the field in which each term can be found. Furthermore, it may be possible to search on terms in specified relational positions (for example, records might only be required in which the term market is immediately preceded by the term software). In this case the index file must also contain information about the word position within a field for each term. Nevertheless, the basic principles governing the operation of inverted files can be grasped from the above description.

Boolean Operators

When a search is made for records containing 'market' and 'software', as in the earlier example, the computer compared record numbers to find which were listed at the locations for each term. Online search services usually make this kind of comparison with the help of boolean operators (although other matching algorithms can be employed and these are discussed in Chapter 13). It is therefore important for the online searcher to gain a clear understanding of the way in which these boolean operators are used.

George Boole was a 19th-century British mathematician and logician who employed mathematical symbolism to express logical processes. His three boolean operators – AND, OR, NOT – provide a flexible way of combining two or more sets in order to produce a required final set. Whenever a search involves looking for more than one term – oil and pollution; oil or coal; coal not anthracite – then some method must be used to match the sets produced for each term. Boolean operators are the chosen method for most online services (although some search systems call these operators by slightly different names instead of using AND, OR, NOT).

The AND operator is used when two terms are to be combined so that records are found which contain both these terms; records which contain neither of these terms or only one of these terms are not required. A search to find all records about oil pollution must identify only those records which contain both 'oil' and 'pollution'. The set containing records on oil is matched with the set containing records on pollution using the AND operator:

OIL AND POLLUTION

so that all records in the oil set are identified so long as they are also present in the pollution set. This boolean relationship is often represented by a Venn diagram which should help to clarify the AND operator. All the records about oil are represented by one circle and all the records about pollution are represented by a second circle. Some of the oil records do not deal with pollution, and some of the pollution records are not concerned with oil. Those records represented by the shaded area of overlap between the two circles, however, include both the term 'oil' and the term 'pollution'; these are the ones which the AND operator finds.

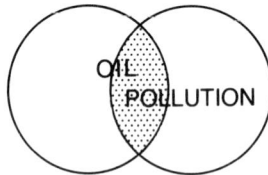

A search for records dealing with either oil or coal requires a different operator; in this case it is not the intersection of records which is sought but the total collection (union) of records on each term. All records on oil and all records on coal, whether or not they deal with both oil and coal, are needed and can be found by combining the terms with the OR operator:

OIL OR COAL

This can also be represented by a Venn diagram. The entire area of each circle is shaded and not just the intersection because all records contained in either set are wanted.

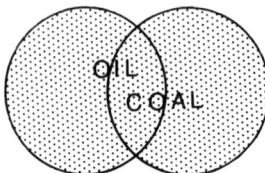

The OR operator is often used to link semantically related terms (including synonyms, and singular and plural forms of a term).

The third operator, NOT, is used when it is desired to exclude from a set of records those which contain a second set. For example, all records about coal may be required except those that deal with anthracite coal:

COAL NOT ANTHRACITE

This is represented by another Venn diagram. In this case, the shaded area comprises that part of the coal set except where it overlaps with the anthracite set.

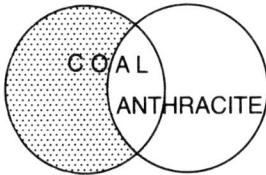

COAL   ANTHRACITE

These three operators are sufficient to handle complex searches where terms are combined in various ways using AND, OR and NOT to locate just those records which are needed. Great care must be taken, however, when using boolean operators; in particular it is quite easy to confuse the AND with the OR operator. The Venn diagrams above have illustrated the very different results which are obtained by using different operators. Use of the wrong operator will produce in all probability a result which bears little relationship to that intended. The use of boolean logic is discussed further in the next chapter where its application is illustrated in a number of simple searches.

References

Garman, N. (1988) An inside look at an online database. *Database*, **11** (2), 50–56

Levine, G.R. (1981) Developing databases for online information retrieval. *Online Review*, **5** (2), 109–120

Salton, G. and McGill, M.J. (1983) *Introduction to Modern Information Retrieval*, Chapters 1–2. London: McGraw-Hill

Further Reading

Davis, C.H. and Rush, J.E. (1979) *Guide to Information Science*, Chapter 8. London: Library Association

Flynn, R. (1987) *An Introduction to Information Science*, Chapters 8–10. New York: Dekker

Harter, S.P. (1986) *Online Information Retrieval: Concepts, Principles, and Techniques*, Chapter 3. Orlando: Academic Press

Chapter 4

Basic Searching

The previous chapter discussed the ways in which information is organized in databases so that discrete data elements can be found when required. It also looked at the way in which terms are selected to represent the major concepts in a search query and explained how occurrences of those terms could be sought in different fields within a record. This chapter concentrates on the searcher's interaction with the retrieval system to find records containing those search terms – that is to say, the mechanics of online searching.

Command-Driven Systems

Any online information retrieval system must provide some method for the searcher to issue instructions to the computer and in return receive messages back from it. The searcher may want to issue an instruction to look at a particular database (the computer might provide access to many databases), to find out which records contain one or more terms or match a particular characteristic (language, type of publication, etc.) or to display records on a screen or on a print-out.

In some cases this dialogue between the searcher and the computer is conducted through a series of menus which present the searcher with choices from which a selection must be made. This menu-driven approach will be considered in more detail at the end of this chapter. Alternatively, interaction between the searcher and the computer may be command-driven. This approach is still more commonly encountered in online search services than the menu approach, and any would-be online searcher will need to acquire some grasp of the techniques used in command-driven systems if access is to be vouchsafed to a range of databases and online search services.

Rather than using a series of menus, the searcher communicates more directly with the computer by using what is called a command language. This language, which uses its own vocabulary and syntax, must be mastered by the user before searches can be carried out. Mistakes in the use of the command language will result either in error messages from the computer, or search results other than those intended. But once mastered, the command language provides a flexible and powerful means of interrogating the computer.

There are almost as many command languages in existence as there are online search systems; in order to search a database on a system it is necessary to use the latter's command language. The need to learn one or more command languages before an online search can be carried out is one of the reasons why many searches, particularly on bibliographic databases, have been undertaken by experienced information intermediaries rather than the people who actually want the information. Various attempts are being made to circumvent the problems caused by command languages (see Chapters 8 and 13) but command-driven systems still occupy a central role in online searching.

In fact, the problem of language multiplicity is not quite so serious as it might seem at first glance. Although there are certainly many command languages, the retrieval systems themselves tend to operate essentially in the same manner. That is to say, individual commands may differ (see below) but the operations they control are similar from system to system. Once one command language for one search system has been mastered it is relatively straightforward to learn other command languages.

Rather than choosing one actual command language in this chapter to demonstrate the principles of online searching, an imaginary language is used, though one closely resembling the Common Command Language (CCL) devised by the Commission of the European Communities for use with European online search services. (The CCL was only adopted by a few of the European hosts and even they tended to adapt it to their own existing command languages, thereby destroying the common element). Searches from three online services are also included later in the chapter to provide some real examples.

Pre-Search Preparation

As with so many other tasks, the quality of the final product from an online search – the search results – will in large part be determined by the care which has been shown at the planning and preparation stages. Pre-search preparation, including the establishment of precisely what is wanted from the search, choosing the best database(s) and online service(s) on which to conduct the search, and planning the strategy in order to get the desired results, are all discussed elsewhere in this book (and especially in Chapters 6 and 8). The importance of this preparation cannot be overestimated and must be completed before any thought is given to sitting at the keyboard and actually beginning the search.

The Search

The search proper begins after the user has logged on to the search service. On some hosts log-on is followed by news from the host about such matters as amendments to the list of databases available, and changes to the command language or network protocols. Once any news items have been displayed, the user will be prompted by the host to enter the first step in the search strategy.

Database selection

Many online services provide access to more than one database; the larger services may include several hundred databases covering many subject areas and including different types of information – full-text, numerical and bibliographic. Some online search services only permit searches to be made on one database (or strictly speaking one file if a database is broken into two or more parts because of its large size) at a time. If a search has to be made in several files then it will be necessary to repeat the search in each one. Other search services offer the chance to search several databases simultaneously. The cluster facility on ESA-IRS is one example; users can create a megafile including up to eight separate files which can then all be searched at once. The OneSearch facility on Dialog works in a similar fashion, users specifying the individual databases which are to be searched collectively (in this case up to a total of 20 databases). One point to note about such multi-database searching is that the same record could be found several times because it happens to exist on several of the databases.

Some online services (for example, Dialog) require that each password issued to a customer should be linked to a default file.

The file so nominated by the customer is then entered automatically at the outset of every search. If the search is to take place in the default file, the user can immediately begin to interrogate the database; otherwise, the first step in the search is to select the database. A file is usually chosen as the default because it is frequently used and therefore in many searches it will not be necessary to bother selecting a file as the prelude to the search. A different reason for choosing a file as the default is to reduce log-on costs. If the service charges for the time during which it is displaying its news it is best to be logged on to a cheap file; the cost of reading the news will then be charged at this rate rather than the rate of a more expensive file. Remember that the difference in hourly connect rates between the cheapest and the most expensive database on a service may be very great.

A different approach has been taken by ESA-IRS. It has designated a special file (File 32) as a parking file. After logging-on to the service the user is immediately placed in the parking file and remains in it until one of the data files is selected. Finally, some search services do not use any kind of default file. Log-on to Data-Star, for example, does not immediately provide the user with access to any file – this only happens when the user chooses one of the files available.

If the service does not provide a default file, or if the user wants to search in a file other than the default, then the first step in the search must be to select the database (normally the identity of the default file is displayed after log-on as a reminder). The user will either be asked to choose a file or else be presented with a general system prompt which indicates that the host computer is awaiting an instruction from the user.

In Search Example 4.1, the user has been placed in a parking file after log-on. The first step, then, is to respond to the system prompt (in this case a question mark) by instructing the service that the search is to be conducted in a bibliographic database, FUEL ABSTRACTS. Several points should be noted. Firstly, until the user responds to the prompt nothing further can happen in the search. Secondly, in this example the database must be identified by a reference number allocated to each database by the search service. Thus the database FUEL ABSTRACTS has been assigned the number 14 and is always identified when searching by this number. Some real services use this device (for example, Dialog and ESA-IRS); others require either the full name of the database or an assigned abbreviation of it to be input (for example, Data-Star and BLAISE). The user must follow precisely the instructions of the search service in this matter. If a database is to be identified by its reference number then its name will not be accepted by the host computer and some kind of error message will be generated. Such error messages can be more or less helpful depending upon the design of the particular service being used. Thirdly, in Search Example 4.1 the database must not only be identified by a number, but that number must be preceded by a command – in this case the command BASE. This tells the service that '14' is a database number and not, for example, a term to be looked for in the database. The vocabulary used to choose a database in this example, then, is a command, BASE, and a database number, 14. The user must know this vocabulary in order to carry out a search. Furthermore, the user must also know the rules for putting together the vocabulary into meaningful statements – the syntax of the command language. In this case the command must precede the number and there must be a space between the two parts of the statement. Fourthly, the system responds to the user input (BASE 14) by confirming that the required database has been selected for searching. It also in this example indicates that the database is online from 1970 and was last updated in January 1989. Finally, the system displays the prompt (?) which indicates that the last instruction (to choose a database) has been carried out and the next instruction from the user is awaited.

PARKING FILE

? **BASE 14**

FILE 14   FUEL ABSTRACTS   1970–1989 (JANUARY)

?

Search Example 4.1   *Selecting a file*

Selecting search terms

Once a file has been selected it is then possible to begin the search proper. The procedure is best illustrated by working through an example: a search is being conducted to locate references in FUEL ABSTRACTS to documents on oil spillage in the Atlantic Ocean.

A strategy has been designed for this search which calls for records to be retrieved which include the following terms: oil, spillage and Atlantic (using terms included in the original query formulation) together with spills and leaks which were not in the query but which are possible synonyms or near-synonyms for 'spillage' (other search terms could be added for comprehensiveness but for this example these five terms are adequate). The term 'ocean' has not been included because 'atlantic' expresses sufficiently well the concept of the Atlantic Ocean. It is useful to group together those terms which represent the same concept; this produces three groupings:

> oil spillage atlantic
>   spills
>   leaks

These terms can then be linked by using one of the boolean operators discussed in Chapter 3. Terms in the same column should be linked by the OR operator because they are alternatives; terms in different columns should be linked by the AND operator because they represent different concepts each of which must be present in any retrieved records.

Although many online search services allow terms to be linked by more than one kind of operator in the same search statement (x AND y OR z) care must be taken if the desired result is to be achieved (see Chapter 5). It is therefore recommended that the novice searcher only links terms in one search statement with one kind of operator. Following this advice, the first step in the search on oil spillage in the Atlantic Ocean will be to find all those records on the database which include either the term 'spillage', the term 'spills' or the term 'leaks'. These terms, then, must be linked together with the OR operator. In the same way as a command was needed before the database number in order to select a database, a command is again needed in front of the search terms to notify the system that those terms are indeed to be searched for in the database. This command in our imaginary search service is FIND. Search Example 4.2 demonstrates the first stage of the search. The command, followed by the three search terms separated by the boolean OR operator, are entered. Once again, the syntax of the command language is as important as its vocabulary. A space must be left on each side of the two operators so that the system can identify them as operators; if no spaces were left then the system would believe it was being asked to search for one term – 'spillageorspillsorleaks'. Online systems normally treat the words 'and', 'or' and 'not' as stop words (that is, non-indexable words) so that they cannot be confused with search terms (see

Chapter 3). The search service makes no distinction between upper-case and lower-case letters, and either can be used.

? **FIND SPILLAGE OR SPILLS OR LEAKS**
    SET 1   324   SPILLAGE
    SET 2   208   SPILLS
    SET 3   159   LEAKS
    SET 4   570   SPILLAGE OR SPILLS OR LEAKS
?

Search Example 4.2   *Selecting terms with the OR operator*

The host computer responds to the search statement by checking the postings file of the FUEL ABSTRACTS database and displaying the number of records which contain each of the terms in the statement. The database therefore includes 324 records with the term 'spillage', 208 records with the term 'spills' and 159 with 'leaks'. The statement asked that the results from the three stages of the search be combined with the OR operator; 570 records contain at least one of the three terms. The sum of these postings for the three terms is in fact 691 and not 570; this difference is accounted for by the fact that 121 of the records must contain more than one of these terms and therefore only 570 *different* records are found.

The system labels each group of postings as a set; thus it identifies the postings for spillage as set 1, for spills as set 2 and for leaks as set 3. Finally, it labels as set 4 the combined postings for these three terms. These set labels can be used if necessary at later stages in the search to recall these results. It is faster to recall postings than to repeat the search for the term (but note that many search services clear this storage space when the user changes from one file to another as well as when leaving the service altogether at the end of a search). The final point to notice in the search example is that the sought term is displayed after the postings figure; this acts as a useful check that the computer has correctly received the term. If the system echo is incorrect then it is always worthwhile to re-input that term. Unfortunately, it cannot be assumed that if the echo is correct then the term was correctly received; any unusual response (for example, a very low posting for a term like 'schools' on an educational database) is always worth checking by repeating the statement.

The remaining two terms, 'oil' and 'atlantic', can now be input using the same command, FIND, but this time combined with the

AND operator (see Search Example 4.3). This produces three new sets – one for each of the terms and a third for the combination of the two. The sets in a search are consecutively numbered and therefore continue on from the earlier fourth set.

? FIND OIL AND ATLANTIC
```
SET 5   725   OIL
SET 6    53   ATLANTIC
SET 7    26   OIL AND ATLANTIC
?
```

Search Example 4.3   *Selecting terms with the AND operator*

The final step in the search is to match together the final sets of each step; the result of ORing spillage, spills and leaks (set 4) must be combined with the result of ANDing oil and atlantic (set 7). The AND operator is used because records are required which are about spillage of oil in the Atlantic. The result of ANDing sets 4 and 7 finds those records which contain the terms oil and atlantic and either spillage or spills or leaks. This produces a final set 8 which includes just six records (see Search Example 4.4). Note that the word 'set' had to be included in this FIND command; otherwise the computer would have confused these characters used as set numbers with their use as numerals (FIND records containing '4' and '7').

? FIND SET 4 AND SET 7
```
SET 8     6   SET 4 AND SET 7
?
```

Search Example 4.4   *Combining two sets with the AND operator*

Looking at retrieved records

It is now possible to examine some or all of the six records in set 8 to establish whether they are relevant to the initial search query. If not, then the search strategy would have to be amended (see below). Perhaps additional terms should be included as synonyms (leakage, seepage) or new concepts added (discharge, fuel). One of the advantages of online searching is that the search strategy can be amended as the search progresses in the light of the results achieved. An examination of the six retrieved records might well reveal new terms which could profitably be included in a revised search strategy.

The contents of any set – either an intermediate one (like set 2 in the earlier example) or a final set (set 8) – can be examined but before this can be done the user must decide three matters: the physical form in which the records are to be output; the format in which the records are to be output; and the number of records to be output from the set.

It is possible to display records on a screen (and simultaneously to download them to a local storage medium such as a micro-computer hard disc), to print them during the online search or to order offline prints which are then mailed by the search service. An online search provides an opportunity to examine large numbers of records very rapidly and to select just those records which match certain search parameters. The user would normally want to view sample records retrieved at various stages in the search to check that they are indeed relevant to the information request. The search service may offer one command to print the records and another command if they are merely to be displayed on the screen (whether or not the search is downloaded) but not printed. The distinction between display at the screen and print online is that the former command will display records one screen at a time rather than scrolling the screen as records are typed. If a printout is not being produced then it is better to use a display command rather than a type command as it can be difficult to read records, let alone make notes on them, if they are constantly scrolling off the screen.

If the user instead chooses offline prints then the advantage of immediate access to the retrieved records is lost. The search service stores the search results, prints them at an off-peak time and mails them to the user. Offline print costs are lower than the equivalent online print costs, and it is therefore cheaper to pay for offline costs than to spend time online while records are printed or even downloaded to disc, especially if the records are long or numerous and the file has high connect rates. The user would always, of course, be well-advised to check a few of the records online before ordering offline prints to ensure that the search has produced the desired results.

Once the output mode has been decided, it is necessary to choose in which format the records will be viewed. Records are divided into fields (see Chapter 3) and it is normally possible to choose which fields will be output. Some search services (like ESA-IRS) offer a variety of record formats which can be selected for outputting, and some provide complete flexibility in outputting fields as well as several default formats (Dialog and BLAISE).

Different formats are suited to different purposes. In the case of records on bibliographic databases, for example, it may be useful at an early stage in the search to check just the titles of records retrieved to confirm that they are relevant. If controlled rather than free-text terms are being used in the search (see Chapter 6) it might be useful to view a format which includes the controlled terms field. Alternatively, the abstract field might be a useful source of additional words to include in a free-text search. At some stage a format must be used which includes the bibliographic citation field if the actual documents described in the record are to be located in the library. A cheap way of finding records is to output only the accession number field if the accession numbers of the online database match those used in any printed version (which is not always the case) and the printed copy is readily available in which to track down the records from their accession numbers. Some services (like ESA-IRS) provide a special download format which includes field mnemonics, extremely useful if the downloaded records are to be reconfigured in a local database (see Chapter 10).

Finally the searcher must choose how many of the records in a set are to be output, as it is not necessary to output the entire set. If records are only being checked to confirm their relevance then it will prove much cheaper to look at just a few rather than the entire contents of a large set. Most services load records in such a way that the most recently added are at the top of the set; in other words, displaying the first three records in a set would display the last three to be added to the database (though this is not necessarily the same as the most recently published).

In order to provide the user with the means to implement these decisions, several commands are required and a syntax in which they can be expressed. To display records screen by screen at a screen the command might be SHOW. This would be followed by an indication of the set to be displayed as any set, and not just the last set created, can be output. Next it would be possible to indicate the format to be used (or perhaps the field labels for individual fields to be output from the record) and finally the range of records to be output from the set. So,

SHOW S=8; F=3; R=1–4

might be used to instruct the system that it is to display (SHOW) from set 8 (S=8) in format 3 (F=3) records 1 to 4 inclusive (R=1–4). As with the other commands introduced earlier, the precise syntax must be followed. In this example, each step must be separated by a semi-colon and spaces must not be left between characters within a step. A service which allows the user to specify which precise fields are to be output might adopt this alternative command structure:

> SHOW S=8; F=AN,TI; R=1–3

where AN and TI are the mnemonics for the accession number and title fields respectively.

SHOW has been used to display records a screen at a time; a different command is required to print online (accompanied by a scrolling display on the VDU); the command TYPE might be used:

> TYPE S=8; F=4; R=1

This would print the first record from set 8 in format 4. The command to order an offline printout would again be different, but the other parts of the output statement would retain the same syntax:

> PRINT S=8; F=4; R=1–6

where printouts of all six records in set 8 are requested to be prepared offline and mailed to the searcher.

Amending search strategy

Reference was made earlier to the heuristic nature of online searching: the searcher can react to the search as it develops and modify the strategy in the light of its results. For example, it might be decided that the search for records on the FUEL ABSTRACTS database dealing with oil spillage in the Atlantic Ocean which found just six records should be widened to include the Caribbean. The search strategy therefore needs amendment to take account of this new concept.

It can be difficult to keep track of a search whilst online, especially if numerous sets have already been created. Many services take account of this difficulty by providing a partial search recall facility which enables the contents of each set to be listed. This can prove a useful *aide-memoire*. In Search Example 4.5 the system prompt has been followed by the command DISPLAY SETS, an instruction to recap on the search to date. Only the set numbers, postings and terms are given; other parts of the search such as any output commands are not listed, and neither are the records themselves. Nevertheless, this kind of list is often sufficient to guide the user on to the next step in the search.

? **DISPLAY SETS**

SETS	POSTINGS	TERMS
1	324	SPILLAGE
2	208	SPILLS
3	159	LEAKS
4	570	SPILLAGE OR SPILLS OR LEAKS
5	725	OIL
6	53	ATLANTIC
7	26	OIL AND ATLANTIC
8	6	SET 4 AND SET 7

Search Example 4.5   *Search recapping*

If the search is to be extended to the Caribbean Sea as well as the Atlantic Ocean then it is necessary to introduce the term 'Caribbean' – as was the case with 'ocean', it is not really necessary to include the term 'sea'. Records are now being sought which deal with oil spillage in either the Atlantic or the Caribbean (see Search Example 4.6). This requires 'Caribbean' to be grouped with 'Atlantic', that is to say, combined using the OR operator. Rather than selecting a term for a second time, it is quicker (and therefore better) to use set 6 which already contains all records including the term 'Atlantic'. This produces a ninth set for 'Caribbean' with 24 records and a tenth set of 71 records including one or the other (or both) terms.

? **FIND CARIBBEAN OR SET 6**

SET 9   24   CARIBBEAN
SET 10   71   CARIBBEAN OR SET 6
? **FIND SET 10 AND SET 4 AND SET 5**
SET 11   13   SET 10 AND SET 4 AND SET 5
?

Search Example 4.6   *Developing a search strategy*

Search Example 4.6 illustrates the need to exercise care when the search strategy grows more complex. Set 10 must be ANDed with set 5 (oil) as well as set 4 (spillage or spills or leaks); set 7 cannot be used because although it ANDs oil and atlantic it does not enable the term 'oil' to be ANDed with 'Caribbean'. The searcher must think logically through each step of the search to ensure that the correct terms are being combined by the correct operators. The nature of inverted files (see Chapter 3) means that when ANDing sets together it is better to put the smallest set at the beginning of the statement and the largest at the end, as in Search Example 4.6. The word 'caribbean' is rather easy to mis-spell, and it is worth emphasizing that an online system will usually search for the term input regardless of whether it has been spelled correctly or incorrectly (by the same token, a word which was mis-spelled when entered into the database record will only be retrieved when similarly mis-spelled by the searcher).

A different way of adjusting the strategy is to narrow rather than broaden the scope of the search. This could be done, for example, by including more terms to be ANDed with the existing terms. Alternatively, one or more additional terms could be combined with the NOT operator. This has the effect of excluding any records containing these terms (see Chapter 3). For example, Search Example 4.6, which deals with oil spillage in the Atlantic Ocean and Caribbean Sea, could be narrowed if the searcher decided that records were not of interest which dealt with a certain part of the Atlantic – the Bay of Biscay. The term 'biscay' could be included in the strategy as shown in Search Example 4.7. Set 11 now deals with oil spillage in the Caribbean and the Atlantic except the Bay of Biscay.

The NOT operator should always be used with care as it may inadvertently exclude records which could have proved relevant. In Search Example 4.7 all records which include the term 'biscay' will be excluded even if they also deal with other parts of the Atlantic; thus a record comparing oil spillage in the Atlantic Ocean off the Azores with spillage in the Bay of Biscay would be lost.

```
? FIND SET 11 NOT BISCAY
  SET 12    7   BISCAY
  SET 13   12   SET 11 NOT BISCAY
?
```

Search Example 4.7 *Use of the NOT operator*

Terminating a search

After a search strategy has been executed and any relevant records ouput in some kind of way, the search can be terminated. This can be done in two ways. The user may transfer to another file on the same search service, either to repeat the search on a different database or to carry out a different search. It will depend upon the service as to whether such a transfer automatically deletes from the host computer the search which has just been completed. The search service documentation should be checked before any file transfer is attempted if there is a possibility that it might be necessary to return to the original search. Some services (for example, Dialog) do provide a way of transferring to another file without deleting the results of an earlier search, but a special command must be used. Otherwise, a straightforward transfer to a different file is normally accomplished simply by using the command to choose a file together with the identification of that file (see Search Example 4.1 above). Such a command terminates the session in the first file and enters the second file. It may also produce such information as the length of time that was spent in the first file and the costs involved. For the second file, information about its online availability may be provided, exactly as if the user has initially logged-in to this file, before the system prompt indicates that the search can now be commenced.

? **LOGOFF**
SESSION TERMINATED AT 1037 12 MARCH 1989
TOTAL ONLINE CONNECT TIME 09.37

Search Example 4.8   *Leaving the search service*

Alternatively, the online session may be terminated altogether by disconnecting from the online search service. This procedure is termed logging-off, and can normally be executed at any point in a search. In Search Example 4.8 the command to log-off (in this example LOGOFF) is entered after the system prompt. The online service responds by confirming that log-off has been completed, and possibly also supplying information about the cost of the session and the total time spent online. The workstation will be automatically disconnected from the search service and any telecommunication networks used; the search is completed.

Search Examples from Command-Driven Services

Dialog Information Services

The examples used above were not taken from an actual online search service, although they resemble several real services. The great number and variety of search services preclude any attempt to provide here more than a few sample searches from some representative services. They should serve to illustrate, however, the ways in which command languages can be used to carry out simple searches to retrieve records on particular subjects. More sophisticated techniques are reserved for Chapters 5 and 6.

The first search is taken from Dialog Information Services, a large vendor of bibliographic, full-text and numerical databases (see Search Example 4.9). Its objective is to trace documents dealing with the effects of nuclear fallout on sheep farming. To achieve this objective it has been decided to match records containing the terms 'nuclear' with records containing either the terms 'fallout' or alternatively 'pollution' and records also including 'sheep'.

Three databases have been chosen for the search: ENVIRO-LINE, produced by the Environment Information Center in the United States and offering an interdisciplinary coverage of scientific, technical and socio-economic aspects of environmental and resources literature; POLLUTION ABSTRACTS, produced by Cambridge Scientific Abstracts and dealing with environmentally related technical literature on pollution, its sources and its control; and CAB ABSTRACTS, a database of agricultural information produced by CAB International (CAB ABSTRACTS is divided into two files – the one used in this search example which covers 1984 until the present, and the other which covers 1972 to 1983).

The first step is to log-on to Dialog. Once the log-on procedure has been completed the system prompt (?) appears to inform the user that Dialog is awaiting an instruction. Unless the default file is to be searched, the first step is to choose the database or databases which are required. Dialog through its OneSearch facility permits a search to be carried out in several files simultaneously. The user enters the command BEGIN followed by the Dialog identification numbers for the three chosen files: ENVIROLINE (40), POLLUTION ABSTRACTS (41) and CAB ASTRACTS (50). Dialog responds by providing information on the length of time already spent online in these three files during this initial stage and the costs so far incurred. It reminds the user that OneSearch is operational and displays information about the online availability of each file; ENVIROLINE, for example, is online from 1970 and was last updated in December 1988 (this search was undertaken in February 1989).

?begin 40,41,50
    13feb89 12:23:16 User012345 SessionB999.9
      $0.17 0.011 Hrs File40
  $0.17 Estimated cost File40
      $0.17 0.011 Hrs File41
  $0.17 Estimated cost File41
      $0.20 0.013 Hrs File50
  $0.20 Estimated cost File50
    OneSearch, 3 files, 0.034 Hrs FileOS
  $0.54 Estimated cost this search
  $0.77 Estimated total session cost   0.049 Hrs.

System:OS – DIALOG OneSearch

    File 40:ENVIROLINE – 70–88/DEC
        (COPR. R. R. BOWKER COMPANY 1988)
    File 41:POLLUTION ABSTRACTS – 70–89/JAN
        (C. CAMBRIDGE SCIENTIFIC ABSTRACTS)
    File 50:CAB ABSTRACTS – 1984–89/JAN
        SEE ALSO FILE 53 (1972–1983)

        Set   Items   Description

?set detail on
DETAIL set on
?select nuclear
40: ENVIROLINE – 70–88/DEC
          6750   NUCLEAR
41: POLLUTION ABSTRACTS – 70–89/JAN
          5950   NUCLEAR
50: CAB ABSTRACTS – 1984–89/JAN
          3357   NUCLEAR

TOTAL: FILES 40,41,50
    S1   16057   NUCLEAR
?select fallout or pollution
40: ENVIROLINE – 70–88/DEC
          350   FALLOUT
      24609   POLLUTION
      24881   FALLOUT OR POLLUTION
41: POLLUTION ABSTRACTS – 70–89/JAN
          752   FALLOUT
      29659   POLLUTION
      30307   FALLOUT OR POLLUTION
50: CAB ABSTRACTS – 1984–89/JAN
          129   FALLOUT
       7262   POLLUTION
       7331   FALLOUT OR POLLUTION

```
TOTAL: FILES 40,41,50
                  1231   FALLOUT
                 61530   POLLUTION
        S2       62519   FALLOUT OR POLLUTION
```
?select s1 and s2
```
40: ENVIROLINE – 70–88/DEC
                  6750   S1
                 24881   S2
                   931   S1 AND S2
41: POLLUTION ABSTRACTS – 70–89/JAN
                  5950   S1
                 30307   S2
                   700   S1 AND S2
50: CAB ABSTRACTS – 1984–89/JAN
                  3357   S1
                  7331   S2
                    95   S1 AND S2

TOTAL: FILES 40,41,50
                 16057   S1
                 62519   S2
        S3        1726   S1 AND S2
```
?select s3 and sheep
```
40: ENVIROLINE – 70–88/DEC
                   931   S3
                   178   SHEEP
                     2   S3 AND SHEEP
41: POLLUTION ABSTRACTS – 70–89/JAN
                   700   S3
                   270   SHEEP
                     1   S3 AND SHEEP
50: CAB ABSTRACTS – 1984–89/JAN
                    95   S3
                 21053   SHEEP
                     5   S3 AND SHEEP

TOTAL: FILES 40,41,50
                  1726   S3
                 21501   SHEEP
        S4           8   S3 AND SHEEP
```
?type s4/6/1–8
```
4/6/1          (Item 1 from file: 40)
0190795        Enviroline Number: *87–038281
  MAY SHEEP SAFELY GRAZE?

4/6/2          (Item 2 from file: 40)
0138932        Enviroline Number: 79–006084
```

THE 1953 NUCLEAR BLAST THAT KEPT ECHOING FOR YEARS

4/6/3   (Item 1 from file: 41)
88–07416
A reassessment of oastrointestinal dose from a continental United States nuclear weapons test

4/6/4   (Item 1 from file: 50)
0665695   OD050–01539
Transport of the radioisotopes iodine-131, cesium-134, and cesium-137 from the fallout following the accident at the Chernobyl nuclear reactor into cheese and other cheesemaking products.

4/6/5   (Item 2 from file: 50)
0574117   OV057–03930; OI055–00006; OD049–06907
Contamination of foods of animal origin with radionuclides. Preliminary results from Lower Saxony after the Chernobyl nuclear reactor accident.
Belastung vom Tier stammender Lebensmittel mit Radionukliden. Erste Untersuchungsergebnisse aus Niedersachsen nach dem Reaktorungluck von Tschernobyl.

4/6/6   (Item 3 from file: 50)
0274207   OV055–01206; OI053–00003; OS048–02057
Radionuclide levels and distribution in grazed saltmarsh in West Cumbria.

4/6/7   (Item 4 from file: 50)
0272239   OG055–00695; OW034–00616; 7Q011–00985;
                 7G008–00950
Annual report 1984.

4/6/8   (Item 5 from file: 50)
0262246   OV055–00507; OI053–00002
Recent occurrence of radioiodine in sheep thyroids from England. [Abstract].

?type s4/5/1

4/5/1   (Item 1 from file: 40)
0190795   Enviroline Number: *87–038281
MAY SHEEP SAFELY GRAZE?
HOWARD BRENDA ; LIVENS FRANCIS
INST OF TERRESTRIAL ECOLOGY, UK.
NEW SCIENTIST, APR 23, 87, V114, N1557, P46(4)
JOURNAL ARTICLE   THE INSTITUTE OF TERRESTRIAL ECOLOGY (ITE), UK, SURVEYED THE DISTRIBUTION AND MOVEMENT OF RADIOACTIVE FALLOUT IN BRITAIN FROM THE CHERNOBYL ACCIDENT BY COLLECTING VEGETATION

FROM 500 LOCATIONS, 10–15 DAYS AFTER THE ACCIDENT.
REGIONS THAT RECEIVED THE HIGHEST DEPOSITS OF
CESIUM-137 AND CESIUM-134 WERE THREE LARGE AREAS IN
THE UPLANDS USED MAINLY FOR SHEEP GRAZING:
WESTERN CUMBRIA, THE SHETLANDS, AND NORTH WALES.
MATHEMATICAL MODELS DEVELOPED FOR PREDICTING
CESIUM AMOUNTS IN SHEEP OVER TIME WERE ERRONEOUS
IN PREDICTING CESIUM LEVELS IN SOILS, VEGETATION AND
SHEEP IN THE UPLAND AREAS. ITE WAS COMMISSIONED TO
STUDY A FARM IN THE UPLANDS TO DETERMINE THE
RELATIONSHIPS OF RADIATION DIFFERENCES IN UPLAND
AND LOWLAND PASTURES, CESIUM LEVELS IN VEGETATION
AND SOILS, AND CESIUM LEVELS IN SHEEP. THE STUDY WILL
LOOK AT HOW SOIL AND PLANTS INFLUENCE THE
MOVEMENT OF CESIUM BETWEEN SOIL, PLANT AND
ANIMAL, AND COLLECT DATA TO EXTEND THE
MATHEMATICAL MODELS FOR ASSESSING POTENTIAL
RESULTS OF ANOTHER NUCLEAR ACCIDENT. (6 PHOTOS)
  Descriptors: *UNITED KINGDOM ; *NUCLEAR ACCIDENTS ;
*RADIATION, ATOMIC DOSES ; *CESIUM 134 ; *CESIUM 137 ;
*SHEEP ; *AREA COMPARISONS ; CHERNOBYL ;
MONITORING, ENV-RADIATION
  Review Classification: 14
?**logoff**
    13feb 89 12:26:43 User012345 Session B999.9

Search Example 4.9   *OneSearch on Dialog*

The user now responds to a second Dialog prompt by entering
the command SET DETAIL ON. This instructs Dialog to display
separately for each of the three files the number of records
(postings) containing any search terms input. If this command had
not been entered then Dialog would only have displayed the total
number of postings in all three files for each search term.
    The search terms can now be entered. The command SELECT
is followed by the first term 'nuclear'. The individual number of
postings found in each file is displayed followed by the total
postings for all three files (16057) labelled S1 (set 1). The SELECT
command is then used a second time, in this case to find records
either containing 'fallout' or 'pollution'; the terms are linked by
the OR operator. Once again individual postings for each file are
followed by the combined postings for all three files, labelled S2
(62519 records). The next step is to match these two sets, S1 and
S2, using the AND operator in order to isolate those records which
contain the term 'nuclear' and either 'fallout' or 'pollution'; 1726

records meet this requirement and are identified as S3. The final stage in the strategy is to link this set 3 with all records containing 'sheep' using the AND operator. This reduces the final set (S4) to just eight records, two from ENVIROLINE, one from POLLUTION ABSTRACTS and five from CAB ABSTRACTS.

The searcher now decides to look at the titles of all eight records in set 4. This is done by entering the command TYPE followed by the set number (S4), the format number which indicates that the title only is required (format 6) and the range of records (1–8). It should be noted that OneSearch may retrieve the same record from more than one file; it is not unusual to find duplicates on files covering similar subject areas, and OneSearch will not eliminate them. In this particular search no duplicates were found amongst the final eight records (a discussion of this and other aspects of using OneSearch rather than a simple search in just one file can be found in Pagell, 1988). The first record looks particularly interesting and it is printed in the fullest format (5). The searcher is satisfied with this result and now terminates the online session by entering the command LOGOFF.

European Space Agency Information Retrieval Service

The next search was conducted on the European Space Agency's Information Retrieval Service (ESA-IRS). This large European online search service, based in Italy, offers a large range of databases. Its search software, QUEST, is derived from an earlier version of Dialog's software, and therefore considerable resemblances will be noted between the command languages of Dialog and ESA-IRS, as well as some differences.

Once the log-on has been completed, the user is prompted to enter the number of the database to be used in the search for bibliographic items on stress in concrete bridges. Although ESA-IRS, like Dialog, allows users to search more than one database at a time, this option has not been chosen on this occasion; the search is conducted on just one database: COMPENDEX (Computerized Engineering Index), produced by Engineering Information Inc. This is selected by using the command BEGIN followed by the COMPENDEX database number (4) on ESA-IRS. After preliminary information about costs incurred so far, measured in European Space Agency accounting units (AU), the user is told that COMPENDEX is online since 1969 and the last update was number 12 for 1988.

? **begin 4**
--------13Feb89 18:10:02 User00999--
   0.09 AU 0.55 Minutes in File   4
   0.09 AU approx Total
File   4:COMPENDEX:1969–88.12
SET ITEMS DESCRIPTION (+=OR;*=AND;–=NOT)
? **find concrete**
   1 29240 CONCRETE
? **find stress**
   2 76718 STRESS
? **find bridge or bridges**
   3 9204 BRIDGE
   4 7388 BRIDGES
   5 12161 3+4
? **combine 1 and 2 and 5**
   6   155 1 AND 2 AND 5
? **find road or roads**
   7 8775 ROAD
   8 7118 ROADS
   9 13142 7+8
? **combine 6 and 9**
   10   8 6 AND 9
? **type 10/s/1–8**

                    TYPE 10/S/1–5
                    Compendex
      CONCRETE TRUSSED ARCH BRIDGES IN CHINA

                    Compendex
      ARCH RAILWAY BRIDGE OVER THE PONTEBBANA STATE ROAD

                    Compendex
      SAFETY OF ROAD BRIDGES SUBJECTED TO VIBRATION

                    Compendex
      Viaduct Over the Cellina Creek for the State Road N. 291 By-Pass at
      Montereale Valcellina (Pordenone)
         VIADOTTO SUL TORRENTE CELLINA PER LA VARIANTE DELLA
      STRADA STATALE N. 291 A MONTEREALE VALCELLINA
      (PORDENONE)

                    Compendex
      Construction of the Coatzacoalcos II Bridge
      CONSTRUCCION DEL PUENTE COATZACOALCOS II

                    TYPE 10/9/6–8
                    Compendex
      MINIMAL REINFORCEMENT OF RIGHT SLAB BRIDGES

Compendex
HIGH STRENGTH REINFORCING STEEL FOR ROAD BRIDGES
Compendex
Developments in measurement of strain and stress in concrete bridge
structures
? type 10/r/8

TYPE 10/R/8
69X1–40986 Compendex 69024536
Developments in measurement of strain and stress in concrete bridge
structures
TYLER RG
Great Britain. Ministry of Transport–Road Research Laboratory–Report
LR189, 1968, 62 p
? logoff
———13Feb89 18:14:02 User00999

Search Example 4.10   *COMPENDEX on ESA-IRS*

After the system prompts in each case, the command FIND is
used to isolate those records containing first the term 'concrete'
and then the term 'stress' (sets 1 and 2). The user decides it is
necessary to locate records containing the term 'bridge' in either its
singular or plural form, and therefore searches for both variants,
linking them with the OR operator. Both terms have been used in
the database and this was therefore a wise precaution. It is now
necessary to combine the concepts represented by 'concrete',
'stress' and 'bridge OR bridges' to find those records which include
all three concepts by using the AND operator. This produces a
sixth set containing 155 records. This is too large a number of
records for the enquirer who in any case is really interested in road
bridges rather than bridges in general. A final concept is therefore
introduced in both its singular and plural forms (road or roads); it
should be noted that if the enquirer were to be interested in
American as well as British information sources it might have been
as well to have used the additional terms highway and highways.
This ninth set is finally combined with set 6 to produce just eight
hits in the tenth set. These eight records are examined by using the
TYPE command together with the set number (10) in the scan
format (title only). The final record looks particularly interesting
and the bibliographic details are retrieved by examining this
record in the reference (R) format. The search now completed,
the user logs off from ESA-IRS.

Profile

The third search, on Profile Information Service, owned by the *Financial Times* and based in London, is looking for full-text information rather than bibliographic information. The request is for recent news items dealing with oil pollution in Antarctica. It is decided to conduct the search across a number of daily and Sunday British newspapers, although this cross-file searching can only be undertaken on issues published in the last few months (in this instance over 13 months since January 1988). The alternative would be to search longer runs of back-issues but separately in each newspaper.

As with the other searches, the first step is to choose the database or databases; in the case of Profile they are selected by entering an acronym (uknews) rather than a database number as on Dialog and ESA-IRS. The newspapers included in this group are listed before the prompt (>) invites the user to input a search term. The command GET is followed by the term antarctica and retrieves 111 news items. It should be noted that Profile does not assign them a set number. The user now wishes to refine the search by adding the concept 'oil' to the search. The command PICK is used with the new term. PICK refines the search by retaining from the original 111 records on Antarctica only those which also include the term 'oil' (on Dialog or ESA-IRS this would be accomplished by inserting the boolean AND operator between the terms Antarctica and oil). This now reduces the retrieved set to 17 items. The headlines from just the first five items are displayed (HEADLINE 1–5) and the user then decides to examine the second item in more detail. By using the command CONTEXT, the sections of the news article around the sought term(s) are displayed (the full news item, of course, might be quite long). The search terms are capitalized in the display. The user could have gone on to look at the complete item by using the command TEXT, but context proves sufficient; the user logs off from Profile by entering the command END.

select uknews

```
SELECT UKNEWS
GROUP FILE UKNEWS:
THE DAILY AND SUNDAY TELEGRAPH      from Jan 1988   Q1   TEL
THE FINANCIAL TIMES      from Jan 1988   Q1   FT
THE GUARDIAN      from Jan 1988   Q1   GDN
TODAY      from Jan 1988   Q1   TDY
THE TIMES AND THE SUNDAY TIMES      from Jan 1988   Q1   TIM
```

"For information from before the above dates, select files individually"
CHARGE GROUP(S):Q1
>
get antarctica

GET ANTARCTICA
    111 ITEMS RETRIEVED
>
pick oil

PICK OIL
    17 ITEMS RETRIEVED
>
headline 1–5

HEADLINE 1–5
SORTING

1   GDN 04 Feb 89 US emergency crews head for Antarctic OIL spill
        (224)
2   TDY 03 Feb 89 Sea vacuum to save OIL slick penguins: A two mile
        OIL slick which is threatening to wipe out wildlife in
        ANTARCTICA could be vacuumed away (532)
3   FT 03 Feb 89 World News in Brief: Antarctic OIL Spill (33)
4   GDN 02 Feb 89 OIL leak 'disaster' for Antarctic ecology (589)
5   FT 02 Feb 89 Fears Diminish Of OIL Damage to ANTARCTICA (222)

All material subject to copyright
>
context 2

CONTEXT 2

2 . . . .
        TDY 03 Feb 89 Sea vacuum to save OIL slick penguins: A two mile
            OIL slick which is threatening to wipe out wildlife in
            ANTARCTICA could be vacuumed away (532)
    . . .
    A TWO-MILE OIL slick threatening to wipe out wildlife in
    ANTARCTICA could be vacuumed away.
    . . .
    The team should be ready to begin the operation by Monday, but OIL is
    already being washed ashore on Anvers Island where the Americans
    have a research station.
    . . .
    He said: 'Once that has been done the skimmer is sent out with diesel-
    powered pumps to collect the OIL up into deflated containers. These
    are then towed either ashore or aboard the nearest ship.

. . .
'If the OIL is not dispersed there will be very serious consequences for wildlife.'
**PRESS RETURN TO CONTINUE, N FOR NEXT ARTICLE, OR X TO EXIT

. . .
Much of the OIL and propane gas on board was stored in drums which may leak slowly, but hundreds more gallons of fuel are believed to have gushed free immediately.
. . .
It formed an inch-thick slick stretching at least two miles, although one vessel reported seeing OIL 12 miles away.
. . .
Scientists at the base have seen whales thrusting themselves out of the water, behaviour rarely observed. They believe the huge mammals may be trying to move the OIL from the surface.
. . .
They will conduct a detailed investigation of the effects of crude OIL on fish and other species.

All material subject to copyright
>
end

END
TIME IN UKNEWS   01 MINS 45 SECS TOTAL SESSION TIME   02 MINS 29 SECS
*SIGN OFF   9:37:13   14 FEB 89

Search Example 4.11   *UKNEWS on Profile*

  These three examples illustrate both the differences in the commands used by the online search services and the underlying similarities in their approach to information retrieval and display. The command language of each service must be mastered before searching can be done, but it is not too difficult to learn new languages once the principles upon which the services operate have been grasped. Before searching on any online service it is strongly recommended that its search manual is studied in order to establish exactly how its command language should be used. A very useful comparative guide to command languages has been published by the United Kingdom Online User Group (Arthur, 1989).

Menu-Driven Services

At the beginning of this chapter command-driven retrieval systems were contrasted with menu-driven systems. The major purpose of the latter is to obviate the need to learn a command language. By so doing it is intended that access to the service will be simplified and that custom will be attracted particularly from end-users who, unlike professional information intermediaries, are less willing to spend time on the mastery of a command language.

Call connected to remote address

ENTER BRS PASSWORD
MMMMMMMMM
ENTER SECURITY PASSWORD

__: MMMMMMMMM

*****WELCOME TO BRS!
THE BROADCAST MESSAGE WAS LAST UPDATED ON 02/16/89 AT 09:20
ENTER Y OR N FOR BROADCAST MESSAGE.__: **n**

ENTER DATABASE NAME__: **menu**

*SIGN ON   11:01:15   02/16/89
MENU
                WELCOME TO BRS/MENUS
                    MAIN MENU
        SERVICE   NUMBER

        Search Service   1

        BRS/MENUS Update (12/1/88)   11
        How to use BRS/MENUS   12
        Customer services   13

        Return to Command-driven BRS 99

        ENTER SERVICE NUMBER OR H FOR HELP → **1**

        BRS/MENUS SEARCH SERVICE LIBRARIES

LIBRARY NAME   LABEL
Business and Finance   BUSI
Medicine and Pharmacology   MDPH

Physical and Applied Sciences   PHAS
Life Sciences   LFSC
Education   EDUC
Social Sciences and Humanities   SOCS
Reference and Multidisciplinary   REFE
Practice Databases   PRAC

ENTER LIBRARY OR DATABASE LABEL, OR M TO RETURN TO MAIN
MENU → **lfsc**

      LIFE SCIENCES   SCREEN 1 OF 2

DATABASE   LABEL

AIDS Abstracts from the Bureau of   AIDD
Hygiene & Tropical Diseases
AGRICOLA (1980 to Date)   CAIN
      (1970 to 1979)   CAIB
BioBusiness   BBUS
BIOSIS Previews (1978 to date)   BIOL
      (1970 to 1977)   BIOB
      (1970 to date)   BIOZ
CAB Abstracts   CABA
Current Contents: Agriculture, Biology AGRI
   & Environmental Sciences
Current Contents: Life Sciences   LIFE
Dissertation Abstracts Online   DISS

ENTER LABEL, L TO RETURN TO LIBRARY MENU, OR PRESS ENTER
FOR MORE →

      LIFE SCIENCES   SCREEN 2 OF 2

DATABASE   LABEL

FAIRBASE   FAIR
National Environmental Data Referral   NEDS
  Service
NTIS Bibliographic Database   NTIS
Pollution Abstracts   POLL
Zoological Record Online   ZREC

ENTER LABEL OR G TO GO BACK → **biol**

BIOL BIOSIS PREV 78–FEB 89

ENTER Y TO DISPLAY DATABASE DESCRIPTION OR PRESS ENTER TO
BEGIN SEARCHING → **y**

The BRS/BIOSIS Previews Database provides easy access to biological
and medical information gathered from government documents, journals

and books, as well as hard-to-find symposia and proceedings. Produced by BioSciences Information Services this database covers biology, research medicine, taxonomy and instrumentation from 1978 to date and is updated monthly. For biological information from 1970–1977 use the database label BIOB.

```
DISPLAY OPTIONS: SHORT: AU,TI,SO,AN
              MEDIUM: AU,TI,SO,KW,MJ,MN,CC,BC,AN
              LONG: ALL FIELDS
```

ENTER SEARCH TERMS, COMMAND, OR H FOR HELP
SEARCH 1 → **alligators**

ANSWER 1 129 DOCUMENTS FOUND

ENTER SEARCH TERMS, COMMAND, OR H FOR HELP
SEARCH 2 → **breeding**

ANSWER 2 63540 DOCUMENTS FOUND

ENTER SEARCH TERMS, COMMAND, OR H FOR HELP
SEARCH 3 → **h**

```
              BRS/MENUS SEARCH HELP
       FOR HELP WITH:                          ENTER:

       Basic Commands (H, S, D, PC, R, C, M, L, O)1
       Search Terms                          2
       Connectors (OR, AND, SAME, WITH, NOT) 3
       Truncation ($)                        4
       Searching Specific Fields
          (e.g. YEAR, AUTHOR, TITLE)         5
       Advanced Commands                     6
```

FOR MORE HELP ENTER: A NUMBER, ANY COMMAND, ANY CONNECTOR, OR ENTER X TO EXIT HELP → **3**

```
       HELP            CONNECTORS   SCREEN 1 OF 8
```

Use CONNECTORS to link search terms in a single document.

CONNECTOR	EXAMPLE	DOCUMENT CONTAINS
AND	car and race	Both terms
SAME	car same race	Both terms in same field or text paragraph
WITH	car with race	Both terms in same sentence
OR	car or automobile	Either term or both terms
NOT	car not race	Car without mention of race Use NOT with caution.

PRESS ENTER TO CONTINUE, ENTER A CONNECTOR, G TO GO
BACK OR X TO EXIT HELP → **x**

ENTER SEARCH TERMS, COMMAND, OR H FOR HELP
SEARCH 3 → **alligators and breeding**

ANSWER 3 4 DOCUMENTS FOUND

ENTER SEARCH TERMS, COMMAND, OR H FOR HELP
SEARCH 4 → **h**

        BRS/MENUS SEARCH HELP
FOR HELP WITH: ENTER:

Basic Commands (H, S, D, PC, R, C, M, L, O)	1
Search Terms	2
Connectors (OR, AND, SAME, WITH, NOT)	3
Truncation ($)	4
Searching Specific Fields	
(e.g. YEAR, AUTHOR, TITLE)	5
Advanced Commands	6

FOR MORE HELP ENTER: A NUMBER, ANY COMMAND, ANY
CONNECTOR, OR ENTER X TO EXIT HELP → **1**

        BRS/MENUS BASIC COMMANDS

FOR HELP WITH: ENTER:

Help	H
Search	S
Display Documents	D
Print Documents Continuously	PC
Review Search	R
Change Databases	C
Return to Main Menu	M
Change Libraries	L
Sign Off	O

FOR MORE HELP ENTER ANY COMMAND, PRESS ENTER TO
CONTINUE, ENTER G TO GO BACK OR X TO EXIT HELP → **d**

HELP D:DISPLAY DOCUMENTS   SCREEN 1 OF 4

To display documents, enter the command, D at a search prompt:

        SEARCH 3 → **d**

BRS/MENUS will then prompt you for the number of the search
answer containing the documents you wish to see:

ENTER ANSWER NUMBER →

Next, you will be asked for the format in which you want the documents displayed:

TI (title only)
S (short format)
M (medium format)
L (long format)
TD (tailored display)

PRESS ENTER TO CONTINUE, ENTER G TO GO BACK OR X TO EXIT HELP → **x**

ENTER SEARCH TERMS, COMMAND, OR H FOR HELP
SEARCH 4 → **d**

ENTER ANSWER NUMBER → **3**

ENTER TI (TITLE ONLY), S (SHORT FORMAT), M (MEDIUM FORMAT), L (LONG FORMAT)
TD (TAILORED DISPLAY) → **m**

ENTER DOCUMENT NUMBERS → **1–4**

1
AN 85002982.8801.
AU HUANG-Z. LIN-H. ZHANG-S.
TI ANALYSIS OF THE LANDSAT REMOTE SENSING IMAGES OF THE TYPES OF HABITATS OF YANGTZE ALLIGATORS.
SO CHIN J OCEANOL LIMNOL.
4(4). 1986 (RECD. 1987). 360–371.
KW FRESHWATER BREEDING SITE ENDANGERED SPECIES UNITED NATIONS CHINA.
MJ ECOLOGY: AQUATIC WILDLIFE MANAGEMENT (MJ07516).
GENERAL BIOLOGY: CONSERVATION,RESOURCE MANAGEMENT (MJ00512).
AEROSPACE/UNDERWATER BIOLOGY: GENERAL STUDIES;METHODS (MJ06002).
ECOLOGY: LIMNOLOGY (MJ07514).
REPRODUCTIVE SYSTEM: GENERAL STUDIES;METHODS (MJ16501).
CHORDATE TAXONOMY: REPTILIA (MJ62516).
MN GENERAL BIOLOGY: INSTITUTIONS,ADMINISTRATION, LEGISLATION (MN00508).
BC CROCODILIA (BC85404).

2
AN 83074317.8704.
AU H0-S-M. LANCE-V. MEGALOUDIS-M.

TI PLASMA SEX-STEROID BINDING PROTEIN IN A SEASONALLY
  BREEDING REPTILE ALLIGATOR-MISSISSIPPIENSIS.
SO GEN COMP ENDOCRINOL.
  65(1). 1987. 121–132.
KW SEX DIFFERENCE.
MJ ENDOCRINE SYSTEM: GONADS,PLACENTA (MJ17006).
  GENETICS/CYTOGENETICS: SEX DIFFERENCES (MJ03510).
  METABOLISM: PROTEINS,PEPTIDES,AMINO ACIDS (MJ13012).
  REPRODUCTIVE SYSTEM: PHYSIOLOGY,BIOCHEMISTRY
  (MJ16504).
MN ECOLOGY: BIOCLIMATOLOGY,BIOMETEROLOGY (MN07504).
  BIOCHEMICAL STUDIES: PROTEINS,PEPTIDES,AMINO ACIDS
  (MN10064).
  BIOCHEMICAL STUDIES: STEROLS,STEROIDS (MN10067).
  BLOOD/BODY FLUIDS: BLOOD,LYMPH STUDIES (MN15002).
BC CROCODILIA (BC85404).

    3
AN 82091645.8611.
AU LANCE-V-A. ELSEY-R-M.
TI STRESS-INDUCED SUPPRESSION OF TESTOSTERONE SECRETION
  IN MALE ALLIGATORS.
SO J EXP ZOOL.
  239(2). 1986. 241–246.
KW RADIOIMMUNOASSAY USA.
MJ ENDOCRINE SYSTEM: GONADS,PLACENTA (MJ17006).
  PHYSIOLOGY: STRESS (MJ12008).
  METABOLISM: STEROLS,STEROIDS (MJ13008).
  REPRODUCTIVE SYSTEM: PHYSIOLOGY,BIOCHEMISTRY
  (MK16504).
MN RADIATION BIOLOGY: RADIATION,ISOTOPE TECHNIQUES
  (MN06504).
  BIOCHEMICAL STUDIES: STEROLS,STEROIDS (MN10067).
  IMMUNOLOGY/IMMUNOCHEMISTRY: GENERAL
  STUDIES,METHODS (MN34502).
BC CROCODILIA (BC85404).

    4
AN 30042748.8603.
AU MCNAMEE-L-L.
TI ARTIFICIAL INSEMINATION EXPERIMENTS WITH FLORIDA
  ALLIGATORS.
SO AGRIC BIOTECHNOL NEWS.
  2(5). 1985. 8–9.
KW CAPTIVE BREEDING ZOO AQUACULTURE USA.

MJ ECOLOGY: AQUATIC WILDLIFE MANAGEMENT (MJ07516).
   REPRODUCTIVE SYSTEM: GENERAL STUDIES;METHODS
   (MJ16501).
   VETERINARY SCIENCE: GENERAL STUDIES,METHODS (MJ38002).
   CHORDATE TAXONOMY: REPTILIA (MJ62516).
BC CROCODILIA (BC85404).

END OF DOCUMENTS IN LIST
ENTER SEARCH TERMS, COMMAND, OR H FOR HELP
SEARCH 4 → **o**

*CONNECT TIME 0:04:56 HH:MM:SS   0.082 DEC HRS   SESSION 12
*SIGN OFF   11:07:02   02/16/89

Search Example 4.12 *BRS User-friendly menus interface to BIOSIS PREVIEWS*

Search Example 4.12, a search for records dealing with the breeding habits of alligators, uses one such menu-driven service, the BRS User-Friendly Menus Interface. The user is prompted to enter the name of the required database. Instead of entering a database name the user enters 'menu'. The Main Menu is now displayed offering the user a choice of options including an explanation of how to use BRS/MENUS or transfer to the command-driven search mode. The user chooses to begin a search using BRS/MENUS and is now offered help on the selection of a suitable database. A list of broad subject areas is displayed from which the user selects life sciences. Yet another menu is now displayed which includes the databases on BRS which are relevant to the life sciences; the user chooses BIOSIS PREVIEWS from 1978 to date (a very large biosciences database). It is interesting to note, then, that help is given in the selection of a suitable database but even so the final choice must be made by the user; the software does not ask the user about the search query and then use that information to choose a database.
   The user can now either obtain a description of BIOSIS PREVIEWS or proceed to the actual search. The user chooses to look at the description and is then prompted to enter a search term (or a command if the user knows the command language). At each step the menu also offers the user the opportunity to request help. The first search term, alligators, is entered and produces a set of 129 records, too many for the user who in any case is really interested in the breeding habits of alligators. A second term,

breeding, is therefore entered, producing an enormous set of 63540 records.

The inexperienced user would now be faced with a problem. How can the records about alligators be combined with those on breeding to isolate those records concerned with breeding and alligators? The user decides to request help, and is then presented with a new menu which is not very user-friendly; the user is expected to know what is meant by *basic commands*, *connectors*, *truncation*, etc. In this case the user guesses that *connectors* is the correct option and receives a brief explanation of various logical operators including AND. This operator is then used to link alligators and breeding which retrieves four records.

The user now wants to look at these records but again does not know how to proceed. Help is once more requested but which option will explain how to display records? In fact, it is now necessary to look at the Basic commands option, which calls up yet another menu of commands including 'Display Documents'. The selection of this option provides information on how to display records, and at last the user can enter the correct command (d). The user is then asked which set is to be displayed, which format is to be used and how many documents in that set are to be displayed. The user displays all four records in the medium format. Finally, the user wishes to log off BRS; fortunately the command to execute this operation was noted by the user from the earlier help screens (thereby avoiding yet another request for help) and the session is terminated.

This simple subject search illustrates some of the strengths and weaknesses of menu-driven systems. The user does not need to know the command language used by BRS, although considerable initiative and perhaps even a little luck or trial and error would be required by the totally inexperienced user. Boolean operators must still be used and the brief description provided on the relevant help screens may not prove adequate for all users. Indeed, some users may not realize they are looking for guidance on the use of connectors and may therefore not find their way through the sequence of menus to this description. Some help is given on database selection, and this may be enough for the end-user; nevertheless, the user must ultimately choose a database for the specific search in hand. No help is given in the selection of search terms suitable for that search nor on how to combine them in an effective search strategy. Nor is any help given on how to modify that initial strategy if it does not produce the desired results. Use of the help screens certainly increases the duration (and therefore the cost) of the search and on occasions several levels of help menu must be navigated before the answer to a problem is revealed – and this was a very simple and short search strategy.

Menu-driven searching, then, takes some of the effort out of online information retrieval but certainly does not solve all the user's problems. A preliminary study of the menu section of the BRS *Manual* would help, but this is an admission that the menu system is not self explanatory. It may be that such menu systems work best for the experienced online searcher who knows how to carry out searches in general but does not happen to know the command language of that particular service. End-users are likely to struggle with most menu-driven systems unless training is provided (see Chapter 8).

This chapter has outlined the steps which would be taken in a typical online search to accomplish a simple subject search. Most services offer more sophisticated searching facilities, however, which reduce searching time as well as providing more powerful and selective retrieval capabilities. These facilities are considered in the following chapter.

References

Arthur, A. (1989) *UKOLUG Quick Guide to Online Commands*, 2nd edn. London: Institute of Information Scientists
Pagell, R. (1988) OneSearch: how and when to use it. *Database*, **39** (2), 39–46

Chapter 5

Retrieval Facilities

Introduction

Currently, command-driven online search services offer a range of retrieval facilities. Such facilities include ways of entering and listing search terms, displaying and printing retrieved records, and controlling the retrieval process as effectively and efficiently as possible. The provision of sophisticated techniques which offer powerful and selective retrieval seems to require complex command languages which are not easy to learn or remember and may have syntax prone to human error. There are often several different ways of achieving a given result and experience quickly reveals short-cuts and reduces keyboarding time (and therefore sometimes costs).

Some idea of the varieties of vocabulary and syntax employed by different command languages is given in Table 5.1 which lists eleven features of any command language and compares seven different languages representing most of the families of language used by the main search services. The seven command languages are:

1. BASIS – used by PFDS.
2. BRS/Search – used by BRS, and by Data-Star.
3. Dialog Version 2 – used by Dialog, and in a modified form (known as Quest) on ESA-IRS.
4. European Common Command Language (CCL) – offered as an alternative command language on European search services such as ESA-IRS and DIMDI.
5. ORBIT – used by the ORBIT search service, and in a modified way by BLAISE.
6. Profile – used by Profile Information.
7. Questel-Plus – used by Télésystèmes-QUESTEL.

Even the most basic command features, such as the prompts given by the system to the user, how to enter a specified database, or how to end a session are done in quite different ways in nearly all

	BASIS	*BRS/Search*	*DIALOG Version 2*
1. User prompt	/	-: / ..:	?
2. Enter file	FILE TEST	..:/TEST	BEGIN 1
3. Command stacking	;	/	;
4. Enter terms (ANDed)	S SOFTWARE AND INDUSTRY	SOFTWARE AND INDUSTRY	SS SOFTWARE AND INDUSTRY
5. Display index and field	E AU=FRENCH J	ROOT FRENCH-J	E AU=FRENCH, J
6. Enter term and field	S TT=SOFTWARE	SOFTWARE.TI.	S SOFTWARE/TI
7. Enter stem	S MARKET*	MARKET$	S MARKET?
8. Enter phrase	S WN2 MARKET, PLANNING	MARKET ADJ PLANNING	S MARKET(W)PLANNING
9. Display record titles	D6 TTL/1-3	..P6 TTL/1-3	T S6/6/1-3
10. Recap strategy	LS	..D ALL	DS
11. End session	LOGOUT	..OFF	LOGOFF

European Common Command Language	*ORBIT*	*Profile*	*Questel-Plus*
1. ?	USER:	>	?
2. BASE1	FILE TEST	SELECT TEST	..F1 TEST ER
3. !	;	unavailable	
4. F SOFTWARE AND INDUSTRY	SOFTWARE AND INDUSTRY	GET SOFTWARE+INDUSTRY	SOFTWARE AND INDUSTRY
5. D AU=FRENCH, J	NBR FRENCH, J/AU	EXPAND FRENCH	..IND /AU= FRENCH J
6. F SOFTWARE(TI)	SOFTWARE/TI	GET SOFTWARE @ TITLE	SOFTWARE/TI
7. F MARKET$	MARKET:	GET MARKET*	MARKET+
8. F MARKET PLANNING	MARKET(W)PLANNING	GET MARKET PLANNING	MARKET W PLANNING
9. S S=6;F=TI;R1TO3	PRT SS6 TI 1-3	TITLE 1-3	..LI SS6 TIT 1-3
10. F? ALL	HIS	REVIEW n	..HI
11. STOP	STOP Y	END	..ST EN

Table 5.1 *Comparative examples of facilities of seven command languages*

of the command languages illustrated. This variety is surprising and most unwelcome, especially since most command languages offer the same standard retrieval facilities of the kinds illustrated in Table 5.1.

The retrieval facilities offered and their implementation in particular command languages are topics difficult to keep separate, so a selection of illustrations will be given when describing a facility. The examples of search statements given in Table 5.1 would all be appropriate to a search for the sample document record given in Chapter 3 in Figure 3.6. The main varieties of structure, in terms of vocabulary and syntax, in command languages can be seen from Table 5.1 if the reader appreciates that the terms being entered are FRENCH J, SOFTWARE, INDUSTRY, MARKET, and PLANNING, the database is number 1 and called TEST, and search set 6 produces records to be displayed; hence everything else in the body of the Table is part of the command language.

Six of the command languages illustrated in Table 5.1 allow several search statements to be entered on one line with an approved separating symbol, a technique known as stacking. Search Example 4.9 in the last chapter could have used abbreviated commands and stacking such as:

> S NUCLEAR AND (FALLOUT OR POLLUTION) AND
> SHEEP; T S1/6/1–8

Facilities standard to all command languages will now be described and illustrated using Dialog Version 2 (Dialog Information Services, 1987) unless indicated otherwise.

Standard Retrieval Facilities

The basics of an online search have been outlined in Chapter 4. Commands are provided to log-on and then perhaps to change default values, such as screen width and length. News and information can be obtained, as well as specific help information. During keyboarding it is very useful to have immediate access to conventions for typing corrections (deleting a character is usually done by the backspace key or by the CONTROL key plus letter H), cancelling a line, interrupting the output, cancelling or re-starting the output, and methods for entering lines longer than the screen width.

Entering search terms and boolean operators

The fourth feature compared in Table 5.1 shows how terms may be entered and linked by boolean operators in the various command languages; the terms SOFTWARE and INDUSTRY linked with the boolean AND, thus matching the record in Figure 3.6 have been chosen to illustrate this. The match is achieved by the appearance of both terms somewhere in the record. Some command languages require an explicit command to enter a search term, such as S (SELECT) – BASIS, Dialog; SS (SELECT STEPS) – Dialog; F (FIND) – CCL; GET – Profile. In BRS/Search, ORBIT and Questel-Plus no explicit command is needed.

The search systems have a basic index which allows the entry of single words to match with titles, abstracts, and the single word components of any subject descriptors assigned by indexers or the full-text of records. So a response of zero items will mean that the inverted file does not contain the word, so no records can be matched. This can sometimes be caused by mistyping the term, or the term could be on a stoplist. A search on BRS, for example, for ON AND LINE AND RETRIEVAL will match with no items as the term ON is on the stoplist. Most search systems provide no warning about this nor do they automatically offer any help by suggesting alternative spellings or by offering words that are similar in spelling. Compound words containing a hyphen will usually match only if entered separately, although it must be remembered that hyphenated words often appear as single words as well (for example, the words on-line, online, on line). Terms that are names of people, countries, languages, or controlled vocabulary descriptors will have to be entered exactly as the system expects in order to establish a match. Entering search terms that are phrases, or entering several words to be matched only if they appear as phrases in the items will be treated later in this chapter.

The boolean operators AND, OR NOT, are subject to a few variations: for example, BASIS employs AND NOT, and Profile only allows abbreviated forms $+$, $-$. This conflicts with Dialog abbreviations * for AND, + for OR. Multiple use of one operator in a search statement causes no problems; thus entering terms for Stress in Bridge(s) could be

S STRESS; S BRIDGE OR BRIDGES; S S1 AND S2

But a problem of priority in execution arises if different operators are used in a statement. Dialog would give an incorrect result with

SS STRESS AND BRIDGE OR BRIDGES

because the ANDed set is processed before OR; the resulting set would contain correctly matched items containing Stress AND Bridge but also unwanted items which contain Bridges but have no reference to Stress at all. One solution is to learn the priority and enter terms accordingly. Alternatively, parentheses may be used to indicate which terms are to be processed first. The statement

SS STRESS AND (BRIDGE OR BRIDGES)

would produce the required result. Parentheses are the best general method (but angular brackets < > have to be used in the case of BLAISE) if operators are to be mixed. There are four different conventions of priority in the seven languages in Table 5.1, including that of priority being determined from left to right as the operators are entered.

Most languages now allow search statements to contain both terms and boolean operators, but to give every intermediate term a set number in Dialog the SS (SELECT STEPS) command must be used rather than S (SELECT). Such set numbers can be used later in a search with a saving of time. Dialog Version 1 and ESA-QUEST did not have this facility and hence had to employ the command C (COMBINE) with set numbers:

S STRESS; S BRIDGE; S BRIDGES; C 1 AND (2 OR 3)

However, users of ESA-QUEST may employ the Common Command Language F (FIND) to mix terms and operators and give intermediate set numbers, as Search Example 4.10 showed.

Displaying search term listings

It is often necessary to be able to display the alphabetically ordered list of index terms to determine the exact form for entry of terms or to discover extra terms useful to a search. There are five different commands to achieve this listing in the command languages shown: E (EXPAND), ROOT, D (DISPLAY), NBR (NEIGHBOR), ..IND (..INDEX). Every language shown has a different layout, shows a different amount of entries, and puts the term entered in different positions in the display.

If the term entered is not to be found in the index it still appears with zero items indicated. Various command conventions are employed to see more of a display, to go *down* to see further entries, or sometimes *up* as well to see earlier entries.

The response to the Dialog command E (short for EXPAND) for one database is shown in Search Example 5.1. The different word forms and phrases are shown.

?E MARKETING

Ref	Items	Index-term
E1	2	MARKETINC
E2	2	MARKETINDEX
E3	118666	*MARKETING
E4	2	MARKETING & CONSUMER SERVICES
E5	77	MARKETING COMPUTER SYSTEMS
E6	173	MARKETING CONSULTING SERVICES
E7	271	MARKETING MANAGEMENT
E8	87	MARKETING MANAGEMENT DEVELOPMENT˙
E9	48	MARKETING MANAGEMENT NEC
E10	15	MARKETING NEC
E11	84	MARKETING PERSONNEL
E12	54015	MARKETING PROCEDURES

Enter P or E for more

Search Example 5.1 *Display of index terms from the PTS PROMT database on Dialog*

The reference codes (E1, E2, . . .) allow speedy selection of specific terms with automatic boolean ORing, thus

    S E7–E9, E11

following the display is equivalent to

    S MARKETING MANAGEMENT OR MARKETING
    MANAGEMENT DEVELOPMENT OR MARKETING
    MANAGEMENT NEC OR MARKETING PERSONNEL

Specifying fields to be matched

It is often necessary to retrieve records by matching specific fields such as author, publication date, classification code, price or country. This is usually achieved by prefixing or suffixing the search term with a code to identify the specific field. Examples of how the various command languages allow the display of index terms close to a specific author (J. French) are shown in Table 5.1, for example:

    EXPAND AU=FRENCH J (BASIS)
    ROOT FRENCH-J (BRS/Search)
    E AU=FRENCH, J (Dialog)

Also there are examples in Table 5.1 of the term SOFTWARE being matched only with the title field, for example:

F SOFTWARE(TI) (Common Command Language)
SOFTWARE/TI (ORBIT and Questel-Plus)
GET SOFTWARE @ TITLE (Profile)

To achieve all the correct field matches it is always necessary to know which fields are only phrase indexed and not word indexed: authors are almost always just phrase indexed (see Chapter 3). This may be seen for the ERIC database on Dialog in Search Example 5.2.

?E AU=FRENCH, J

Ref	Items	Index-term
E1	1	AU=FRENCH, H. WELLS
E2	1	AU=FRENCH, HELENE
E3	0	*AU=FRENCH, J
E4	1	AU=FRENCH, J. C. R.
E5	1	AU=FRENCH, J. L.
E6	2	AU=FRENCH, JAMES
E7	1	AU=FRENCH, JAMES R.
E8	1	AU=FRENCH, JANE
E9	1	AU=FRENCH, JANET
E10	2	AU=FRENCH, JIM
E11	1	AU=FRENCH, JOHN C.
E12	1	AU=FRENCH, JOHN D.

Enter P or E for more

Search Example 5.2   *Display of authors' names from the ERIC database on Dialog*

There is no standardization by the database producer at the input stage and so the entry AU=FRENCH, JAMES could well refer to the same author as AU=FRENCH, JAMES R. or AU=FRENCH, JIM or even AU=FRENCH, J. C. R. The value of such a listing in matching with variant forms of names is obvious. More than one person with the same name cannot usually be distinguished however. Other database producers and search services adopt different conventions for indexing fields and so it is always necessary to check the details of how a particular database has been loaded when searching specific fields. Figure 5.1 shows a sample record of the Heilbron database of properties of chemical compounds, and Figure 5.2 shows how on this database on Dialog particular fields have been indexed as Word only, Phrase only, or Word & Phrase.

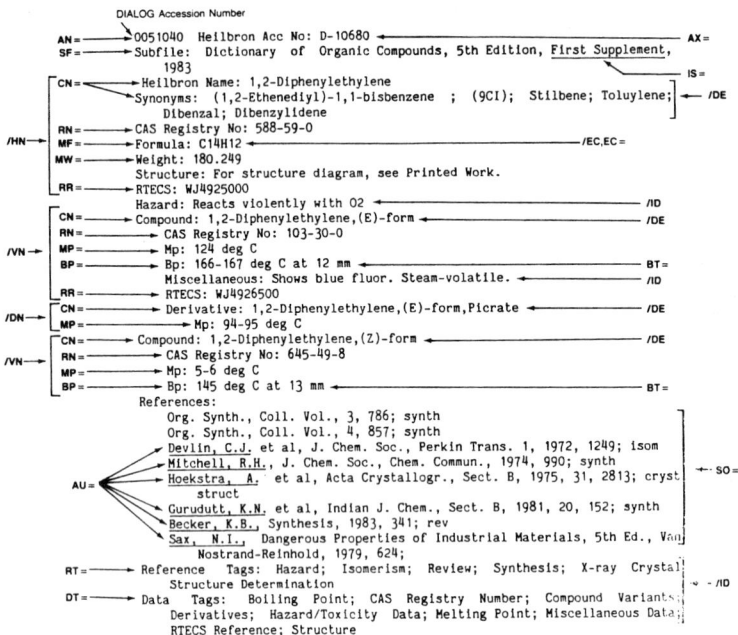

Figure 5.1   *Record structure of the HEILBRON database on Dialog*

In some command languages (for example, Profile) fields cannot be specified. In such cases the single inverted file contains all indexed terms from all fields, although the distinctive form of some fields makes them recognizable. In Profile, however, no phrase indexing is carried out on any field, hence displaying listings from the one term file would do no more than reveal that there are items for the word FRENCH.

In command languages which allow a basic or general index as well as specific indexes for certain fields it is very important indeed to know what the basic or general index contains: if it does not include all fields, which are included? In such cases the usual general answer is *subject aboutness terms that are text in nature*: in bibliographic files this would involve titles, abstracts, descriptors and identifiers, and other notes or subject headings. Figure 5.4 shows that three fields are included in the basic index for the Heilbron database on Dialog. Where there is a basic index of text

BASIC INDEX

PAGE	SUFFIX*	FIELD NAME	INDEXING	SELECT EXAMPLES
303-8	/DE	HEILBRON Name, Variant Name, Derivative Name, and Synonyms[1,2]	Word & Phrase	S STILBENE/DE S 1,2-DIPHENYLETHYLENE/DE
303-13	/EC	Element Count[2]	Word	S C14/EC
303-12	/ID	Compound Type, Hazard Information, General Information, Source of Substance, Use/Importance, Miscellaneous, Reference Tags, Data Tags, and Physical State[2,3]	Word	S VIOLENTLY(1W)02/ID

* If no suffix is specified all Basic Index fields are searched.
[1] Also searchable using CN =.
[2] Terms can be qualified to any one of three levels using one of the following suffixes: /HN to restrict retrieval to the Main HEILBRON substance information, /VN to restrict retrieval to the Compound Variant substance information, and /DN to restrict retrieval to the Derivative substance information (e.g., MP = 24/VN retrieves compound variant substances with a melting point of 24).
[3] Reference Tags, Data Tags, and Physical State may also be searched using the prefixes RT =, DT =, and PS = respectively.

ADDITIONAL INDEXES

PAGE	PREFIX	FIELD NAME	INDEXING	SELECT EXAMPLES
303-49	AN =	DIALOG Accession Number	Phrase	S AN = 0051040
303-43	AU =	Author	Phrase	S AU = SAX, N?
303-50	AX =	HEILBRON Accession Number	Phrase	S AX = D-10680
303-26	BP =	Boiling Point[2]	Phrase	S BP = 166 S BP = 165.5:167.5
303-26	BT =	Boiling Point Text[2]	Word	S BT = (13(W)MM)
303-15	CN =	Complete Substance Name or Synonym[2,4]	Phrase	S CN = 1,2-DIPHENYLETHYLENE
303-16	DR =	Derivative CAS Registry Number[2]	Phrase	S DR = 38608-87-6
303-52	DT =	Data Tags[5]	Phrase	S DT = 'HAZARD/TOXICITY DATA'
303-20	EC =	Element Count[2]	Phrase	S EC = C0014
303-29	FP =	Freezing Point[2]	Phrase	S FP = -5.5 S FP = -.05:1.5
303-23	GN =	Group Number[2]	Phrase	S GN = A7
303-52	IS =	Issue/Edition	Phrase	S IS = FIRST SUPPLEMENT
303-22	ME =	Molecular Element[2]	Phrase	S ME = CHBR
303-19	MF =	Molecular Formula[2]	Phrase	S MF = C14H12
303-29	MP =	Melting Point[2]	Phrase	S MP = 94 S MP = 123.5:125
303-30	MW =	Molecular Weight[2]	Phrase	S MW = 180.249 S MW = 179:182
303-31	OP =	Optical Rotation[2]	Phrase	S OP = 0.10 S OP = 50:51
303-31	OT =	Optical Rotation Text[2]	Word	S OT = (NA(W)LINE)
303-23	PI =	Periodic Index Term[2]	Phrase	S PI = A56B8TU
303-34	PK =	Dissociation Constant[2]	Phrase	S PK = 9.46 S PK = 8.5:8.7
303-45	PN =	Patent Number	Phrase	S PN = DE 2102811
303-35	PS =	Physical State[2,5]	Word	S PS = CRYST
303-23	PT =	Periodic Transition Row	Phrase	S PT = T1
303-36	RD =	Relative Density[2]	Phrase	S RD = 1.399 S RD = 1.2:1.3
303-16	RN =	CAS Registry Number[2]	Phrase	S RN = 588-59-0
303-48	RR =	RTECS Reference	Phrase	S RR = WJ4925000
303-47	RT =	Reference Tags[5]	Phrase	S RT = SYNTHESIS
303-51	SF =	Dictionary Name (Subfile)	Phrase	S SF = DICTIONARY OF ORGANIC COMPOUNDS
303-36	SL =	Solubility[2]	Word	S SL = (HOT(W)H₂O)
303-41	SO =	Bibliographic Source	Word	S SO = (DANGEROUS(S)MATERIALS)
303-54	UD =	Update	Phrase	S UD = 8512

[4] Also searchable in the Basic Index with /DE or /DF.
[5] Also searchable in the Basic Index with /ID.

LIMITING[2]

Sets and terms may be limited by Basic Index suffixes, i.e., /DE, /EC, and /ID (e.g., SELECT S4/DE), as well as by the following features:			
PAGE	SUFFIX	FIELD NAME	EXAMPLES
303-54	/DOC5	Dictionary of Organic Compounds	SELECT S7/DOC5
	/HZ	Hazard/Toxicity Data available	SELECT S9/HZ
	/NOHZ	Hazard/Toxicity Data unavailable	SELECT S2/NOHZ

Figure 5.2 *Indexed fields in the HEILBRON database on Dialog*

terms there will be other indexes (Dialog's additional indexes, for example) to gain access to things such as names (authors, companies, journals, languages) and dates (publication, updates to a database), for example. Dialog's pattern of suffix codes for the fields covered by the basic index and prefix codes for the additional indexes is illustrated generally in Table 5.2, and does attempt to aid the memory by its choice of two-letter code. The idea of distinguishable fields (variously called indexes, sections, paragraphs, etc.) is very important to successful retrieval in some databases: ESA-IRS, for example, has a general specification of some 90 standard fields for its database records and even so some database producers include additional, non-standard fields.

Basic index field specifications (*suffix coded*)		Additional index field specifications (*Prefix coded*)	
Abstract	/AB	Author	AU=
Descriptor	/DE	Company name	CO=
Full descriptor	/DF	Corporate source	CS=
Identifier	/ID	Document type	DT=
Full identifier	/IF	Journal name	JN=
Note	/NT	Language	LA=
Section heading	/SH	Publication year	PY=
Title	/TI	Update	UD=

Table 5.2 *Some of the index field suffix and prefix codes used in bibliographic databases on Dialog*

Combinations of field codes may be needed, and can be stated together with operators; the following statements could be used to retrieve records with either the term DOLPHIN or the term PORPOISE in the title or abstract field:

> SS (DOLPHIN OR PORPOISE)/TI,AB (Dialog)
> /TI,AB DOLPHIN OR PORPOISE (ORBIT)

In ORBIT and BLAISE, entering a term with no field specification results in a message indicating that the term matches with various fields (if that is the case). Search Example 5.3 shows a search on the BNB MARC database on BLAISE for books on 'pencils' where matches were found on the following fields:

(TS) – Title subject keywords.
(PD) – PRECIS descriptors.
(PW) – PRECIS keywords.
(SH) – Library of Congress subject headings.
(SW) – Library of Congress keywords.
(TW) – Title words.

SEARCH 1?
USER:
PENCILS

PROG:
TERM (PENCILS) APPEARS IN (6) CONTEXTS

	NO. OF ITEMS	TERM
1	1	PENCILS (TS)
2	1	PENCILS (PD)
3	6	PENCILS (PW)
4	1	PENCILS (SH)
5	1	PENCILS (SW)
6	10	PENCILS (TW)

SPECIFY NUMBERS, ALL, OR NONE.

Search Example 5.3   *A search term matching six fields from the BNB MARC database on BLAISE*

But it must always be remembered that fields, their codes, and whether they are searchable at all are specific to both particular databases and services. For example, LISA (Library and Information Science Abstracts) can be searched under classification code in ORBIT, but not in Dialog, and under source publication year the reverse is the case. Another phenomenon to watch out for is that where field codes are used to control the parts of records to be displayed or printed out, the actual codes for a given field may differ from those used in entering and displaying terms (for example in BLAISE and ORBIT especially). Table 5.3 shows the various codes used for printing and searching the database of monographs held at the British Library Document Supply Centre (BLDSC); this database is available for searching on BLAISE.

Limiting

Limiting is a short-cut to enable certain field content to apply to a given search statement or even to a whole search. In Dialog, for example, the use of LIMITALL/ENG would cause every subsequent set to include only items written in English; thus being equivalent to incorporating in each set AND LA=ENG. In many command languages the limit command can specify a set number to act upon. With dates or accession numbers, ranges can be

Print qualifier	MARC field	Full name	Search qualifiers
AC	110	Corporate author	(AU), (CW)
AP	100	Personal author	(AU)
BL	024	BLAISE no	(BL)
CB	015	National Bibliography no	(CB), (CN)
CI	021	ISBN	(CI), (CN)
CL	010	LC card no	(CL), (CN)
CS	022	ISSN	(CN), (CS)
DSC	092	BLDSC shelf mark	
EC	710	Corporate name AE	(AU), (CW)
ED	250	Edition	
EP	700	Personal name AE	(AU)
ET	745	Title AE	(TW)
IC	008	Information codes	(DA), (IC), (DA)
MDV	111	Meeting date/venue	
N00	500	Notes	
PA	248	Title – part	(TW)
PU	260	Publ, distr, manuf	(PU)
RC	910	Corporate name ref	(AU), (CW), (TW)
RCN	001	Record Control No	(RCN)
RP	900	Personal name ref	(AU), (TW)
SE	490	Series	(TW), (VOL)
TI	245	Title	(TW)

Table 5.3 *Examples of search and print codes for the British Library Document Supply Centre monographs database on BLAISE*

specified, and for numerical data some languages allow greater than or less than operators, using GT or LT for example. The statement

..LIMIT/2 YR GT 86

in Data-Star would limit the items retrieved in set number 2 to those items which had 87 or greater in the YR (year) field. Table 5.4 shows a selection of eight of the Dialog limit qualifiers.

Limit qualifiers (suffix coded)	
Abstract provided	/ABS
English language	/ENG
Human subject	/HUMAN
Major descriptors	/MAJ
Not English language	/NONENG
Patents document type	/PAT
Publication year	/1984
Accession numbers	/nnnnnn–nnnnnn

Table 5.4   *Some of the suffix codes used for limiting sets used in bibliographic databases on Dialog*

Entering search term stems

A quick method of matching such terms as markets, marketed and marketing is to employ a device which allows the word 'Market' to match both as a word and the stem of several others. But such a stem might match unexpected words such as marketplace and might fail to match a mis-spelling such as markest. However, a shorter stem such as 'Mark' would retrieve irrelevant terms such as marks, markush, etc. Table 5.1 shows five different command language symbols which implement what is variously called truncation, root, stem, and conflating or confounding word forms. More accurately these are examples of open right-hand truncation. Another technique might be

S BRIDGE? ?

to restrict the suffix to one letter, thus matching Bridge, Bridges, Bridged and not Bridging. The restriction could be of several letters and some command languages require this to be specified as a number. Open truncation may be especially useful for phrase indexed field matching. For example, entering an author name where only a first initial is known, if safe to do, might proceed as

S AU=FRENCH, J?

But as Search Example 5.2 shows, this would effect a match with far too many different people (such as Jane French, Janet French, etc.).

Some command languages (but not BRS or Profile) allow internal truncation, variously called masking, embedding, universal character, etc. Variant spellings can be handled quickly

S ADVERTI?ING

would match ADVERTISING as well as ADVERTIZING. Many symbol conventions exist in the languages, and it must also be clear whether the character(s) masked can be absent altogether – for example, on ORBIT the term ALUMIN:UM correctly matches both forms of the word (ALUMINUM and ALUMINIUM) whereas ALUMIN?UM on Dialog would not. It is less common to provide the facility of left-hand truncation, but in the services or databases where this is available, it is an especial advantage for matching with chemical names.

Entering search term phrases

The content of records, particularly bibliographic ones, comprises words and phrases. There may be text fields with sentences and paragraphs, also controlled vocabulary fields containing words and short phrases assigned by indexers, and name fields in which multiword constructions are essential to retain proper sense. Searchers wish to be able to match the words and phrases of search queries to preserve correct meaning, although inverted file access is often easier, quicker and cheaper to provide as single words only. The need for correct phrase matching can be seen in a search for items on search strategies for information retrieval: the statement S SEARCH AND STRATEGIES can produce many irrelevant records, even with both terms appearing in titles such as *In Search of Excellence: Practical Strategies for . . .* and *Developing Strategies for the Job Search.*

As Chapter 3 explained, in principle, field content can be phrase indexed, single word indexed, or both. In addition to this the word indexed fields can also contain positional information (such as a position number indicating the place of a word within a sentence, or within a field) that permits a special kind of phrase matching. For example, the first title above contains the word Search in position 2 and Strategies in position 6: so a search statement could be made demanding the words to be adjacent and in order, in which case neither record with the above titles would be retrieved. Some command languages permit the number of intervening words to be specified, and even the appearance of the words in either order, to try and match 'Strategies for Search' for example. Table 5.1 shows search statements that specify 'Market Planning' to be just that phrase, the words to be adjacent and in order. The syntax required for this will be discussed shortly.

Since phrases are conventionally represented in records by words separated by single spaces, one approach to making phrase indexed fields instantly recognizable is the replacement of the spaces by a character such as a hyphen. A bibliographic record such as that in Figure 3.6 could have the phrases marked and stored as Market-Planning, French-John, Planning-Quarterly, etc. BRS adopts this approach. Matching with such phrases requires accurate entry of the full phrase, or truncation can be used to aid matching, such as FRENCH-J$. This approach cannot be adopted for the longer free-text fields, so the adjacency or proximity method mentioned can then be used, with a search statement in BRS such as SOFTWARE ADJ INDUSTRY used to match this phrase accurately, or the interposed proximity operators WITH or SAME used to relax proximity to WITHin a sentence or anywhere in the SAME field or paragraph.

The same kind of approach to phrase indexing and proximity indication is adopted by Dialog, but fields which are phrase indexed cannot be recognized visually from the item display but only from information given in the documentation for each database and also from the display of search terms prompted by the use of EXPAND. Table 5.5 gives a general example of the kind of information which would be provided for a particular database and shows the pattern that predominates in bibliographic databases.

Search Example 5.1 gave an example of an EXPAND display of the basic index where it can be seen that many phrases are in the index (marketing management, marketing procedures, etc.) presumably as a result of their being allocated by indexers in phrase indexed fields. Figure 5.2 showed the indexing strategy adopted for the fields in the Heilbron database on Dialog.

Because some entered phrases do match with items it is neither easy to grasp that the item count can easily be increased nor remember why some phrases match with no items unless indexing techniques are understood. Search Example 5.4 shows alternative ways of phrase searching. The search phrase SEARCH STRATEGY might well result in no items being retrieved due to the fact that the phrase is not in any of the phrase indexed fields. SEARCH STRATEGIES might result in 1415 records being retrieved. However, if the statement SEARCH STRATEGIES/DE,ID (to

Basic index	Indexing type	Additional indexes	Indexing type
Abstract	Word	Author	Phrase
Descriptor	Word and phrase	Corporate source	Word
Identifier	Word and phrase	Country of publication	Word and phrase
Note	Word	Document type	Phrase
Section heading	Word and phrase	Journal name	Phrase
Title	Word	Language	Word or phrase

Table 5.5 *Some typical kinds of indexing used in bibliographic databases on Dialog*

limit the search to descriptor and identifier fields only) also retrieved 1415 records, then it can be seen that in the particular database being searched only the descriptor and identifier fields are phrase indexed. The statement SEARCH(W)STRATEGY might result in 196 matches with word indexed fields whereas SEARCH (W)STRATEGIES might result in 1499 matches with word indexed and phrase indexed fields. SEARCH(W)STRATEG? shows how more records would be matched with truncation being used.

?**DS**

Set	Items	Description
S1	0	SEARCH STRATEGY
S2	1415	SEARCH STRATEGIES (COMPREHENSIVE PLANS FOR FINDING INFORMATION)
S3	1415	SEARCH STRATEGIES/DE,ID (COMPREHENSIVE PLANS FOR FINDING INFORMATION)
S4	196	SEARCH(W)STRATEGY
S5	1499	SEARCH(W)STRATEGIES
S6	1557	SEARCH(W)STRATEG?

Search Example 5.4   *Some phrase searching examples from the ERIC database on Dialog*

In several command languages the number of intervening words can be specified in a phrase search; for example, TAMING (2W) SHREW could be used to match with *The Taming of the Shrew* even though the intervening two words (of, the) might be on a stoplist. The W adjacency operator is usually used to specify that the words must be in that order; the N adjacency operator can be used to indicate that the words can be in any order. Thus if searching for the phrase 'concrete bridges', CONCRETE (2N) BRIDGES would match most short phrases including 'bridges constructed from concrete'.

In Table 5.1 it can be seen that adjacency is specified in five different ways, mostly by the interfixed character W meaning Word or Within. In BASIS Within is a prefix, WN2, and the comma is the interfix. In the Common Command Language and in Profile the space between the words is the interfix, meaning completely adjacent: schemes of dots (for CCL) and slashes (for Profile) relax this.

Searching the additional indexed fields which are only phrase indexed does benefit greatly from search term displays and from truncation used with care. Combinations of facilities are increasingly available as command languages are developed, thus permitting a statement such as

> S AU=FRENCH, J? AND SOFTWARE(3N)MARKET?/
> TI,ENG

using field prefix, truncation, boolean, proximity, field suffix and limit suffix. However, if the phrase indexed authors had no space following the surname, zero items would incorrectly result. Such complexity may well be counter productive for all but the most experienced searchers. It is often better to adopt a simple step-by-step approach to searching.

Another technique less commonly used for phrase matching is known as string searching, which involves sequentially searching a pre-retrieved subset held in the print file (see Chapter 3). From a searcher's viewpoint it differs from proximity specification in that it has to be applied to an appropriate set of documents already selected and of reasonably small size. Even then it is often very slow. BLAISE does not have proximity searching, so this kind of sequential scan of particular records and fields may be the only way of accurately matching some phrases, though it may take some time to perform and therefore be costly. BASIS and ORBIT and DIMDI's GRIPS language have both proximity and string searching. Since the latter can work as a kind of truncation, a search for a character string such as :ETHYL: may prove beneficial in some databases.

Displaying records and printing offline

When a search retrieves some records which it is desired to inspect, commands are needed to display such records, download them or print them whilst online, or to have them printed offline by the search service and mailed to the searcher. There is quite a variety of commands used for displaying records online as can be seen in Table 5.1 with DISPLAY, PRINT, TYPE, SHOW, and LIST in their full form. Offline display command examples are PRINT, PRINT OFFLINE, and OFFLINE. It can be seen that there are three specifiable elements to the typical command to display records.

The first is the number of the search statement, or set, from which items are to be displayed, often specified as an S or SS number. Profile can only display the last set created by GET, so no set can be specified. In some command languages no set need be specified if the last one created is to be displayed. The second specifiable element is the format in which the item records are to be displayed. Total records can, of course, be presented, in which case the format can be specified as ALL, MAX, FULL, or as an appropriate numbered format. In Table 5.1 just the titles of the bibliographic records are to be output, hence the use of F=TI, TI, TTL, TIT, and the specification /6/ in the search statements.

The third matter to be specified is which items or records are to be displayed. This can also be ALL, or can specify the numbers and ranges, such as 1–3,5. A particular record viewed initially in say, title format, can then be seen in fuller format if its number in the set is specified. These three components of set, format and items are usually specified in an identical manner for ordering offline prints.

Increasing flexibility is appearing in command languages to help this display facility. In some languages the three specifiable elements can be placed in any order. In Data-Star, using just the command . .P invokes the system to provide two useful prompts, one for format (paragraphs) and the other for records (documents). Defaults are nearly always available so that say, just the latest set, in title format, and the first record, can be displayed with a single letter command. User-defined formats are becoming more common, both in the ability to specify exactly which record fields are to be displayed (and sometimes in which order), and in making a permanent numbered format tailored to a given database and user. More services now offer formats that especially aid subsequent processing of records after downloading, so that field ends are marked, for example. Special formats are available on BLAISE, such as an option to have the field names displayed in full, or the field content in the case of MARC records to include the tags. This can be seen in Search Example 5.5.

```
SEARCH 7?
USER
print full marc
PROG:
1
001          68868374#
015.00:0/0    $ab8868374#
081.00:0/0    $a741.9$b41$c18#
082.00:0/0    $a741.941$b074$c19#
```

```
083.00:0/0    $aBritish drawings$b} Catalogues#
245.30:0/0    $aPencil pen & brush$bmodern British drawing#
260.00:0/0    $aLondon$d42 Inverness St., NW1 Gillian$bJason Gallery
              $c[1986?]#
300.00:0/0    $a[45]p$bill$c24cm$epbk#
350.00:0/0    $aNo price#
500.00:0/0    $aCatalogue of an exhibition at the Gillian Jason Gallery,
              London, 1986#
```

Search Example 5.5   *A record displayed in MARC format on BLAISE*

Printing offline proceeds in the same general way as displaying online, but with cost estimates given for the specified printouts and an option to cancel. There may be layout options which can improve the appearance of the search results, and special mailing addresses and headings can be specified. The records can usually be sorted into order on the contents of a particular field, perhaps to arrange a bibliography by author or by publication date.

Recapping, deleting and saving search statements

It is often necessary to be able to recap and see a list of search statements used during an online search. Table 5.1 shows the commands to do this with the full form commands being LIST, DISPLAY, DISPLAY SETS, FIND?, HISTORY and REVIEW. The search statements usually listed by these recap commands are those that created item sets, not those which may have logged-on to a database, displayed search terms, or displayed item records. The statements to be listed can be all of them, which sometimes needs specifying, sometimes does not, or can be a selection specified by number or number range.

Search statement deletion is another facility commonly available. Using commands such as ERASE, KEEP, DELETE, and PURGE, sets may be removed from a current search either because the limit to the number of sets allowed in one session is being reached, or in order to present just the successful parts of the search for a tidy result or for subsequent re-use.

The saving of a number of search statements for automatic re-use is a most valuable facility. One circumstance would be the need to briefly terminate a search before completion perhaps in order to consider whether it could be improved by talking to the requester or consulting documentation. Another would be the immediate application of one search strategy to several different databases, where no more convenient form of multifile searching is possible. Yet another would be later application of the strategy in some weeks or months time to have database updates produce new items. Many search services offer a temporary save, for a few minutes, hours or days, and a permanent save together with methods of amending and deleting. Practices vary over the charge made for using these facilities, from no charge for saving for just ten minutes and charges for anything longer, to complete absence of charges.

The operation of the save facility requires each saved strategy to have a unique code or name, sometimes assigned by the searcher, sometimes by the system. Then the use of a saved search may involve the obligatory re-use of every statement in the strategy, or may permit selective use, such as a line at a time until no more are needed. The formulation of a strategy to be re-used on different databases often needs some care, so that what is only appropriate to all the databases is included. For example, it is usually difficult to utilize search statements designed to match with additional indexes, such as names, because of the different phrase-indexed formats which may be encountered.

Special Retrieval Facilities

In addition to the commonly-encountered standard facilities just described, there are many additional facilities which may either be confined to particular databases or may be offered only by some search services. A selection of these will now be described.

The online thesaurus

A facility confined to some command languages and certain databases is that of displaying entries from a thesaurus during a search. The 17 terms in the ERIC Thesaurus linked to MARKET-ING may be displayed using the Dialog command EXPAND (MARKETING) as shown in Search Example 5.6. Each term is identified by type following the conventions of U (Used for), N (Narrower Term), B (Broader Term), and R (Related Term). The value of such a display lies in the quick identification of possible terms to use in the search, their easy selection in the case of Dialog's 'R' number, and the currency of the item postings which will be better than those which may be given in the printed version of the particular thesaurus. It must be realized, however, that because Dialog's phrase and word indexing fields are put into one basic index, the item postings shown for single words relate to their total use in all the basic index fields, including title and abstract. In the 30 or so Dialog databases which offer this facility, EXPAND with the term in parentheses or with the term chosen by its Ref number from a conventional search term display must be used, for example, E E3 following the result in Search Example

?e (marketing)

Ref	Items	Type	RT	Index-term
R1	3424		17	*MARKETING (AN AGGREGATE OF FUNCTIONS INVOLVED IN THE TR. . .)
R2	0	U	1	DISTRIBUTION (ECONOMICS)
R3	621	N	16	MERCHANDISING
R4	361	N	9	RETAILING
R5	419	N	12	SALESMANSHIP
R6	70	N	5	WHOLESALING
R7	22658	B	68	TECHNOLOGY
R8	21100	R	29	BUSINESS
R9	4367	R	19	BUSINESS EDUCATION
R10	647	R	13	CONSUMER PROTECTION
R11	384	R	12	COOPERATIVES
R12	1062	R	20	DISTRIBUTIVE EDUCATION

Enter P or E for more

?e zz=market

Ref	Terms	Index-term
E1	114	ZZ=MARITIME
E2	18	ZZ=MARITIME EDUCATION
E3	7205	*ZZ=MARKET
E4	2765	ZZ=MARKET// LABOR
E5	3424	ZZ=MARKETING
E6	609	ZZ=MARKING
E7	58	ZZ=MARKING// DIACRITICAL
E8	21	ZZ=MARKSMANSHIP
E9	2984	ZZ=MARRIAGE
E10	607	ZZ=MARRIAGE COUNSELING
E11	1654	ZZ=MARRIED
E12	133	ZZ=MARRIED STUDENTS

Enter P or E for more

Search Example 5.6 *Examples of thesaurus displays from the ERIC database on Dialog*

5.1 would do this. Other databases with thesauri online include INSPEC, SOCIOLOGICAL ABSTRACTS, SPORT, WORLD TEXTILES, MEDLINE, EMBASE and CANCERLIT.

Search Example 5.6 also shows another thesaurus-derived display. This is of the rotated or permuted descriptor list showing every descriptor which contains a particular word. In this example the term 'Market' occurs as a descriptor and in 'Labor Market'. Selection can again be by means of the Ref Number. This feature is a prefix indexed field in Dialog.

One other similar facility which is sometimes provided is the ability to have sets of narrower terms automatically included in the search. For example, in a medical database all the disease names in a given category might be needed to be included in a logical OR relationship. This feature is sometimes known as EXPLODE, and can use named terms or special *tree numbers* taken from a hierarchical listing in the controlled vocabulary.

Advanced display options

In many cases retrieved records exceed the display capacity of the workstation screen, and in full-text databases (containing the original text) facilities are needed to enable speedy browsing through just the portions of the record relevant to the search. Record display options usually provide the option for the display to stop as soon as a screen is filled, or to stop whenever a particular key is depressed, but beyond this the need is to jump backwards and forwards through a large record or to be presented just with the portions wanted, before perhaps the whole record is displayed or printed offline.

One approach divides text records into numbered *text paragraphs*, and first gives a list of these numbered paragraphs in which the search terms occur. Then, particular paragraphs may be selected to be displayed, or every paragraph with matching terms can automatically be displayed. The search terms that are in the record are themselves highlighted in some way, usually by being surrounded by extra spaces and perhaps the asterisk as a masking character. Even this technique may present several screens-full of information, so browsing features may put a *banner line* at the top of each screen to record what the search is and how many screens there are. To avoid continually re-keying fairly complex display commands, short-cuts may be provided to invoke the last display command and move from a single field to the full text or any identifiable field.

Another means of displaying matching search terms is not dependent on the text being divided into paragraphs because a *window* is given on the bits of text with the matching terms surrounded by just a sentence or two. In one example of this, up to 30 words either side of the matches are displayed, and this window size can be set to any amount within this maximum range. This technique of displaying the context is reflected in one such command label KWIC, Key Word in Context, but unlike printed indexes produced traditionally by this technique the matching key words are not sorted into any order but presented in the order of their occurrence in the record. Search Example 5.7 shows the display in KWIC format of five records retrieved from a search for 'microwave ovens' on the CONSUMER REPORTS full-text database on Dialog.

File 646:Consumer Reports Full-Text 1982–Dec 88
    (Copr. 1988 Consumers Union)
    Set   Items   Description
    ─   ───   ─────────
?S MICROWAVE(W)OVEN?
          59   MICROWAVE
          84   OVEN?
    S1   47   MICROWAVE(W)OVEN?
?TYPE S1/KWIC/1–5

1/KWIC/1

   . . . purchases for your gift list. This year, along with high-priced items like TVs and microwave ovens, we've selected a good number of lower-cost, life-simplifying products like kitchen timers . . .

1/KWIC/2

   . . . heavyweight fabrics. Its rough surface snags the little devils and rips them off.

   Full-sized microwave ovens These models are roomy enough for just about any dish. We suggest three top-performing . . .

   IDENTIFIERS: . . . Litton 2494 microwave oven; . . . Whirlpool MW8900XS microwave oven; . . . KitchenAid KCMS135 microwave oven;

   DESCRIPTORS: . . . Microwave ovens;

1/KWIC/3

. . . the Welbilt.

The Panasonic/National is a white chest about the size of a compact microwave oven. It turns out rectangular loaves that are higher than they are wide and weigh just . . .

1/KWIC/4

. . ..a heart patient with a pacemaker implant. Is it safe for her to operate a microwave oven in the kitchen?
COLUMBIA, S.C.; C.B.

A. Yes. Microwave leakage from today's . . .

1/KWIC/5

. . . that polluted the air, blow dryers that sucked in long hair.

We recommended against buying microwave ovens when they first came out, saying they leaked a worrisome amount of radiation. The FDA and the industry took notice, and now microwave ovens leak only minimally and bear a warning label.

We also reported extensively on lawn mowers . . .

Search Example 5.7 *Display of a record in KWIC format from the CONSUMER REPORTS full-text database on Dialog*

The ability to have a set of records sorted into order online before displaying them is offered by a number of services. There will probably be a limit to the number of items that can be sorted, although this may well be several thousand. The fields on which the records are to be sorted will need to be specified, so specifying this as an author field with the set number and items on Dialog requires a search statement such as

SORT S1/ALL/AU

Numeric or financial data might be best displayed in reverse or descending order, from the highest to the lowest, and this facility is often available. In most services unsorted record display is usually ordered by descending record numbers, to give the items most recently added to the database first. In Profile, however, a sort is performed automatically without any special command which presents output most helpfully in descending order of publication date as Search Example 4.11 showed.

Another facility available on some financial databases is that of statistical presentation and analysis. Tables of data can be compiled from a set of records. For example, Dialog provides an online facility using REPORT. The field codes are specified in the order the data are wanted as columns in the table and by means of the SORT command the data may be displayed in a useful order. Such objectives as market analysis can be helped by extra facilities such as row and column totals by means of a CROSSTAB facility.

Frequency analysis and term extraction

A statistical analysis of a different kind is illustrated by the command ZOOM, available on the ESA-IRS service. Its purpose is to analyse the frequency of occurrence of terms in a set of items in order to select the best terms to enter subsequently. Search Example 5.8 shows a preliminary search for items on 'stress in box-beam bridges' in the COMPENDEX database on ESA-IRS. ZOOM analyses the text (in this case phrase-indexed fields) to show the index phrases used in the references in the set listed in order of frequency of use. It may be seen that more precise phrases are offered such as 'beams and girders' and 'box girder' as well as the plural 'stresses', which could be used in further search statements. ZOOM may be applied to fields other than the phrase-indexed ones and can offer text word analyses and ranked lists of authors or institutional names, for example.

BEGIN 4
```
———31Jan89   14:19:45   User09274–
       0.06 AU 0.39 Minutes in File   32
       0.06 AU approx Total
File   4:COMPENDEX:1969–88,12
SET   ITEMS      DESCRIPTION (+=OR;*=AND;–=NOT)
—     ———        ——————————————
?  F STRESS AND BOX AND BEAM AND BRIDGE?
   1 76718      STRESS
   2  4954      BOX
   3 52838      BEAM
   4 12752      BRIDGE?
   5    13      1*2*3*4
? ZOOM
                    Text Analysis Results
Frq   Words/Phrases
————  ——————————————————————————————————————
   8 BEAMS AND GIRDERS
   8 BRIDGES
   8 STRESSES
   7 STRUCTURAL ANALYSIS
   4 BRIDGES STEEL
```

```
3 BOX GIRDER
3 MODELS
3 STEEL STRUCTURES
3 STRUCTURAL DESIGN
3 SUPPORTS
2 BENDING
2 BRIDGES BOX GIRDER
2 COMPOSITE
2 CURVED
2 DESIGN
2 FINITE ELEMENT METHOD
2 HIGHWAY
2 MATHEMATICAL TECHNIQUES
. . . Pages.Lines: More= 2.13
```

Search Example 5.8 *The use of the ZOOM command in the COMPENDEX database on ESA-IRS*

The extraction of terms from items is available on other search services, sometimes just as a list of terms without statistical frequency information. A further feature sometimes provided is the ability to utilize these extracted terms in a subsequent search without having to enter each one in the normal way. In ORBIT, for example, up to 140 terms may be transferred to a select list from records, which can then be listed and used. Another example is the command MAP on Dialog which extracts terms and then creates a saved search of them. This removes duplicate terms and sorts the list into order for editing or for immediate use. These different methods of term extraction, frequency counts and automatic selection are of special value when applied to carefully coded data field information, such as the chemical registry numbers available in some databases.

Multifile searching

The standard facilities for saving searches have been mentioned, and the use of this technique for repeating a search on another database or file has been commonplace. Which databases to use can now often be determined by use of some kind of database index which gives access to all the dictionary files of all the databases (or a selection of them) in order to give the numbers of items which would be retrieved on each. Each database selected must then be entered in the normal way for the actual items to be displayed.

For example, using Data-Star, determining the best databases for a search on the topic 'Passive smoking', the cross-file index could be entered, the category of databases covering biomedicine selected, then postings in the databases compared as shown in Search Example 5.9. Suitable databases can then be selected and the search profile could be amended or saved for execution on just those databases to retrieve the actual records. In Data-Star, as in other services, selection of the databases to be checked can be by category or by individually selected databases, or a combination of both methods.

```
1   ALL D-S DATABASES
20 ALL D-S BUSINESS DATABASES
2   D-S BUSINESS – YOUR CHOICE OF SERVICE
3   D-S BIOMEDICAL
4   D-S DRUG
5   D-S CHEMICAL
6   D-S TECHNOLOGY
7   D-S BIOTECHNOLOGY
8   YOUR CHOICE OF DATABASES
ENTER NUMBER
3

D-S – SEARCH MODE – ENTER QUERY
    1__: PASSIVE AND SMOKING

AIDS       0
BIOL     321
BIZZ     440
BI84     119
BMAP      60
CANC     139
CAZZ     166
CHIN       2
CHZZ      86
CUBI       0
DHSS      11
DIOG       3
EMED      88
EMZZ     551
EM78      69
EM87     394
ENCY       1
FAIR       1
FDCR       0
FORS       4
```

FSTA	1
GPGP	14
HSLI	53
IOWA	55
IPAB	13
IRCS	0
KOSM	0
LHBU	3
LINE	10
MART	1
MEDL	327
MEZZ	457
ME76	42
ME82	88
NAHL	11
NTIS	11
PHAR	0
PHCO	0
PHIN	0
PSYC	20
RPMS	0
SCCC	12
SCIN	583
SEDB	0
SOCA	1
TOXL	488

Search Example 5.9 *The use of the CROSS FILE index on Data-Star*

The next obvious development in multifile searching is the ability to conduct a search in more than one database without having to enter each one and re-enter the terms or execute a saved strategy. A true multifile search starts by the selection of the databases, by category, by identity, by both, or by the use of an index file perhaps. The search is then conducted using the normal facilities, although different conventions in indexing and field labelling amongst the databases chosen will have to be allowed for. Search Example 4.9 in the previous chapter illustrates the use of Dialog's OneSearch multifile search command. Matching items may be displayed, though in addition, these items will be labelled as to their database of origin. The same item may be retrieved from the different databases, and the automatic removal of these duplicate records may be a future feature of command languages. Whilst within a multifile search it is possible to display records just from particular files, and to have lists of index terms displayed from some or all files, either amalgamated or with files of origin indicated. At the conclusion of the search appropriate connect costs will be calculated.

Special services

There are a number of services in addition to those described which may enhance the supply of results to end-users or provide a cost-effective means of supplying a local service. BLAISE and DIMDI, for example, offer offline searching: that is, search statements are entered and saved in the normal way, but the searches are conducted during off-peak hours and the results supplied by mail. This might be a cost effective way of searching multiple files or could be the only way of searching certain subfiles only available offline.

Another special service is that of processing SDI profiles for the Selective Dissemination of Information. Saved search strategies can be invoked as desired, but an SDI service will offer a regular and cheaper means of batch searching just the latest additions to a file from which the results can be mailed to the user at desired frequencies, say once a month. SDI profiles may, of course, be created, inspected, edited or deleted online at any time with suitable commands. Such a special service is usually restricted to particular databases.

A document ordering service which provides full copies of items identified in an online search may be available. The order may be placed during a search or can be placed later. The document suppliers regularly retrieve the orders left for them by users of the search service, then fulfil the order by mail and make the necessary charges direct to the requester. The commands permit special instructions along with mailing addresses, and the ability to list and review previously placed orders.

Some services offer to mount customer's in-house databases as a *private files service*, with access limited to authorized users. This enables powerful search facilities to be used to access local data, and local data to be shared amongst a particular user group, although the cost of such a service, including the necessary data entry, may well be higher than using local software.

The ability to list the total number of databases available for searching on a particular service is usually provided by a special command (for example, ?FILES on Dialog).

Command Language Problems, Options and Criteria

From Table 5.1 it can be seen that a facility sometimes requires only a command (for example, recapping, LS or DS), sometimes a command plus an argument (for example, SELECT SOFTWARE), and sometimes an argument only (for example, the term MARKET as entered in BRS/Search or ORBIT). Some commands have several components (for example, for displaying or printing records). Some search statements include boolean operators or other indicators: these may be prefixes (for example, AU= FRENCH), or suffixes (for example, SOFTWARE/TI), or inter-fixes (for example, MARKET(W)PLANNING). Combinations of these are often permitted. The vocabulary of the commands usually can be entered in a full or an abbreviated form: mostly the latter have been used in Table 5.1 as abbreviations are often the initial letter of the full form and are thus easy, quick and less error-prone to type. (The Profile Information command language permits almost no abbreviations, however.) The syntax of the commands includes such matters as the mandatory use or non-use of a space, the optional use of spaces, and a host of punctuation symbols.

Errors and messages

Learning accurately to understand statements used by searchers helps a beginner to become proficient, as does the process of trial and error. The precise meaning of the search system's responses must also be understood: often there is an echo of what has just been entered (in full or partial form) plus the response itself (as Search Examples 4.9 to 4.11 illustrated). Search sets are assigned a running number and can usually be re-used later in a search (but not in the Profile command language). They are specified for use sometimes just by their number, and sometimes by Sn or SSn ('sets' are called 'searches' in BLAISE and 'search statements' in ORBIT and Questel-Plus, for example).

When the rules for using a particular command language are not followed the result will not be as wanted. Such an outcome may prompt the display of an error message, or may just give a result different from that desired, an outcome that may or may not be realized at the time. A transmission error due to a telecommuni-cations problem on one system prompts the error message:

   Invalid character in above command (line noise?)

Human errors can occur in any search statement. For example, an invalid command can be used, a non-existent prefix or suffix code may be employed, set numbers or item numbers or format descriptions may be invalid. In using mixed boolean logic the parentheses may not be complete, so preventing the processing to proceed.

Buxton and Trenner (1987) have assessed the friendliness of the error messages provided by a number of different command languages. They identified four friendly features. An error message such as:

> Sorry, not a recognized command. Enter ?HELP for assistance.

would be categorized as polite, specific, constructive and helpful. On the other hand, a message such as:

> ***ERROR (99) Disc overflow. Re-enter query.

would be regarded as hostile due to its emotive vocabulary, cryptic numbered code, cryptic vocabulary and domineering final instruction. Buxton and Trenner examined up to 13 features and gave friendly and hostile scorings, giving overall scores by subtracting the hostile scores from the friendly ones. Table 5.6 presents a selection of their findings comparing five command languages. Considerable improvements were also noted in two instances of revised command languages, so progress is being made.

Search service	Number of facilities examined	Friendly scores	Hostile scores	Overall scores
BLAISE-LINE	13	+18	− 5	+13
BRS	9	+ 7	−18	−11
Data-Star	13	+21	−26	− 5
Dialog	12	+18	− 7	+11
Pergamon InfoLine	12	+ 8	−10	− 2

Table 5.6   *Some results of an assessment of friendliness of error messages on five search services (taken from Buxton and Trenner, 1987)*

Errors which produce no message are often baffling to the searcher. Perfectly valid terms and phrases may be selected and zero items indicated but this may be due to failure to spot words on a stoplist or fields that are not phrase indexed. A command device may not be usable in the position adopted, such as the attempt to use left truncation in a system not offering the facility – the result may just be no items rather than a helpful message. Failure to enter a space between sections of a command when required can prompt an 'unrecognized command' message or the wrong result. Distinguishing between numbers as indexed terms and the set numbers is not always easy: for example, an intended set combination using the search statement 'S 1 and 2' on Dialog will access the inverted file to give the many items indexed by both the numbers 1 and 2 (S S1 AND S2 should have been used). Searchers who use different command languages may use a command on one system that is valid only on another.

Command language options

The rigidity of command languages is sometimes reduced by some degree of command synonymy. For example, Search Example 5.1 shows two alternative single-letter commands (P or E) to see more of a search term display list in Dialog. Other Dialog command options result from the preservation of commands or syntax no longer needed in the current version of the language, but helpfully preserved as many users will be familiar with them. For example, Dialog allows the use of the C or COMBINE command to specify boolean operators and set numbers, and still permits set numbers in the TYPE command to have no 'S' prefix, though both of these options are no longer prominent in its documentation.

There are sometimes optional commands especially for the basic facilities of file selection or session termination. Some languages, for example that used by WilsonLine, offer the facility during a session to alter a command: the RENAME function allows command names, abbreviations or logical operators to be changed to any name or symbol not already in use.

Common command languages

The option to choose which command language to use in a service is available to many European services which provide the Common Command Language in addition to their own. When searching on ESA-IRS, for example, the ESA-QUEST language option also permits the use of some of the Common Commands as well, or another option is the exclusive use of the entire Common Command Language. Unavoidable encounters with several command languages now occur even within one service, as gateway connections force the use of the language provided by the target service rather than the logged-on service. Users of different databases via ESA-IRS can encounter STAIRS, BASIS and Profile in addition to the two mentioned. Comparisons of command languages have been produced in the UK (Arthur, 1989) and in the USA (Conger, Anthony and Janke, 1985).

Work on a common command language in the United States, under the auspices of the National Information Standards Association, has been underway since the mid-1980s and is reported by Klemperer (1987). The commands likely to be included in this language are:

START – to initiate a search.
STOP – to end a search.
CHOOSE – to select a file or database.
EXPLAIN – to obtain information about non-session specific aspects.
HELP – to obtain assistance or instruction specific to the user's situation.
SHOW – to obtain session specific information including default settings.
FIND – to perform a search.
SCAN – to view an alphabetical list of keywords or indexed terms.
RELATE – to view related terms from a thesaurus.
DISPLAY – to view search results online.
PRINT – to print search results offline.
SORT – to sort retrieved items.
FORWARD – to view data following displayed data.
BACK – to view data preceding displayed data.
REVIEW – to view the search history.
SAVE – to save search strategies for future use.
KEEP – to save records from a complete search.
DELETE – to delete search strategies 'saved' or records 'kept'.
SET – to set default options.
DEFINE – to create a sequence of commands as a single word or to rename commands.

Wilcox, Quinn and Jensen (1988) describe the implementation of this common command language by Telebase Systems for accessing a variety of search services including Dialog, VU/TEXT, WilsonLine and BRS.

Criteria for friendly command languages

The divergencies in command languages illustrated in this chapter are marked. Roughly comparable facilities seem to have spawned quite different animals. *Friendliness* can mean several different things, and objective measures of effectiveness, efficiency and preference have yet to be made. Trenner (1987) says that a friendly command language should be simple, logical, memorable, generically structured (with an obvious hierarchy of commands and sub-commands), and consistent. It is widely recognized that requirements conflict and compromises are inevitable. Some users want a small number of commands, or short command codes, but these will be impossible to make really simple or memorable. Other users want operations to be performed by one compound step rather than having to follow many steps. Different levels of users, such as end-users or trained searchers, and regular users or occasional ones, can only really be accommodated by offering optional command conventions, or even a mixture of menus, prompts and commands.

One survey of nearly 7000 logged searches on the MEDLINE database revealed that 60 per cent of the command usage was in search term statements and in displaying records, and some commands were used only infrequently and others not used at all (Cooper, 1983). In a survey of online users' opinions of two different command languages the perceived awkwardness of one language was really due to the lack of use of that service (Krichmar, 1981). It was pointed out, however, that just a few frustrating features can be crucial in acceptance of a language.

The issue of standardization still needs to be tackled. It seems an unnecessary feat of memory to remember that totally different operations are performed, according to the command language in use, by commands such as DISPLAY, LIST, PRINT and ZOOM. Even within families of languages different dialects appear. Changes over time require constant re-familiarization, and even the useful command language comparison charts are always slightly out of date as soon as they appear. Definitive studies have yet to be made of the frustration and failure this causes, although various kinds of *front-end filter* may yet succeed in hiding this blot on the online landscape.

References

Arthur, A. (1989) *Quick Guide to Online Commands*, 2nd edn. London: UK Online User Group

Buxton, A. and Trenner, L. (1987) An experiment to assess the friendliness of error messages from interactive information retrieval systems. *Journal of Information Science*, **13** (4), 197–209

Conger, L., Anthony, L. J. and Janke, R. (1985) *Online International Command Chart*. Weston, Connecticut: Online

Cooper, M. D. (1983) Usage patterns of an online system. *Journal of the American Society for Information Science*, **34** (5), 343–349

Dialog Information Services (1987) *Searching Dialog: The Complete Guide*

Klemperer, K. (1987) Common command language for online interactive information retrieval. *Library Hi Tech*, **5** (4), 7–12

Krichmar, A. (1981) Command language ease of use: a comparison of DIALOG and ORBIT. *Online Review*, **5** (3), 227–240

Trenner, L. (1987) How to win friends and influence people: definitions of user-friendliness in interactive computer systems. *Journal of Information Science*, **13** (2), 99–107

Wilcox, R. O., Quinn, M. E. and Jensen, I. N. (1988) The Telebase implementation of common command language. In *Online Information: 12th International Online Information Meeting Proceedings*, pp. 507–515. Oxford: Learned Information

Chapter 6

Search Strategies

Introduction

What is referred to as the strategy in an online search is the total set of decisions and actions taken throughout the conduct of a search, decisions that affect the outcome in terms of items retrieved and items not retrieved. Although the overall approach may be called the strategy, what will be discussed here is as much the kinds of tactics or heuristics which may be employed to direct the search rapidly to the best achievable conclusion. Provisional strategy decisions should be made at the search preparation stage, but it may also be necessary to amend them during the search process once online. The four aims of a strategy are:

1. To match the desired number of relevant records.
2. To avoid matching irrelevant records.
3. To avoid set sizes which are far too large.
4. To avoid set sizes which are far too small or even empty.

Search concepts, postings information and retrieval facilities have all to be handled competently by a person with sufficient subject skills to identify suitable terminology and evaluate the relevance of retrieved records. Meeting these four aims is not an easy task: corrective action is often needed. The need to narrow or broaden a search is central to strategies and tactics as these actions best describe the ways in which either:

1. Set size is decreased, and hopefully less irrelevant records are retrieved without too many relevant ones being missed.
2. Set size is increased, and hopefully more relevant records are retrieved without too many irrelevant ones.

The task is clearly like being on a tightrope: experience and evaluation studies have shown that achieving a set size that gives just the right number of relevant records with no irrelevant ones at all is not often achievable and the search tends to err from perfection on one side or the other. Appropriate measures of performance are known as recall and precision, with recall representing retrieving relevant items, and precision relating the items retrieved to the number of irrelevant also recovered. These measures will be considered later in this chapter, but first the main methods of narrowing and broadening searches will be discussed.

Methods of Narrowing Searches

At any stage in a search the problem may arise of too many items matched. Search Example 6.1 shows a variety of narrowing methods using the CAB International agricultural database on Dialog. The first three search sets select the concept 'foot disease'. It is not surprising that in this large database there are more than one thousand records matching this concept.

```
File 50:CAB ABSTRACTS – 1984–89/JAN
         SEE ALSO FILE 53 (1972–1983)

      Set     Items   Description
      ___     ____    _____
?SS FOOT AND DISEASE
      S1      2191    FOOT
      S2     35507    DISEASE
      S3      1060    FOOT AND DISEASE
?S "FOOT AND MOUTH DISEASE"
      S4       488    "FOOT AND MOUTH DISEASE"
?S "FOOT AND MOUTH DISEASE" AND CATTLE
               488    FOOT AND MOUTH DISEASE
             43104    CATTLE
      S5       266    "FOOT AND MOUTH DISEASE" AND CATTLE
?S "FOOT AND MOUTH DISEASE" AND CATTLE NOT CALVES
               488    FOOT AND MOUTH DISEASE
             43104    CATTLE
              8466    CALVES
      S6       244    ("FOOT AND MOUTH DISEASE" AND CATTLE)
                      NOT CALVES
?S "FOOT AND MOUTH DISEASE" AND CATTLE/DE
               488    FOOT AND MOUTH DISEASE
             37044    CATTLE/DE
      S7       219    "FOOT AND MOUTH DISEASE" AND
                      CATTLE/DE
?S FOOT AND DISEASE
              2191    FOOT
             35507    DISEASE
      S8      1060    FOOT AND DISEASE
```

```
?S FOOT(1W)DISEASE
            2191   FOOT
           35507   DISEASE
      S9      31   FOOT(1W)DISEASE
?S FOOT(2W)DISEASE
            2191   FOOT
           35507   DISEASE
      S10    875   FOOT(2W)DISEASE
?S S7 AND PY=1987
             219   S7
           99241   PY=1987
      S11     40   S7 AND PY=1987
?S S7/ENG
      S12    155   S7/ENG
```

Search Example 6.1 *CAB ABSTRACTS database on Dialog*

One tactic for narrowing this result would be to look for a concept which might be used as a descriptor in this database and found in a thesaurus. Such a term is 'foot and mouth disease', so using this term instead has the following narrowing effect:

```
S3   1060 FOOT AND DISEASE
S4    488 "FOOT AND MOUTH DISEASE"
```

Postings are more than halved to 488 instead of 1060. The placing of quotes around the descriptor is necessary in this case to cause the selection of the phrase rather than the selection of separate terms 'foot' and 'mouth disease' joined by a boolean operator AND.

```
?E (ANIMAL DISEASES)
```

Ref	Items	Type	RT	Index-term
R1	511		22	*ANIMAL DISEASES
R2	0	F	1	LIVESTOCK DISORDERS
R3	67992	B	35	DISEASES
R4	163	N	2	BEE DISEASES
R5	2088	N	1	CAT DISEASES
R6	9977	N	5	CATTLE DISEASES
R7	5276	N	4	DOG DISEASES
R8	13	N	1	DUCK DISEASES
R9	1562	N	1	FISH DISEASES
R10	15	N	1	FOWL DISEASES
R11	1407	N	1	GOAT DISEASES
R12	3765	N	3	HORSE DISEASES

Enter P or E for more

?P

Ref	Items	Type	RT	Index-term
R13	3272	N	9	POULTRY DISEASES
R14	3288	N	5	SHEEP DISEASES
R15	4483	N	3	SWINE DISEASES
R16	241	N	2	TICKBORNE DISEASES
R17	198	N	5	YOUNG ANIMAL DISEASES
R18	1555	N	8	ZOONOSES
R19	30002	R	24	ANIMALS
R20	3504	R	25	NEOPLASMS
R21	6	R	24	ORGANIC DISEASES
R22	3	R	5	PUBLIC HEALTH LEGISLATION
R23	4	R	5	SYSTEMIC DISEASES

?E (CATTLE DISEASES)

Ref	Items	Type	RT	Index-term
R1	9977		5	*CATTLE DISEASES
R2	511	B	22	ANIMAL DISEASES
R3	183	N	4	ANAPLASMOSIS
R4	191	N	3	ANTHRAX
R5	488	N	4	FOOT AND MOUTH DISEASE
R6	249	N	3	RINDERPEST

Search Example 6.2 *Online thesaurus display from CAB ABSTRACTS on Dialog*

The replacement of one search term or concept by another one has a narrowing effect only if it reduces the size of the matching set. Search Example 6.2 shows how the selection of terms that are broader and narrower in meaning does not always have the same broader or narrower effect on set size. Starting with a term that is obviously broad in meaning, 'animal diseases', the online thesaurus display from this CAB database shows 15 terms that are narrower in meaning (those marked 'N' and numbered R4 to R18). But many of these narrower terms have thousands of postings, such as 'cattle diseases' with 9977, far more than the quite rarely used broad term 'animal diseases' with 511. Thus the use of many of these narrower terms would broaden the search. The opposite effect is also seen in Search Example 6.2 where the descriptor 'cattle diseases' is seen to have four narrower terms (R3 to R6) which do have fewer postings than the nearly ten thousand of 'cattle diseases', such as 488 of the term 'foot and mouth diseases'. The lesson from this example is that postings reflect collection breadth and hence retrieval outcome, whereas the terms exhibit semantic breadth according to their meaning and do not necessarily have the effect their meaning may suggest. Both ideas are, of course, crucial to matching items that are relevant to an enquiry.

The boolean operator AND is often the most drastic and speedy narrowing tactic. Search Example 6.1 starts with:

S1   2191 FOOT
S2   35507 DISEASE
S3   1060 FOOT AND DISEASE

The use of AND always results in postings that cannot be more than the least-posted term in the set and often reduces much more drastically as in this case, with 2191 on FOOT reduced to 1060 in the final set. The searcher can often introduce a new term into the strategy to achieve this desirable narrowing effect as the following search example shows:

S4   488 "FOOT AND MOUTH DISEASE"
S5   266 "FOOT AND MOUTH DISEASE" AND CATTLE

Although 'cattle' is used 43 104 times, it does not always occur together with 'foot and mouth disease', but nevertheless 222 items are removed by this tactic.

The boolean NOT can have an equally strong effect. The concept 'calves' is excluded as follows:

S5   266 "FOOT AND MOUTH DISEASE" AND CATTLE
S6   244 "FOOT AND MOUTH DISEASE" AND CATTLE NOT CALVES

The effect is not particularly marked in this particular case as only 22 documents are removed. The use of NOT in this way in searching can easily remove some records which may be acceptable so it must be employed carefully.

Another narrowing tactic is the restriction of terms to their occurrence in particular fields of the record. These may be the natural language fields such as title or abstract, or the more controlled language fields such as controlled terms, descriptors, or identifiers. The expectation is that some fields will enable matches with fewer records which are of greater relevance to the enquiry. Restricting the term 'cattle' to its appearance as a descriptor in Search Example 6.1 has the following result:

S5   266 "FOOT AND MOUTH DISEASE" AND CATTLE
S7   219 "FOOT AND MOUTH DISEASE" AND CATTLE/DE

Because in this database phrase indexing is confined to the descriptor field the term 'foot and mouth disease' is already matched with descriptors only, but restricting 'cattle' to descriptor matching narrows the search yet again by removing 47 records.

Another important narrowing facility is to enter the search term phrases together with proximity indicators. Search Example 6.1 shows this device:

```
S8    1060 FOOT AND DISEASE
S9      31 FOOT(1W)DISEASE
S10    875 FOOT(2W)DISEASE
```

Set 9 severely narrows set 8 by accepting only one intervening word between 'foot' and 'disease'. Set 10 relaxes this by accepting up to two intervening words, thus matching phrases such as 'foot and mouth disease'. Proximity is hard to use accurately: over-tightness may well lose relevant records and laxity may not have much effect. The command languages which offer this feature all do so in ways that are different from one another and thus may well be difficult to remember and use correctly.

The narrowing tactic of inspecting only recent records is easily accomplished on most systems by viewing just the first few records in a matching set. However, recency is usually the date of accession to the database, so the use of publication year may give a more useful result:

```
S7    219 "FOOT AND MOUTH DISEASE" AND CATTLE/DE
S11    40 S7 AND PY=1987
```

In this database on Dialog the publication year field may be specified either by the strategy AND PY=1987 or by qualifying a set by S7/1987. The limiting of records matched by the language of the original document can be done similarly; in this case only records in set 7 which are in English being retained in set 12:

```
S7    219 "FOOT AND MOUTH DISEASE" AND CATTLE/DE
S12   155 S7/ENG
```

Narrowing tactics can, of course, use more than one of these techniques to achieve the desired end.

Methods of Broadening Searches

Retrieving too few items is as common a problem as retrieving too many. If a search is too narrow and has used any of the narrowing tactics already described then possible broadening tactics might be:

1. Fewer terms joined by boolean AND.
2. The substitution of terms related in meaning but having higher postings.
3. Terms matching several or all fields instead of just one field.
4. Any term proximity is relaxed or replaced just by AND.
5. Any restrictions of date or language removed.

Naturally such tactics depend on the need to preserve accurately the topic of the request. Search Example 6.3 is based on an enquiry received as 'The perceptions and expectations of parents versus teachers concerning the achievements of mentally retarded children'. Using the ERIC database covering education and containing about 700 000 records at the time of searching, the strategy processes the request exactly as received. Even though the postings of the individual terms vary from a minimum of 7319 to a maximum of 92 634, no records whatever match the final set.

File 1:ERIC – 66–88/DEC.

Set	Items	Description

?SS PERCEPTIONS AND EXPECTATIONS AND PARENTS AND TEACHERS

Set	Items	Description
S1	11059	PERCEPTIONS
S2	7793	EXPECTATIONS
S3	23932	PARENTS
S4	92634	TEACHERS ((NOTE: SEE "FACULTY" FOR OTHER SPECIFIC TERM. . .)
S5	36	PERCEPTIONS AND EXPECTATIONS AND PARENTS AND TEACHERS

?SS S5 AND ACHIEVEMENT AND MENTALLY(W) RETARDED(W) CHILDREN

Set	Items	Description
	36	S5
S6	45388	ACHIEVEMENT (LEVEL OF ATTAINMENT OR PROFICIENCY IN RELATI. . .)
S7	7319	MENTALLY
S8	8100	RETARDED
S9	91175	CHILDREN (AGED BIRTH THROUGH APPROXIMATELY 12 YEARS)
S10	1008	MENTALLY(W)RETARDED(W)CHILDREN
S11	0	S5 AND ACHIEVEMENT AND MENTALLY(W)RETARDED(W)CHILDREN

Search Example 6.3   *Using too many ANDs on the ERIC database on Dialog*

Zero postings is not a surprising result. This strategy was constructed to illustrate the need for appropriate query analysis and for a careful use of AND. For instance the search uses every content-bearing word in the query and has joined them with AND even when the query phrase 'perceptions and expectations' does not really imply that both topics must be discussed in the same document for it to be relevant. In the everyday language of speech and writing the use of 'and' often requires a boolean OR to make sense in retrieval logic. Likewise, to link parents AND teachers may well be too strong an initial requirement: the chance of finding a record which highlights the 'teachers versus parents' concept is not great. It could also be argued that the concept of children should be omitted to start with as it could appear in records in so many different synonymous ways, although against this there could be a danger of matching records about mentally retarded adults, presumably not relevant to this query.

The terms have been entered in exactly the grammatical form used in the query: the terms perceptions, expectations, mentally and retarded will never match with their thesaurus descriptor equivalents because they are in a different form, as will be illustrated shortly. The fact that the postings of individual concepts reached as high as 92 634 in one case should not be taken to suggest that any number of terms may be ANDed with probable success, or even that such a term will never need broadening – in the *ERIC Thesaurus* there are 68 descriptors which include the singular form 'teacher' that are not matched at all here. Also missed will be the descriptors PARENT TEACHER CONFERENCES and PARENT TEACHER COOPERATION. Of course the crucial concept is that of mentally retarded (children), central to the query and having the least postings (1008) as entered – if this concept is not broad enough then relevant records are bound to be missed: the thesaural form of its four descriptors all include MENTAL RETARDATION, but a match with these will be impossible as the strategy stands.

File 1:ERIC – 66–88/DEC.

Set	Items	Description

?**SS (PERCEPTION OR EXPECTATION) AND (PARENTS OR TEACHERS)**

S1	18061	PERCEPTION (THE PROCESS OF BECOMING AWARE OF OBJECTS, QU. . .)
S2	3484	EXPECTATION (ANTICIPATION OF FUTURE EVENTS, CONDITIONS, O . . .)
S3	23932	PARENTS

S4	92634	TEACHERS ((NOTE: SEE "FACULTY" FOR OTHER SPECIFIC TERM. . .)
S5	3661	(PERCEPTION OR EXPECTATION) AND (PARENTS OR TEACHERS)

?SS S5 AND ACHIEVEMENT AND MENTAL(W)RETARDATION

	3661	S5
	3661	S5
S6	45388	ACHIEVEMENT (LEVEL OF ATTAINMENT OR PROFICIENCY IN RELATI. . .)
S7	20787	MENTAL
S8	11189	RETARDATION
S9	10862	MENTAL(W)RETARDATION
S10	12	S5 AND ACHIEVEMENT AND MENTAL(W) RETARDATION

?T S10/8/1–3

10/8/1
EJ328937   TM510964
Teachers' Expectations and Attributions for Student Achievement: Effects of Label Performance Pattern, and Special Education Intervention.
Descriptors: Attribution Theory; *Educational Diagnosis; Elementary Secondary Education; Expectation; *Labeling (of Persons); Learning Disabilities; Mental Retardation; Prediction; Special Education; *Student Evaluation; *Teacher Attitudes
Identifiers: *Teacher Expectations

10/8/2
EJ267806   TM507204
An Analysis of Teacher Rating Differences Between First-Grade and Mentally Retarded Children: Were Expectancy Biases Involved?
Descriptors: *Expectation; Grade 1; Grading; *Mathematics Achievement; *Mild Mental Retardation; Primary Education; *Student Evaluation; *Teacher Attitudes
Identifiers: Peabody Mathematics Readiness Test

10/8/3
EJ258093   EC141284
Expectations of Vocational Teachers for Handicapped Students.
Descriptors: Academic Achievement; *Expectation; *Learning Disabilities; Mainstreaming; *Mild Mental Retardation; Secondary Education; Self Evaluation (Individuals); Student Behavior; Student Evaluation; *Teacher Attitudes; *Vocational Education Teachers

Search Example 6.4   *An improved search on the ERIC database on Dialog*

Search Example 6.4 shows a better initial strategy as twelve records are matched. The terms 'perception' and 'expectation' now match with thesaural terms as the display in sets 1 and 2 shows

– part of the thesaurus scope note is supplied on the display. In spite of these thesaural terms having less postings than their natural language versions in Search Example 6.3, set 5 shows a large increase in matching records from 36 to 3661. The thesaurus forms 'mental' and 'retardation' also achieve much better matches and the first three of the 12 matching records are seen to have descriptor matches with these terms. The removal of the term children and the replacement of AND by OR in two cases were also vital to the successful broadening of this search.

The next step would be to check some of the records for relevance and, if need be to broaden the strategy by introducing extra synonyms linked with OR or dropping some ANDed concepts. Synonymous or closely related terms can sometimes be gleaned from the records, sometimes from the searcher's knowledge and sometimes from a thesaurus. Here the descriptor 'Performance' is related to 'Achievement', and is a possible candidate. Returning to the cattle foot diseases search example, a reference retrieved under foot and mouth diseases specified three further animals – buffalo, sheep and goats – so the 'cattle' concept could be broadened simply by using these terms. It is not so easy to trace a

File 1:ERIC – 66–88/DEC.

Set	Items	Description

?**SS (PERCEPTION? OR EXPECTATION?) AND (PARENT? OR TEACHER?)**

S1	26694	PERCEPTION?
S2	9795	EXPECTATION?
S3	41721	PARENT?
S4	158306	TEACHER?
S5	12491	(PERCEPTION? OR EXPECTATION?) AND (PARENT? OR TEACHER?)

?**SS S5 AND ACHIEVEMENT? AND MENTAL?(W)RETARD?**

	12491	S5
S6	46743	ACHIEVEMENT?
S7	22006	MENTAL?
S8	12537	RETARD?
S9	11445	MENTAL?(W)RETARD?
S10	27	S5 AND ACHIEVEMENT? AND MENTAL?(W)RETARD?

Search Example 6.5   *A broader search on the ERIC database on Dialog*

most important synonym for 'foot' – the term 'hoof' – preferred in North American usage. In practice, a large number of ORed terms take time to enter at the keyboard, require care in use of parentheses if other boolean operators are being entered in the same statement, and are thus rather prone to error and costly in connect time.

A broadening facility that can sometimes be more easily used is stem matching. Most singular and plural forms can be conflated in this way (except foot and feet, for example), and other variant suffixes allowed for. In the agricultural search example DISEASE? more than doubles the postings of the untruncated term. Search Example 6.5 illustrates this approach in a third initial strategy for the ERIC search on mental handicap. Each of the seven terms entered can now match with its singular or plural form, all postings are increased, and the answer set now matches with 27 items.

Maximizing Retrieval Effectiveness

The tactics for narrowing and broadening just described are only tools to be used to move a search in what is hoped to be the right direction. Maximizing the retrieval of relevant records and minimizing the retrieval of irrelevant ones is often described as maximizing both Recall and Precision. This is derived from the measures used in evaluation testing, namely:

$$\text{Recall ratio} = \frac{\text{Relevant records retrieved}}{\text{Total relevant records in database}}$$

$$\text{Precision ratio} = \frac{\text{Relevant records retrieved}}{\text{Total records retrieved}}$$

For example, in one test case (McCain, White and Griffith, 1987) 11 online searches in the MEDLINE database retrieved 64 records each on average, of which 36 were judged relevant and 28 were judged irrelevant. The average Precision Ratio was therefore 36/64 or 56 per cent. If all retrieved records had been relevant Precision would have been 100 per cent. Recall is difficult to calculate in practice because determining the total records relevant to a query in a database is impossible by direct inspection. However, estimates are sometimes possible, and in the case of the MEDLINE searches a pool of relevant records was identified by parallel searches across five databases. This pool identified 98 relevant records per search, and thus allowed a kind of recall ratio to be calculated as 36/98 or 37 per cent. (In this case it is unlikely that all the pool of relevant records were in the MEDLINE database at all; hence 100 per cent recall would never be possible.) Retrieval effectiveness for MEDLINE in this test was therefore 37 per cent recall at 56 per cent precision. Another database in the test had lower recall but higher precision: 28 per cent and 70 per cent, respectively.

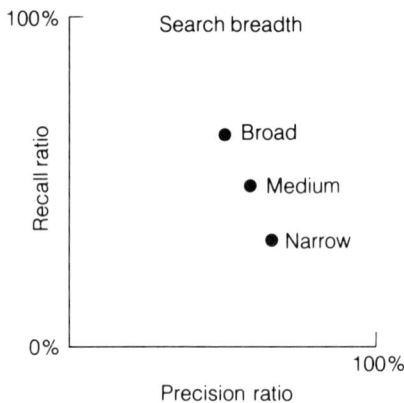

Figure 6.1   *MEDLARS evaluation test data based on 118 searches (taken from Lancaster 1968)*

When such measures can be derived not only from the final outcome of searches, but from searches as they progress, the expectation is that the result will start at low recall and will then increase to the final level obtained. For example, Figure 6.1 plots the average recall and precision results from searches measured at three levels of breadth. These were searches done in the offline batch processed MEDLARS system, the precursor to online MEDLINE. Recall rose from 30 per cent to 48 per cent to 63 per cent as the strategy was broadened, whereas precision fell from 66 per cent to 60 per cent to 51 per cent (Lancaster, 1968). This clearly illustrates the effectiveness law that, on average, an increase in recall can only be obtained at the expense of a decrease in precision, and vice versa. Hence online search strategies will often have to choose between the alternatives of a high recall search with low precision (that is a lot of irrelevant retrieved), or low recall (some relevant not retrieved) with high precision. It must be realized, however, that occasional individual searches may well achieve both high recall and precision, and that improvements in understanding the search query in discussion with the user may well improve both measures. On the debit side, it is not often realized how hard it is to get high recall performances, and results of between 25 per cent and 35 per cent are quite typical.

It should now be clear that tactics for broadening a search may often be described as recall-improving tactics, and those for narrowing a search as precision-improving. The practical evaluation of all types of retrieval system, including online, poses many difficulties, and few valid comparisons have been done even in the controlled conditions of retrieval experiments in the laboratory. Adequate evaluation needs to measure, in addition to recall and precision, criteria such as response time, overall search time, costs, user effort, and perhaps also the database coverage and currency (see Lancaster, 1979).

Retrieval effectiveness can only be maximized by attention to the whole search and its small details from conception to completion. Some important areas requiring attention are now discussed.

Steps in searching

None of the necessary steps in the process of a search should be left out or given scant attention. Lancaster (1979) identified six steps in the search process, namely, information need, stated request, selection of database, search strategy (or formulation), search in database, and screening of output. The cyclical nature of these steps is emphasized: earlier steps are refined by a process of feedback. The subjective nature of users' needs, searcher/system interaction, interpretation of queries and vocabularies, and judgements of relevance of the records selected is an inescapable hazard which can never, in the nature of things, be replaced by objectivity. This analysis of steps is a useful reminder that a final task could well be to mark records for likely relevance to the query, a process sometimes called screening. This task of relevance prediction will be greatly aided by a judicious choice of record display format (to be discussed shortly) and will help decisions regarding the obtaining of the full hard copy of items retrieved where the database is not full-text. Devising a chart of steps in searching can also be useful in training new searchers.

Search formulation

This fourth step in Lancaster's list is the intellectual heart of a strategy and can be broken down into the following decisions:

1. Translation of a query into terms suitable for searching.
2. Extension of a query to include related and substitute terms for use in searching.
3. Combination schemes to make sensible set combinations using boolean AND, OR, NOT.
4. Ordering decisions so that terms and combinations thought most likely to be successful are tried first.
5. Control decisions so that outcomes which will prompt a change of strategy or a termination of the search itself are made.

In practice these decisions are conducted in such a variety of sequences that useful flowcharts of the search process are impossible to construct, but these five decision areas may well prove useful for diagnostic purposes. When a search has failed to meet its objectives, when perhaps recall is too low, or precision is poor, tracing the cause in this way can help avoid the problem in future.

For example, in a query for 'methods of injection used to improve engine performance' a search intermediary expanded the query to include the qualifying term 'fuel injection' without recourse to the enquirer who had wanted cases of 'water injection' and had failed to make this clear. In another case a search for 'uses of aluminium in light aircraft' began on the World Aluminum Abstracts database by:

SS ALUMINIUM AND LIGHT(W)AIRCRAFT

This search statement failed to appreciate the North American spelling of the metal, and in any case it was inappropriate to specify the metal at all in a database devoted exclusively to it: the eight postings under light aircraft would have needed no qualifier to narrow the set anyway.

All five decisions in formulation are prone to human error – not errors in the use of a system and its facilities which would hopefully prompt useful error messages – but mistakes which may not be immediately detected. Decisions regarding the terms to use depend for their success on correct spelling, recognition of which words are stopwords, correct handling of embedded punctuation such as hyphens and apostrophes, and correct appreciation of the effect of word or phrase indexing as implemented in a given system, database and field of a record. The entering of numbers as search terms must not be confused with the identification of sets by number. Decisions about term combinations must correctly use boolean operators and get proximity correct. Premature termination of a search can cause loss in recall: undue continuation of a search can cause loss in precision.

Retrieval approaches

The examples offered so far have all been based on search terms that describe subjects by terms that would be expected to match the basic index of a database, comprising its free-text and controlled terms. Strategies for retrieving known items would be better performed using non-subject fields such as authors, qualified perhaps by equally precisely indexed fields such as corporate source (for example, the name of an institution), journal title or publication year. Such searches stand a better chance of achieving both 100 per cent recall and 100 per cent precision although failures here are not unknown.

However, many searches that are subject-oriented do make use of specially indexed fields: in the sciences it might be a chemical name or patent number; in law it might be a legislation number or case code; in business it might be a trade name or company name; in the humanities a named person or year of birth or death. Other similar fields can be very helpful in narrowing a search, such as a standard industrial classification code of products, a financial data category for trading companies, or a chronological period for literature or history. Retrieval can also be narrowed by choosing categories that often arise from the printed index origin of many databases, such as a particular subfile, a subject classification code or section heading, a hierarchical tree structure code or descriptor code. Document type can sometimes be identified as well.

Another quite distinctive retrieval approach is the use of cited papers, possible only in databases that incorporate citation indexing. The document records in such databases are indexed by all the papers cited by each document, accessed usually by authors' names. Strategies for searching citation databases are discussed by Bawden (1988).

Subject query searching can sometimes be greatly aided by proceeding explicitly from one or more known relevant items to search for similar ones. Enquirers are sometimes aware of papers relevant to their query, so retrieval of these as the first strategy in a search can be followed by an inspection of their total record content to suggest clues for matching other records. This may sometimes be done by means of a preliminary printed index search followed by the use of a unique accession number assigned to the item to find the same record in the database. A prior search of the subject access mechanisms of an appropriate printed index may be of great help to the terminology of the search formulation as well. Inspecting records and analysing their content is increasingly aided by special system facilities such as the ZOOM command on ESA-IRS (see Chapter 5).

The relative merits of approaching retrieval by free-text or by controlled terms is a long-standing debate with a history longer than computer searching (Svenonius, 1986). A number of studies have shown that each approach may often retrieve documents that the other does not; hence a mixed approach will be needed for high recall. The precision-promoting properties of free-text terms were revealed in 40 searches of a legal database where the average precision ratio was 79 per cent but the recall ratio averaged 20 per cent (Blair and Maron, 1985). In other cases free-text has not given such high precision, perhaps because in some subject areas terms are not so precise and considerable skill may be needed to devise good natural language strategies. Controlled language terms may require equal skill in their use, and Bates (1988) describes how effective use may be made of subject descriptions such as category codes, subject headings, faceted classification, descriptors, etc.

Record formats

A good search term strategy needs to be integrated with record display throughout and especially in its concluding phases. Current online interrogation methods fail to integrate term selection with record inspection as closely as do some well-designed printed index layouts searched manually. Failure to select the optimum record formats quickly causes waste of time, an increase in costs, and even the occasional need to re-do a search when the required formats have been omitted by mistake. Now that some database charging structures are related to number of records displayed and their format in both online as well as offline mode, this part of a strategy has great importance.

In bibliographic databases fixed record display options can range from just a record identification number to a full record, with intermediate mixtures available covering combinations of title, abstract, index terms and bibliographic details. If a search formulation retrieves, say, 15 items, two initial display tactics are commonly used. One is to view just one record in fullest format; the other is to look at about five records in title only format. The first tactic is useful when the record structure is new to the searcher, or when the formulation used is judged to be of uncertain accuracy – hence all the help offered by a full record is needed to assist the subsequent strategy. The second tactic of title only is useful to check that a formulation thought likely to produce relevant records is indeed doing so, though its success will depend on the information content of the titles.

Another reasonably brief record format which is helpful in extending a strategy is that of title plus index terms, in the hope that new terms may be spotted to aid a subsequent formulation to improve either recall or precision. Formats which include the bibliographic reference will be essential if it is necessary to retrieve the full-text of the items. Of course, as a search proceeds, selected records may well be viewed in several formats to complete the picture. In formulating subsequent matching sets the NOT operator can be very useful in excluding records already seen and in avoiding duplicate records on the screen or printout. Easy access to the standard and user specifiable record formats for a given system and database may be aided by providing these details on paper as reminders near the workstation.

Large sets of records all believed to be relevant pose a problem. Even the apparently contentless format of just accession number can be useful if the number matches with the accession numbers used in a printed abstracts publication. Retrieved accession numbers can then be searched offline in the printed version. The division of a large set into two or three smaller ones can also be suggested, particularly if the first set can be made the most closely matching records in the fullest format, and perhaps a final set of less closely matching records can be printed in brief format or offline. This kind of approach is called doublelimit (Harter, 1987) and involves using major descriptors or preferred document type to create the first set, particular publication years or certain terms as descriptors to create a second set, and the remainder in an inexpensive yet useful format.

Search Strategy Styles

Some pioneering work by Charles P. Bourne and others (see Markey and Atherton, 1981) on online teaching and practice identified a number of strategy models of the main approaches to searching. The four main types are called Briefsearch, Building blocks, Successive fractions and Citation pearl growing. Table 6.1 offers an overview of these styles with letters standing in place of search terms. In practice searches may incorporate more than one style as they progress.

The essence of a Briefsearch is the use of AND to retrieve a few items quickly without spending time on tracing and using synonyms or alternative terms. The search may well result in a low recall ratio, with only a few of the relevant records found, but this may still satisfy the user or may be followed up by a more comprehensive strategy. Search Example 4.11 matched 17 items by means of the Briefsearch 'antarctica AND oil'. Search Example 4.12 used the terms 'alligators AND breeding' to match just four items.

For the Building blocks approach, each concept of the query is enlarged by synonyms or related terms using the boolean OR. All the concepts are then ANDed to produce the answer set. Search Example 4.9 enlarged one of its three concepts as follows:

> nuclear AND (fallout OR pollution) AND sheep

This resulted in a small answer set of eight items. Had enlargement of all three concepts been necessary, a logical Building block approach could have been:

> S1 nuclear OR radioactive
> S2 fallout OR pollution
> S3 sheep OR lamb OR lambs
> S4 S1 AND S2 AND S3

Although this style of searching is logical in its construction, it does take time to keyboard and requires a sound knowledge of the appropriate vocabulary. Also, it is not easy to modify the strategy if it produces either too few or too many items. But this strategy is often the only way of conducting a comprehensive search on a topic where high recall is required.

The successive fractions strategy is a method of cutting down a large set already created using AND or NOT as the simplest of set narrowing devices. Search Example 1.1 reduced its initial result of 318 postings to just eight by this means in the following way:

Briefsearch
Term A AND Term B = Answer set

Building blocks
Term Aa OR Term Ab OR Term Ac = Set 1 (a large set)
Term Ba OR Term Bb OR Term Bc = Set 2 (a large set)
Term Ca OR Term Cb OR Term Cc = Set 3 (a large set)
Set 1 AND Set 2 AND Set 3 = Answer set

Successive fractions
Term A AND Term B = Set 1 (a large set)
Term A AND Term B AND Term C = Set 2 (a fraction of Set 1)
Term A AND Term B AND Term C NOT Term D = Answer set

Citation pearl growing
Term A = Known relevant pearl record
Term B AND Term C = Answer set (using terms from pearl)

Table 6.1 *The logic of four styles of search strategy*

S1	swimming AND (women OR female)	318 postings
S2	S1 and fit?	29 postings
S3	S2 NOT advanced	8 postings

This strategy is often used as the final focus of the main strategy if the items matched are too many to view or print out. Terms which specify language and date are often useful to achieve this as Search Example 6.1 showed.

Citation pearl growing takes as its starting point a very small initial set, perhaps of just one item known to be relevant to the enquiry. This one 'pearl' is then inspected for suitable terms to be used in pursuing the enquiry. The starting record might well be accessed by author and date. Figure 6.2 shows how this might be done. The record shown is a recent one on an aspect of linguistics research to be found in the PSYCINFO database on Dialog, and is easily retrievable via a well-known author on this subject, Keith Rayner. This record can provide important clues for extending a search to retrieve other items on 'sentence processing research using eye movement methods'. For example, the descriptor 'sentence comprehension' could be used, but the term 'eye movements' is not in the descriptor or identifier fields so might best be searched as a phrase to occur in title or abstract. Further clues might be the other named author, the institution where they work, and the name of the journal. The pearl growing approach would be especially helpful for a search in an area of knowledge not well known to an enquirer or where no thesaurus is available.

75–32203
    Resolution of syntactic category ambiguities: Eye movements in parsing lexically ambiguous sentences.
    Frazier, Lyn; Rayner, Keith
    U Massachusetts, Amherst, US
    Journal of Memory & Language, 1987 Oct Vol 26(5) 505–526 CODEN: JVLBAY ISSN: 00225371
    Journal Announcement: 7511
    Language: ENGLISH   Document Type: JOURNAL ARTICLE
    Descriptors: LEXICAL ACCESS (29293); SYNTAX (51220); STIMULUS AMBIGUITY (49890); SENTENCE COMPREHENSION (46620); ADULTHOOD (01150)
    Identifiers: ambiguous lexical items & syntax, sentence comprehension, adults
    Section Headings: 2720 (LANGUAGE & SPEECH)

Figure 6.2   *Record from PSYCINFO database on Dialog*

References

Bates, M. J. (1988) How to use controlled vocabularies more effectively in online searching. *Online*, **12** (6), 45–56
Bawden, D. (1988) Citation indexing. In *Manual of Online Search Strategies*, edited by C. J. Armstrong and J. A. Large, pp. 44–83. Aldershot: Gower Press
Blair, D. C. and Maron, M. E. (1985) An evaluation of retrieval effectiveness for a full-text document retrieval system. *Communications of the ACM*, **28** (3), 289–299
Drinkwater, C. (1988) Social and behavioural sciences. In *Manual of Online Search Strategies*, edited by C. J. Armstrong and J. A. Large, pp. 469–506. Aldershot: Gower Press
Harter, S. P. (1987) *Online Search Analyst, Version 1.0.* Bloomington: Online Consultants of Indiana, Software package for IBM PC microcomputers or compatibles
Lancaster, F. W. (1968) *Evaluation of the MEDLARS Demand Search Service.* Bethesda, Maryland: National Library of Medicine

Lancaster, F. W. (1979) *Information Retrieval Systems: Characteristics, Testing and Evaluation*, 2nd edn. New York: Wiley

McCain, K. W., White, H. D. and Griffith, B. C. (1987) Comparing retrieval performance in online data bases. *Information Processing and Management*, **23** (6), 539–553

Markey, K. and Atherton, P. (1981) *Online Training and Practice Manual for ERIC Data Base Searchers*, 2nd edn. Syracuse: ERIC clearinghouse on information resources

Svenonius, E. (1986) Unanswered questions in the design of controlled vocabularies. *Journal of the American Society for Information Science*, **37** (5), 331–340

Further Reading

Oldroyd, B. K. and Citroen, C. L. (1977) Study of strategies used in on-line searching. *Online Review*, **1** (4), 295–310

Harter, S. P. (1986) *Online Information Retrieval: Concepts, Principles and Techniques*. Orlando, Florida: Academic Press

Chapter 7

Online Sources

Categorization of Databases

Previous chapters of this book have provided an introduction to the process of online searching. In order to exploit a knowledge of that process, it is necessary to know where to search, that is to say, to have some knowledge about the databases available online. Table 2.1 demonstrated the large number of databases which are publicly accessible. The purpose of this chapter is to provide an introduction for the new searcher to the range of information available online by noting the major databases in a number of subject areas. The areas chosen are: agriculture, energy and the environment, life and health sciences, business, chemistry and the chemical industry, law, news, engineering, information technology, social and behavioural sciences and the humanities. This list of headings is chosen to represent major subjects within the online information industry rather than to offer a uniform set of subject headings. Within each subject area the databases are dealt with in accordance with the categories:

Reference
  Bibliographic
  Referral
Source
  Numeric
  Full-text
  Text-numeric.

Throughout these subjects, it will be seen that there is a great variation in the size of the databases which range from the major bibliographic databases in scientific subjects to tiny referral databases in the humanities. These latter may be highly localized in content such as the contents of a particular museum or art gallery. Such small databases have been omitted from this discussion. It should also be noted that between the subjects there is great variation in the distribution between the types of databases which are available. For example full-text databases are more dominant in business and legal information than in agricultural information. It is important to be aware that there may be considerable overlap between the contents of different bibliographic databases, that is, the same journal paper may be listed in many databases. In addition to categorization of databases by subject areas, there will also be a discussion of bibliographic databases which concentrate on documents of· particular types rather than on particular subjects.

This chapter can achieve no more than provide an indication or a flavour of the range of information available in public databases. More detailed information about the range of databases available can be found in directories such as those produced by Cuadra, Williams (1985), Hall (1986), Brit-line (1988) and in a manual of search strategies (Armstrong and Large, 1988). In addition, the major journals of the online information industry — *Online*, *Online Review* and *Database* – often contain articles about particular databases or the databases available in specific subject fields. The catalogues produced by specific search services are also valuable sources of information and as an example the 1988 Dialog catalogue of available databases extends to nearly 100 pages. Since the online information industry is very volatile, databases may appear on search services other than those indicated in the chapter and may have been removed from some search services.

Agriculture

Agriculture is an excellent example of a multidisciplinary subject. It includes aspects of physical, biological, social and engineering sciences. It is also very obviously a business. The basic activities of producing farm products are supported by a whole range of research, advisory, distribution and marketing support services. All have their own information requirements and many of these can be met from the publicly available online databases.

There are three major bibliographic databases in agriculture: AGRICOLA, AGRIS and CAB ABSTRACTS. AGRICOLA is produced by the American National Agricultural Library and the American Department of Agriculture. It contains references to journal articles, reports, monographs, pamphlets and audiovisual materials on all areas of agriculture and related subjects. Thus as well as references to appropriate material in the animal and plant sciences and production spheres, there is information on agricultural economics, fertilizers, pesticides and even rural sociology. The database contains over 1.2 million references and is updated with approximately 10 000 new items each month. AGRICOLA is accessible on the BRS, Dialog and DIMDI search services.

AGRIS, the International Information System for Agricultural Sciences and Technology, is produced under the coordination of the Food and Agricultural Organization (FAO) of the United Nations. FAO coordinates input from over 100 national and international input centres which participate in this international information system. Given the worldwide data collection and input to the AGRIS system it is less prone to American and European bias in its coverage than many other bibliographic databases. The database is available on Dialog and DIMDI search services and there is a gateway between the ESA-IRS and the INIS/AGRIS computer in Vienna. Subject coverage is similar to that of AGRICOLA. AGRIS contains about 1.3 million items and is growing at about 10 000 items per month.

CAB ABSTRACTS is the online equivalent of the 47 specialized abstracting journals which are published by the various specialized bureaux constituting the Commonwealth Agricultural Bureaux International (CABI). Coverage in this database includes animal breeding, dairy science, soils and fertilizers, agricultural economics, plant pathology, applied entomology, rural development and sociology, and forestry. Some two million references are available covering the literature from 1972 onwards and the database grows by approximately 12 000 references per month. CAB ABSTRACTS is widely available on the commercial search services and can be searched, for example, on BRS, CISTI (Canadian Institute for Scientific and Technical Information), Dialog, DIMDI and ESA-IRS.

It is inevitable with databases of this size that there is considerable overlap in their content as well as significant differences, but attempts to demonstrate the extent of the overlap are fraught with difficulties and thus meaningful figures are impossible to give.

Conceivably these three databases will meet all the requirements for bibliographic information in agriculture. However, it should be noted that there are a number of other bibliographic databases of interest. Some are devoted to all aspects of a particular agricultural product, from basic research on, say, the plant to its marketing and consumption. For example, all aspects of the growth, marketing etc. of coffee are covered by the database COFFEELINE. Those who like their beverages a little stronger may be more interested in the contents of the database VITIS, which includes material on all aspects of wine production and consumption. Some of the larger non-agricultural databases such as CA SEARCH and BIOSIS PREVIEWS will also have much material of interest in agriculture.

Information about current agricultural research projects in the member countries of the European Economic Communities is available through AGREP (AGricultural REsearch Projects). In comparison with the bibliographic databases mentioned earlier, this referral database is much smaller with only some 23 000 items and a growth rate of about 200 items per month. The database includes projects in animal production, fisheries, forestry, land use and conservation. AGREP is available on DIMDI and Datacentralen.

Given the need for information about, for example, pesticides and other agricultural chemicals and about the important business aspects of agriculture, it is not surprising that there are a number of source databases available. AGRA Europe (London) Ltd has built a high reputation for its analysis of the European food and agricultural business. The full-text of its weekly publication *Agra Europe* is available as AGINFO via Telecom Gold, an electronic mail service which is adding access to some information services as a part of its diversification process. AGINFO provides details on prices, trends, market reports and political and legislative issues.

Examples of numeric databases are more common than full-text databases. AGRISTAT provides access to over 600 000 time series on French agriculture. (Time series involve the data being presented over a time period so that variations can be examined.) This database includes production figures and land value figures by departments and regions and is available from at least 1970.

Information of both a textual and numeric nature is to be found in a number of agricultural databases. One obvious area in which text and numeric information are both found in the same database is agricultural chemicals. An example is AGROCHEMICALS HANDBOOK, produced by the Royal Society of Chemistry and made available by Data-Star and Dialog. Details of the physical and chemical properties, uses and toxicity of various agrochemical products are provided. An example of a record from this database as made available on Data-Star is shown in Figure 7.1.

1
AN TAH880200001   3 8807.
AI fosetyl-aluminium (BSI, draft ISO-E).
TP Fungicide.
  Mode of action: Systemic fungicide with protective and curative
  action. Rapidly absorbed, predominantly through the leaves but also
  through the roots, with translocation both acropetally and basipetally.
  Acts by inhibiting germination of spores or by blocking development of
  mycelium.
SY Chemical names: aluminium tris(ethyl phosphonate) (IUPAC, CA).
  Other names: phosethyl AI (draft ISO-F); fosetyl AI; aluminium
  phosethyl.
  Trade names: Aliette; LS 7478   3;
  Chemical group: organophosphorus; organoaluminium.
MO Formula: C6H18AIO9P3; Weight: 354.1.
RN 39148–24–8.
CO Rhone-Poulenc.
PH Form: Colourless crystals.
  Vapour pressure: Negligible at room temperature.
  Stability: Decomposed by strong acids and alkalis. Oxidized by strong
  oxidizing agents. Decomposes above 200.degree.C.
  Corrosiveness: Non-corrosive to metals.
  Solubility: in water at 20.degree.C, 120 g/l. In acetonitrile and
  propylene glycol, 80 mg/l at 20.degree.C. Practically insoluble (<5 mg/
  l) in other organic solvents at 20.degree.C.
  Formulation Types: Wettable powder.
  Compatibility: Incompatible with foliar fertilizers.
AY Analysis of Products: By iodometric titration (Rhone-Poulenc).
  Analysis of Residues: By GLC with phosphorous-specific detection
  (Rhone-Poulenc).
US Control of diseases caused by Phycomycetes (Phytophthora,
  Plasmopara, Bremia spp., etc.) on lettuce, hops, strawberries, pome
  fruit, citrus fruit, pineapples, avocados, vines, cucurbits, onions, cocoa,
  rubber, tobacco, and ornamental plants and shrubs.
TO Toxicity to Mammals: Acute oral LD50 for rats 5800, mice 3700 mg/
  kg.
  Acute percutaneous LD50 for rabbits >2000, rats >3200 mg/kg.
  Non-irritating to skin. In 90/day feeding trials, no-effect level for rats
  was 5000 mg/kg diet, and for dogs 50,000 mg/kg diet. Non-teratogenic
  and non-mutagenic.
  Toxicity to Birds: Low toxicity to birds.
  Toxicity to Fish: LC50 (96 hours) for rainbow trout 428 mg/l.
  Toxicity to Bees: Not toxic to bees.
  Phytotoxicity: Non-phytotoxic when used as directed.
TL Tolerance levels (parts per million): France: Citrus fruit, grapes,
  strawberries, vegetable greens (salad) 5; apples, endives, pineapples,
  tomatoes 1.

Switzerland: Citrus fruits 50; cucumbers, head lettuce, witloof chicory 25; grapes, strawberries 1.5.
Switzerland: Citrus fruits 50; cucumbers, head lettuce, witloof chicory 25; grapes, strawberries 1.5.
MD Antidotes: No specific antidote known. Symptomatic treatment.

Figure 7.1 *A record from the AGROCHEMICALS HANDBOOK database on Data-Star*

Even the crude categorization of databases indicated at the start of this chapter fails to cope with many databases which include information of several types. One example is provided by AGRIBUSINESS USA, which is available on Dialog. This contains full-text of publications from the American Department of Agriculture and bibliographic information on agricultural business. A further example is offered by the AGROCHEMICALS DATABANK, which is available on both Data-Star and Dialog. This contains numeric data and text numeric data about chemicals used in the agriculture industry. Data provided covers nomenclature, chemical and physical properties and an indication of the manufacturers of the product. Clearly the agriculturalist, especially in America, should be able to acquire much of the required information online.

Energy and the Environment

The production and consumption of energy resources and the impact of these and many other industrial processes on environmental quality is a multidisciplinary subject in much the same way as agriculture. The impact of chemicals on delicate ecosystems is a matter of extensive scientific study. The creation of a nuclear power plant is a matter of great engineering complexity. These and countless other examples are influenced by the legislative framework in which they operate. The legislative framework is in turn governed by the pervading social and political environment. Thus it is inevitable that information concerning energy and environmental issues appears in many places. Statistics on, say, coal production, could be found in a general statistical source. References to papers on the environmental effects of using a particular insecticide could equally well be found in a bibliographic database of chemistry or the life sciences. Nevertheless there are a considerable number of databases which are overtly about energy or environmental issues and this section of the chapter is restricted to an indication of some of these.

Much the largest bibliographic database on energy-related matters is DOE ENERGY which contains 1.7 million references and is growing at the rate of about 14 000 items per month. The database is produced by the American Department of Energy with the cooperation of Britain, Denmark, the Federal Republic of Germany, Finland, France, Norway and Sweden. It contains references to papers on all aspects of energy production and use and all actual or potential energy sources are included. Thus there is information from tidal to nuclear power, from electric power engineering to oil shales. The database is available on Dialog and STN International.

ENERGYLINE is produced by EIC/Intelligence Inc and contains approximately 90 000 references to energy-related matters. Coverage includes a wide range of energy sources – solar, nuclear, petroleum, natural gas and electricity amongst them. Material on the political, economic, planning and legal aspects of these energy sources is included in addition to relevant research and development. The database is available via Dialog, ESA-IRS and the ORBIT Search Service.

EIC/Intelligence Inc is also the producer of a major bibliographic database on environmental issues, ENVIROLINE. The database contains about 125 000 items and is accessible via Dialog, DIMDI and ESA-IRS. It contains information about all aspects of pollution, the management of renewable and non-renewable resources and population planning and control. Similar material is covered in ENVIRONMENTAL BIBLIOGRAPHY from the Environmental Studies Institute and available via Dialog. Worldwide literature on pollution, pollution control, pollution research and pollution sources is reported in the database POLLUTION ABSTRACTS. It is produced by Cambridge Scientific Abstracts and is available via a number of search services including BRS, Data-Star, Dialog and ESA-IRS.

In addition to bibliographic databases devoted solely to energy and environmental matters and the large scientific bibliographic databases such as CA SEARCH and BIOSIS PREVIEWS, much environmental and energy information can be located in other databases. For example, water pollution is well documented in AQUATIC SCIENCES AND FISHERIES ABSTRACTS and OCEANIC ABSTRACTS and ecological matters are well documented in LIFE SCIENCES COLLECTION and GEOBASE.

There is a wide range of referral databases in energy and environmental matters. Research projects in the fields of coal science and technology at research establishments and academic institutions in a number of coal producing countries are documented by the International Energy Agency in their database, COALPRO. Interested searchers can use this database via the BELINDIS, CISTI or INKADATA search services. The products of some 550 companies which market more than 2000 products in environmental technology can be located using the DETEQ (Dechema Environmental Technology Equipment Databank) which is available via STN International. It covers instrumentation, laboratory equipment, chemicals and safety engineering equipment. A further example of a referral database in this subject area is NEDRES (National Environmental Data Referral Service), which provides details on collections of environmental data acquired by satellite, buoys, weather stations and environmental observers. The data may be machine-readable or in print format. The database is created by the American National Oceanic and Atmospheric Administration and is searchable on BRS.

Full-text of American state and federal legislative, regulatory and judicial developments are available online in ENVIRONMENT REPORT on Mead Data Central. Full-text of news stories on environmental matters and occupational health is available on ENVIRONMENTAL HEALTH NEWS accessible via the Executive Telecom System to which a subscription is required.

Annual time series of energy balances for worldwide energy sources are available in ENEC (Energy and Economics Databank). The information is compiled by FIZ Karlsruhe in cooperation with the International Energy Agency and is available on INKADATA. The supply and demand for all energy sources in America is provided by two different databases each with the name ENERGY, one available from Sage Data, the other from Chase Econometrics.

Information about the physical and chemical properties of some 1700 coal types, coal liquefaction products and components of coal liquids can be located through COALDATA, available on INKADATA. In addition to such text-numeric data, the database contains citations to the worldwide literature on coal and coal liquefaction. Turning from coal to crude oil, the CRUDE OIL ANALYSIS DATA BASE provides details on approximately 9000 crude oil deposits throughout the world. For each deposit, information available includes location and physical and chemical properties of the deposit. The database is created by the American

Department of Energy and is accessible via that organization's Bartlesville Project Office.

Information about some 63 000 chemicals in the environment can be found in ECDIN (Environmental Chemicals Data and Information Network). The database contains a wide range of information on chemical structures, physical and chemical properties, toxicity and presence in the environment. It is compiled by the Commission of the European Communities and is accessible via Datacentralen. Details of the environmental fate of organic chemicals is available on ENVIRONMENTAL FATE DATA BASES which is both produced and made available by the Syracuse Research Corporation.

Life and Health Sciences

The life and health sciences constitute a vast area of human knowledge, encompassing the scientific study of all known organisms (plant, animals and micro-organisms) and the study of illness and treatment in the human species. There is considerable overlap with databases covered in other sections of this chapter. (For example, biochemistry is treated in depth in a number of chemistry databases and life sciences also overlap to some extent with both agricultural and environmental matters whilst health sciences overlap to some degree with the social and behavioural sciences.)

Within the life and health sciences there are three very large bibliographic databases. BIOSIS PREVIEWS is the online equivalent of *Biological Abstracts* and *Biological Abstracts/RRM*. Examples of a record from this database as it appears on both Dialog and ESA-IRS are given in Figures 3.4 and 3.5. It contains approximately five million references to the literature of life sciences. In addition to core areas such as ecology and microbiology, coverage includes aspects of agriculture, pharmacology and experimental medicine. About 40 000 references are added to the database each month. Inevitably such an important database is available via a range of search services, including BRS, CISTI, CAN/OLE, Data-Star, Dialog, DIMDI, ESA-IRS and STN International. It should be noted that not all the search services necessarily make the complete BIOSIS PREVIEWS (1969–) available online and because of its size many of the search services make the database available as a series of separate files covering specific time periods.

In the health sciences, the major bibliographic database is MEDLINE, produced by the American National Library of Medicine (NLM). This database was one of the first to be available for online searching and NLM has been an important body in the development of the online information industry. The database now contains over five million references and is growing at the rate of approximately 25 000 items per month. It includes material on experimental medicine, clinical practice, medical administration and health policy. Whilst there is emphasis on European and American literature, coverage is worldwide and the database includes references to original literature in more than 40 languages. MEDLINE is available in machine-readable form from 1964, although few search services offer access to all this information. A very important aspect of this database is the in-depth indexing using the associated controlled vocabulary, Medical Subject Headings (MeSH). Each item is indexed by up to 12 terms from this vocabulary to facilitate subsequent retrieval. MEDLINE is widely available and can be accessed through BRS, Data-Star, Dialog, DIMDI, JICST and from the NLM itself.

A second major bibliographic database in biomedicine is EMBASE, produced by Elsevier Science Publishers. It contains about 3 200 000 references and a further 20 000 or so are added monthly. The intention of the producers is to include worldwide literature on human medicine, related biological sciences and pharmaceutical sciences. Coverage also extends to environmental and occupational health and forensic sciences. EMBASE is widely available and can be searched via BRS, Data-Star, Dialog, DIMDI, and JICST. Data-Star is notable because it updates this file on a weekly basis unlike the others which only update monthly.

LIFE SCIENCES COLLECTION is produced by Cambridge Scientific Abstracts and can be searched via BRS and Dialog. It is the online equivalent of 17 abstracting journals. Coverage includes animal behaviour, biochemistry, biotechnology, ecology, genetics, immunology, microbiology and toxicology.

In addition to these large bibliographic databases, there are a considerable number of smaller bibliographic databases in more specific subject areas. A few are noted to indicate the range of sources available. INTERNATIONAL PHARMACEUTICAL ABSTRACTS contains 130 000 references to literature on all aspects of the development and use of drugs, including material on economic and ethical issues of drug use as well as scientific material. The literature from 1970 is covered and the database can be found on BRS, Dialog and ESA-IRS. In addition INTERNATIONAL

PHARMACEUTICAL ABSTRACTS is just one of 13 different files which together make up the NLM's TOXLINE database which provides access to the literature of all aspects of toxicology. ZOOLOGICAL RECORD ONLINE contains approximately 300 000 references to the world zoological literature. The database is accessible via BRS and Dialog. Data-Star and Dialog both make BIOBUSINESS available. This concentrates on the commercial aspects of the exploitation of biological and biomedical research. Areas covered include agriculture, food technology, genetic engineering and pharmaceuticals. Currently the database contains about 100 000 items.

Smaller again are files such as CURRENT BIOTECHNOLOGY ABSTRACTS, which contains about 20 000 items. Dealing with techniques and applications of biotechnology from 1983 onwards, it is available from Data-Star, Dialog and ESA-IRS. The AIDS database contains references to the world literature on Acquired Immune Deficiency Syndrome (AIDS) and is accessible on BRS and Data-Star. The emergence of this new database represents an interesting example of the online information industry reacting rapidly to a relatively recent social and medical problem by the creation of a specialist database.

Research projects in biomedicine and health care within the European Economic Community are noted in the referral database, MEDREP. This is produced by the Commission of the European Communities and can be found on ECHO.

Two important sources of full-text journals in biomedicine are available online. MEDICAL SCIENCE RESEARCH from Elsevier Applied Science Publishers contains the text of 30 original research journals since 1982 and is accessible via BRS, Data-Star and DIMDI. Mead Data Central has made available the large database MEDIS. This includes the full-text of some 60 journals and newsletters and also the full-text of a small number of medical books.

There are examples of textual-numeric databases in the life and health sciences. GenBank (Genetic Sequences Databank) includes bibliographic references and sequence data of reported DNA and RNA sequences. The information is compiled by the Theoretical Biology and Biophysics Group at Los Alamos National Laboratory and is made available on the online service offered by Bolt, Beranek and Newman Inc. The search service Bionet provides access to VECTORBANK which is produced by IntelliGenetics. VECTORBANK contains details of the nucleic acid sequences of more than 130 frequently used cloning vectors. The American

National Biomedical Research Foundation has produced NBRF (Nucleic Acid Sequence Database) and NBRF-PIR Protein sequence database. The former contains the descriptions of some 1800 genetic sequences whilst the latter contains over 3000 partial or complete protein sequences. Both databases are available via Bionet and PIR and NBRF.

Information about approximately 100 000 drugs, including details of tradenames, generic name, mánufacturer, purpose, usage and efficacy data, has been compiled by Paul de Haen International Inc and made available in the database DE HAEN DRUG DATA TRADEMARK by Dialog. Both Data-Star and Dialog provide access to MARTINDALE ONLINE, the machine-readable version of *Martindale: the extra pharmacopoeia*. This reference work provides access to information on nomenclature, actions and uses of more than 50 000 drugs. Farbey (1987) provides greater detail about medical databases and Wyatt (1987) discusses life sciences databases in greater depth.

Business and Finance

The business person or corporate executive may be interested in the contents of databases from any of the other subject areas discussed in this chapter if that subject is one of the interests of the business. However, there are numerous databases which provide information specifically of a business and financial nature. More so than with any other subject these databases tend to appear on specialist search services; many of these have menu-driven interfaces because they are intended for use by the end-user much more than the information professional.

Bibliographic databases such as ABI/INFORM and MANAGE-MENT CONTENTS are on the major search services such as BRS, Data-Star and Dialog. In addition Pergamon Financial Data Services (PFDS) provides access to MANAGEMENT AND MARKETING ABSTRACTS. These databases provide citations to the literature of management on aspects of interest to the corporate executive such as human resource development, decision making and planning. Articles which are relevant to business from the British press and some 100 journals are indexed in the database RIX. This is the online equivalent of *Research Index*. It is produced by Business Surveys Ltd and made available by PFDS.

Beyond the bibliographic databases, the database types enumerated at the start of this chapter are less useful as a means of categorizing business and financial information than in the other subject areas and in this case it is more useful to distinguish between databases providing company information, marketing information, financial information and reports and commentaries.

A major source of information on American companies is DISCLOSURE ONLINE. The database is readily accessible, for example, via BRS, Dialog, Dow Jones, I.P. Sharp and Mead Data Central. It provides detailed information on the financial state of around 12 000 companies including directors, subsidiaries and auditors reports. Information about approximately 120 000 American manufacturing companies can be located in THOMAS REGISTER ONLINE, the machine-readable equivalent of the long established *Thomas Register of American Manufacturing*. It is produced by Thomas Publishing Company Inc and made available via Dialog.

JORDANWATCH, via PFDS, created by the respected business information company Jordans provides information on some 900 000 British enterprises. Dialog and Data-Star provide access to brief details on more than 1.1 million companies from England, Wales and Scotland registered with the (British) Companies House. This information is contained in the database, ICC DIRECTORY OF COMPANIES. Records in this database contain a considerable amount of information about the company. Figure 7.2 contains only an *excerpt* from a record for Laura Ashley plc. Databases

```
AN   01012631 8901 Full Record.
CO   LAURA ASHLEY HOLDINGS PLC
     Public Limited Company
RO   Registered Office: 4TH FLOOR BANK HOUSE
                        CHARLOTTE STREET
                        MANCHESTER
                        M1 4BX
HI   Accounts Reference Date: 01/31
     Date of latest Accounts: 880130
     Date of last Annual Return: 880610
     Date of Incorporation: 710528
     Public Limited Company (PLC)
     Company Status: Live Company
     History: 851119: alteration to memorandum and articles of
     association; 870912: change of directors; 850903: change of
     registered office address; 880611: resolutions re allotment of
     securities by directors (sec. 14, coys act 1980); 860205: plc's
     share allotment returns
```

Company Type: Company registered in England and Wales under Part 1 of the Companies Act 1948.
Quoted: Yes
Accounts lodge name: LAURA ASHLEY HOLDINGS PLC
4th Floor,
Bank House,
Charlotte Street,
Manchester
M1 4BX
Auditors: Deloitte Haskins & Sells
Phone-No: 0686 24050

IN   Trading Address: Station Road,
Carno,
Caersws,
Powys
SY17 5LQ

MM   Secretary: P S Phillips.
Director(s): J M James ; Sir Bernard Ashley ; A R Lofthouse ; P S Phillips ; P Revers ; A Schouten ; M E Smith ; Lord Hooson.

PN   Holding company of a group engaged in design, manufacture, distribution and retail of ladies' and childrens' garments & accessories and home furnishings and perfumery products.

CC   (8396) Central offices not allocable elsewhere; (4536) Womens & girls light outerwear, lingerie & infants wear; (4555) Soft furnishings; (6430) Dispensing and other chemists.

SC   ZCA; LEE; CRE; CLM; CLL.

FF   Consolidated Accounts (000's ukl)
Independent Company

	880130	870131	860125
Date of Accounts	880130	870131	860125
Number of Weeks	52	53	52
Balance Sheet:			
Fixed Assets	70,241	57,292	40,463
Intangible Assets	0	0	0
Intermediate Assets	6,092	3,129	1,476
Stocks	66,824	45,521	35,603
Debtors	3,056	2,459	1,339
Other Current Assets	16,558	15,105	29,934
Total Current Assets	86,438	63,085	66,876
Creditors	16,499	10,899	10,243
Short Term Loans	34,240	7,864	8,877
Other Current Liab	24,738	22,146	19,887
Total Current Liab	75,477	40,909	39,007
Net Assets	87,294	82,597	69,808
Total Assets	162,771	123,506	108,815

Figure 7.2 *An excerpt from a record from ICC COMPANIES database on Data-Star*

designed primarily to report on the credit worthiness of organizations are a very useful source of a much greater range of company information. In Britain such information is available from ADVANCE INFORMATION whilst in the United States the equivalent service is the BUSINESS CREDIT SERVICES DATABASE which is produced and made available by TRW Information Services Division.

A major American source of marketing information is the Predicasts PTS Marketing and Advertising Reference Service which is accessible via Data-Star and Dialog. Dialog also makes available ADTRACK which provides a guide to all advertisements of more than a quarter of a page in size which appear in a range of business periodicals. This database offers unique opportunities to monitor the trends in the marketing efforts of competitors. In Britain, PFDS offers MAID, Market Analysis and Information Databank. This contains analyses of marketing expenditure data together with news of the advertising and market research industries. Similar databases are available from Profile Information (MAGIC) and Harvest Information Services (HARVEST). MAGIC can be seen as a suite of databases which provide information in marketing advertising and public relations whilst HARVEST offers information on marketing, advertising and market research from a variety of sources.

Financial information includes stock market information, foreign exchange and commodities information. Search services providing this type of information can be characterized as dealing in short-life information where the premium is on up-to-dateness. British examples are TOPIC, run by the Stock Exchange, and FINSTAT from the Financial Times. Other search services, for example Datastream, I.P. Sharp and CISI-Wharton, provide historical data and analytical capabilities. Thus their data are often presented as time series and the search service usually provides software for the manipulation of the data for analysis and or graphical or tabular presentation.

The business community is interested in a range of full-text databases. One variety is the wide range of trade and industry newsletters which comment on developments and provide analyses of events within a subject area. An example of this type of newsletter is AGINFO which was noted earlier in the chapter. The search service NewsNet has specialized in the provision of these newsletters. Examples of its offerings are WORLD ENVIRON-MENT REPORT and MID-EAST BUSINESS DIGEST. Further examples are given in the section of this chapter concerned with information technology. The HARVARD BUSINESS REVIEW ONLINE, produced by John Wiley and Sons Inc and made available via BRS, Data-Star, Dialog and NEXIS, contains about 2500 papers from this influential management periodical since 1976. The final area of full-text information which is of interest to the business community is the reports produced by brokers and market research organizations. Some market research reports are made available as a part of other services (for example MAID, mentioned earlier). Both BRS and Data-Star provide access to FROST AND SULLIVAN MARKET RESEARCH REPORTS. This gives informative abstracts of the market research reports produced by this major American market research organization. ICC STOCKBROKER RESEARCH provides full-text of about 1800 original reports from international stockbrokers. These cover reports on both companies and industries. The same database producer, ICC, also produces ICC KEYNOTES MARKET ANALYSIS, containing more than 180 market information reports. Both databases are available via Data-Star. Further information about databases for financial and business information can be found in Bater and Parkinson (1987). Management and marketing information can be followed up in greater detail in Haddon (1987) and the whole area is covered in the book by Walsh, Butcher and Freund (1987).

Chemistry and the Chemical Industry

The major bibliographic database for chemistry and related subjects is the online version of *Chemical Abstracts*. The most widely available version is known as CA SEARCH, produced by Chemical Abstracts Service (CAS), a sub-division of the American Chemical Society. CA SEARCH is accessible on many major search services, including BRS, Data-Star, Dialog, ESA-IRS, ORBIT and Télésystèmes-QUESTEL. The database covers all aspects of chemistry, chemical technology and related subjects and now contains more than 8 000 000 references since 1967 (although some search services only make available items from 1977 onwards). Approximately 40 000 items are added each month and because of its great size the database has been broken into several files by some of the search services. It covers books, conference proceedings, patents, reports and theses in addition to papers from some 14 000 journals and therefore has citations to a wider range of source types than most bibliographic databases. For each item the reference includes the citation, CAS assigned subject terms and the CAS Registry Number. Figure 7.3 provides an example of a bibliographic record from CA SEARCH as made available on BRS. The version of the database available exclusively from STN International is CAS Online. In addition to the information in CA SEARCH, references in CAS Online also contain abstracts for all items added since 1975 and for many of those added prior to that date. The CAS Registry Number has become a vital tool for the indexing of chemicals which may have a number of names, trivial, commercial and structured. The problem of chemical names has become so great that various databases of names have been devised primarily to link together the synonymous names of chemicals. Figure 7.4 provides an example of a record from CHEMNAME on Dialog.

Whilst CA SEARCH is an all embracing database, numerous other databases concentrate on a single area of chemistry. One example is ANALYTICAL ABSTRACTS, produced by the Royal Society of Chemistry and available from Data-Star, Dialog and

AN CA09403011613.
AU TULI-SAROJ. MEHROTRA-K-N.
IN DIV. ENTOMOL. INDIAN AGRIC. RES. INST. NEW DELHI. INDIA.
110012.
TI PERMEABILITY OF CUTICLE OF THE DESERT LOCUST
   SCHISTOCERCA GERGARIA FORSKAL TO CHEMICALS.
SO J. NUCL. AGRIC. BIOL. 9. P99–103. 1980.
YR 80.
LG EN..
CD JNABD..
PT J.
CC CA005004. CA005.
RG ** 62–56–6 CH4N2S. ** 63–25–2 C12H11NO2. ** 121–75–5
   C10H19O6PS2. ** 7664–38–2 H304P.
DE MALATHION PERMEABILITY CUTICLE SCHISTOCERCA.
   GRASSHOPPER CUTICLE SEVIN PERMEABILITY. PHOSPHORIC
   ACID PERMEABILITY CUTICLE SCHISTOCERA. THIOUREA
   PERMEABILITY CUTICLE SCHISTOCERCA.
ST CUTICLE: ANIMAL. INSECTICIDES. SCHISTOCERCA-GERGARIA.

Figure 7.3   *A record from the CA SEARCH database on BRS*

CAS REGISTRY NUMBER: 121–75–5
  FORMULA: C10H19O6PS2
  REPLACED CAS REGISTRY NUMBER(S): 11130–60–2 12737–19–8
  12767–62–3 75513–83–6
  CA NAME(S):
    HP=Butanedioic acid (9CI), SB=((dimethoxyphosphinothioyl)thio)-,
  NM=diethy ester
    HP=Succinic acid (8CI), SB=mercapto-, NM=diethyl ester, S-ester
  with O, O-dimethyl phosphorodithioate
    SYNONYMS: SF 60; 8059HC; ENT 17,034; American Cyanamid
  4,049; S-(1,2-Bis(ethoxycarbonyl)ethyl) O, O-dimethyl
  phosphorodithioate; S-(1,2-Bis(ethoxycarbonyl)ethyl) O, O-dimethyl
  thiophosphate; Carbophos; Compound 4049; Fosfothion; Insecticide no.
  4049; Karbofos; Malathion; Malathion LV Concentrate; Mercaptothion;
  Phosphothion; Ethiolacar; Fosfotion; Malamar 50; Oleophosphothion;
  Sadophos; Siptox I; Sadofos; Cython; O, O-Dimethyl S-(1,2-dicarbeth
  xyethyl) dithiophosphate; Surnitox; Carbetox; Malathion E 50; S-(1,2-Bis
  (carbethoxy)ethyl) O, O-dimethyl dithiophosphate;
  ((Dimethoxyphosphinothioyl)thio)butanedioic acid diethyl ester;
  Insecticide number 4049; Carbofos; Malaspray; Prioderm; Zithiol; Ortho
  Malathion; Fog 3; Malatol; Fyfanon; Moscarda; TM 4049; Malafor; Etiol;
  Vetiol; Carbetovur; TAK(pesticide); Malasol; Extermathion; Forthion;
  Malathyl; Cimexan; Hilthion; IFO 13140; Malataf; TAK; Mavidan;
  Security;

Figure 7.4 *A record from the CHEMNAME database on Dialog*

ORBIT. It contains over 90 000 references to the use of analytical chemistry techniques in a wide range of industries and circumstances. The business aspects of the chemical industry, including products, processes, prices and corporate activities, are covered by the database CHEMICAL INDUSTRY NOTES, which is produced by CAS and available on Data-Star, Dialog and ORBIT. Other bibliographic databases in chemistry include CHEMICAL BUSINESS NEWSBASE, CHEMICAL ENGINEERING ABSTRACTS and CHEMICAL HAZARDS IN INDUSTRY.

A good example of a referral database in chemistry is provided by CHEMQUEST TRADEMARK produced by Molecular Design and available via ORBIT and PFDS. This is a directory of suppliers of approximately 80 000 commercially available chemical substances including biomedical compounds, dyes, organic and inorganic compounds. For each substance, the database provides a description of the compound, its molecular formula, CAS Registry Number, supplier and price. The information is compiled from more than 50 suppliers catalogues and there are facilities for searching by structure, sub-structure and Wiswesser Line Notation (a means of denoting chemical formulae). Information about 15 000 operational chemical production facilities are offered in the CHEMICAL PLANT DATABASE. For each of these facilities the database provides details about location, production capacity (planned and used), contractor, products and trade names. It is produced by Chemical Intelligence Services and is accessible via Data-Star.

Chemical Intelligence Services produce CHEM-INTELL, a database of statistical information about the chemical industry. It contains time series for the production, import and export of over 100 major chemical products by some 70 countries since 1976 and is available on Data-Star and PFDS.

The American Chemical Society (ACS) and John Wiley and Sons Inc both contribute to the database, CHEMICAL JOURNALS ONLINE. This consists of two files, one on chemistry and the other on polymer science. The chemical file contains the full-text of more than 45 000 original papers which have appeared in 18 major primary journals published by ACS since 1982 including *Analytical Chemistry*, *Journal of the American Chemical Society* and *Journal of Organic Chemistry*. The polymer file contains the full-text of more than 3000 papers which have appeared in three primary journals in polymer science and technology published by John Wiley from 1984. The database is accessible via STN International. In addition to the full-text of primary papers, a small number of important chemical reference works are beginning to appear online. The highly respected *Kirk Othmer Encyclopedia of Chemical Technology* is available as one of two files in the database KIRK OTHMER ONLINE. This file contains all the 1200 articles in the third edition of this standard work. The second file consists of the *Encyclopedia of Polymer Science and Engineering*, which is being progressively made available online. The database is available on BRS, Data-Star and Dialog.

Vast quantities of chemical structural information and information on chemical properties are available in the monumental German reference work *Beilstein Handbook of Organic Chemistry*, which seeks to include data about all organic compounds which have appeared in the literature since 1830. It is intended that eventually the database will include information on 3.5 million compounds and at present information about some 700 000 has been incorporated into BEILSTEIN ONLINE SERVICEMARK, available from Dialog, ORBIT and STN International. The

MERCK INDEX ONLINE provides details on the chemical and trivial names, trademarks, formula, properties, CAS Registry Number, action and toxicity of over 30 000 chemicals, drugs, agricultural and veterinary products. The database is available via BRS, and Télésystèmes-QUESTEL. Greater detail about online chemical information is provided by Ash *et al.* (1985).

Law

Computer-based legal information provides a good example of search services which are targeted principally at the end-user rather than the search intermediary (see Chapter 8). The databases are essentially full-text source databases and they are concentrated in the hands of search services (LEXIS and WESTLAW) designed for and targeted at legal firms rather than the library and information community.

The LEXIS service from Mead Data Central provides access to a range of files termed *libraries*. These *libraries* cover the law of specific subjects, for example banking, trade and insurance law. There are also libraries for the laws of individual (American) states and one each for French Law and British Law. WESTLAW is provided by the West Publishing Company and offers similarly comprehensive coverage of both American case law and statutes. Examples of databases on the system are WESTLAW ENERGY DATABASE, WESTLAW COPYRIGHT AND PATENT DATABASE and WESTLAW ENVIRONMENTAL LAW DATABASE. A final example is the database CELEX which has been created by the Commission of the European Communities. This provides full-text of the law of the European Communities. Given the diversity of languages within the community it is interesting to note that it is possible to use versions of the command language in Dutch, English, French, German and Spanish.

Both WESTLAW and LEXIS make available the long established *Shepherd's Citations* in machine-readable form. This database provides citations to histories of cases and to all the subsequent cases which cite a particular case. This method of indexing by creating a forward link between cited case and citing case has been developed extensively in bibliographic databases by the Institute for Scientific Information, some of whose databases are mentioned in other sections of this chapter. One example of a bibliographic database related to law is POLIS (Parliamentary

Online Information System), produced by the (British) House of Commons Library. Its more than 400 000 references include public and general acts, Statutory Instruments and British and European Communities Official Publications. The database also contains summaries of oral and written questions which have been asked in both Houses of the British Parliament. Raper (1988) provides greater detail about legal databases.

News

Not only has the emergence of online search services enhanced the speed and flexibility of searching and increased greatly the range of sources available but also it has allowed the creation of services which were desirable but could not be provided by manual systems. News services which permit access to the full-text of newspapers, current affairs magazines, wire services and specialist newsletters is one such area. The need for up-to-date information and informed opinion has always existed but the necessary manual indexes have not been available and the dedicated searcher has had recourse only to sequential scanning of appropriate sources.

News services are of three types: full-text, summaries and bibliographic. Some databases appear on the general search services such as Dialog whilst others appear on specialist search services such as Profile Information in Britain (see Chapters 2 and 4) or NEXIS in America. A good example of a service providing summaries is Textline, which provides summaries of news from approximately 150 European newspapers and 500 periodicals. It specializes in current affairs, economic, industrial and European Community matters. Textline is accessible both on its own search service and via a gateway from ESA-IRS.

Various American newspapers are available in full-text online versions. Some examples are ARIZONA BUSINESS GAZETTEER, ARIZONA REPUBLIC, THE BOSTON GLOBE, FORT LAUDERDALE NEWS, PHILADELPHIA ENQUIRER and the SEATTLE POST-INTELLIGENCER. All these are accessible via the search service VU/TEXT. Specialist newsletters, which were discussed in the section on business and financial information, could also be considered as news databases. The depth of interest in this type of publication can be gauged from the fact that there are no less than five such newsletters available online which concentrate on the online information industry: ONLINE CHRONICLE (Dialog), ONLINE HOTLINE (Information Intelligence Inc),

ONLINE LIBRARIES AND MICROCOMPUTERS (Information Intelligence Inc), ONLINE PRODUCT NEWS (NewsNet) and ONLINE TODAY ELECTRONIC EDITION (CompuServe).

In addition to these full-text services, there are various bibliographic databases which seek to provide references to the contents of newspapers. Both BRS and Dialog make available NATIONAL NEWSPAPER INDEX. This indexes the major American dailies: the *Christian Science Monitor*, *New York Daily Times*, *Washington Post*, *Wall Street Journal* and the *Los Angeles Times*.

Engineering

Engineering is the application of scientific knowledge to the design and operation of a wide range of structures and machines. This section of the chapter will examine databases in all areas of engineering except electrical and electronic engineering which are dealt with in the next section.

The major bibliographic database in engineering is COMPEN-DEX. It seeks to index the worldwide literature (except patents) for all areas of engineering and related subjects including aeronautical, chemical, civil, electrical and electronic, mechanical, mining and water engineering. The database has approximately 1.75 million references and is growing by some 12 000 items per month. It is widely accessible, being on BRS, CISTI, Data-Star, Dialog, ESA-IRS and ORBIT. There are wide variations in just what part of the database has been made available and the start date for records online varies between 1969 and 1976 on the different search services. Related to COMPENDEX is EI ENGINEERING MEETINGS which contains citations to about 500 000 papers at various conferences, symposia and meetings. Coverage includes most of the major areas of engineering. The database is accessible from CISTI, Data-Star, Dialog, ORBIT and STN International.

In addition to these databases covering all aspects of engineering, there are numerous bibliographic databases which seek to document the literature of specific areas of engineering. The literature relating to the behaviour and applications of fluids in engineering is documented in FLUIDEX. The diverse coverage ranges from flow measurement to port and harbour technology. The database, containing approximately 200 000 items, is produced by the British organization, BHRA, The Fluid Engineering Centre. Access to the database is provided by Dialog and ESA-IRS. Mechanical engineering literature is covered by two databases. There are approximately 200 000 references in the database, ISMEC (Information Service in Mechanical Engineering) which is produced by Cambridge Scientific Abstracts and available on Dialog and ESA-IRS. It is complemented by the French database CETIM, which is produced by the Centre Techniques de Industries Mecaniques; this has about 85 000 items, largely in French and is available via ESA-IRS.

The literature of building and construction engineering is documented in ICONDA which is produced by the Information Centre for Regional Planning and Building Construction of the Fraunhofer Society. It contains about 150 000 items and is available via ORBIT and STN International. The more restricted subject of the provision of electrical and mechanical services in buildings is documented in IBSEDEX which is produced by the British Building Services Research and Information Association and is available on ESA-IRS.

ESA-IRS also provides access to ASIAN GEOTECHNOLOGY containing approximately 35 000 citations to the literature on geotechnical engineering: site investigations, construction methods and equipment and the properties and engineering of soil and rock. ESA-IRS also provides access to BRIX, produced by the British Building Research Station. It contains some 120 000 references to the international literature on building research and all aspects of construction.

Standard specifications, which lay down the performance or quality criteria for products, play an important role in engineering design. Citations to approximately 80 000 standards are provided in INDUSTRY AND INDUSTRY STANDARDS which is available via BRS. As engineering projects have become larger and more complex, project management has become a subject in its own right. The literature on this subject, including project planning techniques, logistics and quality control is recorded in BEFO (Management and Organization), produced and made available by the German search service Fiz Technik. It contains approximately 75 000 items.

Referral databases in engineering exist which refer the engineer to the producers of components, products or tools that may be used in engineering design. The American Ziff-Davis Technical Information Company has produced and made available HAY-STACK. This provides details of standard specifications and also electrical and mechanical parts from manufacturers' catalogues for 13 000 000 products and components. Hoppenstedt Wirtschaftsdatenbank GmbH produces MRA (Measurement, Control, Automation), which provides references to more than 13 000 products used in measurement, control and automation which are manufactured by some 2000 companies in Austria, the Federal Republic of Germany or Switzerland. It is available via Fiz Technik. The American database, VENDOR INFORMATION FILE, provides references to more than 32 000 manufacturers and vendors of industrial products and components for a wide range of largely engineering industries. Entries provide details of the name, address, sales office, product names and tables of contents of the vendor's catalogues. The database is produced by Information Handling Services and is made available via BRS. Finally in this category, ENGINEERING AND INDUSTRY SOFTWARE DIRECTORY has descriptions of more than 4000 computer programs for engineering, industrial and manufacturing applications. Subjects covered include most areas of engineering and information technology. For each program, there is a description of functions and applications, hardware and software requirements, documentation, physical media for distribution, supplier and cost. The database has been produced by Engineering Information Inc and it is made available by Data-Star.

To date, source databases in engineering have not been developed to any great extent. One indication of the possibilities in this field is provided by VDI-N (VDI-NACHRICHTEN) which is available on Fiz Technik. This offers online access to the full text of the German-language weekly newspaper, *VDI-NACHRICHTEN*, which covers the engineering field and is available since 1983.

Information Technology

Information technology can be viewed as the technologies, processes and theories relating to the collection, storage, retrieval and dissemination of information. Thus it includes the converging technologies of computing and telecommunications, emerging disciplines such as artificial intelligence and existing disciplines such as library and information science.

Much relevant information will be located on the general bibliographic databases such as PASCAL and general engineering databases like COMPENDEX. However, the major bibliographic database for this subject area is INSPEC. It provides references to items in physics, electrical and electronic engineering and computers and control engineering. The database now contains approximately three million items and is widely available through search services such as BRS, Data-Star, Dialog, ESA-IRS, ORBIT and STN International. Not surprisingly in such a diverse subject there are also bibliographic databases covering subject areas within information technology. Examples are ARTIFICIAL INTELLIGENCE ONLINE (via ESA-IRS), LIBRARY AND INFORMATION SCIENCE ABSTRACTS (via Dialog and ORBIT), INFORMATION SCIENCE ABSTRACTS (via Dialog) and MICROCOMPUTER INDEX (via Dialog). The database names give some reasonable indication of their content. However, this is not always the case as illustrated by the database ELCOM, which is available via ESA-IRS. This database covers the literature of electronics and communications.

The descriptions of approximately 5000 business systems and utility software programs for all types of computer are given in BUSINESS SOFTWARE DATABASE. Information on each product includes product name, description, supplier details, number of installations and hardware and software requirements. The database is accessible via BRS, Data-Star, Dialog and ESA-IRS. Dialog also provides access to MICROCOMPUTER SOFTWARE AND HARDWARE GUIDE. This lists approximately 35 000 software packages and provides details of hardware and operating system requirements, release date, price and publisher contact information.

The COMPUTER INSTALLATION DATAFILE combines both numeric and text information about computer installations. Approximately 150 000 installed systems at more than 100 000 business locations in America and Canada are listed. For each system details are given of location, manufacturer, peripherals, operating systems and software packages used. The database is compiled by Computer Intelligence, which also makes it available on its own search service. A final example of source data of the text-numeric variety is offered by EMIS (Electronic Materials Information Service) which is produced by INSPEC and made available by ESA-IRS. This provides details such as preparation and properties of materials which are used in electronic components.

Social and Behavioural Sciences

There is rarely agreement about the precise boundaries of the social and behavioural sciences. In the context of this section they can be taken to comprise sociology, psychology, political science, education, human geography and economics. In the case of economics the context is restricted to the theoretical aspects of economics as an academic subject.

Two general bibliographic databases seek to cover all the social sciences. SOCIAL SCIENCES INDEX on WilsonLine contains over 35 000 references to literature from more than 300 English language periodicals from 1984 onwards. On a much larger scale SOCIAL SCISEARCH from the Institute for Scientific Information contains more than 1.8 million references to articles from over 1400 major social science journals. In the case of this database the social sciences include linguistics, business management and marketing in addition to the topics mentioned at the start of this section. The database is available via BRS, Dialog and DIMDI.

ERIC (Educational Resources Information Center) contains over 20 years' references to literature on education and related topics. Thus it includes subjects such as educational psychology, education management, communication skills, languages and linguistics. It is the online equivalent of two printed publications, *Resources in Education* and *Current Index to Journals in Education*, which provide access to the report and journal literature, respectively. The database is available via BRS, Dialog and ORBIT.

Access to the literature of psychology and behavioural sciences since 1967 is provided by PSYCINFO. It now contains more than 500 000 items and increases by about 3000 items per month. Very recent material is noted in the companion database PSYCALERT. Both databases can be found on the BRS and Dialog search services whilst PSYCINFO is also accessible via Data-Star and DIMDI.

The major bibliographic database in sociology is SOCIOLOGICAL ABSTRACTS, which now includes approximately 200 000 items. Coverage includes methods, theories, history and research in sociology. It includes references to the literature from 1963 to the present day. It can be found on a number of search services including BRS, Data-Star and Dialog.

The theory, history and development of economics as an academic discipline is covered by ECONOMIC LITERATURE INDEX, which corresponds to the *Journal of Economic Literature* from 1969 to the present date. The database now contains over 130 000 references and is accessible via Dialog.

The major bibliographic database in political science contains references to more than 30 000 items. This is United States POLITICAL SCIENCE DOCUMENTS, which covers the contents of the major American political science journals. The database is accessible via Dialog. References to contemporary social and political issues are recorded in PAIS INTERNATIONAL. This database contains approximately 250 000 references and is available on BRS, Data-Star and Dialog. ESA-IRS provides access to about 100 000 items related to urban studies in ACOMPLINE. Many aspects of human geography as well as some aspects of physical geography are covered by GEOBASE, which is accessible via Dialog.

In addition to these discipline-orientated bibliographic databases, there are a number of problem-oriented databases. Examples are CHILD ABUSE AND NEGLECT and FAMILY RESOURCES, both of which can be found on Dialog.

In some areas of the social sciences a particular national perspective may be important. The databases noted so far in this section have a heavy American, British and English language bias. It is important to note that there are bibliographic databases covering the social sciences literature of other countries and languages. For example, a series of databases called FRANCIS covers anthropology, economics, geography, education and sociology amongst other subjects which are produced by the French Centre National de Recherche Scientifique (CNRS). These are made available on the French search services G-CAM Serveur and Télésystèmes-QUESTEL.

Social scientists make much use of statistical information. There are now a considerable number of online sources. The CENSUS REPORTING PROGRAM from the American Census Bureau provides details from the 1980 American census which can be accessed on the search service, Executive Telecom System Inc. DONNELLEY DEMOGRAPHICS, from Donnelley Market Information Services and accessible via Dialog, contains current year estimates and five-year projections of demographic data based upon the 1980 American census. CRONOS-EUROSTAT is produced by the Statistical Office of the Commission of the European Communities and contains over 900 000 time series of economic and general data for the EEC countries. Data include general statistics such as population and also details of national accounts, balance of payments, foreign trade, industries and agriculture. Many of the data are available via a number of search services: ADP DataServices, CISI-Wharton Econometric Forecasting, Datacentralen and GSI-ECO. CISI-Wharton produces time series of economic data on a number of areas of the world (for example, the United States, Latin America, the Middle East and the Pacific Basin). CENDATA from the American Census Bureau and available via Dialog contains full-text and some numeric data from the Census Bureau, economic and demographic reports and press releases. Further details can be located in a variety of sources such as the chapter by Foster (1984).

Humanities

The humanities are taken to include art, music, philosophy, languages, religion and history. There are far fewer databases in the humanities than in the social sciences or the natural sciences or technology. Furthermore the databases tend to be smaller than in the other subject areas and the bibliographic databases tend to cover only the more recent literature and for a shorter time span. The relative paucity of humanities databases is largely a matter of economics. Humanities research is not funded on anything like the same scale as research into scientific subjects and the need and ability to pay for up-to-date information are much less than is the case with business and financial information. However, there are now an increasing number of bibliographic databases in the humanities and a small number of referral and full-text databases.

Probably the largest bibliographic database in the humanities is ARTS & HUMANITIES SEARCH which is produced by the Institute for Scientific Information and available via BRS. Approximately 900 000 items from about 1300 journals cover material on folklore, linguistics, language, music, philosophy and the visual and performing arts amongst other subjects. The British Library has produced the EIGHTEENTH CENTURY SHORT TITLE CATALOGUE and made it available on the BLAISE-LINE search service. It contains detailed notes and bibliographic information on some 200 000 printed materials (including lists, advertisements and songs as well as books) from the 18th century. An example of a record from this database is given in Figure 7.5. HUMANITIES INDEX is produced by H.W. Wilson and made available via WilsonLine. It contains approximately 40 000 items from many areas of the humanities for example, religion, philosophy, folklore and the performing arts. There are a whole series of databases available on the major French search service Télésystèmes-QUESTEL covering various subjects within the humanities: FRANCIS: ART ET ARCHEOLOGIE, FRANCIS: ETHNOLOGIE, FRANCIS: HISTOIRE ET SCIENCES DE LA LITTERATURE, FRANCIS: HISTOIRE ET SCIENCES DES

RELIGIONS: FRANCIS: PHILOSOPHIE, FRANCIS: PRE-HISTOIRE ET PROTOHISTOIRE, FRANCIS: REPERTOIRE D'ART ET D; ARCHELOGIE and FRANCIS: SCIENCES DU LANGAGE are all produced by the Centre National de la Recherche Scientifique Centre de Documentation.

RCN – n032376
AP   – Chetham John
TI   – A book of psalmody, containing, variety of tunes, for all the common metres of the Psalms in the old and new versions, and others for particular measures, with chanting-tunes for Venite exultemus, . . . and fifteen anthems, . . . The tenth edition, with large additions, and corrected. By the Reverend Mr. John Chetham.
PU   – Leeds printed and sold by G. Wright and Son: sold also by the booksellers in Leeds; N. Binns and W. Edwards, Halifax; J. Meggitt and G. Newton, Wakefield; J. Bent and J. Cockshaw, Barnsley; W. Ward, Sheffield; [and 1 each in York, Manchester, Huddersfield, Bradford, Pontefract, Knarebro', Newcastle, and Kendall; and 3 in London, including F. Newbery]   1779
PH   – [4],viii,186,12,[2]p.   music 8:

Figure 7.5 *A record from the EIGHTEENTH CENTURY SHORT TITLE CATALOGUE database on BLAISE*

ART LITERATURE INTERNATIONAL is a bibliographic database which is produced by the J Paul Getty Trust and available via Dialog. It consists of approximately 90 000 references to literature in art history, sculpture, painting and photography. A related database, ART INDEX, is produced by the H.W. Wilson Company and is available on WilsonLine. More than 13 000 art sales catalogues are noted in the database, SCIPIO, produced by the American Research Libraries Group (RLG) and available via its service RLIN. Non-RLG members must pay a subscription.

The literature of history is documented in two databases from the same producer, ABC-CLIO. HISTORICAL ABSTRACTS covers all aspects of economic, political and social history of the world outside North America and AMERICA: HISTORY & LIFE contains material about the history of Canada and the United States. Both databases can be found on Dialog. The literature on languages and linguistics can be located via MLA BIBLIOGRAPHY, produced by the Modern Language Association of America and accessible via Dialog. LINGUISTICS AND LANGUAGE BEHAVIOUR ABSTRACTS also provides access to literature in this area. It is produced by Sociological Abstracts and can be found on BRS and Dialog. Access to the literature of music, including historical musicology, ethnomusicology and the theory, practice and performance of music is provided by RILM ABSTRACTS (Repertoire International de Litterature Musicale). The database is produced by the City University of New York and made available by Dialog. Another American university, Bowling Green State University, through its Philosophy Documentation Center, has produced PHILOSOPHERS INDEX, once again searched on Dialog.

The few referral databases in the humanities tend to be small in scale and regional in character. Examples are a catalogue of art works in Spanish museums and a catalogue of mosaics from ancient Greece. More details can be traced in the directories of databases.

Full-text humanities databases are now becoming available. On Dialog, it is possible to search the modern revision of the King James version of the Bible. The American search service, THE SOURCE, makes available the database RELIGION-ONLINE. This includes news and feature articles on religious affairs.

Bibliographic Databases Covering Particular Forms of Materials

Most bibliographic databases are distinguished by the subject matter which they include within their remit. However, there are a small number of bibliographic databases which are distinguished not by their subject coverage but by the document types which they cover. For example all dissertations accepted at American and over 200 non-American educational institutions are recorded in DISSERTATIONS ABSTRACTS ONLINE, which is accessible on BRS and Dialog. Dialog and ESA-IRS make available CONFERENCE PAPERS INDEX from Cambridge Scientific Abstracts. The database provides citations to a million papers presented at regional, national and international meetings, conferences and symposia. CONFERENCE PROCEEDINGS INDEX on BLAISE-LINE contains citations to 230 000 conferences, the proceedings of which can be borrowed from the British Library Document Supply Centre. An example of a record from this database is given in Figure 7.6. Much government sponsored research, especially within aerospace, defence and related areas is published in the report literature rather than the journal literature.

Citations to more than 1.2 million publicly available reports from largely American government sponsored research are listed in NTIS (NATIONAL TECHNICAL INFORMATION SERVICE). This can be accessed via BRS, CISTI, Dialog, ORBIT, STN and other search services. STN, along with BLAISE-LINE and INKADATA, also provides access to SIGLE (System for Information on Grey Literature in Europe). This documents the grey literature (conferences, reports etc.) published within the countries of the European Communities.

```
RCN  – G00941229
IC   – 871103 b
BL   – 18611793 +CON
DSC  –   Plastics 85/22975
MDV  –   MAR 1985 London
TI   – Plastics for pipeline renovation and corrosion protection
         in UK and overseas  Joint symposium   Papers
EC   – Plastics and Rubber Institute
EC   – Institution of Public Health Engineers   Metropolitan
         District Centre
EC   – Institution of Water Engineers and Scientists
IT   – PLASTICS
IT   – PIPELINE RENOVATION
IT   – CORROSION PROTECTION
```

Figure 7.6   *A record from the CONFERENCE PROCEEDINGS INDEX database on BLAISE*

Details of monographs are listed in LCMARC and UKMARC. The former contains more than two million references to books published since 1968 and catalogued by the American Library of Congress; the latter contains more than one million references to books published in Britain since 1950.

The other document type for which specific bibliographic databases have been developed is patents. Patents exist to provide legal protection and commercial benefit to inventors in return for sharing their inventions with the community at large. The encouragement is in the form of the exclusive right to the commercial exploitation of the invention for an agreed period of time in a particular geographical area. This legal right to exclusive commercial exploitation is granted in exchange for the publication of the details of the invention in the form of a patent. Thus patents

ACCESSION NUMBER   80–64317C/37 (64317C)
TITLE   Metal spigot and socket pipes for underground
                   pipelines – where each pipe is connected by cable to
                   anode used for cathodic protection of pipe against
                   corrosion
DERWENT CLASSES   M14×12 R41 R51
PATENT ASSIGNEE   (THON/) THON J
INVENTORS   THON J
PATENT FAMILY   DE2907368–A 80.09.04 (8037)
                  DE2907368–C 83.10.27 (8344)
PRIORITY   79.02.24 79DE–907368
INT'L. PATENT CLASS.   C23F–013/00 H01B–007/28 H02G–015/18
ABSTRACT   The pipes have rubber seals, and possess an
                  electrically insulating outer sheath, plus >=1 anode
                  which is inserted in the earth for cathodic protection of
                  each pipe. The anode is pref. a rod which is located inside
                  the pipe while the latter is transported; and the rod is
                  pref. connected by a cable to a conductor shoe spot
                  welded onto the end of the socket on each pipe.
                      During the transport of the pipe, the anode is pref.
                  surrounded by an elastic cushion which fills and closes
                  the end of the pipe, which pref. has a rounded internal
                  flange on the end of the socket. The anode is taken out of
                  each pipe for assembly of the pipeline.
                      After laying a pipeline, it is normally necessary to
                  employ specialist firms to provide cathode protection.
                  The invention provides anodes and cables fixed on the
                  pipes before the latter leave a factory, so the pipelayers
                  can install the anodes.

Figure 7.7 *A record from the WORLD PATENTS INDEX on
ORBIT Search Service*

are documents, which contain elements of science and technology, law and commerce. Clearly patents are important sources of scientific and technological information; less obviously they are also important sources of commercial information since they provide details of the new inventions and research directions of competitors. In order to acquire adequate legal protection, it is necessary for the inventor to file a patent in all those geographic areas (usually countries) in which legal protection is sought. Thus it is necessary for the compilers of patent databases to provide links between different patent documents in different countries which refer to the same invention. The documentation of patents is clearly a complex situation and the searching of patent literature is tailor made for the use of online searching.

The technological content of patent specifications from 34 patent-issuing authorities is recorded in WORLD PATENTS INDEX, which is produced by Derwent Publications Ltd. It is available via Dialog, ORBIT and Télésystèmes-QUESTEL. An example of a patent from this database on the ORBIT search service is provided in Figure 7.7. Patents issued in some 51 countries and by the European Patent Office and the World Intellectual Property Organization are included in INPADOC. This can be searched on either INKADATA or ORBIT. EDOC, available via Télésystèmes-QUESTEL, contains about five million records which provide links amongst more than 14 million patent documents issued in many countries for the same inventions. A detailed discussion of patents and patent databases is beyond the scope of this book and the interested reader is referred to Simmons (1988) for greater detail and to Marchant (1987) for more guidance on available databases.

Whilst many databases have been mentioned in this chapter in an attempt to help the newcomer to online searching become familiar with online sources, it must be remembered that these databases are but the tip of a digital information iceberg. Whole disciplines such as physics and metallurgy have been ignored and only a selection of databases has been mentioned from the disciplines chosen for inclusion.

References

Armstrong, C. J. and Large, J. A. (1988) Editors. *Manual of Online Search Strategies*. Aldershot: Gower
Ash, J. *et al.* (1985) *Communication, Storage and Retrieval of Chemical Information*. Chichester: Ellis Horwood
Bater, P. and Parkinson, H. (1987) *Business and Company Databases*. London: Aslib
Brit-line. Directory of British Databases (1988). Horley: EDIP
Cuadra Directory of Online Databases. Cuadra/Elsevier (twice per annum)
Farbey, R. (1987) *Medical Databases*. London: Aslib
Foster, A. (1984) *Databases and Databanks*. In *Information Sources in Economics*, edited by J. Fletcher. London: Butterworths

Haddon, A. (1987) *Management and Marketing Databases*. London: Aslib

Hall, J. L. (1986) *Online Bibliographic Databases*, 4th edn. London: Aslib

Marchant, P. (1987) *Patents and Trademarks Databases*. London: Aslib

Raper, D. (1988) *Legal Databases*. London: Aslib

Simmons, E. S. (1988) *Patents*. In *Manual of Online Search Strategies*, edited by C. J. Armstrong and J. A. Large, pp. 84–156. Aldershot: Gower

Walsh, B.P., Butcher, H. and Freund, A. (1987) *Online Information: A Comprehensive Business Users Guide*. Oxford: Basil Blackwell

Williams, M. E. (1985) Editor. *Computer Readable Databases: A Directory and Sourcebook*, 2 volumes. Chicago: American Library Association

Wyatt, H. V. (1987) Editor. *Information Sources in Life Sciences*. London: Butterworths

Chapter 8

Searching and the Search Process

Intermediaries and End-Users

One interesting fact about online searching is that traditionally it has often been done by librarians or information scientists – professional intermediaries – on behalf of clients (often referred to as end-users). These end-users have tended to delegate their online searching to intermediaries even though they would often do comparable manual searches for themselves.

Some information specialists may spend a high proportion of their working week acting as intermediaries, but many only devote a small part of their time to this activity, the remainder being given to other library or information duties. In a 1980 survey of 407 intermediaries employed in British libraries and information units, the mean time spent in online and related work was just under eight hours per week. This figure included preliminary discussions with the client, pre-search preparation, related work and follow-up work; in fact, the mean time spent in online searching itself was only 1.5 hours per week, or around 75 hours per year (Keenan and Hargreaves, 1980). A survey by the Online Information Centre in 1982 found that 76 per cent of British users spent 100 hours or less per year in online connect time (Deunette and Hall, 1983). More recently, in 1986, Aslib (the Association for Information Management) conducted a survey amongst its 1500 members in Britain which achieved a 24 per cent response rate. It revealed that 21 per cent spent less than 26 hours online per year and a further 18 per cent spent between 26 and 50 hours per year. Only just over 2 per cent of the Aslib respondents spent more than 200 hours per year online (Sippings, Ramsden and Turpie, 1987). American searchers may spend somewhat more connect time online; in 1985 the *Marquis Directory of Online Professionals* reported that 22 per cent of (mainly American) users searched more than 20 hours per month, that is, more than 240 hours per year (*Key Note Report,* 1987).

It is not too difficult to see why online searching should have been concentrated in the hands of professional intermediaries. Firstly, the early commercially available online databases were largely (though not exclusively) bibliographic, and therefore fell squarely within the domain of the library and the librarian, at whom they were primarily marketed. It is not surprising that the online terminals were located in the library alongside printed abstracting and indexing journals and were controlled and largely used by library staff; users were (and still often are) discouraged from conducting their own online searches as actively as they were encouraged to conduct their own searches of the printed equivalents.

Secondly, the majority of online search services used command languages with their own vocabulary and syntax (although menu-driven services are becoming more widely available). The searcher must learn a command language in order to communicate with the host computer. Furthermore, different services employ different command languages, and the searcher may need to gain a proficiency in several such languages to access databases scattered over several search services. Although such command languages are not very difficult to learn (see Chapters 4–6), some time must nevertheless be devoted to initial training, as well as to updating if the command languages themselves change (as many have in order to provide ever more sophisticated retrieval techniques). For the information specialist, getting to grips with command languages is a part of the job, but for others it is a time-consuming activity which must be slotted into a busy schedule.

Thirdly, the successful online searcher must not only be familiar with the subject scope of individual databases but also with their individual features: searchable and non-searchable fields; indexing policies; print formats, and so on. Anyone can acquire and maintain a familiarity with the idiosyncracies of different databases, but, again, this takes time and effort; in practice, the information professional is more likely to do this than end-users.

Fourthly, the successful searcher must be able to transform a search query into a coherent search strategy, and furthermore be capable of amending that strategy whilst online in the light of search results. Again, this is a skill which must be learnt and practised; it is not always easily grasped by the occasional searcher but should become second nature to the experienced intermediary.

Finally, and perhaps most persuasively, both online search services and the communication networks used to access these services have traditionally based most of their charges on connect time – the time spent by the searcher online to the host computer. This has placed a premium on quick and efficient searches by experienced practitioners rather than fumbling, uncertain and slow searches by occasional users who may be unfamiliar with the database, the search service, or both. The intermediary, in other words, would be expected to find information much more quickly than the end-user. This is likely to be an important factor whether the search costs are borne by the library or passed on to the client. In the former case, the library has a strong incentive to retain control over expenditure and insist that the search is done by one of its staff; in the latter case, the end-user might well prefer to use the skills of a professional intermediary who can keep online connect costs to a minimum.

Despite these points in favour of intermediary searching, some end-users have always conducted their own searches. This is particularly true in the case of numerical databases which have tended to be searched by scientists, economists, statisticians and managers rather than librarians or information scientists. End-user searching in this case can largely be explained by the need for subject expertise if these databases are to be properly exploited.

In all kinds of searching, of course, subject expertise is an essential ingredient. The selection of database and search terms as well as the assessment of retrieved data depend upon subject knowledge. Generally speaking, the end-user client is likely to have a better grasp of the subject than the librarian intermediary, and this applies to all kinds of database searching. It is a measure of the skills needed to search effectively on many online services that the skills of the intermediary have so often outweighed the greater subject knowledge of the client. In the case of numerical databases, however, it is often possible to process the raw data retrieved in the search by using, for example, correlation or forecasting software; this can only be done by a searcher who has a very clear idea of the uses to which the data are to be put as well as a knowledge of statistical or econometric techniques.

The growth in the number of numerical databases available online has undoubtedly increased the number of end-user searchers. A second factor has been the growth in the number of full-text databases; although bibliographic and referral databases – the traditional strongholds of the intermediary – remain very important, a growing number of records and searches fall into the numerical and full-text categories. Not only is the end-user familiar with the idea of looking through the printed versions of newspapers, journals and documents which might now be available online, but much of the publicity and marketing drive from their publishers is targetted at the end-user as well as or even at the expense of the information specialist.

Another factor encouraging end-user searching is the increasing availability of menu-driven search software rather than or as well as command-driven software (see Chapter 4). The end-user does not have to learn a command language but can make choices from a list (or menu) in order to conduct a search. Although such menu-driven services are often aimed specifically at the end-user and certainly do obviate the need to learn commands they still require some feel for information retrieval as well as being rather slow and tedious to use repeatedly.

End-user searching is also likely to increase with the growth of CD-ROM databases. Whittall (1989) reports on the searching of the LIFE SCIENCES database on CD-ROM at Beecham Pharmaceuticals Research Division by scientists ranging from project managers to junior technicians. Generally these end-users found it easy to use and appropriate for quick and easy searches for specific items of information.

It is also important to remember that online services are not working in a technological vacuum. Microcomputers are widely available at home, in school, in the office and laboratory and on the shopfloor. Locally-generated information, including bibliographic information, is stored on in-house databases and records from external databases can be downloaded and integrated with local data. All kinds of people are now used to searching on computers for data and can see no reason why a distinction should be made between local and external databases, especially when the same workstation can probably be used for both purposes. As Martin and Dutton (1985) remarked:

> Scientists who regularly use microcomputers for other purposes show a strong motivation to do their own literature searches. As microcomputers become more widely available within large organizations we expect this trend to expand to include managers, sales staff and many other traditional non-users of technical information services.

End-user familiarity with an in-house information retrieval system has been exploited in one experiment where special software (front-end software) is used to convert the commands of an in-house system (the Deco text storage and retrieval package) into the commands used by several major online services such as

Dialog and BRS. The scientists and engineers who already know how to use Deco can then search on these external services without the need to learn several new command languages (Teskey, Henry and Christopher, 1987). More will be said about such front-end software towards the end of this chapter.

These factors have undoubtedly encouraged a growth in end-user searching, further stimulated by sustained marketing campaigns by the online search services and database producers aimed at the potentially enormous end-user population. The Aslib survey mentioned earlier found that British library and information professionals in 1986 still carried out 91 per cent of online searches and only 11 per cent were done by end-users (Sippings, Ramsden and Turpie, 1987). It is interesting to note, however, that a survey of a similar target group in 1982 (Deunette and Hall, 1983) found that only 4 per cent of searches were done by end-users; in other words, although intermediary online searchers still predominate, end-user activity does appear to be increasing. Of the new users signed up in 1986 by one search service, Dialog, 80 per cent were reported as being end-users (*Key Note Report*, 1987).

Librarians as a whole reacted enthusiastically to the introduction of online services. It is perhaps surprising that a profession not renowned for its radical views should have accepted new technology so readily, but online services did offer librarians new opportunities. They made available to the smallest library or information unit the kind of information resources hitherto found only in the very largest collections. Furthermore, these sources could be searched in very sophisticated ways at high speeds. In general, librarians enjoyed carrying out online searches and they also believed that new technology was enhancing their professionalism and raising the status of the library or information service.

The current growth in end-user searching may pose a long-term threat to this sense of heightened professionalism. Faibisoff and Hurych (1981) note that "The concept of end-users searching online bibliographic databases touches many sensitive chords . . . [which] range from doubts that end-users can master the intricacies of searching to fears that librarians will no longer be needed if end-users undertake their own searches". Yet as Dutton (1987) has summed up, "Whatever the views of professional intermediaries on the desirability of end-user search, and these vary from enthusiasm to concern, the consensus is that it is here to stay".

In contrast with online searches, manual information searches have always been conducted by end-users as well as information professionals. In many cases the end-user is quite prepared to undertake a search through printed bibliographies, abstracting journals, periodicals, newspapers or whatever. In other cases, the information professional will encourage users to search the printed sources for themselves, perhaps after initially showing them where and how to look. But there are always those end-users who prefer someone else to do the search for them rather than spend their own time, or else call upon the special skills of a professional if the search proves difficult for them to undertake alone. There is no reason to suppose that the situation with online searches will be markedly different. The approach adopted will depend upon the circumstances and personalities involved. Some end-users will never be happy to hand over responsibility to an intermediary while others would cheerfully accept almost any search results rather than perform a search themselves. In the latter category, for example, might be found the managers at the Orion Royal Bank in London; it has been reported that they would rather spend their time analysing and manipulating data than searching databases. This decision was not taken because they found it too difficult to search online but because they preferred to delegate information work to the staff specially hired for the job; as the information manager expressed it, "although a manager knows how to make a coffee, he doesn't do it himself" (Nicholas, Erbach and Harris, 1987). In part, the attitude of the user can be accounted for by personality, but the particular context in which the search takes place, as Williams (1977) argued, also plays its part:

> At one extreme is the research worker who has been active in a particular subject for some time. He is well aware of the literature in his field and usually knows where he can find the answer to queries as they arise . . . He might well be quite reluctant to give responsibility for searching for references to an intermediary [although] . . . if a query arises in a peripheral or a new area, the advice of someone familiar with the literature sources is invaluable . . . At the other extreme is the manager . . . Characteristically he requires information rapidly, but the subjects of the queries may vary widely, making it very difficult for him to be sufficiently familiar with the specialist literature each time. These requirements are most easily met by using an intermediary.

End-user searching is likely to continue its expansion, but the role of the intermediary is unlikely to disappear. Attempts by end-users to conduct their own searches may lead in practice to an enhanced appreciation of the scope and complexity of the search process and hence to increased demand for intermediary searches

(Dutton, 1987). Witiak (1988) reports that end-users in her organization have a better appreciation of the capabilities and the limitations of online searching after attending an online workshop presented by the information staff, and if the end-users still prefer to have their online searches done by intermediaries, they are easier to work with than untrained users. Reporting on a project conducted in a medical library to introduce medical staff to online searching, Reed (1987) concludes:

> The library as a central resource of information can extend its role into one of a gateway to online databases . . . It should be emphasized that this does not replace the librarian, but is an enhancement of his role. Although most end-users wanted to continue conducting their own online searches, only a minority wanted to continue without some assistance from the librarian . . . If end-user online searching within the library becomes the norm then it may be necessary to train more library staff in online search skills.

It may be, though, that the intermediary has to become more specialized, dealing with those queries which baffle the client and which require the specialist skills of an information professional. To some extent Warr and Haygarth Jackson (1988) found this to be true in their large chemical company, although they do concede that "it is difficult to draw conclusions from searches that are never seen in the Information Unit". They add that chemists appreciate their limitations but "in many cases they are happy with a selection of leading references or a more restrictive search than the information scientist would have done".

There will also be new opportunities to set up and run both initial and update training programmes for end-users such as the one discussed by Steffen (1986), and to act as consultants, advising on such matters as database selection and strategy construction (the Unilever case study in Chapter 14 also provides an example of the information department playing a central role in the implementation of end-user searching).

Searcher Characteristics

What characteristics should be sought in a good online searcher? This question has exercised the minds of a surprisingly large number of observers. In fact, most of the characteristics which have been suggested (usually with the intermediary in mind, though many of them would equally apply to the end-user) are of a general nature; they would probably be considered highly desirable in most professions. Van Camp (1979), for example, suggests that the good searcher should have self-confidence, a logical and inquiring mind, common sense, a retentive memory, perseverance, patience, a good sense of humour, efficient work habits and be people-oriented. To these, Dolan (1979) has added flexibility of thinking together with basic spelling and grammar skills. These all seem admirable traits and accomplishments, and it would be difficult to argue very persuasively against any of them.

Bellardo (1985) has reviewed this extensive literature on searcher characteristics as well as looking at the findings of several research studies on searching performance. She argues for "caution and restraint" in discussions about what makes a good online searcher. Further, she recommends that "Educators, trainers, advisors, and supervisors responsible for staffing and training decisions should also be cautious in deciding who should search, and should provide encouragement even for those who might not appear at first to be suited to the task, particularly if they are highly motivated and interested".

The major conclusions that can be drawn from lists of ideal characteristics and studies into searcher behaviour are that online searching does require personal as well as technical attributes (such as knowledge of command languages or database organization, and keyboarding skills) and that it is by no means an easy task to carry out well. There are good and bad online searchers, and organizations employing searching intermediaries should select their personnel with care. They are the interface between the client and the system and no matter how sophisticated the search software or excellent the database, the results obtained are largely determined by the skills of the searcher. As in so many other areas, a good operator can to some extent compensate for poor facilities, but the best facilities are of little use in incompetent hands.

The Search Process

The process of conducting a search includes five stages:

1. Establishing the client's precise information request.
2. Choosing the information source(s).
3. Preparing the search.
4. Conducting the online search.

5. Presenting search results (in the case of a search by an intermediary).

All are important and it would be negligent to concentrate on the search itself at the expense of the other stages.

Establishing the information request

At the outset the intermediary must establish exactly what the client wants. As in other kinds of client–professional dialogue there is ample opportunity for misunderstanding and confusion. The literature of the reference interview as conducted at the library reference desk prior to manual searches is highly relevant (see especially Davinson, 1980; and Grogan, 1979) and highlights the many problems which the intermediary can encounter in establishing precisely what the client does want. Perhaps foremost among these problems is the tendency for a client to express a general request for information on a broad topic when in fact a very precise question lies behind this request (for example, the request might initially be for anything on musical instruments when the client really wants names and addresses of companies which manufacture high output pickups for bass guitars). The intermediary must demonstrate skills in asking the right questions as well as patience if the actual information request is to be correctly identified. The very powerful retrieval capabilities of online search systems make it especially important that the search is not conducted on a much broader topic than is really necessary lest a deluge of irrelevant information be retrieved.

The intermediary will not always be familiar with the subject area of the search, although ideally intermediaries should know at least something of the basic terminology and main information sources involved. In the absence of subject knowledge it is especially important that the intermediary establishes precisely what the client requires. Any temptation to hope for the best should be resisted; without a clear understanding of the topic the search cannot be successful, and it is better to admit ignorance at the interview than to reveal it when the search results are presented to the client. The wise intermediary would consult the client on suitable search terms (including synonyms for the client's initial suggestions) and any relevant references which could be located online in order to look at how they have been indexed (see the pearl growing search strategy in Chapter 6). Some clients may also be able to give advice about suitable databases on which the search might be conducted.

This initial stage should also be used to establish any other parameters which the client wishes to set. It is always useful to know whether a search should be confined to information produced in particular time periods, languages or forms of publication. The level of treatment should also be determined (specialist or popular) and the exhaustiveness or selectivity of the search. A strategy to retrieve a few, highly relevant, popular items may be very different from one aimed at a comprehensive search on technical data.

The pre-search preparation has a particularly vital role if the client is not to be present at the search itself (see below) but it should not be neglected just because the client is to attend the search. The intermediary should always have a clear idea of the query before planning the search strategy and going online. It is also worth emphasizing that end-user searchers must also decide upon the points outlined above even though in this case the 'interview' will take the form of self-questioning.

The interaction between the intermediary and the client can be catered for by a person-to-person interview during which all relevant points are discussed. Such interviews, incidentally, also offer opportunities for the information specialist to meet users and to publicize other information services. A bonus, in other words, can accrue in the form of a better understanding between the library or information unit and its users. Interviews, though, are demanding of time both for the intermediary and the client; Somerville (1977) estimates that anything from five minutes to an hour can be required, with the majority ranging from 20 to 40 minutes. Nevertheless, interviews are to be recommended whenever possible.

Alternatively, the interview can be conducted remotely by sending the client a search form to complete. This form should be easy for the client to understand and complete, and should collect all the information necessary to design a strategy for the subsequent search. Even when a personal interview is held, intermediaries may find an interview form useful; it can ensure that the interview has a structure and will remind the intermediary of the information which must be obtained. An example of such an interview form is given in the Case Study from Birmingham Public Libraries (see Appendix). Although it might seem reasonable to suppose that a personal interview between client and intermediary would produce a clearer idea of the former's information demand, this may not necessarily be the case. Evidence from a Medlars evaluation indicates that search results for those scientists who completed search forms and mailed them to the information unit were more effective than the results delivered to scientists who had been interviewed. As Lancaster (1979, pp. 149–150) reports, "this discovery was unexpected", suggesting as it does that scientists are able to communicate their information needs better in writing than in person.

End-user searching was discussed in an earlier section of this chapter. The intermediary would not hold a pre-search interview with clients who intend to do their own searches, but might instead use what Janke (1985) has called *pre-search counselling*. He defines this as "the process whereby a librarian, acting in a purely *advisory* role, assists the client searcher in devising his or her search strategy, before that searcher goes online". As in the pre-search interview, such a counselling session would be used by the information professional to define as clearly as possible the client's search topic. Unlike the pre-search interview, however, the counselling session is used to ensure that the client understands the steps required to perform the search, including the required commands and boolean operators. The client should be "heavily implicated at every step in the evolution of the search strategy". As Janke argues, the purpose of pre-search counselling is to encourage clients to run their own searches rather than resorting to an intermediary searcher. An alternative (or, indeed, a supplement) to the provision of such counselling is the organization of end-user online training courses, although such courses cannot be used to discuss problems arising from specific searches which are about to be undertaken.

Choosing information sources

The pre-search interview has one other very important task: to establish whether a search on an external online search service is indeed the best way of meeting the client's needs or whether it would be better to conduct the search in a different way – by using printed sources, databases on CD-ROM, or even by consulting informal sources. The wide range of information available online now means that many information queries can be answered from online sources. Nevertheless, some searches are more cheaply and even more quickly completed from printed sources if these are readily to hand. Many quick reference questions would fall into this category. Printed sources are also likely to provide a longer retrospective coverage than their online counterparts. If sufficient retrospective coverage is available online, however, then this medium is particularly attractive for retrospective searching because a search can be carried out in one step compared with the need to repeat the search in successive issues of a printed source.

It is normally possible to search online using free-text terms as well as or instead of assigned index terms. This can prove a distinct advantage. Free-text terms are particularly useful when new terminology is being used which may not have entered indexing languages or in subjects where concepts cannot easily be represented by a set of index terms, no matter how well chosen. Printed sources can be browsed (an approach which is virtually impossible online) but this method of free-text searching is time-consuming and rather hit and miss. Usually it is necessary to search a printed source for a specific item of information by using its indexes, where reliance must be placed upon the accuracy and reliability of the index terms.

It is normally relatively straightforward when online searching to combine a variety of search concepts (for example, several subject terms plus the language or literary form in which the retrieved data must be presented). This is much more difficult and certainly more laborious to do in printed sources. Online searches, then, can be more specific than manual searches.

In some cases the online database may be more up-to-date than its printed equivalent, but this is not necessarily the case. Often both forms are updated simultaneously, although postal transmission may delay the receipt of the printed copy (it has not been unknown, of course, for technical problems to hold up the appearance of the online version).

Finally, an increasing number of online databases do not have printed equivalents (for example, ABI/INFORM, CHEMICAL BUSINESS NEWSBASE and BIS INFOMAT) and in other cases the online version is not identical with its print counterpart (as with PSYCINFO which contains additional records not available in its print equivalent, *Psychological Abstracts*).

A number of studies have been made to compare online and manual retrieval systems. One of them, undertaken by Johnston and Gray (1977), investigated several agricultural information sources. They found that manual searches tended to have higher precision than online searches of the same data, with online searches tending to have higher relative recall. In fact, high recall was best achieved by using both printed and online sources. They concluded that the differences in retrieval performance were due to differences in entry points available for searching between the printed and the online versions and that these differences were peculiar to each source: "The key to choosing between manual and computer searching of a particular database lies in detailed knowledge of the difference in entry points between the two forms of the database, and of the ease of expressing the concepts of the search in terms of these entry points".

Increasingly it will also be necessary to choose between an online search on a remote database and an in-house search of the same data on CD-ROM. Although the number of databases available online still far exceeds that on CD-ROM, the latter are proliferating and many of them are already available online. It should be noted, however, that the retrospective coverage might not be identical on the two media (in particular, despite the impressive storage capacity of a CD-ROM – currently 550 megabytes or about 200 000 pages of A4 text – the larger databases are still too big to fit on just one disc). Furthermore, online databases can be much more easily updated than CD-ROM databases (which is not to say that this necessarily happens). Information which requires very frequent updating (like news wire services) is therefore better suited to online whereas more static information (such as might be found in an encyclopaedia) is eminently suitable for CD-ROM.

The high annual subscription costs of CD-ROMs will probably ensure that only those databases likely to get heavy use will be purchased. Searches on the less commonly used databases will still be carried out on remote search services where payment is by usage. Where an organization has access to a database both online and on CD-ROM the latter is likely to be selected just because incremental usage does not add to costs once the disc has been purchased. The fact that response time on CD-ROM is typically somewhat slower than on a remote service is unlikely to outweigh the financial incentive to use the in-house system. CD-ROM also eliminates the need to cope with the uncertainties of telecommunication networks. As regards retrieval facilities, CD-ROMs typically offer menu-driven searching (sometimes at several levels of sophistication) as well as or instead of command-driven searching. On-screen, context-sensitive help is also frequently available on demand to simplify the searcher's task. CD-ROM is therefore likely to prove particularly attractive to end-users.

Search preparation

Once the intermediary has a clear idea of the client's information needs, suitable database(s) and service(s) can be selected. The client may have suggested one or more databases, but the intermediary should also draw upon personal experience of online sources as well as database directories and online indexes. There is no point in choosing databases which are only available on services for which no password is held or which are unfamiliar to the searcher. Some databases, of course, are loaded on several services in which case a choice of search service must also be made. Factors such as familiarity with the command language, search software facilities, telecommunications and database connect costs, and quality of support documentation and help desk should all be taken into account when making this choice.

The strategy to be used in the search can now be worked out. The searcher must decide whether to use controlled or uncontrolled terms; if the former are chosen then any available printed thesauri should be consulted. Even if the search is to use natural language terms it might be worthwhile looking in a thesaurus to identify synonyms and to suggest broader and narrower terms. The search terms should then be assembled using the correct boolean operators (see Chapters 4–6). It is also a good idea to think at this stage of alternative strategies which can quickly be employed if the search results are initially unsatisfactory. The searcher must strike a balance between underpreparation and overpreparation. Whilst it is very unwise to embark upon an online search without an initial strategy, the interactive nature of online systems cannot be exploited if the searcher remains too inflexibly tied to a prepared strategy which is implemented willy-nilly, regardless of results.

The online search

The online search itself is described in other chapters and will not therefore be discussed here. One preliminary decision which must be taken, however, is whether the intermediary should conduct the search in the presence or absence of the client. There is much to be said for the client being present in order to evaluate results as they appear and to help in any readjustment of the initial strategy. In some cases, of course, the client may be too busy to attend, and in other cases the personal preferences of one or both of the participants may suggest that a search by the intermediary alone would be the better choice.

Presentation of search results

The final stage in the search process is to present the client with the results. A printout of the search output can be produced as the search takes place; this printout can then simply be handed over to the client. Alternatively, if a microcomputer with suitable software is used to carry out the search it is possible to download the entire search on to the storage medium (hard disc, floppy disc, etc.) used by the microcomputer. This offers the advantage that the search can now be edited using a word-processing package before it is delivered to the client. Unwanted parts can be deleted; for example, search command statements can be removed to leave only the retrieved records, or duplicate records (the same record retrieved from two or more databases) can be eliminated. It is also possible to annotate the results; in the case of a bibliographic search, for example, an indication can be given of whether or not the retrieved citations are to be found locally in the library or must be requested through interlibrary loans.

The presentation of results also provides an opportunity to gain oral or written feedback from the client on the efficacy of the search. This is especially important if the client was not present during the actual search. The intermediary should always try to establish the success or otherwise of the search; if the results are not entirely successful the client may be able to shed light on the source of the problem and suggest new approaches to be taken in a follow-up search. Customer satisfaction is the ultimate test of a service, and the intermediary should be prepared not only to listen to (or read) search evaluations but also to learn from them.

Hardware and Software Search Aids

A series of barriers impedes the exploitation of online search services, including complicated log-on procedures to communication networks and computers, multiplicity of command languages and complexities in the retrieval process. In an endeavour to reduce, if not eliminate, these barriers, a variety of tools have been provided by the database producers, the search services, user groups, library schools and so on.

One of the major ways of breaking down barriers to online use – training courses (including self-instructional software) – is discussed in Chapter 9 and will not therefore be considered in this chapter. Concern here is rather with the hardware and software developments which are intended to make online searching simpler, especially for the end-user who is less willing than the intermediary to persevere with complicated and inconsistent procedures.

Hardware

The need to learn a command language before an online search can be conducted is a deterrent to searching, especially for end-users who might be reluctant to invest time in mastering the necessary vocabulary and syntax. One answer to this problem, chosen by a few online search services, is to provide dedicated workstations with keyboards specifically designed to simplify the search process: individual keys are assigned specific retrieval functions. To take one example, Mead Data Central offers a dedicated workstation from which to search LEXIS, a full-text legal database (although since 1985 it has also been possible to use an IBM or compatible microcomputer with suitable software). Mead specifically intended LEXIS to be used by lawyers rather than information intermediaries, and saw the design of dedicated hardware as a way of simplifying searching. The LEXIS terminal has many special function keys such as 'print case', 'next page' or 'prev doc' which eliminate the need to type command statements (when accessing LEXIS through a personal computer the special functions are duplicated by using dot commands such as .np for next page or .pd for previous document). Part of the undoubted success achieved by LEXIS in attracting end-user searchers can be attributed to the simplified access offered by such a dedicated workstation (Gray, 1988). The case study of the accountancy firm, Binder Hamlyn, in the Appendix provides another example of end-users' positive reactions to simplified searching via a dedicated workstation; although employees at Binder Hamlyn are encouraged to do their own searching on all online services, only Textline is much used, and this is the only one available to them which uses a dedicated workstation. In an investigation of end-user online searching in the financial institutions of the City of London, Nicholas, Erbach and Harris (1987) found that Textline was probably the most popular of the services offered and that one of the reasons for this popularity was its dedicated workstation "with function keys doing all the hard work".

Software

A different way of simplifying online searching, again usually with the end-user very much in mind, is through software rather than hardware provision. This has taken a number of different forms. In some cases the online search service itself has tried to simplify its search software; a remote intermediary assistance service has provided software to simplify searching and to log the user on to an actual search service; or software has been designed (in some cases by a search service) for installation on the user's local microcomputer where it acts as a front-end interface between the user and the remote online search service.

The online search services have adopted two major strategies to assist users who are logged on to their host computers. The first has been to persist in the use of a command language but to simplify the language, usually by reducing it to a subset containing only the most important and basic commands. Dialog, for example, has introduced a service aimed specifically at home users. This service, called Knowledge Index, provides evening and weekend access at a reduced cost to just some (but the most frequently used) of Dialog's databases. The searcher must still learn a few Dialog commands as well as how to use boolean operators, but assistance can be obtained online by typing HELP followed by the appropriate command or facility. The drawback here is that the user must still grapple with the problems of commands, albeit with a smaller number than a full Dialog user, as well as the mechanics of constructing and implementing a search. The advantages are that the repetitiveness of menu-driven systems is avoided and response time is generally faster.

The second strategy adopted by the online search services has been to eliminate the need to learn a command language at all by replacing it with menu-driven searching. BRS/After Dark is an example of a service largely based on such a menu-driven approach. In this case the searcher works through a series of menus, at each stage selecting one option from a number of choices until the desired search strategy has been executed. Although menus obviate the need to learn command languages, they are slow (and therefore expensive) to use and can become tedious with repeated usage. A fuller discussion of menu-driven retrieval systems is provided in Chapter 4. A simplified command language offers the advantage that time and patience are not expended in working through several levels of menu, but expects some learning effort by the user. The menu approach offers users the advantage that they do not have to learn any commands, but they must then tolerate a slow and inflexible service. Neither, in other words, is entirely satisfactory.

A number of gateways now exist between different search services. For example, PFDS and ESA-IRS operate a gateway service between their two systems. It is only necessary to sign a contract with one of them. Using the assigned password, the other service can be accessed via the contracting service. Similarly, only one bill will be received from the contracting host even if the user has carried out searches using both services. Such a gateway undoubtedly simplifies the management and accessing of online services (see Chapter 9) but does not help the user overcome the major problem of multiple command languages. The user of the PFDS/ESA-IRS gateway, for example, must learn both command languages in order to use databases on both host computers.

A remote intelligent gateway service provides a different solution to that offered by the search services. In this case the user logs on initially not to an online search service but to the gateway service's computer which in turn connects the user to a suitable online service.

EasyNet, offered by the American company, Telebase Systems, is one example of such a service which provides access to around 12 major online search services (EasyNet can be accessed from Britain via InfoSearch, a service of Istel Ltd based in Redditch). Once logged on to the EasyNet computer the user is given the choice of EasyNet I, II or III.

EasyNet I offers extensive help to the novice searcher who on logging on to the service is presented with a series of menus which first of all identify the database on which the search is to be conducted. Access cannot be obtained to all the databases on the search services but the main database in any particular subject area is included (currently 163 databases are available). Next the user enters the search topic and is helped to construct a search strategy. EasyNet then translates the strategy into the command language of the search service it has selected and logs on to that service (if the database is available on several services EasyNet shares searches amongst the different services in turn). After the search is completed and the data downloaded to EasyNet's computers, the user is logged off from the search service (but not from EasyNet). Only the first 10 or 15 records retrieved in the search are downloaded; once the user has viewed them it is possible to ask for the next 10 or do another search. In either case EasyNet must then reconnect to the search service, upload the strategy once more and subsequently download the retrieved data.

EasyNet II enables the more experienced searcher to go directly to any of the hundreds of databases available on the various search services accessed via the EasyNet gateway (users of EasyNet II benefit because they only need sign up with EasyNet and receive just one bill from it no matter how many search services are used).

EasyNet III permits searching on most of the EasyNet databases/ search services using one command language based on the European Common Command Language (CCL). This offers a common terminology for the basic search operations available on most of the search services. EasyNet then rapidly converts the CCL commands into the search service's own language.

Commenting on EasyNet, O'Leary (1988) admits that "there are many kinds of highly sophisticated searches which it cannot handle". He adds, however, that it is intended "to provide both end-users and professional searchers with options which most now lack – for end-users to get powerful searching capabilities otherwise available only to professionals, and for professional searchers to do expert searching on [search services] otherwise unavailable to them". EasyNet, then, offers considerable benefits to all users, and especially to the novice. It employs clever and sophisticated software which removes much of the burden from the inexperienced searcher. Yet it cannot really match the skills of a proficient human intermediary. One evaluation of end-user searching on EasyNet (Larsen, 1987) has commented upon a number of common problems encountered during searching. In particular users found it difficult to know what to do when the search results were poor. Instead of modifying their strategy they often concluded that no information was available on the topic. At the same time, the evaluation did find that "even in the cases where the quality of participants' search results seemed to be rather poor from a professional searcher's point of view, the users were satisfied". In other words, end-users may often be content as long as some relevant information is found; they remain blissfully ignorant of the additional data which a professional might have found. An evaluation of EasyNet via its British gateway, InfoSearch, found that for fairly simple searches it could produce the same results as going direct to the hosts but at a higher cost (Buxton, 1988). It concluded:

> Organizations making frequent use of online information will
> probably find it more economical to use a trained intermediary
> for searching . . . Its main value is probably giving access to
> hosts needed only very occasionally.

So far the software developments discussed have all been implemented on remote mainframe computers to which the user must connect via a telecommunication network. Growing numbers of software packages are now available, however, for the user's own microcomputer which simplify online searching in several ways. In addition to making the microcomputer behave like a terminal (terminal emulator), many communications packages can be purchased which will store and send the long alpha-numeric strings required to log-on to data communication networks and online search services (see Chapter 9). Some packages enable the user to prepare a search offline and then rapidly upload it to the search service after log-on. This reduces the stress and costs of keying the search strategy whilst online but also retains the interactive properties of online searching because the prepared strategy can be interrupted and amended if necessary. Any results from the search can then be downloaded to the microcomputer's disc for subsequent offline use.

Communications software simplifies connection to a host computer but does not assist the user in the actual construction of the strategy. Other *gateway software* is available, however, which attempts to remedy this shortcoming by providing easy access to remote services. This software is installed in front of the actual search software to act as an interface between the host computer and the searcher and is therefore often called *front-end* software. A useful discussion of such software is provided by Hawkins and Levy (1985). It would be possible to mount such front-ends on the search service's mainframe computer but in practice most of these packages are designed for the searcher's microcomputer and are menu-driven.

Some front-end microcomputer software, such as Sci-Mate, can be used to search on several services. Other front-end microcomputer software has been produced by a particular search service for use only with its service. An example of such a package is WilSearch, produced by the H.W. Wilson company for use with its WilsonLine online search service. WilSearch guides users in the selection of databases and helps with the preparation of a search strategy by, for example, automatically inverting personal names and right-hand truncating Dewey classification numbers. The user is then automatically logged on to WilsonLine, the search executed and the user asked how many of the retrieved records are wanted. These are downloaded after which WilSearch disconnects from WilsonLine. The records are then displayed locally one at a time and the user prompted to indicate whether they are relevant. Finally, the subject headings from all the relevant records are displayed as possible terms to use in a follow-up search (Janke, 1988).

Despite the impressive sophistication of WilSearch (and similar packages) it can no more replicate an experienced human searcher than EasyNet. Unless very simple subject searches are conducted, the user will still be required to exercise considerable skills in the construction of the search strategy despite all the help WilSearch can offer (O'Leary, 1986).

Front-end search software can make a valuable contribution to online searching, particularly for end-users who do not wish to devote time and energy to training courses. It is important, however, to appreciate current shortcomings and to evaluate carefully all such packages. As Levy (1984) suggests, they should be considered in terms of ease of use, existence of cost and time saving features, the extent to which they exploit the range of search capabilities available on the actual search services and the utility of any auxiliary programs (such as the capability to create in-house databases provided by micro-DISCLOSURE or on-screen help and a short training program on Sci-Mate).

Teskey, Henry and Christopher (1987) point out, furthermore, that easy access to online services is only achieved at the price of restricting the type of searching and level of interaction that the user can achieve: "We believe that for many professional users, these restrictions will be unacceptable". They argue that not only the intermediary but even end-users (for whom front-end software is primarily designed) who already search in-house retrieval systems will miss facilities like truncation and field searching which are available on many in-house retrieval packages as well as on external retrieval services but which cannot be used on those external services via most front-end software packages.

Although front-end software has been quite successful at automating what Hawkins (1988) calls "the mechanical portion of the search process" it has left virtually untouched the potentially much more troublesome intellectual area of search strategy construction. As Fenichel (1981) has argued, "Research has shown that for both experienced and inexperienced searchers the major problems are not with the mechanics of the system command language but with search strategy". Yet packages like EasyNet typically stop at the point where the user needs guidance in the formulation of a strategy, merely requesting the user to enter the strategy rather than offering any help on how this might be done.

It is the difficulty of designing front-end software which can convert the novice searcher's request into an effective online strategy which has stimulated interest in expert systems as a possible solution. A well-known example is CANSEARCH, a rule-based expert system written in Prolog and developed by Pollitt (1986). CANSEARCH enables medical practitioners to search the literature of cancer therapy by interaction with an expert system front-end. Such expert systems tend to operate in very limited domains (for example CANSEARCH interacts only with the MEDLINE database and only contains knowledge about one subject – cancer therapy) and are only now beginning to pass from research prototypes to commercial products.

One product being marketed for searchers in the electrical, electronic and communication technology industries, Tome Searcher, applies an expert system to elicit information from the user about the search objectives. In particular, a set of questions is posed to the user even before the query is input in order to clarify eight points (Vickery, 1988):

1. Is the user an experienced or first-time user?
2. Is the ensuing search to be by author or subject?
3. Should a subject search be limited in any way (by date, language, document type, treatment)?
4. Should it be precise or broad?
5. How many items should the search aim at?
6. What output format is required?
7. Should the results be printed or downloaded?
8. What databases should be searched?

Tome Searcher then accepts a natural language expression of the query, asks the user for clarification if necessary, develops a search strategy and modifies it in accordance with its probable hit rate before going online. Tome Searcher then logs on to the search service, chooses the database(s) according to requirements, uploads the search, offers the user an option to browse the retrieved records, downloads any required records and logs off.

In Search Example 8.1 Tome Searcher has converted a natural language request for information about 'The use of optical fibre in local area networks but not in Ethernet' into a search strategy and has added the correct commands for a search on INSPEC using ESA-IRS. It has taken account of the variant spellings (fibre/

fiber), the abbreviation of local area network (LAN), used truncation, inserted the correct operators and overriden operator priority by the correct use of brackets. It has also limited the occurrence of terms to the title field (as instructed by the user at the set-up stage). In this instance, all the retrieved records seem relevant (only three of which are included in Search Example 8.1), although it cannot be assumed that all search requests will be handled so successfully.

BEGIN 8
```
--------17Feb89   11:57:49   User0999--
      0.03 AU 0.18 Minutes in File   32
      0.03 AU approx Total
File    8:INSPEC:1969-89,06
SET  ITEMS     DESCRIPTION (+=OR;*=AND;-=NOT)
----  --------  --------------------------------------------
```
? F (NETWORK+NETWORKS)*(OPTICAL FIBRE?+OPTICAL FIBER?)* (LOCAL AREA+LAN+LANS)
```
  1  94202    NETWORK
  2  78610    NETWORKS
  3  20052    OPTICAL(W)FIBRE?
  4   7639    OPTICAL(W)FIBER?
  5   8424    LOCAL(W)AREA
  6   4031    LAN
  7   1700    LANS
  8    850    (1+2)*(3+4)*(5+6+7)
```
? F ETHERNET
```
  9   1365    ETHERNET
```
? F 8-9
```
 10    788    8-9
```
? L10/TI
```
 11     31    10/TI
```
? T11/4/1-31

```
              TYPE 11/4/1
B89018968, C89014200 INSPEC Conference Paper Issue 8906
89059309
Applications of plastic optical fiber to local area networks
   Scholl, F.W.; Coden, M.H.; Anderson, S.; Dutt, B.
   Codenoll Technol. Corp., Yonkers, NY, USA
   FOC/LAN '88 Proceedings. The Twelfth International Fiber Optic
Communications and Local Area Networks Exposition
   Atlanta, GA, USA 12-16 Sept. 1988
   1988, p.338-43, 3 Refs, Country of Publ.: USA
   Publisher: Inf. Gatekeepers. Boston, MA, USA
   Pages: xix+349
```

Berube, R.; Mahoney, P.; Polishuk, P. (Editors)
Treatment: A (APPLICATIONS); P (PRACTICAL)

Gives a review of each of the communications systems components. Following this the authors describe the LAN applications in which POF seems most likely to contribute. Since costs are important, comparison will be made between present-day glass fiber LANs and projected costs for POF systems. The view for future systems is that POF will dominate in the most cost sensitive areas, predominently short distance applications, whereas glass fiber systems will be favored for applications requiring longer distance between DTEs

Classification Codes: B6260 ; B4125 ; B6210L ; B0560 ; C5620L
Controlled Terms: local area networks ; optical fibres ; optical links ; plastics
Uncontrolled Terms: plastic optical fiber ; local area networks ; LAN ; costs ; short distance applications

TYPE 11/4/2
B89011470, C89007887 INSPEC Conference Paper Issue 8904
89036541
Optical fiber multichannel local area networks
Camarda, P.; Castagnolo, B.; Leaci, G.
Dept. of Comput. Sci., California Univ., Los Angeles, CA, USA,
IEEE International Conference on Communications '88: Digital Technology – Spanning the Universe. Conference Record (Cat. No.88CH2538–7)
Philadelphia, PA, USA 12–15 June 1988
1988 p.1514–18 vol.3. 13 Refs. CCCC: CH2538–7/88/0000–1514$01.00.
Country of Publ.: USA
Publisher: IEEE. New York, NY, USA.
Pages: 3 vol. xxx+1783
Sponsor: IEEE
Treatment: T (THEORETICAL/MATHEMATICAL)

The throughput and average delay for a fiber-optic multichannel local area network (LAN) is derived. This system, which can be seen as an extension of the classical single-channel local area networks, provides fault tolerance and reliability as well as better capacity and throughput characteristics than single-channel networks. The average system delay is smaller only at high load and larger at low load. Expressnet and Fasnet, two round-robin protocols specifically designed for unidirectional systems, are considered in detail for nongated sequential service (NGSS). The developed analysis is easily extended to any round-robin protocol

Classification Codes: B6260 ; B6210L ; B6150 ; C5620L
Controlled Terms: local area networks ; optical links ; protocols

Uncontrolled Terms: optical fibre multichannel LAN ; local area networks ; throughput ; average delay ; fault tolerance ; reliability ; capacity ; throughput ; system delay ; Expressnet ; Fasnet ; round-robin protocols ; nongated sequential service

TYPE 11/4/3
B88067436, C88058095 INSPEC Conference Paper Issue 8822
88217498
Low loss optical fiber system and cost optimization for local area networks
Das, A.K.; Mandal, A.K.; Banerjee, S.; Ganguly, A.K.
ETCE Dept., Jadavpur Univ., Calcutta, India
WESCANEX 88: Digital Communications Conference Proceedings (Cat. No.88CH2595–7)
Saskatoon, Sask., Canada 11–12 May 1988
1988, p.129–34, 18 Refs, CCCC: CH2595–7/88/0000–0129$01.00, Country of Publ.: USA
Publisher: IEEE. New York, NY, USA
Pages: v+182
Sponsor: IEEE
Treatment: P (PRACTICAL); T (THEORETICAL/MATHEMATICAL)
The authors describe processes for minimizing the insertion losses for biconical fiber couplers used as optical switches or Tee or directional couplers. Also described are ways to minimize the joining losses in local area networks. Empirical formulas are derived for the cost of optical fiber, transmitter, and receivers as functions of their dependent parameters

Classification Codes: B6260 ; B4125 ; B6210L ; B0260 ; C5620L ; C1180
Controlled Terms: local area networks ; optical couplers ; optical fibres ; optical links ; optical losses ; optimisation
Uncontrolled Terms: low loss optical fibre system ; cost optimization ; local area networks ; insertion losses ; biconical fiber couplers ; optical switches ; directional couplers ; joining losses
: : :
? **LOGOFF**

Search Example 8.1   *Tome Searcher (only 3 of the 31 records actually retrieved have been reproduced here)*

One of the problems involved in the design of expert systems for online searching, as Kehoe (1985) points out, is "the lack of extensive knowledge gathered from experts about how they search". Whether gratifying or disappointing, the human expert still seems to have the edge over existing software when it comes to retrieving specific information from large databases.

References

Bellardo, T. (1985) What do we really know about online searchers? *Online Review*, **9** (3), 223–239

Buxton, A. B. (1988) A quantitative evaluation of Infosearch multi-host access (EasyNet). *Online Information 88: 12th International Online Information Meeting Proceedings*, pp. 715–722. Oxford: Learned Information

Davinson, D. E. (1980) *Reference Service*, Chapter 6. London: Bingley

Deunette, J. and Hall, S. (1983) *1982 Survey of UK Online Users: A Report On Current Online Usage*. London: Online Information Centre

Dolan, D. R. (1979) The quality control of search analysts. *Online*, **3** (2), 8–16

Dutton, B. (1987). End-user online search. *Aslib Information*, **15** (11/12), 284–285

Faibisoff, S. G. and Hurych, J. (1981) Is there a future for the end user in online bibliographic searching? *Special Libraries*, **72** (4), 347–355

Fenichel, C. H. (1981) Online searching: measures that discriminate among users with different types of experiences. *Journal of the American Society for Information Science*, **32** (1), 23–32

Gray, R. (1988) Law: British and European legal systems. In *Manual of Online Search Strategies*, edited by C. J. Armstrong and J. A. Large, pp. 507–536. Aldershot: Gower

Grogan, D. J. (1979) *Practical Reference Work*, Chapter 4. London: Bingley

Hawkins, D. T. (1988) Applications of artificial intelligence (AI) and expert systems for online searching. *Online*, **12**(1), 31–43

Hawkins, D. T. and Levy, L. R. (1985) Front end software for online database searching. Part 1: definitions, system features and evaluation. *Online*, **9** (6), 30–37

Henry, W. M. *et al.* (1980) *Online Searching: An Introduction*. London: Butterworths

Janke, R. V. (1985) Presearch counseling for client searchers (end-users). *Online*, **9**(5), 13–26

Janke, R. V. (1988) Systems and databases for home and office use. In *Manual of Online Search Strategies*, edited by C. J. Armstrong and J. A. Large, pp. 679–715. Aldershot: Gower

Johnston, S. M. and Gray, D. E. (1977) Comparison of manual

and online retrospective searching for agricultural subjects: *Aslib Proceedings*, **29** (7), 253–258

Keenan, S. and Hargreaves, P. (1980) A profile of the online intermediary. *Proceedings of the 4th International Online Information Meeting*, pp. 181–186. Oxford: Learned Information

Kehoe, C. A. (1985) Interfaces and expert systems for online retrieval. *Online Review*, **9** (6), 489–505

Key Note Report (1987) *Online Databases: An Industry Sector Overview*, 3rd edn. London: Key Note Publications

Lancaster, F. W. (1979) *Information Retrieval Systems: Characteristics, Testing and Evaluation*, 2nd edn. New York: Wiley

Larsen, G. (1987) Searching the intelligent gateway EasyNet – the end-user's point of view. *Electronic Library*, **5** (3), 146–151

Levy, L. R. (1984) Gateway software: is it for you? *Online*, **8** (6), 67–79

Martin, J. F. and Dutton, B. G. (1985) Online end-user training: experiences in a large industrial organisation. *Program*, **19** (4), 351–358

Nicholas, D., Erbach, G. and Harris, K. (1987) End-users: threat, challenge or myth? *Aslib Proceedings*, **39** (11/12), 337–344

O'Leary, M. (1986) WilSearch: a new departure for an old institution. *Online*, **10** (2), 102–107

O'Leary, M. (1988) EasyNet revisited: pushing the online frontier. *Online*, **12**(5), 22–30

Pollitt, S. (1987) CANSEARCH: an expert systems approach to document retrieval. *Information Processing and Management*, **23** (2), 119–138

Reed, S. (1987), "Where's the lady with the toy?": implementation of an end-user project. In *Online Information Retrieval in Practice*, edited by Linda Dorrington, pp. 3–11. London: Taylor Graham

Sippings, G., Ramsden, H. and Turpie, G. (1987) *The Use of Information Technology by Information Services: The Aslib Information Technology Survey 1987*. London: Aslib

Somerville, A. N. (1977) The place of the reference interview in computer searching: the academic setting. *Online*, **1** (4), 14–23

Steffen, S. S. (1986) College faculty goes online: training faculty end users. *Journal of Academic Librarianship*, **12** (3), 147–151

Teskey, N., Henry, M. and Christopher, S. (1987) A user interface for multiple retrieval systems. *Online Review*, **11** (5), 283–289

Van Camp, A. (1979) Effective search analysts. *Online*, **3** (2), 18–20

Vickery, A. (1988) The experience of building expert search systems. *Online Information 88: 12th International Online Information Meeting Proceedings*, pp. 301–313. Oxford: Learned Information

Warr, W. A. and Haygarth Jackson, A. R. (1988) End-user searching of CAS ONLINE: results of a cooperative experiment between Imperial Chemical Industries and Chemical Abstracts Service. *Journal of Chemical Information and Computer Science*, **28** (2), 68–72

Whittall, J. (1989) CD-ROM in a specialist environment. *Proceedings of the Third Annual Conference on Small Computers in Libraries, London, February 1989*, pp. 119–121. London: Meckler

Williams, P. W. (1977) The role and cost effectiveness of the intermediary. *Proceedings of the 1st International Online Information Meeting*, pp. 53–63. London: Learned Information

Witiak, J. (1988) What is the role of the intermediary in end-user training? *Online*, **12**(5), 50–52

Chapter 9

Management Aspects of Using External Search Services

Introduction

Previous chapters have discussed the process of online searching. This chapter seeks to examine the management aspects of using external search services. Management considerations fall into three broad areas and the chapter is divided accordingly: firstly, issues relating to the planning for and implementation of online searching within an organization; secondly considerations relating to the smooth operation of online searching facilities and finally the very important subject of education and training for the use of online search services. Whilst the discussion focuses on the management issues relating to the searching of external databases in libraries, many of the issues raised in this chapter will have to be addressed by anyone using external databases regardless of the organizational context.

Planning and Implementation

The need to use external search services

Before proceeding further, it is important to be certain that online searching is appropriate for the needs of the organization. Is access to external search services the most appropriate way to satisfy an information need or could it be more appropriately solved by printed sources or CD-ROM? Does access to external databases meet a real need of the organization or extend the services which that organization seeks to provide? Clearly the answer to these questions must be an unequivocal *yes* before further planning and preparation is undertaken. The wide and expanding range of material available online was indicated in Chapter 7 and the major directories from which more information about online sources can be gained were noted in that chapter.

The choice of databases and online search services

Having decided to make use of online search services, an early decision must be taken about which databases and therefore which search services are most likely to be used. It is possible that the use of some search services may require specialized equipment for their adequate exploitation. For example, it is necessary to have a particular type of terminal or terminal emulator software to take advantage of the chemical structure search and display facilities offered by search services CAS ONLINE or by the DARC system on Télésystèmes-QUESTEL. A further alternative may be to gain access through gateway services such as EasyNet which was discussed in Chapter 8.

The decision about which online search services to use will be determined by a number of factors. Obviously it is necessary to use a search service or services which provide access to those databases which it is known are to be used. The range of databases available on the various search services should be considered. Frequently once searching begins, a wider range of databases will be utilized than had originally been envisaged. This is particularly the case where bibliographic databases are being accessed. Thus it is sensible to ensure that the search services with which contracts are signed initially, provide access to a wide range of databases. It is for this reason, amongst others, that the so-called supermarket search services such as Dialog are so popular. Other factors to be taken into account when deciding upon search services include:

1. The cost of using the required databases, including the cost of connect time and print charges and any relevant discount arrangements.
2. The number of years' data which is available online.
3. The quality of the documentation.
4. The facilities provided by the command languages, for example, variations in the boolean search capabilities or the manner in which word proximity searching is provided.
5. Help and training facilities offered by the search service.
6. The way that required databases have been made available on

different search services, for example, variations in the manner in which the basic index has been constructed.

7. The quality and reliability of the telecommunications link.

It should be noted that in any attempt to judge the differing costs of accessing the various search services, the appropriate tele-communications and telephone charges must be considered as well as the costs for connect time and information display. Communications costs may vary considerably both between and within countries.

Increasingly the online search services are extending the range of facilities and services offered to their customers. Thus user-friendly interfaces for inexperienced searchers such as BRS/Menus or the reduced and simplified command language offered by Dialog's Knowledge Index, electronic mail facilities and online document ordering are now available on a number of search services. In some cases, the presence of such additional services may be helpful and should be taken into account in deciding with which search service a contract should be signed.

All these points can be considered and their relative importance taken into account when one has gained some experience of online searching. Making an informed decision and accurately assessing the factors set out above may be very difficult for the newcomer to online searching. The decision may well be aided by discussion with more experienced practitioners. Such people can usually be contacted through local, regional or national online user groups or possibly through a national online centre. A very useful guide to starting online searching is given by Turpie (1988).

Telecommunications access

Once arrangements have been made to sign contracts with appropriate search services then similar arrangements must be made to gain access to the relevant national telecommunications network(s). In the corporate environment such access may already be available as a part of the organizational information technology infrastructure. Unless the organization has a direct link to the national data communications network(s), arrangements must be made to dial the nearest access points (or nodes) of that service. Thus the installation of a telephone is essential. It may be considered desirable that a direct line is installed for online searching. This has the advantage that calls and therefore searches do not pass through a switchboard and are less likely to be cut-off. On the other hand if the searching is performed through the organizational telephone system then the cost of telephone calls to the data communications network may well be lost in the corporate telephone bill. In either event it is sensible to have a line solely for online searching so that incoming calls are not interrupted.

Workstations

Once an initial choice of search services has been made then a choice of equipment for online searching can be made although it should be noted that increasingly this is already in place for other applications. The minimum equipment necessary is a workstation, and if necessary a telephone line and modem. In the early days of online searching, the workstations used were almost exclusively dumb terminals whilst nowadays the workstations are almost exclusively microcomputers. Some helpful guidance on the requirements for an online searcher's workstation has been provided by Huffmann and Leigh (1986). Typical prices are from £500 upwards.

It is necessary to use a microcomputer with either twin floppy disc drives or a hard disc. Whilst the former is adequate, the latter gives greater scope for downloading and local processing of search output. A printer is essential for creating a paper copy of the search. A wide range of printer types, for example dot-matrix, daisywheel and laser printer, are available at a wide range of prices (£200 to £2000). It is helpful to use a printer which operates at a reasonable speed so that if it is being used to give simultaneous print output at search time the printer speed does not slow down the search. So a reasonably rapid dot-matrix printer with a capability for near letter quality typeface is a sensible option.

In addition to the technical considerations, a range of other factors should be considered in selecting a microcomputer for online searching. The first and probably most important of these is any policy on microcomputer purchase in the organization. Purchasing equipment which falls within an agreed organizational policy has a number of advantages to the online searcher. Firstly, the equipment may be available at a reduced price as a result of organizational buying power. Secondly it is possible that the organization has in-house repair and support facilities. Thirdly there will be a user base for that particular computer within the organization. Thus the newcomer either to microcomputers or the particular machine will have access to a number of experienced users who may be a source of invaluable advice.

The novice online searcher, who is neither aided nor constrained by organizational policy on microcomputer purchase, should pay particular attention to ensuring that a reliable and reputable workstation is selected. It is also important that it is purchased from a reliable and reputable local dealer who will provide necessary support, particularly in the early stages. It should be noted that it makes good sense to pay rather more than the lowest available prices for equipment if the slightly higher payment ensures that the equipment is purchased from a supplier who provides the necessary support. If the equipment is to be purchased by a newcomer and from a local dealer then time spent perusing the computing press and introductory guides to micro-computers will be time well spent. This should enable the purchaser to acquire familiarity with the barrage of jargon which may be used by sales staff.

It is useful to sign a maintenance contract with the equipment supplier. This may be anything up to 15 per cent of the purchase price of the equipment per annum.

Search software

The microcomputer will need to be supplied with appropriate software for online searching. Sometimes when a microcomputer is purchased it is supplied with a quantity of software, apparently free of charge. This is sometimes referred to as 'bundled' software. This may include terminal emulation software. Whilst this software may be adequate for online searching, it is not as useful as software which has been designed specifically for this purpose. Software of the latter variety enables the search to be simplified and the connect time reduced. Typically such search software enables the searcher to create a search strategy offline and then transmit the strategy to the search service either as an entire strategy or in a number of elements. The strategy will be transmitted at the speed of the data communications network rather than at the typing speed of the online searcher. This can make a significant reduction to search costs. Online search software should also permit the downloading of data from the search service to the local microcomputer for local offline processing, perhaps for the elimination of duplicate records before the search output is presented to the requestor. Online search software also helps to simplify the process of logging on to the various search services. The search software should enable the complex process of dialling telephone numbers and logging-on to data networks and remote hosts to be reduced to a small number of keystrokes. This type of search software is exemplified in Britain by HEADLINE from Head Computers. A comparison of these types of packages has been made by Ramsden (1987). Examples of communications software widely used in the United States include Crosstalk and Smartcom.

Whilst this type of search software is intended for the professional search intermediary, there is a growing category of software which provides greater help with the search process. This software is aimed at the end-user or the occasional searcher. It is known as 'gateway software'. This software should not be dismissed by the professional searcher since it may have a role to fulfil in providing simplified access to search services which are only used occasionally. Some examples of this type of software are discussed in Chapter 8.

Modems

If access to the data communications network is gained via the public telephone network then it is necessary to obtain a piece of equipment, known as a modem, to translate digital computer signals into audio signals which can be passed along public telephone lines. Modems are now reasonably priced and offer a wide range of facilities. As with microcomputers, some time spent perusing appropriate articles and advertisements in the micro-computer press before purchasing this equipment is time well spent. At the time of writing, rapid developments are taking place in modems and so advice is restricted to a number of general points. It is most important to ensure that the modem which is selected for purchase is one which has been approved for use with the telephone and telecommunications networks with which it will be used. In this respect great care should be exercised in the reading of advertisements and if there is the slightest doubt, it is wise to consult the relevant telecommunications authorities. It is important to ensure that the modem chosen can transmit and receive data at the speeds at which the search service and the telecommunications network operate. Usually this will mean 300 baud or 1200 baud and possibly 2400 baud. These transmission speeds are also known by the CCITT standards v21 (300 baud), v22 (1200 baud), v22bis (2400 baud) and v23 (1200/75 baud) or by their American equivalents from Bell. It is also important to ensure that the modem can operate in the required transmission mode (full and/or half duplex). Finally it is sensible to acquire a modem which is compatible with the Hayes protocols. These protocols define the way in which the communications software and the modem communicate with each other. They are named after the American company which produced the first intelligent modems and whose protocols have become a *de facto* international standard. A simple modem operating to v21 and v23 standards can be purchased in Britain for £75 whilst a modem capable of operating at v22 standards costs approximately £250.

Location of facilities

Discussion of equipment for online searching leads logically to a consideration of the location of the online searching facilities. The number of potential locations will be restricted by other tasks within the organization and by locations to which it is possible to supply telephone lines, power supplies and appropriate cabling. An important policy decision at this stage, especially in the context of libraries and information centres, is the visibility of the search workstation. Should it be located in a public place or alternatively should it be given a quiet location behind the scenes? Another alternative which becomes increasingly viable is that the remote search service can be accessed from a number of workstations within the organization.

Whilst the visibility of online search capabilities has obvious attractions and the notion of searching from a number of workstations at various locations has attractions, on balance it makes more sense to have a fixed location for online searching and one which is not too public. It should be apparent from earlier chapters and in particular from Chapters 5 and 6 that successful online searching is a complex process which involves flexible interaction with the search service, the user (if present) and a range of documentation. Coping with these interactions is demanding enough without the added burden of doing so in a public place where the searcher may be subjected to interruptions from casual passers-by. The cost and volume of the documentation required for access to a number of databases and search services dictates a fixed location for online searching since all but the simplest of searches is likely to require some consultation with the documentation. In addition, keeping accurate records of searches at several locations is an additional problem.

Whatever location is chosen, it is important to provide adequate space for the storage of documentation and a work area which enables the searcher to use the manuals being consulted as the search strategy is performed. It is wise to purchase appropriate computer furniture rather than to use other library or office furniture which rarely provides adequate workspace for both workstation and documentation. Some guidelines on the requirement of an online searcher's workstation and some possible layouts are provided by Morris, Dyer and Dowling (1987).

Who should search?

In some organizations there will only be a single online searcher. However, in many situations there may be a requirement for a number of staff to act as online searchers as a part of their duties. The question of who should be an online searcher is inextricably linked with the question of how online searching is to be integrated into the functions of the organization. For example, in a public reference library, if it is deemed that access to remote databases is a logical extension of the reference and information services provided then it follows that the searching of those databases ought to be the province of all the professional and possibly some of the non-professional staff. To argue that the searching of remote databases should only be carried out by some of the reference staff is to imply that the service is in some way special. A similar argument can be made in the case of academic libraries, many of which are organized on a subject specialist basis, which mirrors the organizational structure of the parent institution. If these subject librarians are not concerned with the provision of all services to the appropriate clientele then their credibility with that clientele is undermined. Thus they must necessarily be involved with the searching of remote databases. Nonetheless, the policy of treating online searching as an activity to be totally integrated into the operation of the library is not without its consequences. It is possible that some of these consequences may be detrimental to the service offered. One inescapable consequence is that the more searchers there are in a particular organization the less searching each individual searcher will perform and this may impair the quality of searching performed. A second inescapable consequence is that the process of keeping all searchers informed about relevant developments with the various search services and databases becomes more complex. Finally there is an extensive literature about the attributes of a good online searcher (see Chapter 8). Whilst no definite conclusions have been reached, it is inescapable that some people are less effective and comfortable as online searchers than others. It is possible that it is doing neither them nor the organization any good by causing them to perform online searches.

Fee or free?

Many libraries face a difficult decision about whether to make online searching freely available or to charge a fee. In favour of making online searching available freely to all readers is the notion that libraries offer free access to information. Protagonists of this view argue that there is no more reason to require readers to pay for information which is obtained from a computer than there is to make them pay for information which has been obtained from a book in the library's stock. Others argue that whilst this may be the case in an ideal world, the world is far from ideal and in order to take advantage of new technological opportunities it is necessary to make some charges. The situation in British university libraries has been reviewed by Mowat and Cannell (1986). In this sector approximately 25 per cent of libraries perform searches freely whilst the remaining 75 per cent make some sort of total or partial cost recovery. It was noted that in those libraries which charged more than 10 per cent of the actual cost there was less likelihood of searches being requested than in those which made no charges. Some organizations, particularly academic libraries, may restrict access to online searching to certain categories of reader. For example, searches may only be available to institutional staff, thus excluding students. Alternatively arrangements may be made to make access available only to postgraduate or final year students or students may have a certain amount of connect time or 'money' allocated beyond which payment must be made.

When equipment has been installed, contracts signed and staff trained, the service should be announced to potential customers. All publicity such as posters, leaflets or press releases should be professionally produced in the appropriate house-style. The level of publicity given to a new online search facility will be governed by the level of financial and staff commitment made to the service. It would be a serious error to promote the new service with a blaze of publicity only to find that the demand generated could not be met because of financial or staffing constraints. As with many services, satisfied clients will provide the best publicity.

Operation

Once online searching has been introduced into an organization, a number of regular tasks must be undertaken to ensure the smooth running of the service.

Costs and payments

The first task relates to the charges incurred in searching. The search services currently charge for access to their databases by a combination of connect time charges and charges for online or offline display of the information retrieved. In the early days of online searching, the major component of the charge was the connect time charge but in recent years there has been a trend towards recouping a greater amount of the costs via charges for information display. It is argued that it is the information and not the time spent searching for it for which the searcher should incur most cost. An analogy is sometimes made with shopping where the customer only pays for the goods obtained and not for the length of time selecting them from the supermarket shelves. Typically the connect charge will be in the range £20 to £140 per hour and the display charge in the range £0.16 to £0.80 per item but there may be exceptions and some charges related to highly valued business information may be higher. Some search services offer inducements to pay in advance for searching. The inducement is a reduced charge for searching. The advantage to the customer is that more connect time can be bought for the same amount of money whilst the advantage to the search service is that the money is paid in advance at the beginning of the financial year. In addition to these charges, search services often make an annual subscription charge for the provision of documentation updates; $50 is a typical figure.

It is important to install a system for recording all searches which are performed. This should include details of the search service and database used, the date and time of the search and an estimate of the cost and/or connect time of the search. These elements are all important for ensuring that the subsequent monthly bills from the various search services are accurate and only contain charges for searches which were undertaken within the organization. Such a system can be implemented easily using either record sheets or a log-book. It is important that all searchers are aware of the necessity to keep these records. Examples of record sheets are shown in the case studies. When these are received they should be checked against the search log and any discrepancies noted and the problem resolved with the searcher concerned or the search service before the bill is passed to the accounts department for payment. Most host systems have mechanisms for automatically chasing unpaid accounts. Thus it is important to clear a bill as soon as possible, otherwise the administrator risks inundation with reminders and threats to terminate the service. The payment of accounts in foreign currencies can be a slow process and this is a further reason why bills should be cleared as soon as they are received and rapidly paid. This may be facilitated by the use of standing orders.

Documentation

Each search service and many database producers sell significant amounts of documentation. This is usually in the form of loose-leaf manuals. An initial collection of these materials will be acquired when an organization commences online searching. This will consist of the user manuals for the search services with which contracts have been signed and documentation such as user manuals and/or thesauri of those databases which it is anticipated will be regularly used. There will be a steady stream of updates to be incorporated into this documentation. It is important that these updates are read, assimilated and filed as soon as possible for use by all searchers. In addition to their basic documentation, the search services and some database producers send out regular newsletters to searchers. Again it is important that time is set aside to read these newsletters, to assimilate relevant details and to arrange for the newsletters to be brought to the attention of other searchers within the organization, possibly by circulation.

Procedures manual

Each organization which begins online searching should consider compiling a policy and procedures manual for online searching. This may take the form of either a separate manual or a chapter within an existing staff manual. Such a document should explain which search services are available and note access routes and passwords. It may list local searching expertise in particular search services and databases. Local policy about the offering of online searching to the clientele should also be explained.

In addition, the service will operate smoothly if time is spent ensuring an adequate supply of consumables such as printer paper and ribbons and any internally produced documentation.

Impact of using external search services

The use of online search services will inevitably have an impact on the organization. One obvious consequence of searching biblio-graphic databases is to draw to the attention of people, who could make use of them, relevant documents which are not available locally. Thus the use of online search services will probably have an impact on document borrowing or purchase costs.

A second impact of the use of online search services is to call into question the need for access to some information held locally in print format. Published evidence of any causal relationship between cancellation of print-based material and its availability online is at best flimsy (Lancaster and Goldhor, 1981; Sperr, 1983). However, the suspicion remains that as budgets become even tighter and online services are now readily accepted, their influence on subscriptions to the print equivalent is increasing and will continue to do so. The position is now further complicated by the increasing availability of information on CD-ROM. Cannell (1989) has reported that the introduction of CD-ROM in one medical library has reduced online searching costs by 50 per cent whilst the Plymouth Polytechnic case study reports cancellation of some print products when their CD-ROM equivalents were made available.

Policy and operation review

The online information industry is changing rapidly. This makes it particularly important that there are mechanisms for regularly reviewing the use of online searching within the organization. Any review should be aimed at ensuring that:
1. The search services used are the most appropriate, that is, they are the most economical and offer access to the required databases.

2. Contracts with unused search services are ended since there is an overhead in keeping knowledge and documentation up to date.
3. New training requirements are identified and met.
4. Existing policy and practice are amended as necessary.
5. Effects of the introduction of online searching on other activities within the organization are identified.
6. The views of clients on the service are monitored, perhaps by questionnaire.

In short, all aspects of online searching should be kept under continuous review.

Education and Training

The early chapters of this book make it clear that there is much information to assimilate and many skills to be acquired in order to become a successful online searcher. Since the online information industry is continually changing, it is important to recognize education and training of searchers as a continuing process. Education can be taken to mean a general awareness of online searching and ought to enable recipients to answer the question 'What is online searching?' Thus it would include an awareness of computer held databases, command languages, telecommunications networks and the equipment necessary to access the databases. It would also include an awareness of the type of information which might be accessed by online searching. In any organizational context, it should include as far as possible an awareness of the availability of online searching within that organization, the search services and databases accessible, to whom the service is available and under what conditions. That is, anyone within the organization might reasonably be expected to know that organization's policy towards online searching. Perhaps most difficult of all, it is necessary for all concerned to be educated about the complexity of online searching and the need for appropriate and adequate training in both search services and regularly used databases if optimum search results are to be achieved. This awareness of online searching clearly applies both to library and information centre staff and to their clientele.

Training for online searching can be defined as the acquisition of the knowledge and skills necessary to realize the potential offered by online searching. Thus training can be expected to enable searchers to learn the command languages of specific search services and to gain a detailed knowledge about how particular databases are made available by a given search service. It is important to recognize that in a subject where there are continuous changes, it is not sufficient to learn about a particular search service, its command language and available databases at a particular point in time but it is also necessary to keep abreast of recent developments. In short, effective education and training is not a one-off process but a continuous activity.

Training packages

A wide range of tools and techniques have been tried in the education and training of online searchers. Since the beginning of online searching, the expense of connect time and communications costs, especially outside the United States, has been a serious problem. These expenses have inhibited the use of live searches by library schools in their education programmes. The use of 'live' searching in library schools has been inhibited further by technical problems such as the unreliability of communications networks. The unsympathetic nature of the command languages to learners and the nature of the learners themselves have also been given as reasons why other training aids have been developed (Guy, 1983). Nevertheless most courses on online searching include an element of live searching.

In order to contain the costs of courses in online searching a number of teaching packages have been developed, in particular by library schools but more recently also by the search services. It should be noted that these packages complement rather than act as an alternative to live searches. These packages have been reviewed by Guy (1983) and Wood (1984). There have been a wide range of non-interactive packages such as tape-slides and videos. These have the advantage that they can be used with a wide audience and they provide the possibility of a glimpse 'behind the scenes'. However they are expensive and may date rapidly. Possibly the most ambitious training package is a disc-based interactive video program which was developed from a detailed in-house training programme at University College Cardiff (Smith and Roach, 1984). Other teaching packages can be divided into three types, computer-assisted instruction, simulation and emulation (although there are packages which combine more than one of these techniques). Computer-assisted instruction packages test students' understanding of the command language and basic concepts of online searching. A negative feature of this type of package is that it may not explain learner errors adequately. Simulations operate by guiding the student through a prerecorded search and correcting student errors; they do not have a database or a command language of their own. A disadvantage of simulations is that the learner must follow a predefined route through the search and no latitude is allowed to deviate from that route.

Emulations incorporate a command language which is as close as possible to that of a particular search service and a database, albeit usually a very small one. In Britain emulations have been implemented on both microcomputers and mainframes. An emulation of Dialog, DIASIM, which was developed at Leeds Polytechnic, has now been implemented in Britain, Norway and Australia as a teaching aid. The system has been described by Livesey (1984). At the College of Librarianship Wales, an emulation of the ESA-IRS system has been developed as a part of a larger training package which also includes computer-assisted learning modules. The package runs on IBM-PC XT and compatibles (Armstrong and Large, 1986). This package recognizes that the need for training stretches beyond the training of intermediaries since it was specifically designed for the training of end-users. This is a trend which has been reported by others, for example, Ostrum (1987) and Tillman (1987).

Emulations and simulations offer students the opportunity to work at their own pace, to gain keyboarding experience (which is still important in some contexts) and to become familiar with the command languages of particular systems. The fact that this experience is gained without the expense of connect time and telecommunications charges enables students to become familiar with online searching in a more relaxed manner than if they were connected to remote hosts. However, even systems based on mainframes do not necessarily provide all the facilities found in the command language of an online search service. For example, DIASIM, does not permit SUPERSELECT, SELECT STEPS or word proximity searching; further, they do not provide access to databases of a realistic size. Hence useful as these tools are in education and training they should not be seen as replacements for access to host systems and *live* searching. Whilst emulations have generally been used to a greater extent in Britain than in America, an American microcomputer-based emulation of Dialog has recently been reported (Broadway, 1987).

The increasing availability of text retrieval software (some of which are versions of the software used by the search services) for the creation and searching of in-house databases was noted in Chapter 1 and is discussed further in Chapter 10. It would seem reasonable that these systems would provide an environment in which the principles of online searching can be taught without the costs incurred or the technical problems of searching external databases. However, there is little evidence that this is occurring. Presumably this is caused by a combination of:

1. Difficulty and/or cost of acquiring a database of a suitably large nature.
2. The cost of implementing a search capability for a number of simultaneous searches whether on a local area network or by a series of standalone microcomputers.
3. The available software to date has not been sufficiently easy in use for this option to commend itself to educators.

It is reasonable to suppose that this situation is now changing and the advent of CD-ROM (see Chapter 10 for more details) may have a large impact on the education and training of online searchers in the near future. Clearly the storage capabilities of CD-ROM enable large databases to be made available for searching. Software producers are beginning to learn from the earlier attempts of the search services and the producers of software for in-house systems and the software for searching on CD-ROM is rather easier to use. This may be a further advantage in the immediate future. Against this must be set the fact that the cost of installing the necessary equipment is not trivial and currently CD-ROM is a single user device. However, experience of using these systems in the education of online searchers has been reported by Day (1988) and, for end-user training, by Whitsed (1989).

As the industry has matured, the online search services have offered an increasing range of help to educators and trainers of online searchers. One approach has been to provide training files containing a limited subset of a particular database, perhaps the records from a single year, at a greatly reduced connect charge. There are normally some restrictions on the command language facilities which can be used with these training files, for example, it may not be possible to order offline prints or to set up SDI profiles. Nevertheless, they offer a useful means of gaining experience of live searching at a greatly reduced cost. The widest range of these training files is probably the ONTAP (*ON*line *T*raining *a*nd

Practice) files offered by Dialog but similar files are offered by other search services. Some search services, of whom Data-Star is one, have developed workbooks aimed at new searchers in particular subject areas such as biomedicine or business to introduce the basics of online searching with worked examples in particular subjects. Data-Star has produced several floppy disc-based introductions to the fundamentals of searching whilst BRS has produced a multivolume multimedia training programme.

A range of features provided by the search services as part of their support to searchers can properly be seen as extensions to their training function. The search service documentation, both the system manuals and the detailed descriptions of each database, can be read and consulted with profit by all searchers. The various search service newsletters should be seen as a regular source of up-to-date information and their regular perusal is an important part of the continuing education and training of the online searcher. It is common practice for a search service to allow free search time on a database which has just been released for searching by its users. This may last for the first month of the availability of the database. Whilst this might be seen as a marketing ploy on the part of the search service, it does offer the online searcher the opportunity to explore a new database at relatively little cost and thus to extend knowledge of available information. Finally, the search service help desks can be seen as a source of extending the knowledge base of the individual searcher and therefore should not be overlooked as a part of the education and training process.

The trainers

A number of organizations are involved in the provision of education and training courses for online searching. From the outset, online search services have been heavily involved in training online searchers. A glance at the list of forthcoming courses in the newsletters of many of the major search services will give an indication of the scale of this effort. There are courses on a regular basis at numerous locations across the United States, at various centres in Britain and Europe and increasingly in other parts of the world such as Japan, Australia and Mexico. Some of the larger search services now present their courses in a variety of languages. In many cases the online search services have developed a whole range of courses for different types of user (beginners and experienced searchers), particular databases and particular market sectors such as business or chemistry. Most of these courses are single day but occasionally they may extend over two days or only half a day. Typically they consist of 60 per cent lectures, 20 per cent demonstrations and 20 per cent practical work. Requirements for a good training course have been suggested by Wood (1987).

Producers of the larger databases, for example INSPEC or Chemical Abstracts Service, also provide courses though on a lesser scale than the host systems. Such courses concentrate on a detailed exposition of the coverage and special features of their particular database or range of databases. On occasions they examine differences in the way in which the particular databases have been made available by different search services.

The various local, regional, national and subject-based Online User Groups perform a useful education and training function. The contribution of these groups in the area of continuing education and training is particularly important. Since the early days of the online industry, the various professional associations such as the American Library Association and the Institute of Information Scientists have played an important role in the education and training of online searchers. Latterly, these bodies have been rather less involved in the provision of such courses. Courses offered by search services, database producers and professional bodies have been reviewed by Buxton (1984).

The library schools have been involved in education and training for online searching in two ways. The provision of introductory courses in online searching has been important in the continuing education programmes of many schools (Guy, 1982). In the longer term the incorporation of online searching into the curricula at both undergraduate and postgraduate levels has been of greater significance. One approach has been to offer special courses in online searching whilst another has been to incorporate online searching into appropriate existing courses, such as information sources, information storage and retrieval or even library automation. Whatever approach is adopted, it is now the case that virtually all students leaving library schools in Britain and America have received a basic education and training in online searching.

Whilst this chapter has provided general guidelines on the process of going online it should be noted that the specific approaches adopted will be dictated by local circumstances. It may be the case that local considerations outweigh all other factors, for example, the lack of availability of a particular currency, political considerations or free access may in different circumstances all have a major impact on the choice of search service.

References

Armstrong, C. J. and Large, J. A. (1986) From middle-man to end-user: the changing market for online training. *Proceedings of the 10th International Online Information Meeting*, pp. 307–316. Oxford: Learned Information

Broadway, M. D. (1987) Dialtwig: a mini-Dialog in a controlled microcomputer based environment. *Database*, **10** (6), 122–128

Buxton, A. B. (1984) Online training courses in the UK. *Proceedings of the 8th International Online Information Meeting*, pp. 503–509. Oxford: Learned Information

Cannell, S. (1989) User reactions to CD-ROM in a medical library. *Proceedings of the Third Annual Conference on Small Computers in Libraries, London, February 1989*, pp. 115–118. London: Meckler

Day, J. M. (1988) CD-ROM – an online training tool? *Education for Information*, **6** (4), 403–410

Guy, R. F. (1982) Short courses in online searching: continuing education and the library school. *Proceedings of the 6th International Online Information Meeting*, pp. 143–153. Oxford: Learned Information

Guy, R. F. (1983) Training aids for online instruction: an analysis. *Proceedings of the 7th International Online Information Meeting*, pp. 353–360. Oxford: Learned Information

Huffman, G. D. and Leigh, W. E. (1986) The well equipped searcher's support station. *Microcomputers for Information Management*, **3** (1), 59–68

Lancaster, F. W. and Goldhor, H. (1981) The impact of online services on subscriptions to printed publications. *Online Review*, **5** (4), 301–311

Livesey, J. B. (1984) DIASIM: a Dialog simulator. *Program*, **18** (4), 347–350

Morris, A., Dyer, H. and Dowling, R. (1987) Workstation design for the online searcher. *Online Information 87. 11th International Online Information Meeting Proceedings*, pp. 227–239. Oxford: Learned Information

Mowat, I. R. M. and Cannell, S. E. (1986) Charges for online searches in university libraries. *Journal of Librarianship*, **18** (3), 193–211

Ostrum, G. K. (1987) Computer assisted training of infrequent users of CAS Online. *Proceedings of the 8th National Online Meeting*, pp. 375–377. Medford, NJ: Learned Information

Ramsden, A. (1987) Five communications software packages reviewed: Communique, Connect, Datatalk, Headline, Information Transfer. *Program*, **21** (3), 245–259

Smith, N. R. and Roach, D. K. (1984) An interactive videodisk training programme for online information retrieval. *Proceedings of the 8th International Online Information Meeting*, pp. 493–501. Oxford: Learned Information

Sperr, I. L. (1983) Online searching and the print product; impact or interaction? *Online Review*, **7** (5), 413–420

Tillman, H. N. (1987) Teaching online searching to teachers in training. *Proceedings of the 8th National Online Meeting*, pp. 445–449. Medford, NJ: Learned Information

Turpie, G. (1988) *Going Online 1988*. London: Aslib

Whitsed, N. (1989) CD-ROM, an end-user training tool? The experience of using Medline in a medical school library. *Program*, **23** (2), 117–126

Wood, F. E. (1984) Teaching online information retrieval in the United Kingdom library schools. *Journal of the American Society for Information Science*, **35** (1), 53–55

Wood, F. E. (1987) Training courses. *UKOLOG Newsletter*, **49**, 8–9

Chapter 10

Online Searching of Locally Stored Databases

Introduction

Much of the discussion of online searching so far in this book has related to the searching of publicly available databases on remote online search services. This chapter will concentrate on aspects related to searching databases on local computer systems. The *local* databases may be publicly available ones or may be generated in-house and they may be stored on magnetic or optical disc.

Early techniques for using computers to store and retrieve bibliographic data developed from the work of Luhn (1957) at IBM. Initially this involved using the computer to generate index entries from keywords in the title of a document and to print out a list in sorted keyword order; this became known as a KWIC (Keyword in Context) type of index. Figure 10.1 shows entries generated in a KWIC-type index for four document titles. By the mid to late 1960s some large organizations had begun to use their local mainframe computers to store and retrieve information which had previously been stored and retrieved on various types of card (for example, edge-punched cards or 80-column punched cards). Such cards would have previously been processed using electro-mechanical devices such as card sorters. The computer systems were initially used to produce printed products, such as information bulletins giving details of recently acquired items, KWIC-type indexes, for running selective dissemination of information (SDI) services and sometimes for running batch retrospective searches of the whole machine-readable collection of records. One example of software developed originally in the late 1960s specifically for this sort of work is ASSASSIN (which was originally an acronym from Agricultural System for the Storage and Subsequent Selection of Information) developed by ICI's

Agricultural Division. Clough (1986) describes the development of ASSASSIN and how it was used initially for the processing of public databases (such as INSPEC and Chemical Abstracts Condensates) in-house.

Walks in west Wales	1
Hiking up hills in Wales	2
Hill-walking: some useful hints	3
Wales: a guide to walking in the hills	4
GUIDE	
Wales: a guide to walking in the hills	4
HIKING	
Hiking up hills in Wales	2
HILLS	
Hiking up hills in Wales	2
Wales: a guide to walking in the hills	4
HILL-WALKING	
Hill-walking: some useful hints	3
HINTS	
Hill-walking: some useful hints	3
WALES	
Hiking up hills in Wales	2
Wales: a guide to walking in the hills	4
Walks in west Wales	1
WALKING	
Wales: a guide to walking in the hills	4
WALKS	
Walks in west Wales	1
WEST	
Walks in west Wales	1

Figure 10.1 *A simplified KWIC-type index*

By the mid-1970s many information units and special libraries had started to use the remote search services for online searching of public information but still required systems for the storage and retrieval of local or private information such as company reports, laboratory tests, market surveys and so on. Tedd (1979) reports on the use, by 12 information units in Europe, of computers (both remote and local) to assist with the retrieval of public and private bibliographic information. Some of the remote search services provide facilities for users to store private data which can then be searched and retrieved using the appropriate command language and telecommunications system. However, with the rapid developments of local computing resources during the 1980s there has been a tendency to search local databases in-house on microcomputers. Resulting from the decrease in cost of computing power many organizations have become involved in using software for in-house processing of such information. This software is often referred to as information management software which Kazlauskas (1987a) defines as:

> . . . computer software which facilitates the creation, manipulation and maintenance of and product generation from, variable length textual records. These records typically include such data as names, titles, dates, publication information, source and origin, location, index terms, abstract, text and numeric content information, and identifying numbers. These data are found in descriptions and the full contents of: books, documents, reports, audio-visual and magnetic media, articles and reprints, memoranda and correspondence, contracts, briefs, litigation support and other legal materials, and a multitude of reference and referral data sources.

Kazlauskas estimates that in the late 1970s in North America there were only about 20 commercially available packages for the creation of information management databases; by 1984 there were about 100 such packages whereas over 200 packages are listed in his 1987 directory (Kazlauskas, 1987b). Kazlauskas (1987a) categorizes the information management software as follows:

1. File manager software.
2. General database management software.
3. Specific database management software.
4. Library/records/information centre subsystem applications.
5. Integrated library/records/information centre systems.
6. Text retrieval.

Text retrieval software tends to provide the search functions similar to those encountered when searching the remote online search services and so this chapter will concentrate on the use of such software for local searching. The development and use of text retrieval software (such as Sci-Mate, STAIRS and CAIRS) in Britain is described by papers in Rowlands (1987) with a detailed directory of such packages being provided by Kimberley (1989). In Australia, Frey (1987) outlines the growth of the use of microcomputer text retrieval packages such as Micro-CAIRS and Micro-STATUS.

Some organizations are acquiring databases on CD-ROM for local searching. In such cases the search software (usually text retrieval software) is provided along with the data. Bristow (1988) describes the practical experiences of the reference department in Indiana University at Bloomington in the United States in using various CD-ROM products.

This chapter covers various aspects related to local online searching of publicly available data on CD-ROM as well as of locally produced databases.

Local Record and Database Structure

Records on CD-ROM databases

Many of the databases currently available on CD-ROM are also available for searching on the remote online search services. However, there are sometimes differences, maybe slight, between the structure of the records and the ways in which they may be searched, in the different systems.

Figure 10.2, for instance, shows an example of a LISA (Library and Information Science Abstracts) record on the CD-ROM database produced by Silver Platter and on Dialog. Detailed information on how to search a given database on a given system is, of course, given in the main systems manual. However, a manual prepared by the database producer often includes useful comparisons which may affect the searcher's decision of which system to use (*LISA Manual*, 1987). It can be seen from Figure 10.2 that hyphens have been inserted on the CD-ROM version on several occasions to enable phrase retrieval, for example, Online-Computer-Library-Center, Bulletin-des-Bibliotheques-de-France and Information-storage-and-retrieval. Also, the CD-ROM version includes the author's affiliation (where the author works) in the author field (in this case D-B-M-I-S-T) whereas this is not included in the Dialog records. Another small difference is that the CD-ROM version has an explicit date field (DA) whereas in Dialog this information is implicit (as it is also in the CD-ROM database) in the accession number. All the major indexing decisions are taken by the database producer (in this case the British Library Association) but the detailed decisions on search codes, search fields, print formats, etc. are taken by the organization loading the database, be it a CD-ROM producer (such as Silver Platter) or a search service (such as Dialog).

(a) Silver Platter CD-ROM

SilverPlatter v1.4   LISA (1/69 – 9/88)

TI: The **OCLC-DBMIST** agreement
TO: L'accord **OCLC-DBMIST**
AU: **Darrobers,-Martine**;
   D-B-M-I-S-T-(Direction-des-bibliotheques,-des-musees-et-de-l'infor-
   mation-scientifique-et-technique),-France; Online-Computer-Library-
   Center-(**OCLC**)
SO: Bulletin-des-Bibliotheques-de-France, 30 (6) 1985, 537–538. 3 refs
PY: 1985
LA: French
AB: At the end of 1985, the French Directorate of Libraries, Museums,
   and Scientific and Technical Information (DBMIST) signed an
   agreement with the US Online Computer Library Center (OCLC) to
   cooperate in provision of cataloguing services and research projects.
   OCLC's international data base already includes 700,000 French
   notices, and provides content summaries and locations as well as
   bibliographic descriptions. This step will allow France to develop its
   own national catalogues, and although the move may be opposed on
   the grounds that it means abandoning French standards for American,
   the move to adopting international practices is essential now that
   databases are internationally accessible on-line
FH: On-line Cooperation. France. Direction des bibliotheques des
   musees et de l'information scientifique et technique and Online
   Computer Library Center
DE: France-; Technical-processes-and-services; Information-storage-
   and-retrieval; Information-retrieval; Cataloguing-; Computerised-
   cataloguing; On-line-cataloguing; Cooperation-
CC: TogsNccD44 Togs
DA: 1987
AN: 87–1485

(b) Dialog

179715   87–1485   Library and Information Science Abstracts   (LISA)
   The OCLC-DBMIST agreement
   L'accord OCLC-DBMIST
   Darrobers, Martine
   Bulletin des Bibliotheques de France
   SOURCE: 30 (6) 1985, 537–538. 3 refs
   LANGUAGES: French
   At the end of 1985, the French Directorate of Libraries, Museums, and
Scientific and Technical Information (DBMIST) signed an agreement with
the US Online Computer Library Center (OCLC) to cooperate in provision

of cataloguing services and research projects. OCLC's international data base already includes 700,000 French notices, and provides content summaries and locations as well as bibliographic descriptions. This step will allow France to develop its own national catalogues, and although the move may be opposed on the grounds that it means abandoning French standards for American, the move to adopting international practices is essential now that databases are internationally accessible on-line

NOTE: D.B.M.I.S.T. (Direction des bibliotheques, des musees et de l'information scientifique et technique), France; Online Computer Library Center (OCLC)

DESCRIPTORS: France; Technical processes and services; Information storage and retrieval; Information retrieval; Cataloguing; Computerised cataloguing; On-line cataloguing; Cooperation

SECTION HEADINGS: CATALOGUING

SECTION HEADING CODES: TogsNccD44

Figure 10.2 *LISA record on (a) Silver Platter CD-ROM and (b) Dialog*

Records on in-house databases

A crucial stage in the setting up of a local database for online searching is the design of the record – the number of fields to be included, their possible length, the method of indexing those fields and so on. Datta (1987) describes the setting up of an in-house database, using the CAIRS software package, at the Overseas Development Natural Resources Institute (formerly TDRI) Library. Figure 10.3 shows the record structure, known in CAIRS terminology as Screen Definition Table, which for each of the 32 fields defines various parameters such as the name of the field, the three-letter abbreviated form, the size of the field and the way in which the field is indexed. The CAIRS package provides several ways of generating search terms: those used are:

A (Automatic) –all words (apart from those in a stop-list) are included.
F (full field) – the complete contents of the field are entered as a search phrase in the index.
M (Manual) – search terms are allocated manually.
T (Tagged) – words or phrases are tagged (by being enclosed in < >) and then are entered as a search term in the index.

Screen pages (VDU)	Field Nos on screens	Field No in synonym file	Fields	Window Sizes × no of windows	Synonyms	Type of indexing	Terminator set
Page 1	02	1	Accession number	7 × 1	acc		
	03	2	Spare Field 1	1 × 6			
	04	3	Security Code	1 × 8	sec	F	
	05	4	Acc Bull Heading	4 × 1	abh	F	
	06	5	File Code	6 × 1	fil	F	
	07	6	Spare Field 2	1 × 6			
	08	7	Spare Field 3	1 × 1			
	09	8	Spare Field 4	1 × 1			
	10	9	Spare Field 5				
	11	10	Location	56 × 2	loc	F	
	12	11	UDC No	63 × 2	udc	F	
	13	12	Date	63 × 2	dat	A	..
	14	13	Author	4 × 1	aut	T	..
Page 2	02	14	Title	223 × 2	tit	T	
	03	15	Reference	383 × 3	ref	T	
Page 3	02	16	Publisher	222 × 2	pub	T	
	03	17	Collation	222 × 2	col	T	
	04	18	Author Cat	298 × 4	auc	F	
	05	19	ISBN	1 × 1	isb	T	
	06	20	Language Text	20 × 1	lat	A	..
	07	21	DOC Type	58 × 2	doc	A	..
	08	22	Spare Field 6	27 × 2			
	09	23	TDRI Project No	20 × 2	pro	F	
	10	24	Bull Heads	5 × 1	buh	F	
Page 4	02	25	Access Bull	58 × 3	acb	F	
	03	26	Staff Loan	58 × 2	lon	A	..
	04	27	Return Date	50 × 2	rdt	F	
	05	28	Section Headings	50 × 1	shd	A	
	06	29	Spare Field 7	210 × 1			
	07	30	Spare Field 8	1 × 1			
		31	Spare Field 9	1 × 1			
Page 5		32	Descriptors	1 × 1	des		..

A = Automatic; F = Full field; M = Manual; T = Tagged.

Figure 10.3   *Example of a record structure in CAIRS*

Some local databases may be much simpler in format than that shown. Figure 10.4 shows an example on walks perhaps available at a tourist information centre – giving details of the type of walk, length, features and so on.

```
NAME:         BROBRYN
LENGTH:       5
TERRAIN:      Moor
MAP:          OS 135
AGE:          8+
FEATURES:     Waterfall; Mine; Birds of prey
DETAILS:      Start at National Trust car park (SN      ) and
              proceed on marked path to. . . .
```

Figure 10.4 *Sample simple record*

Teskey (1984) states that there are often problems in appreciating the impact that decisions made when designing the record structure will have on the future performance of the retrieval system. Often small changes in the record design can have a major effect on the time taken to retrieve items.

Standards for record structure

Although there is a great variety of record structures amongst even databases in the same general category (bibliographic, numerical and full-text) some attempts have been made to introduce national or even international standards into this confusing picture. The use of standard record structures makes it easier to become familiar with a new database, and such standards are essential if information is ever to be transferred easily from one database into another.

Standardization is particularly important for bibliographic records. Many countries, for example, produce machine-readable national bibliographies which seek to list books published within their borders; the resulting records could then be merged into one enormous universal bibliography listing all documents published throughout the world, an objective which has been pursued since the middle ages. Such an exchange of bibliographic records is much simplified if all countries generate bibliographic records with identical structures – the same fields in the same order. In an endeavour to promote this objective a standard for bibliographic records was agreed between Britain and the United States in the late 1960s. This standard is called MARC (MAchine Readable

Cataloguing) and contains a large number of fields and sub-fields.

Although MARC has now been adopted as a standard in many countries, unfortunately it still cannot function as a proper international standard because of the national variations which have been introduced to meet the precise requirements of individual countries. As a consequence, another standard, UNIMARC, has now been developed which is intended to act as an international standard. Some countries have agreed to adopt it for their national bibliographic systems; additionally, UNIMARC can act as a pivot or intercode, enabling different variants on MARC to be converted into any other variant via UNIMARC. This would mean that any MARC format only required software to convert it into UNIMARC; from UNIMARC it could then be re-converted into any other MARC format.

An international standard, ISO 2709, has been designed for the interchange of bibliographic records on magnetic tape. This standard is widely accepted and used, especially for MARC records. The MARC format, however, is designed principally for the exchange of machine-readable records about books; it is not really appropriate for recording details of journal articles. To overcome this problem the Common Communication Format (CCF) has been designed under the auspices of Unesco in conjunction with the International Council of Scientific Unions Abstracting Board (ICSU-AB), the International Federation of Library Associations and Institutions (IFLA) and the International Standardization Organization (ISO). Unesco has concerned itself over the years with the setting up of local databases in developing countries, which – for reasons such as high cost and poor telecommunications facilities – cannot easily access the remote online search services. Thus the CCF is an exchange format intended for use by organizations within the information community that wish to exchange bibliographic records with each other. Hopkinson (1985) describes this format in more depth.

Local database structure

The text retrieval type of software which is mainly described in this chapter is based on an inverted file of searchable terms as was described in Chapter 3. Ashford (1984a) lists the typical facilities of such a database:

1. The text of the information is held in a single flexible record with field or record markers for structure.

2. Access to the stored information is made through an inverted file of pointers to all the significant words in the body of the text.
3. The searcher addresses the system via a command language which will have facilities for boolean logic, display of records, access to the postings frequency of words in the inverted file and so on.
4. The software deals with the maintenance of the inverted file when records are added, modified or deleted.

Widely used text retrieval packages that are used for producing local databases include ASSASSIN, CAIRS, POLYDOC, STATUS and their microcomputer counterparts.

Other types of information management software as described by Kazlauskas (1987a) are based on different database structures. The file or data manager software is used for the creation and manipulation of single, unrelated files. The database management systems (DBMS) vary in complexity, and the phrase has come to mean different things to different people. DBMSs were originally developed during the 1960s by those involved in working in mainframe computer departments who wished to generate a single database (say of items produced in a factory) for various applications in different departments (say for sales, marketing, production and research and development). Thus DBMS software in the mainframe and minicomputer environment (for example, ADABAS, FOCUS, IDMS and TOTAL) is complex and is often seen as a framework to assist those writing applications programs rather than as software that might be used by an end-user or novice searcher for the retrieval of information. Koenig (1985) provides a tutorial on the structure of databases in DBMS systems. A particular type of DBMS is the relational DBMS or R.DBMS, which involves information being represented in the form of tables, the columns of which correspond to fields in conventional records and the rows of which are the records themselves. Oxborrow (1986) gives further details of the ways in which database systems may be implemented and used efficiently.

There is a growing number of what is now known as DBMS software available for use with microcomputers. Chen and DeYoung (1984) provide a good description of such software including packages such as PFS, and the dBase family. Woodrow (1986) describes the use of dBase II for a database of local societies created and maintained by Hertfordshire County Libraries in Britain.

Tagg (1985) compares and contrasts text retrieval software and DBMS software and describes some of the moves towards their integration. INFOText, for example, is a package which consists of a text retrieval facility added on to a standard DBMS package, INFO. Ashford and Willett (1989) provide an introduction to this fairly complex area of text retrieval and document databases.

Searching Local Databases

The search facilities available for local databases are often similar to those which are available from the remote search services. Some of the text retrieval packages are directly linked to the software used by the remote services. For instance, Micro-Questel, produced by Télésystèmes-QUESTEL, incorporates similar search commands to the remote service and it also includes commands for the uploading of documents for use by the Questel search service. Similarly BRS/Search has similar search commands to the BRS search service. Some of the remote search services have entered the CD-ROM market. Dialog, for instance, markets various CD-ROM databases (some are shown in Table 10.1) which incorporate search facilities similar to (and therefore familiar to users of) the remote service. In addition a CD-ROM disc, Dialog On Disc Discovery Preview, is available for practice and training in searching. Some producers of text retrieval software have made

Name of database	Subject
AGRIBUSINESS USA	Agricultural industry
CANADIAN BUSINESS AND CURRENT AFFAIRS	Canadian national and provincial information including company, product, industry and financial information
ERIC	Education
MEDLINE	Biomedical literature
MEDLINE CLINICAL CONNECTION	Clinical medicine
NTIS	US government-sponsored research and development
STANDARD AND POOR'S CORPORATIONS	Details of public and private companies

Table 10.1　*Some of Dialog's CD-ROM databases*

their packages available for searching CD-ROM databases as well as for locally stored databases. Harwell Computer Power, for instance, markets STATUS and Micro-STATUS and has collaborated with the Dutch firms Samsom and Philips to produce CD-ROM databases that may be searched using the STATUS commands. Details of the search facilities available in a variety of text retrieval packages are given in Kimberley's (1989) directory.

Command language

Most text retrieval packages use a command-driven approach, although sometimes menu screens are used to act as prompts to show the commands available. Micro-CAIRS, for instance, includes menu screens to provide direct access to functions that can be used to set up and modify the database, enter and modify records, search, design output formats, generate indexes and so on. TINman, however, has no recognizable search commands; the users are able to browse through ordered lists of information and then navigate to an item of interest by pressing a single key (Noerr and Bivins-Noerr, 1985).

The commands available for searching Silver Platter's CD-ROM databases are:

HELP –	for help about system functions.
FIND –	for entering search terms (words or phrases).
GUIDE –	for help about the database in use.
SHOW –	to display the retrieved record, or part of it.
INDEX –	to look at the inverted file of search terms.
PRINT –	to print retrieved records.
RESTART –	to end a session.
XCHANGE –	to switch to another Silver Platter CD-ROM disc.
PREVIOUS –	to display previous record.
NEXT –	to display next record.

Use of boolean operators

Most text retrieval packages offer some form of boolean searching. However, the ability to nest search statements and input the request all on one line (as described in Chapter 5) for example:

(COMPUTERS OR MICROCOMPUTERS) AND (SOFT-WARE OR PACKAGE) AND RETRIEVAL is available on packages such as CAIRS, BRS/Search, STATUS and INMAGIC. In other cases a boolean search may be undertaken in a more roundabout way.

Search Example 10.1 shows the output from a search of a collection of audio-visual materials at the College of Librarianship Wales (CLW) library using the CARDBOX-PLUS package. The first record shown, a film (*Archive film and the study of war and society*), is the first one in the database of 933 records. The user is asked to enter a command.

```
Cardbox-Plus file = C:CLWLIBAV.FIL          READY              R/01
LEVEL 0 – RECORD 1 OF 933
*****************************************************************
*                   CLW LIBRARY AUDIO VISUAL MATERIALS         *
*       TITLE:ARCHIVE film and the study LOCATION:Film–073      *
*       of war and society.              DATE:1972             *
*       PLACE:Bletchley                                         *
*       PUBLISHER:Open-University                               *
*       DESCRIPTION:25 min. sd. b. & w. 12mm.                   *
*                                                               *
*       CREDITS:                                                *
*                                                               *
*       NOTES:                                                  *
*                                                               *
*                                                               *
*       KEYWORDS:Archives Films Historical-Sources Arthur-      *
*       Marwick War Society                                     *
*                                                               *
*       CLASS NO:001.432                                        *
*****************************************************************
Enter command: SELECT /ONLINE
    Enter the word to be found.       (hit RETURN at end, or F2 for preview)
    "?" matches any letter, "+" any sequence of letters.



Cardbox-Plus file = C:CLWLIBAV.FIL          READY              R/01
LEVEL 1 – RECORD 1 OF 37
*****************************************************************
*                   CLW LIBRARY AUDIO VISUAL MATERIALS         *
*       TITLE:OCLC'S strategic planning   LOCATION:VHS/C–623    *
*       challenges.                       DATE:1985             *
*       PLACE:Dublin, Ohio                                      *
*       PUBLISHER:Online-Computer-Library-Center, Inc.,         *
*       DESCRIPTION:1 videocassette (VHS) (88 min.): sd., col.  *
*       NTSC standard.                                          *
```

```
*                                                          *
*   CREDITS:By Rowland-Brown                               *
*                                                          *
*   NOTES:An OCLC Video Communications Program. N.B.       *
*   NTSC standard: must be played on multistandard player in*
*   academic block.                                        *
*                                                          *
*   KEYWORDS:OCLC Cataloguing Online Housekeeping          *
*   Automation USA                                         *
*                                                          *
*   CLASS NO:021.650973                                    *
*                                                          *
```

Enter command: **INCLUDE /DIALOG**
    Enter the word to be found.   (hit RETURN at end, or F2 for preview)
    "?" matches any letter, "+" any sequence of letters.

Cardbox-Plus file = C:CLWLIBAV.FIL   READY   R/01
LEVEL 2 – RECORD 2 OF 40

```
*                                                          *
*          CLW LIBRARY AUDIO VISUAL MATERIALS              *
*   TITLE:The DIALOG of information   LOCATION:VHS/C–362    *
*   retrieval.                        DATE:1981            *
*   PLACE:Palo Alto                                        *
*   PUBLISHER:Dialog-Marketing-Department                  *
*   DESCRIPTION:1 videocassette (VHS) (15 min.): sd., col.,*
*                                                          *
*   CREDITS:                                               *
*                                                          *
*   NOTES:                                                 *
*                                                          *
*                                                          *
*   KEYWORDS:DIALINDEX DIALORDER Databases USA             *
*   Online Dialog Computers                                *
*                                                          *
*   CLASS NO:024.04                                        *
```

Enter command: **INCLUDE KE/DATABASE+**
    Enter the word to be found.   (hit RETURN at end, or F2 for preview)
    "?" matches any letter, "+" any sequence of letters.

Cardbox-Plus file = C:CLWLIBAV.FIL   READY   R/01
LEVEL 3 – RECORD 1 OF 49

```
*                                                          *
*          CLW LIBRARY AUDIO VISUAL MATERIALS              *
*   TITLE:DATABASES.                  LOCATION:Tape/S–341   *
*                                     DATE:1985            *
*                                                          *
```

```
*                                                              *
*    PLACE:London                                             *
*    PUBLISHER:Prismatron                                     *
*    DESCRIPTION:59 slides: col. + 1 sound cassette (22 min.):*
*    1 7/8 ips, mono                                          *
*    CREDITS:                                                 *
*                                                             *
*    NOTES:Computer awareness series                         *
*                                                             *
*                                                             *
*    KEYWORDS:Database-Management-Systems Cataloguing        *
*    Books Structure DMS DBMS                                *
*                                                             *
*    CLASS NO:001.6442                                        *
*                                                             *
****************************************************************
```

Enter command: **QUIT**
        (now hit RETURN)

Search Example 10.1   *CARDBOX-PLUS search*

SELECT/ONLINE

This results in 37 records containing the word online being
retrieved, and one is displayed, a videotape of OCLC's strategic
planning strategies.
    The next command:

INCLUDE/DIALOG

adds in to the already retrieved set extra records which include the
term DIALOG, thus giving a new set of 40 records. The second
record in this set 'The DIALOG of Information Retrieval' is
displayed using the → key to move from the first record to the
second. The next command:

INCLUDE KE/DATABASE+

is used to add in records which include the stem 'database' in the
keyword field; this results in 49 records, the first of which is a tape-
slide programme on databases. Although no boolean operators
were used this search is equivalent to SELECT (ONLINE OR
DIALOG OR KE/DATABASE+). The SELECT command in
CARDBOX-PLUS also acts like a boolean AND, and the NOT
function is achieved using the EXCLUDE command. The com-

mand QUIT is used to leave the CARDBOX-PLUS search software.

Limiting by search field

The ability to limit the search by specifying a particular field (as in limiting the search to the keyword field in Search Example 10.1) is available in many packages.

Proximity searching

The ability to search for terms either adjacent to each other or within a given number of words of each other is available in some packages such as ASSASSIN, BASIS, CAIRS, INMAGIC, MINISIS and POLYDOC. For example, the operators used for this with the INQUIRE package are:

ADJ – to look for adjacent terms.
SEN – to look for terms in the same sentence.
WITHIN ± N words – to look for terms within a specified range.

This type of facility is particularly useful for searching full-text databases.

Truncation and spelling variations

Many packages offer the facility of right-hand truncation. Left-hand truncation is not so common but is often required if searching chemical names.

e.g. SEARCH ?SULPH?

to match with METABISULPHATE, SULPHUR, SULPHUROUS etc. Terms like SULPHUR also pose problems of variations in spelling. When records are input to a local database from various sources, perhaps by downloading, it is necessary to have the available search facilities to retrieve records including the variations. Some packages have a *character masking* or *wild card* feature to solve this.

e.g. SEARCH SUL*UR

to match with SULFUR or SULPHUR. One package, Superfile from Southdata Ltd matches spelling variations using a phonetic retrieval technique. Thus, a search for THOMSON would match with Thompson, Tommson, Tomson, Tomasson etc. Superfile is being used by many libraries in the Netherlands for searching large databases on WORM discs produced for the Dutch Ministry of Welfare, Health and Culture.

Range searching

Because of the need to search for numeric data (by date or by price etc.) the facility to search by range – using operators such as GE (greater than or equal), EQ (equals), LT (less than) etc. – is often available in text retrieval packages. For example, the command FIND PRICE LT 60, might be a command to retrieve records which have a number less than 60 in the price field. Some packages (like Micro-CAIRS and InMAGIC-Micro) enable the searcher also to carry out simple calculations based on numeric values.

Ability to consult a thesaurus

Some packages enable a thesaurus to be created and maintained which can then be used to assist with searching. In some cases this might be a list of current search terms (sometimes referred to as a *go* list) whilst in other cases a more complete thesaurus may be created which indicates the relationships (broader, narrower, related, synonymous) between search terms. Using a thesaurus at the search stage can improve the retrieval performance; alternatively the thesaurus may be used at the inputting stage in assisting with the allocation of descriptors or keywords to an item. Pasqual (1986), writing on the use of STATUS at the Western Australia Department of Agriculture describes how the thesaurus capability within STATUS enables the search

　　　Q Wheat disease?

to match with all the specific (narrower) terms related to wheat diseases in the database. If there is no thesaural control the onus is on the searcher to ensure that suitable broader, narrower, related or synonymous terms are used as appropriate in the search.

Display and browse the index

Most text retrieval packages provide facilities for the display of alphabetic sections of the index, or inverted file, showing the search terms and sometimes the number of postings. Search Example 10.2 shows the index close to the term 'ERYTHROMYCIN' in the Consumer Drug Information on Disk (CDID). CDID, produced by the American Society of Hospital Pharmacists (ASHP), is a database with linked software available on a floppy disc for local searching on an IBM-PC (or compatible) microcomputer. The database is aimed at providing health professionals and the public with a method of retrieving information on commonly prescribed drugs. Recently, ASHP has replaced CDID with MedTeach, a menu-based software product based on the *Medication Teaching Manual*. Search Example 10.2 also shows part of the record retrieved from a CDID search.

Target Term: ERYTHROMICIN

Erypar
EryPed
Erythrityl Tetranitrate
Erythrocin Stearate
Erythromycin
    Erythromycin Base Filmtab
    Erythromycin Estolate
    Erythromycin Ethylsuccinate
    Erythromycin Stearate
Eserine Sulfate

\\\ Page 1 of 5 \\\\\\\\\
and = Moves]F1 = Main Menu]F8 = End Group [
]ENTER = Choose]F2 = Summary]F9 = Item [Please select a term
]Alt-C = Colors]F3 = Page Back]F10 = Help [
]Alt-A = First]F4 = Page Ahead] O = Group Items [
]Alt-Z = Last]F7 = Group Items]Type a Response [

+++++++++++++++++++++++++++++=
CONSUMER DRUG INFORMATION ON DISK – page 1
+++++++++++++++++++++++++++++=

£ 1 of 2 . . . .

MONOGRAPH TITLE: Erythromycins (eh rith roe mye' sins)
GENERIC NAME: Erythromycin Ethylsuccinate/ Erythromycin Stearate/ Erythromycin/ Erythromycin Estolate

DRUG CLASSIFICATION: Erythromycins
MEDICAL CONDITION: Infections-General
ROUTES AND DOSAGES: Oral Capsules/ Oral Tablets/ Oral Liquid,
Solution, Syrup, etc
REGISTRY NUMBER: 41342–53–4/ 643–22–1 / 114–07–8 / 3521–62–8

PRODUCT INFORMATION. . . . . . .

E-Mycin/ ERYC/ Ery-Tab/ Erythromycin Base Filmtab/ Ilotycin/ PCE/
Robimycin/ RP-Mycin/ Ilosone/ EES/ E-Mycin E/ EryPed/ Pediamycin/
Wyamycin/ Bristamycin/ Eramycin/ Erypar/ Erythrocin Stearate/ Ethril/
Pfizer-E/ BK-Erythromycin/ Wyamycin S/ Pediazole

USES . . . .

The erythromycins are available in a number of chemical forms, including
erythromycin (base), estolate, ethylsuccinate and stearate. All of these
forms of erythromycin share the same uses, side effects and precautions
except erythromycin estolate/, which produces liver problems more
frequently than other erythromycins (see Undesired Effects and
Precautions).

The erythromycins are systemic antibiotics used to treat a wide variety of
infections, including throat, ear and skin infections, pneumonia and
diphtheria. They are considered good drugs to treat or prevent ""strep""
infections in people who have a history of rheumatic fever or rheumatic
heart disease and who may be sensitive or allergic to penicillins.

The erythromycins are the preferred drugs to eliminate diphtheria-
causing bacteria from people who show no signs of the disease but are
infecting others. There is some evidence that erythromycins are
effective against Legionnaires' disease.

Search Example 10.2 *CONSUMER DRUG INFORMATION*
database

Once a local database has been created it is often used for the
production of various printed lists, indexes or cards as well as for
online searching. Indeed the impetus for using a computer in the
first place may have been to assist in the production of the printed
products, and the ability to carry out online searches of the
database is therefore an added bonus. Users may be able to define
which fields are to be printed as well as their layout. In some
packages stored text and headings can be incorporated. Datta
(1987) includes examples of a printed accessions bulletin (with
bold type and underlining), catalogue cards and general lists that
are produced from a local database using CAIRS. Green (1988)
describes the use of a general R.DBMS, Paradox, and the word-

processing package WordStar on a microcomputer for creating an in-house database (in an engineering research centre library) that is used for running an SDI service, printing a current awareness bulletin and for retrospective searching. Some packages, for example, ASSASSIN-PC, enable keyword type indexes to be printed.

Many of those using text retrieval packages in special libraries or information units may have been accustomed to alerting their users to newly published or newly acquired material that is of direct relevance to individual users; this is generally known as selective dissemination of information or SDI. SDI facilities are available from the remote search services (as described in Chapter 5) and they are also sometimes available in the local text retrieval packages. The basic requirement is the ability to store search profiles that may be matched, perhaps by selecting appropriate date ranges, with records recently added to the database.

One development of searching local databases is the growing use of special devices to assist the interaction between the searcher and the computer system.

Many microcomputers, such as the IBM-PC or its compatibles, have special function keys which can be pre-programmed to store specific commands or groups of commands. These may be used to save the searcher typing in the specific commands of the system. For example, Search Example 10.3 shows the introductory screen of the LISA CD-ROM database available from Silver Platter; this briefly describes the use of some of the function keys. The system is in FIND mode at the start of the search and so the first search phrase HOSPITAL-PATIENT-LIBRARIES (a phrase in LISA's list of descriptors) is input. The next term is the truncated term, CHILD*, and then the two concepts are linked using the boolean operator AND. The first of the 23 retrieved references is displayed using the F4 (for SHOW) function key with the terms which have been used to retrieve this record highlighted.

Another device that may be used to assist searching is to use the ↑ , ↓ , →, ← keys to move the cursor to a specific part of the screen. Again the aim is to minimize the amount of pressing of keys by the searcher. Fries and Brown (1987) describe the use at Dartmouth College, New Hampshire, USA, of the Datext Corporate Information CD-ROM database (now known as Lotus' CD/CORPORATE), which integrates bibliographic, textual and numeric data on over 10 000 American public companies from various databases such as Predicasts' PROMT, DISCLOSURE II, INVESTEXT, ABI/INFORM, MEDIA GENERAL'S

SilverPlatter v1.4   LISA (1/69 – 9/88)

TITLE SCREEN	1 OF 1

The LISA Database
1969–September 1988

The LISA Database contains summaries of the world's literature in librarianship, information science and related disciplines,

To search LISA: type your search request, then press RETURN

To learn about the system: press F1 (HELP)

To learn about the LISA database: press F3 (GUIDE)

FIND:

Type a search request, then press RETURN; or press F1 for HELP.

SilverPlatter v1.4   LISA (1/69 – 9/88)

No.	Request	Records
£1:	HOSPITAL-PATIENT-LIBRARIES	124
£2:	CHILD*	4516
£3:	£1 and £2	23

SHOW fields:ALL   Records: ALL

Press RETURN to start with the first record; or press F1 for HELP.

SilverPlatter v1.4   LISA (1/69 – 9/88)

```
                                                        1 of 23
TI: Hospital outreach programme at the Montreal Children's
Library
AU: Walsh,-Molly; Montreal-(Quebec-Province)-Children's-
library
SO: Bulletin-ABQ/QLA-Bulletin, 30 (1) Jan-Apr 88, 21–22
PY: 1988
LA: English
AB: Describes the hospital outreach programme provided by
the Montreal Children's Library which serves several
departments of the Montreal Children's Hospital, Shriner's
Hospital, and schedules visits for Papillon day care groups from
the Quebec Society for Disabled Children.
FH: Hospital patient libraries. Children's libraries. Public
libraries. Quebec Province. Montreal Children's Library
DE: Canada-; Public-libraries; Children-; Welfare-services;
Hospital-libraries; Handicapped-; Institutional-libraries; Isolated-
; Disadvantaged-; Hospital-patient-libraries
CC: HuEfp&   Hu
DA: 1988
AN: 88–3854
:                                                        :
```

SHOW fields: ALL   Records: ALL

Press CTRL F2 to select terms from record for searching
PgDn for more; F10-Next Record; F2-Find- F1-Help; ESC-
Command Menu

Search Example 10.3 *Search of LISA on CD-ROM*

MARKET FILE and WHO'S WHO IN FINANCE AND
INDUSTRY. Search Example 10.4 shows some of the screens
displayed during a search for the Colgate Palmolive Company.
The arrows are used initially to choose a company search; the
specific name is typed, and this results in a display of the portion of
the inverted file of companies alphabetically close to Colgate. The
arrows are again used to move the searcher to the 'profile' option
and the resulting record is displayed.

Another device which may be used for moving the cursor in
local database searching is the *mouse*. This is the name given to a
device consisting of a small box, linked to the workstation by a
long cord, which can be moved around on a firm flat surface to

```
┌──────────────────────────────────────────────────────────────────┐
│  ┌────────────────────┐   ┌────────────────────────────────────┐  │
│  │ Main Menu          │   │ Current Selection                  │  │
│  ├────────────────────┘   ├────────────────────────────────────┘  │
│  │                        │ After selecting a company, you may     │
│  │  Company               │ select from the following options:     │
│  │  Portfolio             │   – Profile                            │
│  │  Industry              │   – Recent Financials                  │
│  │  Line of Business      │   – Historical Financials              │
│  │  Executive             │   – Subsidiaries                       │
│  │  Quit                  │   – Directors                          │
│  │                        │   – Stock Report                       │
│  │                        │   – Recent Articles                    │
│  │                        │   – Article Search                     │
│  │                        │   – Investment Reports                 │
│  │                        │   – Report Excerpts                    │
│  │                        │                                        │
│  └────────────────────────┴────────────────────────────────────┘  │
│  Input text: ■                                                     │
│  Press ← to Select the Current Item.                               │
│  F1 – Help            Technology Disc – January 1986               │
└──────────────────────────────────────────────────────────────────┘
```

```
┌──────────────────────────────────────────────────────────────────┐
│  ┌────────────────────┐   ┌─────────────────────┐    Company      │
│  │ Company List       │   │ Current Selection   │                 │
│  ├────────────────────┘   ├─────────────────────┘                 │
│  │  Cognitronics Corp     │ Colgate Palmolive Co                   │
│  │  Coherent Inc          │                                        │
│  │  Cohu Inc              │ 300 Park Avenue                        │
│  │  Coleman Co Inc        │ New York, NY 10022                     │
│  │  Colgate Palmolive Co  │ Tel: 212–310–2000                      │
│  │  Collagen Corp         │                                        │
│  │  Colonial Penn Group In│ Business: Soap and Other Detergents    │
│  │  Colorocks Corp        │                                        │
│  │  Colt Industries Inc   │ Total Sales ($000's):  4,909,957       │
│  │  Columbia Chase Corp   │ Net Income ($000 s):      71,550       │
│  │  Columbia Data Products│                                        │
│  │  Com Tel Inc           │ Shares Out: 82,669,461  FYE: 12/31/84  │
│  │  Com Vu Corp           │ Traded on:  NYSE   Ticker Symbol: CL   │
│  │  Comarco Inc           │                                        │
│  │  Comcast Cablevision of│                                        │
│  └────────────────────────┴────────────────────────────────────┘  │
│  Input text: Colgate Palmolive Co ■                                │
│  Press ← to Select the Current Item.                               │
│  F1 – Help          Technology Disc – January 1986                 │
│                     ESC – Main Menu                                │
└──────────────────────────────────────────────────────────────────┘
```

```
┌──────────────────────────────────────────────────────────────────┐
│                                               Company              │
│  ┌────────────────────┐   ┌─────────────────┐ Colgate Palmolive   │
│  │ Company Menu       │   │ Current Selection│                    │
│  ├────────────────────┘   ├─────────────────┘                    │
│  │  Profile               │ This report contains the following     │
│  │  Recent Financials     │ information for a selected company:    │
│  │  Historical Financials │   – Basic Identification Data          │
│  │  Subsidiaries          │   – Description of Business            │
│  │  Directors             │   – Lines of Business                  │
│  │  Stock Report          │   – Officers                          │
│  │  Recent Articles       │   – Summary Financial Results          │
│  │  Article Search        │                                        │
│  │  Investment Reports    │                                        │
│  │  Report Excerpts       │                                        │
│  │                        │                                        │
│  └────────────────────────┴────────────────────────────────────┘  │
│  Input text: ■                                                     │
│  Press ← to Select the Current Item.                               │
│  F1 – Help          Technology Disc – January 1986                 │
│                     ESC – Company List                             │
└──────────────────────────────────────────────────────────────────┘
```

Search Example 10.4 *Searching DATEXT CD-ROM database (taken from Fries and Brown, 1987)* move the cursor on the screen. It can, therefore, be used to point to menu items on the screen that can be selected by the pressing of a button on the mouse. The mouse may also be used to *pull-down* or manipulate windows of text or data. Manipulating an interface like this for searching is very different from the usual serial approach to searching available from the remote search services. A further development is the use of *icons* which use pictures rather than words. Thus a file may be deleted by pointing to a file name in a directory window with a click of the mouse, dragging the file name to the corner of the screen, again with the mouse and placing it in the dustbin icon. This type of search environment is known as WIMP, Windows, Icons, Mice and Pointers. Gibb (1989) describes some of the current development in WIMPs and graphical interfaces.

The use of *windows* (without the mouse) is apparent when searching the Bowker's BOOKS IN PRINT PLUS CD-ROM database. The actions are indicated along the top of the screen with SEARCH being the current action. The user can move to other actions by using the ←, → keys. The split screen shows the possible search codes and provides a workspace for the input of a

Search Browse Format Action Options Databases   Books In Print Plus

au=	Author	1. kw = child$ 44805
bn=	ISBN	2. kw = hospital$ 1443
kw=	Keyword	3. cs = 1 and cs = 2 100
lc=	LCCN	
pu=	Publisher	
su=	Subject	
ch=	Children's Subject	
tc=	Title Code	
ti=	Title	
se=	Series Title	
at=	4,4 Author,Title	
tk=	3,2,2,1, Title	
cs=	Combine Set	
ac=	Audience	
gr=	Grades	
il=	Illustration	
la=	Language	
pr=	Price	
py=	Publication Year	

F1 – > Help   ESC – > Menu Bar
Enter new Search Statement & press ENTER . F10 – > Brief Citation
Search Completed

Books In Print Plus

```
                      ┌────────── Search Workspace ──────────┐
                      │ 1. kw = child$                  44805 │
                      │ 2. kw = hospital$                1443 │
          ┌─────────── Brief Citations ──────────────────────────────────┐
   Title                 Author              Price    Date        ISBN
   Children's Hospitals in t   Rothman, David     $40.00    1988   0824076834
     Manual of Pediatric Thera  Children's Hosp   $24.50  08/1988   0316138886
     Pediatric Hospitalization  Knafl, Kathleen              1988   0673397327
 I   What Teenagers Want to Kn  Boston Children   $16.95  05/1988   0316250635
     Your Hospital Stay . . . It 1  Rosenstock, Jud  $4.95  11/1988   0962217204
     Clinical Pastoral Care fo  Hesch, John B.     $9.95  05/1987   0809128713
     Coping with a Hospital St  Carter, Sharon    $12.95  10/1987   0823906825
     Fat Dog's First Visit: A   Krall, Charlott    $4.00  06/1987   0939838230
     For Your Hospital Visit    Gregg-Schroeder          10/1987   0835805700
 I   Going to the Hospital      Civardi, Anne      $2.95     1987   0746000731
 I   The New Child Health Ency  Boston Children   $19.95  11/1987   0385295979
```

Books in Print Plus

```
                      ┌────────── Search Workspace ──────────┐
                      │ 1. kw = child$                  44805 │
                      │ 2. kw = hospital$                     │
          ┌─────────── Brief Citations   Citation(s) Selected : ──────────1┐
   Title                 Author              Viewing :              1
          ┌─────────── Books in Print Format ──────────────────────────────┐
   Ch    │ Krall, Charlotte B. & Jim, Judith M. Fat Dog's First Visit: A Child's View of │
   Ma    │   the Hospital. Hull, Nancy, editor. Hull, Nancy, illustrator. Williams, │
   Pe    │   Michele, illustrator. LC 87–2745. (Illus.). 28p. (Orig.) Juv (ps–3) 06/ │
 I Wh    │   1987. Paperback text edition. $4.00. (ISBN 0–939838–23–0). Pritchett │
   Yo    │   & Hull Associates, Incorporated. │
   Cl
   Co
   Fa
   Fo
 I Go
 I Th
```

Search Example 10.5   *Searching Bowker's BOOKS IN PRINT PLUS™ CD-ROM database*

search. The keyword search for books related to children in hospital is input as shown:

KW = child$
KW = hospital$
CS = 1 and CS = 2

On pressing F10, the function key programmed to set up a display of the brief citations, the window containing that display is pulled down on to the screen. The ↓ key is used to move the cursor to the 8th citation and pressing F10 again provides a display of the full citation of Charlotte Krall and Judith Jim's book *Fat Dog's First Visit: A Child's View of the Hospital.*

As end-users, particularly medics, are beginning to carry out their own searches on CD-ROM some analyses of their search techniques are beginning to appear.

The experiences at the Erskine Medical Library at Edinburgh University in evaluating end-user searches of Medline on CD-ROM show:

1. Searchers repeat terms rather than use OR logic, for example,
   CEREBRAL PALSY AND CHILD ABUSE
   CEREBRAL PALSY AND SOCIAL WORK
   CEREBRAL PALSY AND FOSTER HOME
   CEREBRAL PALSY AND CHILD PRE-SCHOOL
   instead of:
   (CHILD ABUSE OR SOCIAL WORK OR FOSTER HOME OR CHILD PRE-SCHOOL) AND CEREBRAL PALSY
   which would take less time and might not result in duplicate records.
2. Searchers omit relevant synonyms
   TUMOUR
   instead of TUMOUR OR TUMOR OR NEOPLASM
3. Searchers wrongly use truncation
   ETHICS? AND HANDICAPPED
   instead of
   ETHIC? AND HANDICAPPED

The important outcome of such studies shows that most of the end-users are happy with their searches most of the time, however they must be reminded that if a more up-to-date and comprehensive search is required this is probably best done by an intermediary.

Management Aspects

Developing a local database: initial study

The first stage in the setting up of a local database should be a detailed study of the existing system for storing and retrieving information and the requirements for the new system; in effect a feasibility study. It is necessary to collect data on the size and growth rate of the current collection, the average size of the current records, the requirements of the users who will search the database and the likely number of searchers expected at any one time. The results of such a study will help determine the software and the hardware required for the system. Ideally the software should be chosen first and should match with the requirements identified. However, in practice, constraints such as existing hardware and perhaps existing software may pertain. Although special software could be written, this is often an expensive and time-consuming solution.

Eddison (1988) provides some practical advice for planning and building local databases, and emphasizes the importance of planning in determining who wants the database, why it is required, and how it is to be created and maintained. The planning decisions taken for a database to be compiled, maintained and searched by perhaps only one person (say a librarian/information officer working alone in providing a service to a small organization) are very different from those taken for a database to be compiled and maintained by a large number of people and then perhaps searched by a different set of people.

The result of a study such as this should be presented to management and if it is decided that the database be created then a plan (perhaps a critical path chart, or a bar chart) should be prepared, as for any other automation project outlining the steps in the implementation process.

Choosing software for a local database

When choosing a software package for local database searching the main factors to be considered that relate specifically to searching include:

1. How are the index terms created?
2. Is boolean searching available?
3. What other search techniques are available?
4. Is there a thesaurus capability?
5. How is the inverted file displayed?
6. Can the search be carried out on several files?
7. Can the software search for phrases?
8. What are the limits of field, record and file sizes?
9. Can the software search a reasonably sized database in an adequate time? Because many searchers of in-house databases will probably be used to the (usual) rapid response time of the

remote search services it is necessary to ensure that the software and the hardware configuration are sufficient to retrieve information from the local database in an adequate time.

10. Can several people search the database at once? Many of the software packages for use on microcomputers are aimed at a single user searching, or updating, the database at any one time. However by using a multi-user operating system some packages support several searchers at one time. Alternatively microcomputers may be linked together in a network to provide a master copy of the database and 'read only' versions may be searched from individual workstations; packages such as INMAGIC-Micro, TINman, CARDBOX-PLUS and Micro-CAIRS can be used in this way.

11. Is it easy to use?

12. Is the software used by other similar organizations? If so, what are their experiences?

13. How much does the software cost? The variation is great, from hundreds to tens of thousands of pounds. Generally, software for microcomputers is cheaper than software for minicomputers or mainframes; however, there will be different rates for single and multi-user versions. ASSASSIN-PC, for instance, costs £995 for the single-user version and £25 000 upwards for the networked version.

14. Who wrote the software? There are various types of organizations involved in writing software for local database searching. Some, having developed software in-house, have then started to market it; one example of such is the British Food Manufacturing Industries Research Association, which developed CAIRS originally, in the mid-1970s, for use within its information unit. Some firms specialize in this area. Cuadra Associates, for instance, is a firm with staff highly experienced in online searching aspects; it has produced the STAR package, an integrated multi-user hardware and software information management system. The use of STAR by three organizations is described in *Database* (1987). Sometimes national or international bodies are involved in producing software. The International Development Research Center in Canada, for instance, produces MINISIS, a minicomputer version of a package originally developed at the International Labour Office in Geneva. MINISIS is used by various international information systems such as AGRIS (Agri-

cultural Information System) and DEVSIS (Development Sciences Information System). A microcomputer version of MINISIS which is known as Micro CDS-ISIS is available from Unesco and is used in many countries worldwide (Jacso, 1986).

15. Who supplies the software? In some cases the organization which wrote the software is not able to supply and market that software. It is necessary to ensure that the software is supplied by a reputable firm which will ensure that updated versions and new releases will be available if required.

16. What are the hardware and software requirements? Software packages are written in a particular programming language, to run under a particular operating system with a minimum configuration of storage capacity and so on.

17. Can the software be used in a language other than English? Some packages can communicate with the searcher in various European languages; examples of such packages include CAIRS, TINman and STATUS.

18. Is the support adequate? Some suppliers or producers provide detailed support in the form of documentation, help with designing record structures or training in the use of the package. Some users of packages (for example, CAIRS and STATUS) have come together to form user groups which meet periodically to share experiences.

19. Is the warranty adequate?

Further details on aspects involved in choosing a package are given by Ramsden (in Rowlands, 1987), Kazlauskas (1987a), who includes a software evaluation form and Citroen (1989), who also discusses criteria for choosing emulation packages and programs for data conversion.

Finding out basic details of these packages has been made easier since the appearance of directories such as Kazlauskas (1987b) and Kimberley (1989). A selected bibliography of information management software is provided by Ingebretsen (1987). Published comparisons of packages are useful when selecting a package. A comparison of 11 microcomputer packages (including ASSASSIN-PC, CARDBOX-PLUS, dBase III, INMAGIC-Micro, Micro-Questel, Mikro-Polydoc and TINman) has been undertaken by the Netherlands Association of Users of Online Information Systems (VOGIN) and reported by Sieverts and Mastenbroek (1987). Ashford (1984b) compares nine packages (including ASSASSIN, BASIS, INFOText, CAIRS and STATUS) used with mainframe or minicomputers. Critical reviews of software packages are available in some journals; Frey (1986), for instance, describes the use of BRS/Search for creating and searching databases.

Creating a local database

Having selected and acquired suitable software and ensured that it works effectively on the appropriate hardware it is necessary to design the structure of records, input the records and create the database. Great care should be taken in the design of the record structure to ensure that relevant information is recorded about the item so that it may be retrieved when appropriate. Lundeen and Tenopir (1988) discuss various aspects of the design and creation of text databases on microcomputers. Decisions also need to be made regarding factors such as:

1. Acronyms (are they to be used or spelled out? Is there a standard list?)
2. Index terms (are these to be controlled or uncontrolled?)
3. Dates (is there to be a standardized way of referring to dates?)

Eddison (1988) discusses these aspects of local database creation in more depth as well as aspects of quality control, which, it is noted, must start with the first steps of database creation.

The actual mechanics of inputting the records need to be established. In some cases records will be keyboarded directly into the system. Alternatively an outside bureau may be used for the initial creation of records. Another alternative is that some records may be downloaded from a remote online search service for incorporation in a local database.

The legal position of downloading is not too clear and the current copyright implications are discussed by Martyn in Rowlands (1987). Unless permission has been given, it is illegal to take pieces of text, save them on disc, reformat them and perhaps add text. EUSIDIC, the European Association of Information Services, is attempting to persuade the database producers to standardize on their policies with respect to downloading. Gorman (1986) reported on the relevant policies of 65, mainly American, database producers. There are various software packages available such as HEADFORM from Head Computers or FILTER from Information Automation which enable records to be downloaded, perhaps from a remote search service or from a CD-ROM database, and then be reformatted to the necessary structure for a local in-house database.

It is necessary to check carefully all records entered into a local database otherwise they may not be retrieved when required and the old maxim 'Garbage in, garbage out' will pertain. It is often better to proof-read using a printed output, preferably of a high quality, rather than attempting to do this directly on a VDU screen. Software packages for searching and creating local databases usually incorporate facilities for correcting errors in the data, hopefully with a minimum of effort.

Once the data have been captured and verified, the database must be built by generating the necessary indexes and files. The time taken for database loading can vary considerably, as can the size of the final database generated from a given set of records. Sieverts and Mastenbroek (1987) report on comparisons of the time taken to store and index a given number of records using different packages.

Maintaining a local database

Having created the initial database it is important to realize that regular *backups* of the database should be taken in order to ensure that in the event of some corruption of the data, the database can be reconstructed. Backup involves the copying of the database on to a separate disc or magnetic tape, or perhaps printing it out as well. If the database is added to or modified daily, then the backup process should probably be carried out daily too. The decision as to how often the database should be updated is an important one, and depends on the frequency with which new records are received, the need for currency, the time taken to update and so on. It may also be necessary, depending on the type of information included in the database, to remove older data to a suitable archiving medium, at suitable intervals; this is done so that the files do not grow too large which may adversely affect the search speed.

Judge and Gerrie (1986) include papers from a workshop held in Australia for producers of small-scale bibliographic databases and these include practical points on the creation and maintenance of local databases.

Selection of CD-ROM products

Most CD-ROM products currently available offer an alternative means of access to information that is already available via a remote online search service, or in printed form, although it may be packaged differently. The decision relating to whether or not to acquire a CD-ROM database is affected by various factors as discussed by Hatvany (1987) who compares searching on CD-ROM and via the remote search services in terms of capacity, currency, cost, response time and data rates. The general conclusion is that if a searcher uses a given database infrequently it is usually more cost-effective to use a remote service, whereas if much use is made of that database then it might be best to acquire the CD-ROM version.

In order to read CD-ROM discs it is necessary either to buy a CD-ROM drive to link in to an existing microcomputer or to buy an integrated CD-ROM workstation. Philips, for instance, launched such a workstation, during 1988, which incorporates an industry-standard IBM-PC AT, with a single floppy disc drive and a 20-Mb hard disc as well as the CD-ROM drive; this cost about £4000 originally but the price has fallen as the demand has increased. It is necessary to ensure that any CD-ROM drive acquired is capable of reading discs written according to the International Standardisation Organisation (ISO) Standard 9660. Even so, there may be problems of hardware or software incompatibility when CD-ROMs from a variety of producers are used on one disc drive.

To help in the decision relating to what CD-ROM databases should be acquired there are various directories (for example, Emard, 1988) appearing as well as user evaluations; Day (1987) describes her experiences of using LISA on CD-ROM, for instance. Brunell (1988), of the Bibliographical Center for Research, in Denver, states that the four main factors to be considered when choosing a CD-ROM product are:

1. Data files. How far back does the information on the CD-ROM database go? What is the record structure? What fields can be searched? How often is the database updated?
2. Search software. Are beginner and expert modes available? Can it be searched in a similar way to that adopted for searching the remote services? Does it respond within acceptable time limits? Can it link with other software? (The LOTUS CD/CORPORATE database, for instance, can link to the LOTUS 1–2–3 spreadsheet package.)
3. Hardware. Most CD-ROM databases require a hard disc and 640 Kb of RAM; some also make significant use of colour on the screen. Thus the possibility of upgrading existing equipment may add to the cost of setting up the CD-ROM database.
4. Cost and terms of subscription/purchase.

SilverPlatter v1.4   ERIC (1/83 – 3/88)

TITLE SCREEN   1 of 1

The ERIC Database
January, 1981 – March, 1988

The ERIC (Educational Resources Information Center)
database consists of the Resources in Education (RIE) file of
document citations and the Current Index to Journals in
Education (CIJE) file of journal article citations from over 750
professional journals. Sponsored by the U.S. Department of
Education, ERIC is a network of 16 Clearinghouses, each
specializing in a separate subject area.

To search the ERIC database: type your search request, then
press RETURN

To learn about the system: press F1 (HELP)
To learn about the ERIC database: press F3 (GUIDE)

FIND: **dyslexia**
SilverPlatter v1.4   ERIC (1/83 – 3/88)

No.   Request   Records

£1:   DYSLEXIA   200

PRINT   Fields: all   Records: 1
         separate pages: (No) Yes searches: (No) Yes
Press RETURN to start with the first record; or F1 for HELP.

SilverPlatter v1.4   **ERIC (1/83 – 3/88)**

AN: EJ361106
CHN: EC201017
AU: Kelso,-Jill
TI: Nurturing a Special Child.
PY: 1987
JN: Exceptional-Parent; v17 n8 p50–53 Nov-Dec 1987
AV: UMI
DT: Journal Articles (080); Opinion Papers (120)
TA: Parents
LA: English
DE: Personal-Narratives
DE: *Child-Rearing; *Disabilities-; **Dyslexia**-; *Epilepsy-
IS: CIJFEB88
AB: A mother of a son with epilepsy and **dyslexia** offers 10 guidelines
    for parents including: acknowledge your grief; recognize assets and
    limitations; encourage independence; ignore unsolicited advice; be
    proud of your child's achievements; make use of financial aid;
    subscribe to newsletters; get to know your child's physician; and
    make time for yourself. (DB)
CH: EC
FI: EJ
DTN: 080; 120

Search Example 10.6(a) *Search and print of ERIC on Silver Platter*

With some databases now being made available on CD-ROM by a
variety of suppliers, the selection process may become more
complex. MEDLINE, for instance, is available from Silver Platter,
Dialog, OCLC, Ebsco and Cambridge Scientific Abstracts; Kittle
(1988), for example, reviews these products. Search example 10.6
shows the variation in searching for a single term 'dyslexia' on the
ERIC database produced on CD-ROM by Silver Platter, OCLC
and Dialog. The Silver Platter search retrieved 200 records and the
details of the first record (an article by Jill Kelso) are printed
using the function key (F6). The OCLC search, using software
known as CD450, retrieved 235 records and the first record is
printed using the function key (F7). The Dialog OnDisc search has
an 'easy menu' option for the naive user, but in the example the
Dialog commands were used. In this case 280 records were
retrieved and the Kelso article has been displayed. Desmarais
(1988) covers the selection and implementation of CD-ROM
databases in more depth.

Database: CIJE 82-

RETRIEVED Record:	1>**dyslexia**
	F2=Index F3=Fields ↵ Enter Query

Welcome to Search CD 450!

To search the database, enter a word or phrase and press ↵
Search CD450 will locate records in the database containing this
word or phrase.

Search for subject phrases assigned to each record by placing
hyphens between the words in the phrase. The Index <F2> will
help you identify words and subject phrases in the database.

Use ↑ ↓ PgUp   PgDn to scroll text in retrieved records.

Press <F1> for more information about searching the database.

Search CD450   v2.01   F1=Help   F10=Quit

Database: CIJE_82- (CIJE, 1982-Mar 1989)
Query 1:   dyslexia (235)

Accession Number: EJ379115

AUTHOR: Lundquist, Arlene J.
              Nash, Robert

TITLE: Remediating Language Deficient/Dyslexic College Students:
              An Interview with Robert Nash.

SOURCE: Journal of Developmental Education (v12 n1 p16–19 Sep
              1988)

YEAR: 88

Robert Nash responds to questions concerning his personal and
professional background, the Simultaneous Multisensory Instructional
Procedure for Teaching the Complete Sound Structure of the Language,
problems associated with dyslexia, the social/emotional impact of
learning disabilities, and the University of Wisconsin's Project Success
for language inefficient/dyslexic students. (DMM)

NOTE: UMI

MAJOR DESCRIPTORS:
Dyslexia
Language Handicaps
Multisensory Learning
Remedial Instruction
Teaching Methods

MINOR DESCRIPTORS:
College Students
Community Colleges
Remedial Programs
Student Problems
Two Year Colleges

Search Example 10.6(b)   *Search and print of ERIC on OCLC CD-ROM*

```
WELCOME TO DIALOG ONDISC(tm) MANAGER

               Version 2.00 JAN-88
             Serial Number OM0302712001
This software product and the indexing techniques used on
the disc are protected by both United States Copyright Law
          and International Treaty Provisions.

             Written by: Claude Schoch
   Copyright 1985–1988 Digital Library Systems, Inc.
              ALL RIGHTS RESERVED
```

```
        Select Search Mode

    Easy Menu Search
    DIALOG Command Search
    Online Search
    Return to DOS
```

↑ ↓ Move ←—Select

```
                    ERIC
   Current Index to Journals in Education (CIJE)
          Resources in Education (RIE)
 Office of Educational Research and Improvement (OERI)
   More current ERIC records may be found online
                 in File 1, ERIC
   Copyright (c) 1988, DIALOG Information Services, Inc.
  All rights reserved. No claim to original U.S. Gov't works
```

ERIC – CJIE & RIE   1980 – March 1988

Set   Items   Description
___   ___   ___

?SELECT DYSLEXIA

1/2/1 of 280
EJ361106   EC201017
Nurturing a Special Child.
Kelso, Jill
Exceptional Parent, v17 n8 p50–53 Nov-Dec 1987
Available From: UMI
Language: English
Document Type: JOURNAL ARTICLE (080); POSITION PAPER (120)
Journal Announcement: CIJFEB88
Target Audience: Parents
Descriptors: *Child Rearing; *Disabilities; *Dyslexia; *Epilepsy;
Personal Narratives

Search Example 10.6(c)   *Search and print of ERIC via Dialog Ondisc*

There are many developments in progress in the area of online searching of locally stored databases with image-based systems beginning to appear as well as hypertext systems.

References

Ashford, J. A. (1984a) Storage and retrieval of bibliographic records: a comparison of database management systems (DBMS) and free-text approaches. *Program*, **18** (1), 16–45

Ashford, J. A. (1984b) Information storage and retrieval systems on mainframes and minicomputers: a comparison of text retrieval packages available in the UK. *Program*, **18** (2), 124–126

Ashford, J. A. and Willett, P. (1989) *Text Retrieval and Document Databases*. Bromley: Chartwell Bratt

Bristow, A. (1988) Reference sources on CD-ROM at Indiana University. *Electronic Library*, **6** (1), 24–29

Burnell, D. H. (1988) Comparing CD-ROM products. *CD-ROM Librarian*, **3** (3), 14–18

Chen, C.-C. and DeYoung, B. (1984) *Integrating Micro-Based DBMS in Libraries*. West Newton, Mass: MicroUse Information

Citroen, C. (1989) Microcomputer software for information retrieval: how to make a well-founded choice. *Program*, **23** (2), 141–150

Clough, C. R. (1986) The changing role of retrieval systems and specialists. In *Online Information 87: 10th International Online Information Meeting Proceedings*, pp. 175–184. Oxford: Learned Information

Datta, V. K. (1987) Use of CAIRS at the Tropical Development and Research Institute Library. *Program*, **21** (4), 360–375

Database (1987) Database looks at Cuadra's STAR. *Database*, **10** (6), 35–45

Day, J. M. (1987) LISA on CD-ROM: a user evaluation. In *Online Information 88: 11th International Online Information Meeting Proceedings*, pp. 273–284. Oxford: Learned Information

Desmarais, N. M. (1988) *The Librarian's CD-ROM Handbook.* Westport, Connecticut: Meckler

Eddison, E. B. (1988) How to plan and build your database. *Database*, **11** (3), 15–26

Emard, J. P. (1988) *CD-ROMs in Print 1988–1989.* Westport, Connecticut: Meckler

Frey, D. (1986) BRS/Search/Micro/Mini version. *Library Software Review*, 189–193

Frey, C. (1987) Microcomputer software packages for information management: an Australian perspective. *Microcomputers for Information Management*, **4** (1), 11–37

Fries, J. and Brown, J. (1987) Business information on CD-ROM: the Datext service at Dartmouth College, New Hampshire. *Program*, **21** (1), 1–12

Gibb, F. (1989) Developments in WIMPs and GIs. In *Proceedings of the Third Annual Conference on Small Computers in Libraries held in London in February 1989*, pp. 54–58. London: Meckler

Gorman, N. (1986) Downloading . . . still a live issue? A survey of database producers' policies for both online services and laser disks. *Online*, **10** (4), 15–25

Green, K. E. (1988) Selective dissemination of information using a low-cost relational database at GEC's Engineering Research Centre. *Program*, **22** (2), 161–176

Hatvany, B. (1987) Comparison of CD-ROM and online. In *Online Information 87: 11th International Online Information Meeting Proceedings*, pp. 285–290. Oxford: Learned Information

Hopkinson, A. (1985) Standardizing data exchange: the Unesco Common Communication Format. In *Proceedings of the 9th International Information Meeting.* Oxford: Learned Information
Ingebretson, D. L. (1987) Information management software: a selected bibliography. *Database,* 10 (6), 27–34
Jacśo, P., Szücs, A. and Varga, S. (1986) Micro-CDS/ISIS: a bibliographic information management software from UNESCO. *Microcomputers for Information Management,* 3 (3), 173–198
Judge, P. and Gerrie, B. (1986) Editors. *Small Scale Bibliographic Databases.* Sydney: Academic Press
Kazlauskas, E. J. (1987a) Information management software: guidelines for decision making. *Database,* 10 (6), 17–24
Kazlauskas, E. J. (1987b) Editor. *Directory of Information Management Software for Libraries, Information Centers, Record Centers 1987–8.* Studio City, Ca: Pacific Information Inc
Kimberley, R. (1989) Editor. *Text Retrieval: A Directory of Software.* Aldershot: Gower
Kittle, P. (1988) Medline on CD-ROM: a review of six products. *Laserdisk Professional,* 1 (3), 18–28
Koenig, M. E. D. (1985) Data relationships: bibliographic information retrieval systems and database management systems. *Information Technology and Libraries,* 4 (3), 247–272
LISA Online User Manual (1987). Oxford: Learned Information
Luhn, H. P. (1957) A statistical approach to mechanised encoding and searching of library information. *IBM Journal of Research and Development,* 1, 309–317
Lundeen, G. and Tenopir, C. (1988) *Managing Your Information: How to Design and Create Textual Databases on your Microcomputer.* New York: Neal Schuman
Noerr, P L. and Bivins-Noerr, K. T. (1985) Browse and navigate: an advance in database access methods. *Information Processing and Management,* 21 (3), 205–213
Oxborrow, E. A. (1986) *Databases and Database Systems: Concepts and Issues.* Bromley: Chartwell Bratt
Pasqual, G. (1986) Development of an agricultural database for dissemination of research information to research and extension workers using STATUS software. *Program,* 20 (3), 323–331
Rowlands, I. (1987) *Text Retrieval: An Introduction.* London: Taylor Graham
Sieverts, E. G. and Mastenbroek, O. (1987) *Microcomputer Applications for Online and Local Information Systems: A Test and Comparison of 30 Software Packages.* Leiden: VOGIN

Tagg, R. M. (1985) Text retrieval and database management systems – compare and contrast. In *Text Retrieval in Context: Proceedings of the Institute of Information Scientists Text Retrieval '84 Conference*, edited by R. Kimberley, C. D. Hamilton and C. H. Smith, pp. 40–45. London: Taylor Graham

Tedd, L. A. (1979) *Case Studies in Computer-Based Bibliographic Information Services*. BLR&DD Report No. 5463. London: British Library

Teskey, F. N. (1984) *Information Retrieval Systems of the Future*. Library and Information Research Report 26. London: British Library

Woodrow, M. (1986) Case study 1: dBase II for local information files. In *Microcomputer Software for Information Management: Case Studies*, edited by M. Collier, pp. 39–55. Aldershot: Gower

Chapter 11

Videotext and Teletext Systems

Introduction

The online search services which have been discussed thus far were designed and implemented on the assumption that they would be searched by information professionals. More recently attempts have been made to make these search services more accessible to non-information professionals (see Chapter 8). Approximately in parallel with the development of these search services for information professionals, computer-based information systems intended for use by the mass, domestic market were created. These are the videotex and teletext services which originated in Britain but have now spread worldwide. Public videotex and teletext services have tended to develop on a national basis and the treatment in this chapter reflects the fact that systems which were developed initially in Britain have been further developed in both technical and service terms in other countries.

To the searcher, videotex and teletext are immediately different from conventional online search services. The display, which mixes text and graphics and uses colour, is obviously very different from systems using teletype displays. The similarity in videotex and teletext displays results from the efforts of videotex designers to comply with the display standards implemented by teletext operators. The basic interaction has always been the menu rather than the command language. The similarity in screen and in interaction led to some initial confusion between videotex and teletext. However, in the late 1970s the distinctions between videotex and teletext services and between videotex and conventional online search services were relatively clearcut. More recently these distinctions have become somewhat blurred by the introduction of some menu-based interactions in online search services and some use of direct searching in videotex systems.

Nevertheless, the separate origins and intended market of videotex and teletext systems has led to a sufficiently different development path for these systems to merit a separate chapter.

Since the beginning of videotex and teletext, there has been terminological uncertainty and it is as well that the reader is aware of this from the outset. When the then (British) Post Office first developed a public videotex system, it wished to call this service Viewdata. However, this name was not acceptable in Britain as a brand name and the service was rapidly renamed PRESTEL. In Britain, viewdata soon became the generic name for a type of computer-based information system of which PRESTEL was the publicly available system. The broadcast textual information systems, introduced by the two broadcasting authorities in Britain, became known as teletext systems. The name videotex became the generic term which referred to both teletext and viewdata services. However, this use of the term videotex has not been widely adopted outside Britain and the term videotex has become used to refer to the interactive systems known as viewdata in Britain. One helpful distinction which is sometimes made is to refer to videotex systems as interactive videotex systems and teletext systems as broadcast videotex or pseudo-interactive videotex systems. It should be clear from this that the reader is well advised to make certain how a particular author is using terminology. In this book videotex refers to interactive systems only and the broadcast systems are called teletext.

Teletext

Teletext is a text-based information system in which the information is transmitted by the television authorities using spare lines in the television signal. The broadcast signal is received and decoded by a suitably adapted television set. Teletext systems were developed by research engineers of the British Broadcasting Corporation (BBC) and the (British) Independent Broadcasting Authority (IBA). In the early stages of research and development the engineers of the BBC and IBA used somewhat different ways to broadcast the signal. Fortunately a joint technical standard for teletext signals was developed. This permitted the signals from the two authorities to be received and decoded by a single decoder and this enabled the services to begin transmission in November 1976.

The information in teletext systems is structured as a series of pages on the broadcasting organization's computer. These pages are broadcast on the spare lines in the TV signal as a continuous loop of pages. The signals can be received by anyone with a television set which has been fitted with the appropriate teletext adaptor. The user interacts with the system through a numeric keypad. When the user enters a page number, the decoder grabs that page the next time that it is broadcast and displays the information on the screen. From this description, it should be apparent that the user interacts with the broadcast signal and not with the computer system; and thus teletext is sometimes referred to as broadcast videotex or as pseudo-interactive videotex. Since the pages of information are broadcast in a continuous loop, the response time between requesting a page of information and having it displayed on the screen can be anything up to 25 seconds. Such a delay makes the system seem very slow in comparison with more conventional online search services. The mode of display on the screen is an obvious difference between teletext services and online search services. In teletext services the screen is divided into a grid of rows and columns, rather like a spreadsheet, and the resultant cells are used for generating either a character or a simple graphic. In British teletext, a grid of 24 rows with 40 columns in each row is used. Within each cell a matrix of 6 by 10 dots is used to build up characters. Other countries use a similar approach but the precise implementation is different. Details of the French system appear later in the chapter. A more detailed technical description of teletext is beyond the scope of this book but the reader who wishes to know how the information is transmitted and then decoded for presentation on a television screen should consult the book by Money (1979).

Despite a response time which appears slow to users of other online systems, teletext in Britain is proving to be very successful and now has a user base of over 3 500 000 installed receivers. It seems likely that the services are popular because they are available free of charge to viewers with a suitable adaptor on their television set. A further advantage is that as the users are interacting with a broadcast signal rather than a computer system, there are no problems of other users affecting accessibility to the system.

There are now four teletext services in Britain, two from the BBC known as CEEFAX (literally see facts) linked to the TV channels BBC1 and BBC2 and two from IBA known as ORACLE (Optional Reception of Announcements by Coded Line Electronics) which are linked to the commercial channels. All channels offer a basic diet of general news, financial information such as exchange rates and commodity prices, sports news and results, weather and travel news and information related to TV and radio programmes. Some examples are shown in Figures 11.1 and 11.2. Figure 11.1 shows a typical headline page from the ORACLE service. The top line indicates the page number within ORACLE and the date and time. Commodities price information from the BBC City News service on CEEFAX is shown in Figure 11.2. Again the top line indicates page number, date and time. In addition the services provide a certain amount of leisure information/entertainment such as jokes and games for children, gardening and knitting information. Whilst the two broadcasting authorities collaborated on the technical standards which enabled teletext services to be created, they have exploited the services in rather different ways. The BBC through CEEFAX provides a rather more serious news service with a small amount of entertainment on the system. ORACLE provides much more entertainment and superficial information. Since 1981, ORACLE has been a commercially operated service which generates income from a variety of advertising ventures. One of the most successful of these is the provision of a series of regional classified adverts covering such diverse topics as property for sale, motoring and armchair shopping (see Figures 11.3 and 11.4). Information about entertain-

Figure 11.1 *Schematic of headlines on ORACLE*

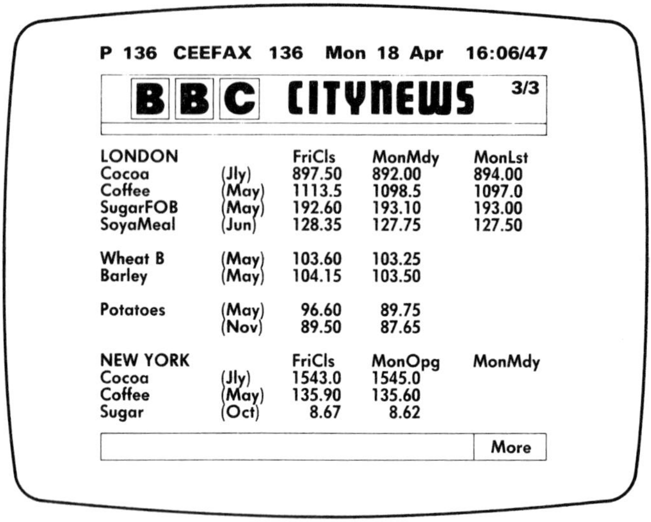

Figure 11.2   *Schematic of commodity prices on CEEFAX*

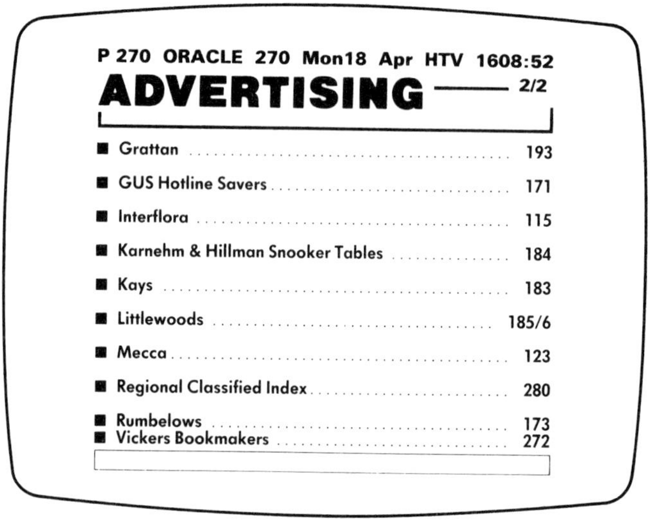

Figure 11.3   *Schematic of armchair shopping on ORACLE*

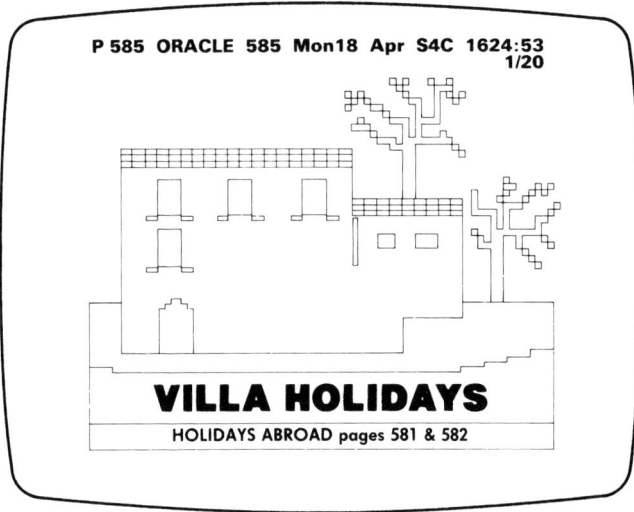

Figure 11.4 *Schematic of holidays advertised on ORACLE*

ment is also provided on a regional basis. Further innovative income generating activities have been the inclusion of 'sponsorship' pages or part pages whereby adverts may be linked to particular editorial sections of the database. This is achieved whilst maintaining editorial independence. A further use has been the provision of *advertorials*, that is pages of specialist information which are presented in editorial format and are relevant to the commercial interests of the advertiser who pays a fee for the presence of this information on ORACLE.

The volume of information available on teletext in Britain is limited. In the case of CEEFAX there is anything between 400 and 600 pages on a given day whilst the equivalent figures for ORACLE are 1000 to 2000 pages. The method of finding and displaying a page precludes many more pages being offered: the resulting delay between selection and display would be unacceptable. The search mechanism is straightforward. The searcher simply keys in a page number via the keypad and this page is then displayed when it is next grabbed by the decoder. The searcher is aided by an initial contents page/menu as indicated in Figures 11.5 and 11.6. Although a certain number of options are provided in this menu, some may not be considered tremendously helpful to the new searcher. What for example is the newcomer to make of the option 'Buzz' on ORACLE? Only the experienced user will know that this is a message service for children. In addition there is an index to the contents. Whilst these access mechanisms may seem rudimentary to the user of command languages, it must be remembered that there is only a small amount of information on teletext systems and research has shown that a significant proportion of regular users memorize the page numbers which they use regularly. Indeed research carried out for ORACLE reports that 38 per cent of users claim to have memorized the entire index (*Videotex Industry Yearbook*, 1987)!

In the United Kingdom, teletext is being utilized for other activities as well as information transmission. For example, it is used for sub-titling some television programmes for the hard of hearing. It is used as a mechanism for the broadcasting and downloading of computer software, particularly aimed at home and school users. IBA is experimenting with the use of 4-Tel, a sub-section of the ORACLE service, to provide a range of programme-related support services and to promote programmes on Channel 4. The BBC is offering Datacast, a data transmission service for private organizations.

Figure 11.5   *Schematic of CEEFAX contents page*

Figure 11.6 *Schematic of ORACLE contents page*

Teletext has spread well beyond the confines of Britain since its introduction in the 1970s. In America, the two major television channels, CBS and NBC, both introduced national teletext magazines in 1983. The CBS service is known as Extravision whilst the NBC service is known as Tempo. There have been other attempts at both national and local teletext magazines, some of which are offered by cable television companies. One ambitious project was mounted by Time Life Books in 1982. Its aim was to produce a 5000-page teletext magazine service which was designed specifically to take advantage of the features of teletext. The intention was to introduce the first full channel broadcast teletext service. However, the service was cancelled after a year's trials because of economic difficulties.

In France, teletext and videotex services have been developed with greater government involvement and direction than in most other countries. After a slow start, the benefits of this central coordination and direction are now visible and are discussed later in this chapter. French teletext services are known as ANTIOPE (Acquisition Numérique et Télévisualisation d'Images Organisées en Pages d'Ecriture). ANTIOPE in fact defines the standard for character and graphic display within the French teletext and videotex services. This differs slightly from the display used in

British systems. In the ANTIOPE standard, the grid is 25 rows by 40 columns and the matrix used within each cell is 8 by 10. The teletext service has been developed as a series of specialized information services rather like private videotex systems or closed user groups (see later in the chapter) on a public videotex service. The name ANTIOPE has been retained in the teletext services whilst the videotex service, which is examined later in the chapter, is known as Télétel. These services are intended for particular audiences rather than aimed at the whole of the market. Some examples are:

1. ANTIOPE-BOURSE transmits financial information to brokers in Paris and Lyon. It is named after the French stock market in Paris.
2. ANTIOPE-METEO is a national weather information service.
3. ANTIOPE-ROUTE provides road information. It is broadcast to road information centres and service stations throughout France.
4. ANTIOPE-SNCF provides tourist information from the French railways.

As with France, there has been considerable government involvement in the development of teletext and videotex services in Canada. This has occurred through the Canadian Department of Communications. The services are known as Telidon which rather than being an acronym emanates from the Greek, tele (at a distance) and idon (I perceive). The government role in Canada has been that of a catalyst encouraging the creation of services rather than acting as a service provider itself. In 1982 the Canadian Broadcasting Corporation (CBC) introduced a 300-page bilingual teletext service which was delivered as a part of the broadcast television signal nationwide but also as a part of a cable television service in Calgary, Montreal and Toronto. Since 1983 the Ontario Telidon Network has provided a 100-page teletext service carrying general and local news. Other countries in which teletext is either under development or being tested include Austria, Sweden and Japan. Greater detail on the development of teletext is provided by Binder (1985).

Videotex

Videotex systems were conceived as a method of increasing the use of the telephone system during those hours when it was heavily underutilized, that is during non-business hours. The initial idea was put forward and developed by Sam Fedida of the (British) Post Office; the historical development of videotex is outlined in Woolfe (1980). The intention was to offer an information service to the mass market which utilized the telephone network as the access mechanism and the television set as the terminal. The assumptions were that most homes had both a television set and a telephone and therefore it ought to be possible to provide an information service that was accessible from most homes. The information was to be stored on remote computers. The computers storing the information are those of the suppliers of telephone services in a country; in many countries this is the national telecommunications authority whilst in others such as America it is private companies like Bell. Since the system was intended for the mass market it was necessary to have a simple search mechanism and so access was provided by means of a menu. However, videotex systems have many similarities with conventional online search services; examination of the representation of a videotex system given in Figure 11.7 demonstrates this point.

Whilst some of the introductory information and guidance around the system is provided by the system operator, most of the information available on the British public system is provided by third parties known as Information Providers (IPs). IPs are analogous to the database producers in the conventional online information world. There is a wide diversity of companies within the ranks of the Information Providers; some are offshoots of established media companies such as East Midlands Allied Press, others are new organizations set up to exploit the possibilities offered by videotex systems, yet others are hoping to use their presence on a videotex service to improve the sales of their products, for example, mail-order catalogue companies and travel and insurance companies. Finally, a substantial amount of information is made available on PRESTEL by government, both local and national.

The information in a videotex system is stored as a series of pages. Each page can be divided into a number of frames of information. A frame is one screenful of information. The pages are structured hierarchically and a hypothetical example is provided in Figure 11.8. Videotex systems are searched by taking options from menus. The searcher progresses through the database by taking a series of options from menus until such time as the required information is located. Whilst this search mechanism appears simple to use, it is not without its problems as is noted later in the chapter.

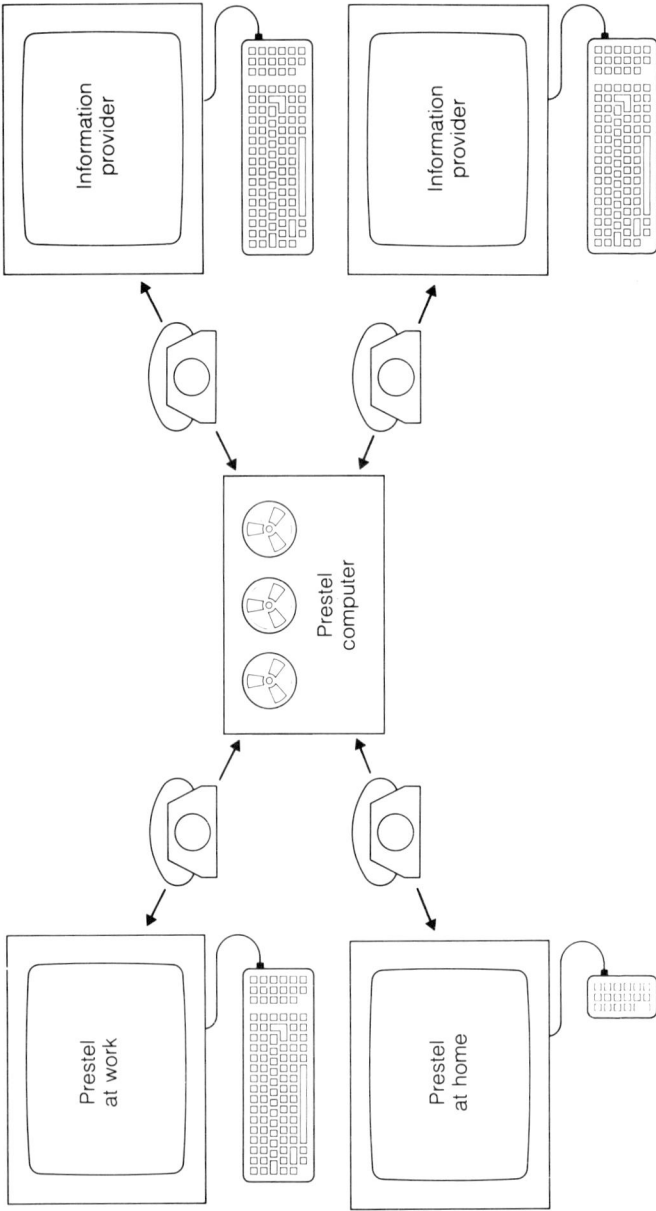

Figure 11.7   *How the PRESTEL system works*

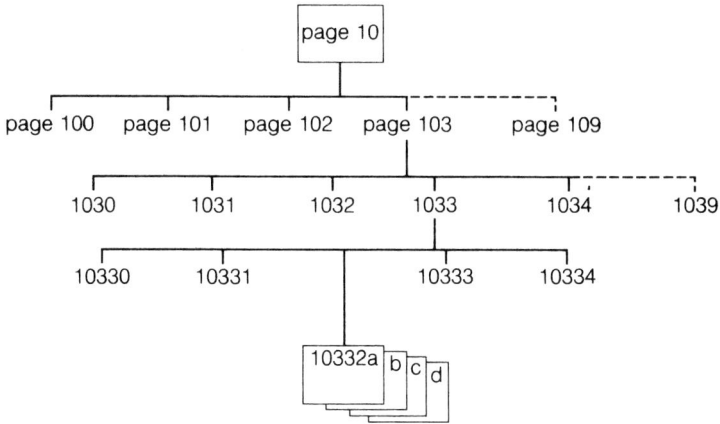

Figure 11.8 *Videotex page structures*

The manner in which the information in videotex systems is presented on the screen is much more akin to that which has already been seen in teletext than that used by the conventional online search services. Indeed it has already been noted that the standard for character display for the French videotex and teletext systems were developed together as a single standard. Further, commonality with the standard used for character generation in the British teletext services proved to be a greater influence than did the possibility of cooperating on the development of a European videotex standard as far as the developers of PRESTEL were concerned. The British and French method of character and graphic display is known as alphamosaic since the relatively crude graphic capabilities produces a tiled or mosaic effect on the screen. A much superior image is produced by the Canadian Telidon system which is known as alphageometric. In this system a series of graphics primitives or building blocks are defined by Picture Description Instructions (PDIs). Complex pictures can be constructed from a surprisingly low number of these building blocks which include point, line, arc and rectangle. Whilst the quality of image is undoubtedly higher so is the cost of the necessary terminal. Further information can be obtained about videotex displays from Martin (1982) and Woolfe (1980).

Whilst the initial intention was for the domestic television set to act as the terminal, dedicated videotex terminals soon appeared in the marketplace. These were aimed at the business user of videotex systems. These terminals were soon followed by software which enabled domestic microcomputers to act as videotex terminals. Thus the prospective user of videotex systems has a range of possible terminals to consider. A detailed consideration of the advantages of the three approaches to videotex terminals has been provided by Forster (1987) in a report which acts as a sourcebook on the products available in Britain.

The initial view that videotex services would unleash a large latent demand for information services delivered to the home has not been borne out in practice, at least as far as the pioneering PRESTEL system is concerned. The initial expectation that millions of homes would make use of videotex services not long after their introduction has proved to be a gross overestimate. This has led to a reconsideration of the marketing strategy employed by the service supplier, British Telecommunications (BT). The strategy now is to target specific market sectors where there is evidence that videotex services will meet a need. The information available on the system has been restructured and changed to meet this different perception of how PRESTEL will succeed. At the end of October 1987, there were 310 000 frames of information available on the PRESTEL system (*Videotex Notes*, November 1987). There is information covering general news, sports news and results, weather forecasts and travel news, and a wide range of information regarding leisure activities which varies from pop charts to theatre listings. In addition to this general information, there is information specific to the particular market sectors which have been targeted for development, including agriculture, business, banking, education, insurance, microcomputing, tele-shopping and travel. The diversity of available information can be illustrated by examining in slightly greater depth the information provided for users in some of these sectors. In agriculture, for example, there is information about current market and commodity prices, regional weather forecasts and pest reports. Information provided by a range of agricultural advisory bodies such as the Milk Marketing Board, the Meat and Livestock Commission and the Agricultural Development and Advisory Service is available via PRESTEL. Subscribers to the PRESTEL Farmlink service also have access to some computer programs to aid farm management, for example, a program which calculates livestock ration formulations or a program which calculates dairy herd costings.

In the teleshopping section, it is possible to order goods from a range of mail-order catalogues and arrange payment by credit card. In addition, it is possible to order a number of other products from specialist suppliers, ranging from wine through food and plants to office supplies. The business sector is supported by PRESTEL CitiService. This service provides continually updated information on stocks and shares, government stocks, exchange rates, unit trusts, interest rates, commodity prices, specialist news, advice and comment. In addition to its own information, Citi-Service also provides a link to the Stock Exchange's own computerized share system, SEAQ. CitiService is not restricted to information provision and it also offers a telebroking service which enables users to buy and sell shares. Finally, the service offers an individualized portfolio management service which keeps track of the value of the investments of an individual investor.

The cost of accessing a videotex system is cheap in comparison with online search services. On PRESTEL there is a quarterly standing charge of £6.50 for residential users and £18.00 for business users. In addition there is a quarterly line rental of £13.95 for domestic users and £22.55 for business users. Further there is a connect charge of £0.06 per minute during business hours (0800–1800 Monday to Friday). The service is available without connect charges outside this time period. There are page charges which may be levied by the information providers and there is also the telephone call charge. The latter is now at local call rates throughout Britain. Whilst these charges may be comparatively cheap, they appear rather complex and make the control of running costs difficult. This may be unimportant to the business user given the modest charges but the complexity of charges cannot have encouraged potential domestic use of PRESTEL. This is particularly significant when the notion of paying for information was totally new to the domestic user.

An important development in public videotex systems has been the gateway between systems. Much of the impetus for this development came from the public videotex service, Bildschirmtext, offered in the Federal Republic of Germany. In the PRESTEL service gateways are used to good effect in the provision of educational information. For example there are gateways to different computer systems covering full-time higher education, short courses in higher education and educational resources aimed particularly at schools. The French Minitel system has recently begun to provide gateway access to the online search service Télésystèmes-QUESTEL. Initially this gateway offered access to only three databases covering trademarks, French business news and press agency dispatches, but the search service is sufficiently pleased with the impact of this development for it to be planning to increase the number of databases which it makes available via this route (*Questel to make money via Minitel*, 1988). The development of gateways continues and is taking on new forms with a gateway between PRESTEL and a cable television company in Britain and gateways to enable banking transactions announced in Holland, Italy and Norway (*Videotex activity*, 1988).

Whilst it was expected that videotex systems would create a new marketplace by revealing unexpressed demands for information, it has been other functions of videotex which have contributed greatly to their continuing development. In addition to gateways to other systems, it is the provision of electronic mail and transaction processing facilities which enable teleshopping, holiday bookings or other transactions which are influencing the development of videotex. It is not appropriate to explore these developments in a book about online searching but it is important that the reader is aware that its role as an information source is of decreasing importance in the progress of videotex.

The basic search mechanism for using videotex is the menu. The searcher is faced with a menu of options from which a choice is made by entering the appropriate number using the keypad or keyboard. A typical menu from the PRESTEL system is shown in Figure 11.9. In most searches, it will be necessary to go through several menu pages (in effect index pages) before reaching the page(s) with the sought information. Clearly such searching by a menu-based system is straightforward. Whether or not it is effective is somewhat less obvious. If the choices offered within a particular menu are clearcut and for a particular information need, it is apparent that only one option from the available menu is a plausible route to the required information; there should then be no problem. However, this is frequently not the case as a hypothetical example may demonstrate. A searcher requires information on hotel accommodation in the Provence region of France. In the chosen general videotex system, the searcher is forced to choose an option from a menu which includes 'Travel information' and 'Holiday information' along with 'News', 'Weather' and 'Business information' among the limited options available.

Unless the searcher has used the system before, it will not be obvious whether 'Travel information' or 'Holiday information' is the appropriate menu choice for this information requirement or indeed whether the choice is irrelevant because both or neither lead to the required information. Various trials with videotex systems have demonstrated that lack of a clear menu choice can be a real problem and that menu-based videotex systems work best when the searcher has a clear notion of the information available on the system and that information can readily be structured hierarchically. The problems of menu-based information systems and their relationship to the well-known problems of hierarchical classification schemes have been examined by Rowley (1983). In some situations it is necessary to choose from a menu of letters which indicate the first letter of index words (see, for example, Figure 11.10). Unless the searcher is aware of how the required concept is represented, successful choice from such a menu is very difficult. For example, unless the searcher has information from an earlier search, it is not obvious whether to use 'automobiles', 'cars' or 'motor cars' to search for information about cars. Thus successful choice from a menu of letters is difficult.

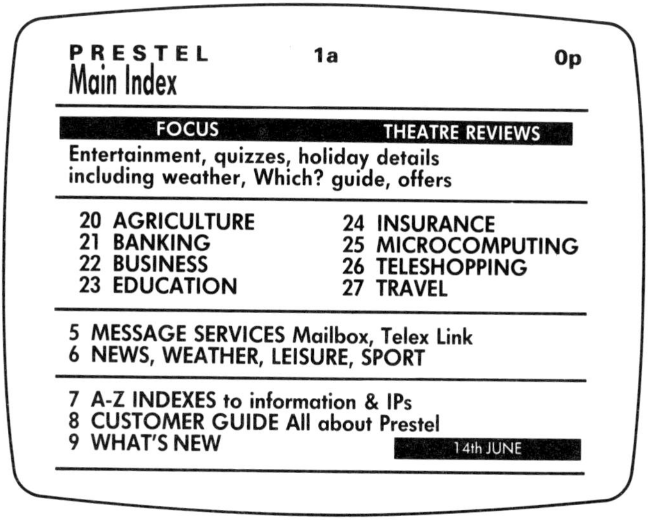

Figure 11.9 *Schematic of PRESTEL main menu*

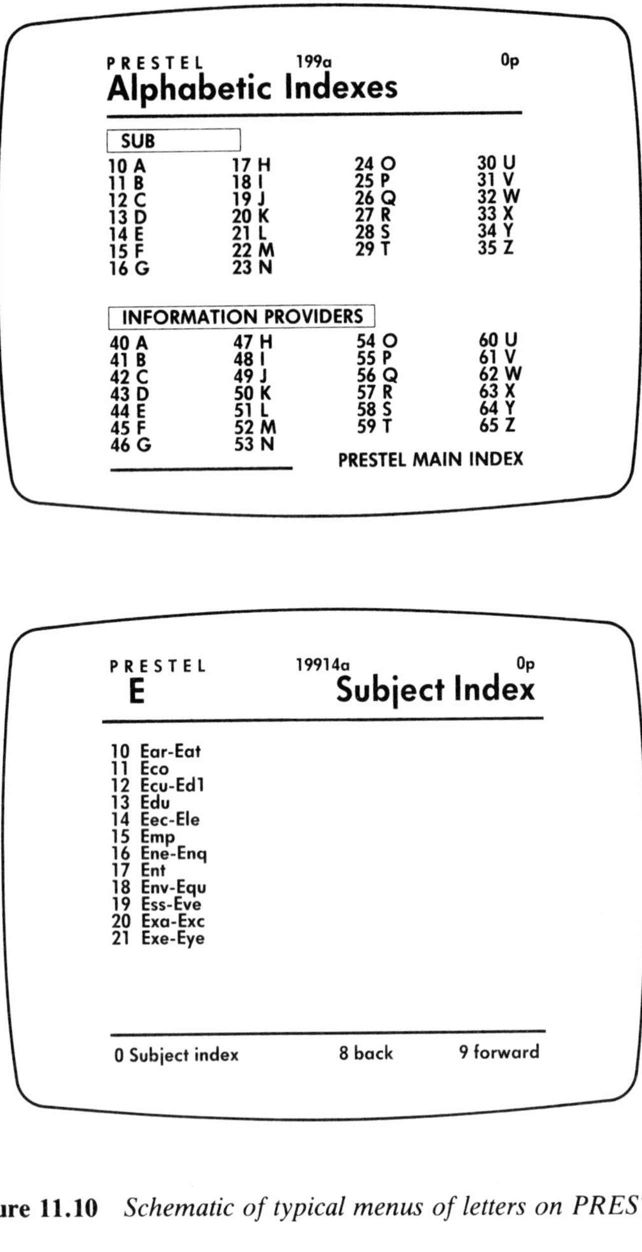

```
PRESTEL        199a              0p
Alphabetic Indexes

  SUB
10 A         17 H         24 O         30 U
11 B         18 I         25 P         31 V
12 C         19 J         26 Q         32 W
13 D         20 K         27 R         33 X
14 E         21 L         28 S         34 Y
15 F         22 M         29 T         35 Z
16 G         23 N

  INFORMATION PROVIDERS
40 A         47 H         54 O         60 U
41 B         48 I         55 P         61 V
42 C         49 J         56 Q         62 W
43 D         50 K         57 R         63 X
44 E         51 L         58 S         64 Y
45 F         52 M         59 T         65 Z
46 G         53 N

                          PRESTEL MAIN INDEX
```

```
PRESTEL        19914a            0p
E                          Subject Index

10 Ear-Eat
11 Eco
12 Ecu-Ed1
13 Edu
14 Eec-Ele
15 Emp
16 Ene-Enq
17 Ent
18 Env-Equ
19 Ess-Eve
20 Exa-Exc
21 Exe-Eye


0 Subject index        8 back        9 forward
```

Figure 11.10   *Schematic of typical menus of letters on PRESTEL*

In a large videotex system which offers information on many subjects, it is relatively easy for the searcher to get lost whilst working through the menus. On some systems it is not easy to retrace the steps of a search to follow up an interesting lead which was noted whilst the searcher was following another path. Most users of videotex systems accessed via a menu have at some time or another experienced the feeling that they were navigating through a maze without a plan. This induces frustration with the search mechanism and the system in general.

It is apparent from this description of searching a menu-based system that it may be painstakingly slow and therefore frustrating for the experienced user of the system. The videotex user who searches regularly, say to check share prices or train times, will soon be frustrated by the simple but tedious access route through a sequence of menus. Many videotex systems enable a searcher to go straight to a known page number by entering that page number in a specific way. For example on PRESTEL, it is achieved by use of *page number#. It was noted with regard to teletext systems that many users soon memorize regularly used page numbers. Presumably too it is easy to create a personal index to frequently used pages. In some instances a printed index may be available, for example, a printed index to the PRESTEL service appears regularly as a supplement to the videotex magazine *Connexions*. This index provides access to the top page of the various information providers and also access to a certain number of subjects but the subject entries in the index only contain a restricted number of cross references so that the onus is on the searcher to think of the various ways in which a subject may be represented in the index.

In a further effort to combat the limitations of menu-based access to a large and diverse system, British Telecom implemented a simple keyword search facility on PRESTEL in early 1987. It is possible to move rapidly to the appropriate header page by means of a single keyword such as *ABERYSTWYTH#. It is possible to combine keywords in an implicit boolean AND search; for example *FRANCE ACCOMMODATION# goes straight to a listing of companies which offer hotel or holiday accommodation in France. In addition there are facilities to simplify the repetition of parts of a search and to tag up to five pages for later retrieval. Further details are available in *Connexions* (1987).

Keyword searching requires a keyboard rather than a numeric keypad and thus could be seen as a step away from the initial concept of a mass market information system in which the domestic television receiver acts as the terminal. However Pollitt

(1985) has demonstrated that it is possible to use menus and a numeric keypad to present the searcher with boolean search facilities. The search mechanism provided for the educational services, NERIS and ECCTIS, which are available via gateways from the PRESTEL education service use search mechanisms which have similarities to Pollitt's suggestions but they do require a keyboard rather than a keypad. A review of many search options provided within videotex systems has been provided by Buscain (1985).

It is clear that initial projections for the exploitation of public videotex in Britain proved to be wildly and unrealistically optimistic. Terminals or TV adaptors could only be made available cheaply if there was a high volume of sales. Volume sales would only occur if there was sufficient material on PRESTEL to ensure that considerable numbers of the public felt that it was worth investing in a terminal or adaptor. Information providers would only make the investment necessary to make the service sufficiently interesting when they were convinced that the market was large enough. The situation was aggravated because the medium was new and nobody was certain about how it could be best used or how best to design and present information. Potential information providers had no clear view about what to present, how to present it or to whom they were seeking to present their services. This is in marked contrast to the development of other online search services where there was already a known demand for information, bibliographic, financial or other and online search services or in-house databases simply offered a different access mechanism.

Martin (1982) noted that it was possible that a single application might well trigger an explosive uptake of videotex. In this context it is interesting to note the French approach to the development of videotex. Rather than leaving the development of videotex to market forces, the French government, through its PTT (the Postal, Telegraph and Telecommunications Authority) has provided the catalyst which has enabled videotex to become far more widespread in France than in any other country in the world. That catalyst was the provision of the French telephone directory as a videotex service and the supply of a free videotex terminal known as a Minitel to anyone who was willing to use it rather than the printed directory. This had two effects. The first was to provide a large market for the French companies who manufactured the terminals. It is hoped that from this large domestic base of terminals, these manufacturers will be able to develop export markets. Secondly the appearance of a large and increasing base of installed terminals has provided the impetus for the information providers, or service providers as they are known in France, to offer an increasing range of services over the national videotex service Télétel. In the longer term the French PTT can look forward to the replacement of the printed telephone directory and the expensive directory enquiry service with a solely online service. Whilst the initial name of the French system was Télétel this is increasingly being replaced by the name Minitel which is a testimony to the success of the French approach. In addition to the electronic telephone directory service there are three major services offered on Télétel: Télétel-1 which is aimed largely at the domestic market and whose service providers use it largely as a mechanism for generating extra business; Télétel-2 is aimed at the business community and Télétel-3 is the highly successful kiosque or casual use system whereby the user has access to many services and the bill for their use appears as a part of the telephone bill. The cost for using this domestic service is 0.73FF per minute and the comparable rate for the use of the business service is 1.25FF per minute. Further information about Télétel is available in Binder (1985) and Financial Times Business Information (1986).

Table 11.1 provides data on the number of installed terminals for various national videotex services. The success of the French strategy is clearly demonstrated. The number of subscribers in the United Kingdom and the Federal Republic of Germany are considerable in comparison to many conventional search services yet they are very low in comparison to the early predictions of videotex take up. Use in the other countries listed is clearly in its infancy.

Whilst videotex systems were initially conceived as public mass market information systems, they have also been developed as private in-house information systems in a number of organizations. There are an increasing number of packages available for the creation, maintenance and searching of in-house videotex systems. These can be operated on computers ranging from microcomputers to mainframe computers. An indication of the range of packages available in Britain for the creation of private videotex systems is provided by Yates-Mercer (1985). At the time of writing, this author noted that the cost of software to run an in-house videotex service ranged from approximately £10 000 to several hundred thousand pounds. Private videotex systems are being widely and successfully operated in a range of organizational contexts. In the

Country	Number of subscribers
Australia	30 000
Austria	8 300
Finland	1 100
France	3 000 000
Italy	15 000
New Zealand	6 300
Netherlands	26 150
Norway	2 000
Sweden	13 300
United Kingdom	75 000
FR Germany	99 700

Source: *Videotex Notes*, **43**, February 1988.

Table 11.1   *Videotex subscribers by country*

private sector, their application has been noted in the travel trade, in banking, insurance, the motor trade, the chemical industry, predictably the electrical and electronic industry and in retailing. In the public sector, private videotex systems are being utilized in national government, local government and in education. Yates-Mercer (1985) suggests a number of features of successful applications of private videotex systems. These are:

1. The information on the system is needed by a large number of clearly identifiable people who are frequently spread over a wide geographical area.
2. The users of the system are frequently not a part of the organization providing the service (for example, the use of a tour operator's system by a travel agent).
3. The users are frequently new to the use of computer systems and need systems which are simple to use.
4. The information can be split into small elements, expressed as a few words and structured into a hierarchical tree structure.

These characteristics may help to identify situations in which in-house videotex systems offer more appropriate solutions than other in-house systems (Chapter 10). Details of the types of use to which private videotex systems are being put can be obtained from the book by Yates-Mercer, who has attempted to provide a full survey of the use of private videotex systems in Britain in 1984. Many public videotex services provide facilities for running an information service which are only open to a restricted group of users. Access to the group is usually on payment of a subscription fee. These groups are referred to as closed user groups (CUGs). CUGs offer a halfway house between public and private videotex services. They may be particularly useful in situations where either the user group is geographically very widespread or the service is very new.

This chapter has examined videotex and teletext systems as examples of online information systems. Accordingly it has sought to emphasize the information available through these systems and the search mechanisms for accessing that information. It is very important that the reader should bear in mind that whilst these systems were initially envisaged as mass market information systems, it has become increasingly apparent that the information storage and retrieval aspects of videotex systems, in particular, is but one function of these systems. It is being increasingly recognized that it is the other functions, namely transaction processing and electronic messaging, which are likely to determine the future directions and applications of videotex. After a period of inflated expectations, videotex systems are settling down to be a useful mechanism for transaction processing and information retrieval. Both public and private systems are finding niches where they have a useful role to play as alternatives to both conventional data processing and online search services. Teletext services are finding niches in which they can exploit the fact that information is freely available for much of the day and that since the user interacts with a broadcast signal rather than a remote computer there are few problems of system access. The larger databases and the interactive capabilities of videotex systems have led to these systems receiving much more attention than the relatively humble broadcast services, but this should not be allowed to detract from the utility of the latter.

References

Binder, M. B. (1985) *Videotex and Teletext: New Online Resources for Libraries*. Greenwich, Connecticut: JAI Press Inc

Buscain, A. (1985) Videotex systems and data access methods: a state-of-the-art review. *Aslib Proceedings*, **37** (6/7), 249–256

Connexions (1987) The key to PRESTEL. *Connexions*, May/June 1987, 53–54

Financial Times Business Information (1986) *Videotex and Teletext Markets*. London

Forster, W. A. (1987) *Buyers' Guide to Videotex Equipment.* Hatfield: Cimtech

Martin, J. (1982) *Viewdata and the Information Society*. Englewood Cliffs, N.J.: Prentice Hall

Money, S. A. (1979) *Teletext and Viewdata*. London: Newnes Technical Books

Pollitt, S. (1985) End user boolean searching on viewdata using numeric keypads. In *Proceedings of the 9th International Online Information Meeting*, pp. 373–379. Oxford: Learned Information

Questel to make money via Minitel (1988) *Information World Review*, **25**, April, 1

Rowley, J. E. (1983) PRESTEL and hierarchical classification: an examination of menu based information retrieval systems. In *Proceedings of the 7th International Online Information Meeting*, pp. 185–197. Oxford: Learned Information

Videotex activity (1988) *Information World Review*, **25** i.e. **26**, 3

Videotex Industry Year Book 1987. London: Spicer and Pegler Associates

Videotex Notes (November 1987) **40**, 1

Woolfe, R. (1980) *Videotex the New Television/Telephone Information Services*. London: Heyden

Yates-Mercer, P. A. (1985) *Private Viewdata Systems in the United Kingdom*. Aldershot: Gower

Chapter 12

Online Public Access Catalogues

Introduction

It was noted in Chapter 1 that the catalogues of an increasing number of libraries are now available for searching online. These are known as Online Public Access Catalogues (OPACs). Such OPACs may be searched from a terminal within the originating library, at a terminal elsewhere in the organization or remotely via national and even international telecommunications networks. Obviously searching a library catalogue at a distance marks a notable development in the use of library catalogues.

The availability of OPACs represents a significant development in online searching yet it has occurred almost in isolation from more conventional online search services. Whether such separate development is inherent in the differences between OPACs and conventional online search services is a moot point. Nevertheless that separate development dictates separate treatment in this book.

This chapter seeks to examine OPACs from the viewpoint of the searcher, not that of the catalogue creator. In the next section of this chapter, OPACs are set into context with discussions of OPACs in relation to library catalogues, library automation and online information retrieval systems. This is followed by an examination of the records at the heart of OPACs in which the differences between them and records in conventional online information retrieval systems are discussed. The searching of OPACs is then considered in terms of the types of searches performed and the interaction between user and OPAC. Throughout the intention is to relate OPACs to online searching rather than to produce a comprehensive review of OPACs, their design and implementation. The reader who wishes to consider OPACs in greater depth could usefully start with the text by Matthews (1985), the research report by Mitev, Venner and Walker (1985) or the special issue of the journal *Library Trends* (*Library Trends*, 1987).

OPACs in Context

OPACs and catalogues

The library catalogue exists primarily to indicate the books available in a particular library or library system. The objectives of the library catalogue, first set out by Cutter in 1867 (Cutter 1904), have stood the test of time:

1. To enable a person to find a book about which one of the following is known
    the author
    the title
    the subject.
2. To show what the library has
    by a given author
    on a given subject
    in a given kind of literature.
3. To assist in the choice of a book
    as to its edition
    as to its character — literary or
    topical.

In order to meet these objectives a series of widely used standards or rules about the content of catalogue entries and the access points within catalogues to those entries have emerged. The most widely used set of standards at present is the second edition of the Anglo-American Cataloguing Rules (AACR2). Library catalogues have traditionally provided access points in their files by author, by title and by subject. In the United States the subject is represented by subject headings, often the Library of Congress Subject Headings, and the entries by author, title and subject are filed into a single sequence, the so-called dictionary catalogue. In Britain the subject is represented by the classification number, frequently assigned from the Dewey Decimal Classification Scheme. The catalogue is then organized into two sequences, the first an alphabetical sequence, contains the entries by author and title (if given) and the second sequence is presented in the classification number order (usually with a separate index to the classification scheme).

Before the development of OPACs catalogues had appeared in a number of physical formats, including book, card and Computer

Output Microform (COM). These formats were generally unpopular and library users avoided them wherever possible (Lancaster, 1977). In contrast the major survey of OPAC use found that OPACs are used more frequently than other catalogue formats and that they are used with enthusiasm (Matthews, Lawrence and Ferguson, 1983). Thus OPACs have created a situation where library catalogues, which hitherto had been used with reluctance, are now being used with enthusiasm.

OPACs and library automation

Progress in the automation of library housekeeping procedures (acquisitions, circulation control, cataloguing, etc.) has been most marked. In the early 1960s, library automation consisted of pioneering attempts to automate specific housekeeping functions on in-house computers. For example, the first cataloguing systems were based on 80-column punched cards with line printer output. From these early days of batch systems, library automation has progressed through shared networks such as SWALCAP (now SLS Ltd) and BLCMP in Britain or OCLC in the United States to an era where integrated online library systems are becoming the norm. The important point is the linking of the various functions. Thus, it may well be possible to link the catalogue to the circulation file so that not only is it possible to determine whether a book is in the collection of a particular library but also whether or not it is available or on loan at a particular time. It is important to note, therefore, that the OPAC is not designed solely as an information retrieval system but as a module of an integrated library management system. Developments in library automation have been reviewed by Tedd (1987).

The development of intra-organizational communications networks in both the commercial and academic environments means that increasingly the OPAC can be searched by the user from the workplace rather than by a visit to the library. The linking of these networks to national and possibly international networks creates the possibility of searching the catalogue at a great distance. This represents a notable development in catalogue capabilities and a challenge to catalogue designers. However, searching a catalogue remotely without any documentation and possibly without a knowledge of the local implementation of the classification scheme and cataloguing rules is not without its difficulties.

OPACs and information retrieval

OPACs differ from more conventional bibliographic information retrieval systems in a number of ways. The most fundamental concerns the characteristics of those who use them. It was a general assumption, at least in the early days, that online information retrieval systems would be searched exclusively by information professionals. Thus it could be assumed that the searchers would have a knowledge of the principles of information retrieval and would be prepared to learn one and often several command languages. No such assumptions may be made about the searchers of OPACs. Indeed, it must be assumed that the catalogue (that is, database) will be searched by users with a wide range of skills and aptitudes. The interaction between searcher and OPAC must be intelligible to and accepted by users who individually have a wide variation in their

1. Competence in the use of computers.
2. Knowledge of catalogues and cataloguing.
3. Knowledge of information retrieval.
4. Knowledge of the subject on which they are seeking information.

There may be some similarity with the broad range of competences assumed by the designers of videotex systems. These requirements place a heavy burden on the designers of OPACs. Matthews (1985) gives an indication of the variety of solutions adopted by different libraries to the problems of making the OPAC–user interaction acceptable. Some systems use a command language approach, some have adopted a menu-driven approach, whilst yet others have adopted a form-filling approach. Some systems offer both menu-driven and command language approaches. There is usually an inverse relationship between the ease of use of the system and its sophistication. For example, use of a menu system as a means of searching by author or title or subject means that the retrieval of records by a sophisticated combination of search terms from a number of fields is lost.

Many OPACs offer lessons to the designers of conventional information retrieval systems with their attempts to make the interaction understandable to the searcher. Such lessons become increasingly important if there is to be a successful move towards end-user searching of online search systems (see Chapter 8). Nevertheless, it is clear that no operational OPAC can reasonably claim to have solved the problem of providing a user–system interaction which is acceptable to all users of the system. Arguably the nearest to this goal is the experimental OPAC, OKAPI, at the Polytechnic of Central London (Mitev, Venner and Walker, 1985). This system has attempted to remove from the interaction all the jargon of computing, information retrieval and cataloguing, so that the system should be comprehensible to all users without training. Careful attention has been paid to the layout of information on the screen both in the presentation of menus and bibliographic information on the screen. The latter is presented without any labels or tags which are meaningful only to the bibliographic cognoscenti. Much of the interaction is menu-driven, the number of choices available from the menu is limited and the user responds by using one of a restricted number of colour-coded keys. In order to perform a subject search the user merely enters a series of subject words and these are processed by OKAPI. There is no need to understand the concept of boolean searching as it is implicit in the system. The initial screens met in an interaction with OKAPI (first version) are presented in Figure 12.1.

It is generally accepted that an OPAC must include help facilities, that these must be relevant to the particular position within the OPAC from which they are requested (context sensitive) and that they must be presented in a manner which enables the searcher to return to the point in the search from which the help was first called. This is perhaps more important in OPACs than in online search services since it is generally felt to be impossible to provide the searcher of an OPAC with help in the form of printed documentation. It has been argued by some that an OPAC which needs a help facility is a failed OPAC since the interaction ought to be implemented in such a way that it is intelligible to all without recourse to help facilities (Walker, 1986). This is a powerful argument with which it is difficult to disagree. A final point about the OPAC–user interaction is that the system designers must take account of the fact that users already attribute far too great a capability to most computer systems and attempts to provide 'user-friendly' interactions may simply accentuate this problem (Estabrook, 1983).

A second major difference between OPACs and conventional bibliographic information retrieval systems is the subject coverage of the database. A characteristic of most conventional bibliographic databases is that their coverage is limited in subject scope either to a single subject such as chemistry or to a range of disciplines linked to a particular mission, for example, pollution control. (There are a small number of exceptions – databases which concentrate on

```
**OKAPI**

          P.C.L. EXPERIMENTAL ON-LINE CATALOGUE

          This on-line catalogue will help you to find the
          books you are looking for in the P.C.L. libraries.

          Books received very recently are not on the computer :
          but they are included in the microfiche catalogue.

          A small number of books acquired before 1975 are
          still only to be found on the card catalogue.

    IN ORDER TO SEARCH THE COMPUTER, YOU WILL HAVE TO PRESS A
    FEW KEYS.

    For example, when you have finished reading this screen and
    want to go further, press the GREEN KEY on your keyboard . . . ▮
```

```
              P.C.L. ON-LINE CATALOGUE              ** OKAPI

    Do you want to look for :

          1. SPECIFIC BOOK(S)
             (if you know the author and/or title)

          2. BOOK(S) ABOUT SOMETHING
             (any topic(s) you have in mind)

    Indicate your choice by typing 1 or 2 : ▮

    IF YOU HAVE A PROBLEM DURING YOUR SEARCH, PRESS THE
    YELLOW KEY FOR EXPLANATIONS, OR ASK A MEMBER OF THE
                          STAFF.
```

Figure 12.1   *OKAPI introductory screens*

material of a particular type such as conference papers, dissertations or patents.) In contrast, nearly every library catalogue will cover all fields of knowledge. This has consequences in terms of index languages used and the searching of the database. A controlled vocabulary index language covering the whole sphere of knowledge or a significant proportion of it is most unlikely to be as specific as one covering a restricted subject area. A comparison of the term specificity achieved in the INSPEC thesaurus and Library of Congress Subject Headings will illustrate this point. This may lessen the value of that index language in the search process. The very breadth of the subject coverage of the database increases the opportunities for false coordinations of terms and the subject coverage of the database no longer acts as a facet in the representation of the subject. The term 'culture' used, for example, in a biological database would retrieve material in which the word is used in its microbiological sense but would be unlikely to retrieve material in which the word is used in an historical or anthropological sense; but if the term were to be used in an OPAC, it would be likely to retrieve material in which the term is used in all these contexts.

A third major difference between OPACs and conventional bibliographic information retrieval systems relates to the underlying assumption about the use to which the database will be put. Despite the fact that conventional bibliographic databases can be searched by a whole range of features such as author, corporate source, language or document type, the underlying assumption is that most searching will be for documents containing information on a particular subject. On the other hand, the underlying assumption in the creation of library catalogues has been that most searches will be known item searches, that is searches for documents whose bibliographic details are known. The implications of this different assumption and their impact on the records at the heart of OPACs is discussed in the next section of this chapter.

Records

Emphasis in library catalogues is placed on the description and therefore the identification of the physical entity, the book, rather than the content of the document. Nevertheless there is considerable variation between OPACs. At the simple end of the spectrum are those OPACs in which the searching is performed on relatively brief records as in Figure 12.2 (a record from an OPAC based on a

WISE, M. *COMMON FISHERIES POLICY OF THE EUROPEAN COMMUNITY. _____ 1984

1 copy on file

ITEM NUMBER	ISSUE	L/S	USER	OTHER DETAILS
	DATE			

| 80 8412858 4 | | 0 | NOT ISSUED | Classmark: HD9465.E9.W8 |

Figure 12.2 *Typical record details in an OPAC based on a circulation system*

circulation system). Brief records such as the one in Figure 12.2 are often used in library circulation systems but would not be considered *proper* catalogue records by the purists. Although they can be searched by author, classmark and possibly keywords in the title, this represents a very limited approach to the subject content of the documents. At the other end of the spectrum are records which conform to MARC standards (discussed in Chapter 10). An example of this type of record is given in Figure 12.3. Clearly this larger record contains a greater level of detail about the item but much of that detail is about the physical entity not the subject content; thus it will be of interest to only a minority of potential users.

It is appropriate to note that most libraries use a level of description of the physical document and its subject content which lies somewhere between these two extremes. Figure 12.4 represents a typical example. In recent years there has been a vigorous debate between those advocating the use of full MARC records and those supporting the use of much briefer records in library catalogues. A series of experiments conducted by the Centre for Bibliographic Management (formerly the Centre for Catalogue Research) at the University of Bath has indicated that as tools for the finding of known items within a library collection, the briefer records are perfectly adequate. Indeed for the non-bibliographically inclined majority briefer records are probably preferable since they do not contain bibliographic details which are incomprehensible to the majority of catalogue users (Seal, Bryant and Hall, 1982).

Regardless of the depth of physical description in the catalogue record, the subject representation of the document content remains sparse. Rather than the in-depth subject representation

RECORD CONTROL NO	0416323901
INFORMATION CODES	850325s1984 en W 00011 eng b
LC CARD NO	84–573
NAT BIB NO	b8421847
ISBN	0416324002 v pbk No price
BLAISE NO	11294521 +UKX
GEOGRAPHIC AREA	e——
LC CLASS NO	SH254·E87
DEWEY DECIMAL CLASS	338·3 727 094 19
SUBJECT SUMMARY	European Community countries. Fishing industries. Policies of European Economic Community: Common Fisheries Policy
PERSONAL AUTHOR	Wise Mark 1944–
TITLE	The common fisheries policy of the European Community Mark Wise
PUBL, DISTR, MANUF	London Methuen 1984
PHYSICAL DESCR	xvii,316p ill maps 23cm cased
TERMS OF AVAILABILITY	No price : CIP rev.
UNTRACED SERIES	The Methuen EEC series
LC SUBJECT HEADING	Fishery policy European Economic Community countries
PRECIS DESCRIPTOR	01030 European Community countries 11030 fishing industries in s0030 policies of on 31030 European Economic Community 10420 European Economic Community q1030 Common Fisheries Policy
PRECIS SIN NO	3084221
PRECIS RIN NO	0195596
PRECIS RIN NO	0035262
PRECIS RIN NO	090953x
PRECIS RIN NO	001785x
PRECIS RIN NO	0910090

Figure 12.3 *A record in British MARC format showing field labels rather than MARC tags*

which is the norm in many bibliographic databases, the content of the book is usually summarized as a single statement which is then presented in the controlled index language of the particular library system. This is usually the relevant classification number in British libraries or the appropriate subject heading(s) in American libraries. The result of this different assumption about the use of the database in terms of their respective levels of content representation has been graphically charted by McClure (1976). He has noted the fact that in a catalogue database where the typical document is a monograph the subject matter of the document is represented by, on average, 1.3 subject terms. This contrasts starkly with bibliographic databases which frequently

RECORD CONTROL NO	0416323901			
NAT BIB NO	b8421847			
ISBN	0416324002	v	pbk	No price
DEWEY DECIMAL CLASS	338·3	727	094	19
SUBJECT SUMMARY	European Community countries. Fishing industries. Policies of European Economic Community: Common Fisheries Policy			
PERSONAL AUTHOR	Wise Mark 1944–			
TITLE	The common fisheries policy of the European Community Mark Wise			
PUBL, DISTR, MANUF	London Methuen 1984			
PHYSICAL DESCR	xvii,316p ill maps 23cm cased			
TERMS OF AVAILABILITY	No price : CIP rev.			
UNTRACED SERIES	The Methuen EEC series			
NOTES – BIBLIOGRAPHY	Bibliography: p308–309. } Includes index			

Figure 12.4   *Record with medium level of detail*

include a searchable title and abstract and several subject descriptors to represent the content of much briefer documents (for example, journal papers).

Whilst records with this low level of subject representation have been adequate to support known item searching, they are not proving adequate to support the increased level of subject searching which OPAC users are demanding. Markey (1985) has reported that the one thing which OPAC users request most of all is enhanced subject representation in the OPAC record. Whilst this can be taken as an indication of a request for increased subject access in OPACs it is not necessarily an indication of how this should be achieved. In recent years there has been an increasing interest in improving subject searching capabilities in OPACs by enhancing the subject content of the record, by incorporating some controlled index language into the OPAC or by the inclusion of automatic search procedures (Hartley, 1988; Walker, 1988). To date it has not been possible to determine the optimum method of enhancing subject searching in OPACs.

Searching OPACs

Currently available OPACs can generally be viewed as being of two types which are referred to in the literature as first-generation and second-generation OPACs (Mitev, Venner and Walker, 1985). The two generations of OPACs have differing features and capabilities which reflect the underlying philosophy behind their development.

First-generation OPACs

Generally, first-generation OPACs have been derived from traditional, manually searched catalogues or computerized circulation systems. Sometimes they are referred to as phrase-indexed or pre-coordinate OPACs. The number of access keys is limited and they are similar to those in manually searched catalogues, that is to say, author, title (as a phrase), classmark and possibly subject heading (as a phrase). These OPACs may also provide search facilities by *acronym* keys, that is, a combination of a small number of characters from different fields. An example of a search using an acronym key is given in Search Example 12.1. In this example the user has entered the acronym key 'lancinfo'; the first four characters are taken from the author's surname and the second four characters are taken from the first significant word in the title. Two items are retrieved. The user requires the second item. On indicating this, fuller details including availability information are presented. Other characteristics of first generation OPACs are that they expect exact matching on the particular field and are generally intolerant of user mistakes.

This variety of search mechanism is acceptable for specific item searches and Search Example 12.2 provides an example of an author search on a typical early OPAC. Considerable guidance is provided about the exact manner in which the author's name must be entered. At the end of the search, not only has the searcher located details about the required book but the fact that the book is currently in the library has been noted. Whilst the instructions provided on the screen are adequate for this particular example, it is not clear how to search for an author whose name is less straightforward, for example, Charles De Gaulle (in this particular case there was no match on either De Gaulle, C or Gaulle, CD).

First generation OPACs have the benefit that usually something is displayed on the terminal as a result of a search. Thus if there is not an exact match, it may display those records which are nearest to the particular search key. For example, an incorrectly keyed author search entered as 'SMTH' may include in the response a display including items by 'SMYTH'. If there are facilities for browsing backwards and forwards through a sequence this may facilitate the location of items by the desired author 'SMITH'. Unfortunately, these OPACs often merely produce some output and it may not be obvious that there has been an error at the input stage; one discovery of OPAC research has been that many users do not spell accurately (Walker 1986). Thus the OPAC searcher

There are five different ways of searching:

    Q – QUICK search – (only 8 key taps needed!)
    A – AUTHOR (or other name) search
    T – TITLE search (including periodicals)
    K – KEYWORD-IN-TITLE search
    C – CLASSMARK (subject) search
        and L – Logout (PLEASE do so when finished)
Choose one, and enter its letter here: **q**

QUICK search:
    enter first 4 letters of the AUTHOR and first 4 letters of the TITLE
    eg. to find "Ecology" by R.E.Ricklefs, enter RICKECOL
      [or enter H if you want more Help]

Enter AuthTitl: **lancinfo**

Number of matches   2

      1. AUTHOR: Lancaster,FW& Fayen,EG
      DATE:1973
          TITLE: Information retrieval on-line

      2. AUTHOR   Lancaster,FW
      DATE:1979
          TITLE: Information retrieval systems: characteristics, testing
               and eval

EITHER choose a book from this list & enter its number (eg.1),
        OR choose a letter from:
F – go Forwards (seeing 5 records)
B – go Backwards   S – do another QUICK search
X – see the list of search types; or use a search letter now (eg.T)

Enter the number or letter here: **2**

         AUTHOR: Lancaster,FW
          TITLE: Information retrieval systems: characteristics, testing
and evaluation   2ed
        IMPRINT: Wiley   1979
                Number of copies owned by the library or on order = 1

Book no.   Location Shelfmark   Loan category & Status

527582 8 MAIN   Z 699 Lan   LONG   In Library

F – go Forwards (seeing 5 records)   Z – see next record only, in
this format
B – go Backwards   S – do another QUICK search
X – see the list of search types; or use a search letter now (eg. T)
Enter the letter here: **x**

Search Example 12.1 *Acronym search on a first-generation
OPAC*

There are five different ways of searching:

    Q – QUICK search – (only 8 key taps needed!)
    A – AUTHOR (or other name) search
    T – TITLE search (including periodicals)
    K – KEYWORD-IN-TITLE search
    C – CLASSMARK (subject) search
        and L – Logout (PLEASE do so when finished)
Choose one, and enter its letter here: **A**

AUTHOR (or other name) search:
    enter a person's name in the form: surname, COMMA, initials eg.
    SHAW,CM
    or the name of an organisation as it stands eg. LABOUR PARTY
        [or enter H if you want more Help]
                                    especially about people as subjects
Enter Name: **LARGE,JA**

Number of matches   2

        1. AUTHOR: Large,JA
           DATE:1983
               TITLE: The foreign-language barrier: problems in scientific
communicati

        2. AUTHOR   Armstrong,CJ& Large,JA,eds
           DATE:1987
               TITLE: Manual of online search strategies

EITHER choose a book from this list & enter its number (eg.1),
        OR choose a letter from:
F – go Forwards (seeing 5 records)
B – go Backwards   S – do another AUTHOR search
X – see the list of search types; or use a search letter now (eg.T)

Enter the number or letter here: **1**

        AUTHOR: Large,JA
            TITLE: The foreign-language barrier: problems in scientific
communication
        IMPRINT: Deutsch   London   1983
                    Number of copies owned by the library or on order = 1

Book no.   Location Shelfmark   Loan category & Status

577091   3   MAIN   Q 2050 Lar   LONG   In Library

F – go Forwards (seeing 5 records)   Z – see next record only, in
this format
B – go Backwards   S – do another AUTHOR search
X – see the list of search types; or use a search letter now (eg. T)

Search Example 12.2 *Author search on a first-generation OPAC*

LIBRARY USER FACILITIES

CODE
 6 AUTHOR/TITLE ENQUIRY
20 CLASSMARK ENQUIRY

KEY-IN CODE OF FACILITY
  6

DEWIS I DDEFNYDDWYR

RHIF
 6 YMHOLIAD AWDUR/TEITL
20 YMHOLIAD RHIF DOSBARTH

BWYDWCH I MEWN RIF EICH DEWIS

UNION AUTHOR/TITLE ENQUIRY
>**smth**<
 1 SMUEL,R.H. *SELECTED WRITINGS. _____ 1965
 2 SMULLYAN,A. *FUNDAMENTALS OF LOGIC. _____ 1962
 3 SMULLYAN,R.M. *FIRST-ORDER LOGIC. _____ 1968
 4 SMULLYAN,R.M. *THEORY OF FORMAL SYSTEMS. _____ 1961
 5 SMUTS,J.C. *SELECTIONS FROM THE SMUTS PAPERS._____ V1.1966
 6 SMUTS,J.C. *SELECTIONS FROM THE SMUTS PAPERS._____ V2.1966
 7 SMUTS,J.C. *SELECTIONS FROM THE SMUTS PAPERS._____ V3.1966
 8 SMUTS,J.C. *SELECTIONS FROM THE SMUTS PAPERS._____ V4.1966
 9 SMUTS,J.C. *SELECTIONS FROM THE SMUTS PAPERS._____ V5.1973
10 SMUTS,J.C. *SELECTIONS FROM THE SMUTS PAPERS._____ V6.1973

KEY-IN "PAGE+1","EXPAND(LINE NO)",OR "END":**pa**1

UNION AUTHOR/TITLE ENQUIRY
>smth<
 1 SMUTS,J.C. *SELECTIONS FROM THE SMUTS PAPERS._____ V7.1973
 2 SMYSER,W.R. *GERMAN-AMERICAN RELATIONS. _____ 1980
 3 SMYTH;FAMILY *CALENDAR OF THE CORRES.ED.BETTEY. _____ 1982
 4 SMYTH,A.H. *PHILADELPHIA MAGAZINES. . .1741–1850. _____ 1892
 5 SMYTH,A.P. *CELTIC LEINSTER. _____ 1982
 6 SMYTH,A.P. *SCANDINAVIAN KINGS IN THE BRITISH ISLES. _____ 1977
 7 SMYTH,A.P. *SCANDINAVIAN YORK & DUBLIN. _____ V1.1975
 8 SMYTH,A.P. *SCANDINAVIAN YORK & DUBLIN. _____ V2.1978
 9 SMYTH,A.P. *WARLORDS & HOLY MEN. _____ 1984
10 SMYTH,C.H.E. *CRANMER & THE REFORMATION UNDER EDWARD.   1926

KEY-IN "PAGE+1","PAGE−1","EXPAND(LINE NO)",OR "END":**en**

Search Example 12.3 *Incorrectly entered author name; entering author index at incorrect place*

may be misled about the outcome of the search. This is demonstrated in Search Example 12.3 where an inaccurately keyed search request for 'SMTH' produces a display of entries for 'SMUTS'. By moving to the next screen items by 'SMYTH' can be located. However, there is no indication to the searcher that the search term was entered inaccurately. In many cases it would be easy for the searcher to assume that the library did not contain

What type of search do you wish to do?
    1. TIL   –Title, journal title, series title, etc.
    2. AUT   –Author, illustrator, editor, organization, etc.
    3. A-T   –Combination of author and title.
    4. NUM –Classmark or control number.
    5. KEY   –One word taken from a title.
       BYE   –Enter BYE at any time to finish.

Enter number or code, then press CARRIAGE RETURN **5**

Type the title keyword you want to use below.

If you do not know the exact ending for a word use the symbol ú to stand for the unknown letters.
    e.g.: GHANA
    e.g.: TELEVISú (for televised, television, and televisions)

Enter keyword, then press CARRIAGE RETURN
ORGANIC
ORGANIC

Your Title keyword: Matches   361 titles

                                         No. of citations
                                in entire catalogue

	No. of citations in entire catalogue
1 Adsorption of organic compounds on electrodes	1
2 Advanced organic chemistry Part A Structure and mechanisms	10
3 Advanced organic synthesis methods and techniques	1
4 Advances in organic chemistry	1
5 Advances in organic geochemistry proceedings of the Inter>	4
6 The analysis of organic materials 2	22
7 Aqueous-organic systems	1
8 Aspects of the organic chemistry of sulphur	1
9 Aspects of organic photochemistry	1
10 Asymmetric organic reactions	1
11 Basic organic chemicals (except specialised pharmac>	1

Type the number of the book of your choice –OR–
    FOR – move forward in this list   CAT – begin a new search

Enter number or code, then press CARRIAGE RETURN

Search Example 12.4 *Search for a single word from the title in a first-generation OPAC*

material by the sought author, although this is unlikely with a name as common as 'SMITH'. An OPAC searcher who finds that a sizable OPAC does not contain any material by authors with a common surname should be suspicious about the search outcome and consider repeating the search.

What type of search do you wish to do?
    1. TIL   –Title, journal title, series title, etc.
    2. AUT   –Author, illustrator, editor, organization, etc.
    3. A-T   –Combination of author and title.
    4. NUM –Classmark or control number.
    5. KEY   –One word taken from a title.
       BYE   –Enter BYE at any time to finish.

Enter number or code, then press CARRIAGE RETURN **4**

  Which type of number do you wish to search? (choose one)
    1. CAL   –Classmark
    2. CSN   –ISBN or ISSN

Enter number or code, then press CARRIAGE RETURN **1**

    Enter the classmark below, including all punctuation.
    EX: 330.9
    EX: 621.380941

Enter classmark, then press CARRIAGE RETURN **547**

Your classmark: Matches at least   100 numbers

		No. of citations in entire catalogue
1	547	417
2	547. BAN	1
3	547. GIL	1
4	547. KIC	1
5	547. ORG	1
6	547.0014	8
7	547.00212	5
8	547.0024574	4
9	547.0028	22
10	547.00285425	1
11	547.003	8

Type the number of the book of your choice –OR–
  FOR – move forward in this list   BAC – move backward in this list
  CAT – begin a new search

Enter number or code, then press CARRIAGE RETURN

Search Example 12.5 *Classmark search in a first-generation OPAC*

The next two figures demonstrate the limitations of subject searching in early OPACs. One limitation is indicated in the menu at the top of Search Example 12.4. Option 5 in that menu indicates that it is possible to search for one and only one word in a document title. This may be helpful if the document title contained a precise and infrequently used term, for example 'antiforeignism' in the book *Antiforeignism and modernization in China, 1860–1980* by Kuang-sheng Liao (1984). However, it is of no value in searching for books with commonly occurring words in the titles, for example, the classic text *Geography: a modern synthesis* would be very difficult to retrieve by the title words. In Search Example 12.4 the searcher requires an introductory text on organic chemistry. There are 361 titles retrieved. It would be possible, if tedious, to browse through all of these. Certainly none of the items displayed on the first screen meet the requirements of the searcher. It is possible to search on this system by classmark and Search Example 12.5 represents an attempt to answer the same query by using this approach. The result is of no great help to the searcher since it reveals only how many books are classified as organic chemistry. It would be necessary to browse through them until a number of acceptable books were located. In essence, first generation OPACs are like searching a hard copy catalogue but with the searching performed at a terminal. Whilst this may be popular with users and improve the speed of searching it does not necessarily improve the quality of the searching.

Second-generation OPACs

Second-generation OPACs have their origins in the commercial bibliographic information retrieval systems of the 1970s and accordingly have greater similarity to the search services considered in other parts of this book. Second-generation OPACs are likely to be operated by a command language, albeit one which may well be simplified for use by inexperienced users. This generation of OPACs provides keyword searching, that is post-coordinate searching. Thus it offers the attendant benefits of search flexibility but also the possibility of false coordination of terms which are inherent in post-coordinate systems. Second-generation OPACs offer greater opportunities for subject access to the records within the database than do first-generation OPACs, but this improved subject access is inhibited by the lack of detailed content representation within the records, as noted earlier. An example of a search on a second-generation OPAC is presented in Search Example 12.6. Having taken the option to search by keyword, the term 'ecology' was entered by the searcher. This produced 322 items and so the searcher narrowed the search by adding the term 'heathland'. This reduces the number of postings to one and the document description is then examined. The similarity to conventional online bibliographic retrieval systems is apparent. This particular OPAC enables searches to be performed which combine terms from a variety of fields. The search history is presented at every stage. However, no more than five search statements can be made before a new search must be started and a further restriction is that it is only possible to use one or two terms in each search statement. Thus it is not possible to make a search of the variety:

s1 and (s2 or s3)

Second-generation OPACs suffer from two problems. First, it is very difficult to browse through the records in an OPAC of this type. Secondly, the large size and wide subject coverage of many catalogues in comparison with other bibliographic databases probably lead to too many searches suffering from *false drops* and/or too many 'hits'. An example of this is seen in Search Example 12.7 where a search for items on the history of Yorkshire retrieves a book on the birds of Yorkshire. This book is retrieved because it presents a historical treatment of the subject and the term historical appears in the title.

The experimental OPAC, OKAPI, used both keyword and phrase searching at different stages in the search process, although

```
-------------------------- * MAIN MENU *  --------------------------
You can Look at this Library's information page ....................................................I

     Find out which books are issued to you ......................................................R

     Look for a book by its computer book number ...........................................B

     Look for books by keywords (author, words .............................................K
         in the title or classmark)

     Look at the Subject Index ........................................................................S

     Look at external library catalogues............................................................X

     Get help with using the system ...............................................................H

     Exit from the system .........................................................................E
Type the letter indicating your choice and press RETURN K
         LOOKING FOR BOOKS OR JOURNALS BY KEYWORDS

  OTHER OPTIONS: To go back to the Main Menu type G then    RETURN
  For help type H then     RETURN
```

Enter search string 1:

A search string consists of one or two, but not more than two, keywords
A keyword is one of the following:

- An author's name (eg. BADDELEY A D or BADDELEY?)
- A word in the title of a book (eg. PSYCHOLOGY)
- A library classmark (eg. B 2.4 or SK 6?)

If two keywords are used they must be joined by the special words: AND, NOT or
OR (eg. BADDELEY A D AND B 2.4)

Enter search string 1 > **ecology**

Search number	Search string	Matches
S1	ECOLOGY	322

[Note: the search number may be used as a   OTHER OPTIONS
keyword in the following search string   [G – Go back]
to combine an earlier search string with   [H – Help]
a new keyword (eg. S1 AND PSYCHOLOGY)]

Type the search number to display the books found (eg. 3)
       OR enter search string 2>**S1 and heathland**

Search number	Search string	Matches
S1	ECOLOGY	322
S2	S1 AND HEATHLAND	1

[Note: the search number may be used as a   OTHER OPTIONS
keyword in the following search string   [G – Go back]
to combine an earlier search string with   [H – Help]
a new keyword (eg. S1 AND PSYCHOLOGY)]

Type the search number to display the books found (eg. 4)
       OR enter search string 5>**2**

FRIEDLANDER C P. HEATHLAND ECOLOGY. 1960
Shelved at: XC 5.8 FRI
Computer no. C001 4865 00 32   Not issued

Search example 12.6 *Subject search in a second-generation OPAC*

```
-------------------------- * MAIN MENU *  --------------------------
You can Look at this Library's information page ....................................................I

    Find out which books are issued to you .....................................................R

    Look for a book by its computer book number ...........................................B

    Look for books by keywords (author, words ...............................................K
       in the title or classmark)

    Look at the Subject Index ...........................................................................S

    Look at external library catalogues.............................................................X

    Get help with using the system .................................................................H

    Exit from the system ................................................................................E
Type the letter indicating your choice and press RETURN K
          LOOKING FOR BOOKS OR JOURNALS BY KEYWORDS
```

```
 ----------------------------------------------------------------
|  OTHER OPTIONS: To go back to the Main Menu type G then   RETURN  |
|                 For help type H then    RETURN                    |
 ----------------------------------------------------------------
```

Enter search string 1:

A search string consists of one or two, but not more than two, keywords
A keyword is one of the following:

  – An author's name (eg. BADDELEY A D or BADDELEY?)
  – A word in the title of a book (eg. PSYCHOLOGY)
  – A library classmark (eg. B 2.4 or SK 6?)

If two keywords are used they must be joined by the special
words: AND, NOT or OR (eg. BADDELEY A D AND B 2.4)

Enter search string 1 > **yorkshire**

Search number	Search string	Matches
S1	YORKSHIRE	472

[Note: the search number may be used as a   OTHER OPTIONS
keyword in the following search string   [G – Go back]
to combine an earlier search string with   [H – Help]
a new keyword (eg. S1 AND PSYCHOLOGY)]

Type the search number to display the books found (eg. 1)
        OR enter search string 2>**historical**

Search number	Search string	Matches
S1	YORKSHIRE	472
S2	HISTORICAL	1041

[Note: the search number may be used as a
keyword in the following search string
to combine an earlier search string with
a new keyword (eg. S1 AND PSYCHOLOGY)]

OTHER OPTIONS
[G – Go back]
[H – Help]

Type the search number to display the books found (eg. 2)
     OR enter search string 3>**S1 and S2**
Finding this information will take some time. Press RETURN to wait
or G to go back to search string prompt and use a more specific term

Finding this information will take some time. Press RETURN to wait
or G to go back to search string prompt and use a more specific term

Search number	Search string	Matches
S1	YORKSHIRE	472
S2	HISTORICAL	1041
S3	S1 AND S2	5

[Note: the search number may be used as a
keyword in the following search string
to combine an earlier search string with
a new keyword (eg. S1 AND PSYCHOLOGY)]

OTHER OPTIONS
[G – Go back]
[H – Help]

Type the search number to display the books found (eg. 3)
     OR enter search string 4>**3**

Search number 3   S1 AND S2   5 matches

1 HARLAND J> HISTORICAL ACCOUNT OF THE CISTERCIAN ABBEY OF SALLEY IN CRAVEN,

2 YORKSHIRE> HISTORICAL ACCOUNT OF THE LATE ELECTION FOR THE COUNTY OF YORK
3 WAINWRIGHT J> YORKSHIRE: AN HISTORICAL . . . VIEW OF THE WAPENTAKE OF STRAFF

4 EXWOOD J E AND UNWIN R W> YORKSHIRE TOPOGRAPHY: A GUIDE TO HISTORICAL SOUR

5 MATHER J R> BIRDS OF YORKSHIRE: HISTORICAL AND PRESENT STATUS AND DISTRIBU

Search Example 12.7 *False coordination in a second-generation OPAC subject search*

CATALOGUE ENQUIRIES MENU

> Code
> 1 AUTHOR+TITLE enquiry
> 2 AUTHOR enquiry
> 3 TITLE enquiry
> 4 SUBJECT enquiry
> 5 CLASSMARK enquiry
> / Return to main menu
>
> ? Help
> **4**

SUBJECT ENQUIRY

This enquiry looks for TITLES or SUBJECT HEADINGS containing as many as
possible of the words you enter

Enter a brief description of the subject
: **online public access catalogues**

> / to end, or to start a different type of search
> ? for explanations

SUBJECT KEYWORD ENQUIRY   Search Results
"online public access catalogues"
0 items match your search closely (0 records found altogether)

If you display the records the most similar ones should appear first)
> Code
> D to display the records
> B to go back and do a new search of this type
> E to edit or amend this search
> / to end or start another type of search
>
> ? Help
> **B**

SUBJECT ENQUIRY

This enquiry looks for TITLES or SUBJECT HEADINGS containing as many as
possible of the words you enter

Enter a brief description of the subject
: **online public access**
SUBJECT KEYWORD ENQUIRY   Search Results
"online public access"
0 items match your search closely (8 records found altogether)

If you display the records the most similar ones should appear first)
> SUBJECT KEYWORD ENQUIRY   Brief Display   records

"online public access"

----

1 Al-Janabi, Nasser Hussain. Automatic indexing and multi-access on information retrieval of a 1983

2 SCHAFFER, B.. IMPROVING ACCESS TO PUBLIC SERVICES. 1973

3 Public access to library automation. [1981]

4 Elder, Neil Colbert McAuley. Regionalism and the publicity principle. Sweden. 1973

5 Foster, Peggy. Access to welfare. 1983

6 Modern public records / Chairman Sir Duncan Wilson; presented to by the Lord High Chancellor. 1981

Enter   + (next page), LOCATION, FULL, BACK (to search results), /

Search Example 12.8   *Search on an OPAC incorporating some OKAPI features*

in both cases the search mechanism was invisible to the user. It is reasonable to suppose that this is the direction which ought to be taken by the next generation of operational OPACs. Search Example 12.8 shows a search on a system which has incorporated some of the approaches developed in the OKAPI project. A search is performed on the subject 'online public access catalogues' and no items are found. The searcher drops the last term from the search statement and repeats the search. The system responds by indicating that whilst there are no exact matches there are a number of near matches and the first six of these are displayed. At no stage in this interaction has the searcher been required to use any command language or to be involved with any boolean logic. An introduction to systems which do not require the searcher to understand command languages or boolean logic is provided in Chapter 13 whilst further explanation of the operation of the OKAPI system can be gained from Mitev, Venner and Walker (1985) and Walker (1988). The OKAPI projects are leading the way to the eventual implementation of more user-oriented systems which may become known as third-generation OPACs.

This chapter has demonstrated that Online Public Access Catalogues constitute a special type of bibliographic database and that searching these databases has similarities and differences with the searching of more conventional bibliographic databases. Their particular importance would appear to lie in the fact that they must cater for a very wide range of users, most of whom do not have skills in online searching. Thus OPACs are of considerable interest for the lessons which they can provide in the improvement of user-system interaction as end-user searching increases in importance. It should be clear from the sample searches that OPACs are different from each other and that the precise details of the search process varies between systems. The OPAC user must watch the screen carefully, note all instructions and follow them accurately making maximum use of any on-screen help messages.

References

Cutter, C. A. (1904) *Rules for a Dictionary Catalog*. Washington: Government Printing Office

Estabrook, L. (1983) Human dimension of the catalog; concepts and constraints in information seeking. *Library Resources and Technical Services*, **27** (1), 68–76

Hartley, R. J. (1988) Progress in subject access: anticipating the user. *Catalogue and Index*, **88** 1, 3–7

Lancaster, F. W. (1977) *Measurement and Evaluation of Library Services*. Arlington, VA: Information Resources Press

Liao, Kuang-sheng (1984) *Antiforeignism and Modernization in China, 1860–1980*. Hong Kong: Chinese University Press

Library Trends (1987) Public access online catalogues. *Library Trends*, **35** (4)

McClure, C. A. (1976) Subject and added entries as access to information. *Journal of Academic Librarianship*, **2** (1), 9–14

Markey, K. (1985) Subject-searching experiences and needs of online catalog users: implications for library classification. *Library Resources and Technical Services*, **29** (1), 34–51

Matthews, J. R. (1985) *Public Access to Online Catalogs*, 2nd edn. New York: Neal Schuman

Matthews, J. R., Lawrence, G. S. and Ferguson, D. K. (1983) *Using Online Catalogues: A Nationwide Survey*. New York: Neal Schuman

Mitev, N. N., Venner, G. M. and Walker, S. (1985) *Designing an Online Public Access Catalogue*. London: British Library (Library and Information Research Report 39)

Seal, A., Bryant, P. and Hall, C. (1982) *Full and Short Entry Catalogues: Library Needs and Uses*. Bath: Bath University Library

Tedd, L. A. (1987) Computer-based library systems: a review of the last 21 years. *Journal of Documentation*, **43** (2), 145–165

Walker, S. (1986) Ease of use in online catalogues: a plea for the user. *Online Access to Library Files: Proceedings of the Second National Conference (University of Bath April, 1986)*, edited by J. Kinsella, pp. 79–89. Oxford: Elsevier Information Bulletins

Walker, S. (1988) Improving subject access painlessly: recent work on the OKAPI online catalogue projects. *Program*, **22** (1), 21–31

Chapter 13

Beyond Boolean Searching

Introduction

"Present day services are, on the whole, inefficient and over-expensive products, packaged in the shiny wrapping of modern technology, and hostile to end-users" in the view of Cyril Cleverdon (Cleverdon, 1984). He goes on to explain that this is due to the understandable pressures of coping with the literature explosion and that modern technology is indeed needed – but it will be successful only if three changes are made. These are the use of natural language for searching, the provision of an alternative to boolean query formulation, and the marketing of small databases covering just the important journal papers. Cleverdon argues that cost would be relatively low, the recall performance would be quite adequate for most users, the precision performance would be markedly superior to present services, and the resulting system could be really user-friendly.

Cleverdon's first suggestion that natural language searching should replace controlled language searching has been adopted by many database producers and online searchers. Full-text databases such as the news files on Profile do not contain controlled terms and the user has no option but to search with natural language terms. Natural language input is also being tackled by expert systems, as discussed at the end of this chapter. Cleverdon's third idea, selective databases, has not yet become a reality. He suggests that a database to cover the natural sciences would contain about 400 000 papers per year, but to date no such database has emerged. It is not clear how these papers would be selected from the annual output of scientific papers which is considerably larger than this. The CD-ROM medium would seem to be the ideal means of making such databases available. The case for searching mechanisms which do not require boolean operators is made by referring to the results of several research experiments.

Cleverdon's other suggestion, that boolean query formulation be replaced by some other mechanism, has attracted considerable interest over the years. A number of rival methods have been proposed and in some cases retrieval systems have been constructed to put them into practice. It is to this aspect of Cleverdon's thinking that this chapter is devoted.

Boolean Searching Considered

There is an inescapable fuzziness and lack of precision in information retrieval of most kinds, so the critics of boolean searching can easily identify some of its problems. Firstly, it is said to be difficult for novices to learn and easy for them to make simple mistakes. A second problem is the frequent need to adjust the output size to make it larger or smaller, again sometimes requiring difficult decisions about boolean logic and the use of other retrieval facilities such as positional operators.

Thirdly, all output from a given search statement has equal status and no order of inspection is suggested, even though some items may have more terms in common with the query than others. For example, consider two document records with the following terms denoted by letters:

Document 1: A, B, E

Document 2: A, B, C, D, E, F

These two match equally if the search statement is:

A AND B AND (C OR D OR E OR F)

Yet it can be argued that presenting document 2 for inspection before document 1 would be helpful as its likelihood of relevance is higher because document 2 contains all the terms in the query statement whereas document 1 only contains three of the six terms.

A final problem with conventional boolean systems is that all the terms in both document surrogates and query representations are accorded an equal value or weight. It is reasonable to suppose that for both document and query representations some terms are more important than others. For a number of years researchers have investigated methods of giving weights to both query and document terms in an effort to improve retrieval performance and to provide an ordered or ranked output. It is by no means certain that their efforts have yielded a significantly improved performance and in any event the incorporation of weighted terms into conventional boolean searching has yet to be achieved as a different retrieval procedure is needed.

But arguments in favour of boolean searching are not hard to muster either. It is a logical and flexible way of processing queries to match with database records and exploits a quite conventional formal logic. One or more boolean search statements reflects the query structure clearly. Throughout a search what is happening is clear to the searcher as both the matching and non-matching records can be related unambiguously to the search formulation. Finally, as presently implemented on inverted files, a very rapid response to term postings is given and the logic itself is usually implemented rapidly to reveal the matching records. Whatever the merits of these arguments might be, however, alternatives to boolean searching have been formulated.

Automatic Query Formulation

The possibility of formulating and processing queries automatically is an interest of long standing to information retrieval researchers. The user must supply the query and make judgements on the relevance of the items retrieved, but all the processes in between these two activities should be performed by the computer with little human involvement. A simplified and introductory selection of topics in automatic searching will now be given, but van Rijsbergen (1979) and Salton and McGill (1983) should be consulted for more information.

Quorum matching

One alternative to the searcher constructing search statements of the right breadth using boolean operators is for the system to formulate the query automatically in some way. One method is called the quorum function (Cleverdon, 1984), which has been implemented on a trial basis by the ESA-IRS search service (Muhlhauser, 1985). Search Example 13.1 gives an example of a search using what ESA-IRS calls Questquorum. The enquiry is for documents on the use of an expert system or front end in information retrieval. The search commences by connecting to an

File 8:INSPEC: 1969–88, 22
SET ITEMS DESCRIPTION (+=OR;*=AND;–=NOT)

? RUN QUESTQUORUM
SETPAGEMODE Accepted

At any time type HELP for details, HALT to exit or X to go one
level back

Please type the terms which define your search subject
ENTER-**EXPERT SYSTEM FRONT END INFORMATION RETRIEVAL**

SELECTing:

SET	ITEMS	DESCRIPTION
1	11342	EXPERT
2	595796	SYSTEM
3	18688	FRONT
4	43926	END
5	173372	INFORMATION
6	17468	RETRIEVAL

COMBINing sets in quorum logic:

SET	ITEMS	DESCRIPTION	
7	5	01*06*03*04*05*02	*Level 6*
8	5	01*06*03*04*05– 7	
9	0	01*06*03*04*02– 7– 8	
10	1	01*06*03*05*02– 7– 8– 9	
11	24	01*06*04*05*02– 7– 8– 9–10	*Level 5*
12	12	01*03*04*05*02– 7– 8– 9–10–11	
13	43	06*03*04*05*02– 7– 8– 9–10–11–	

You have retrieved 5 relevant items
and 85 with less relevancy

Do you want to:

1 enter other terms
2 get a list of other possible terms
3 look at the items
4 exit
5 comment QUESTQUORUM service
ENTER–**3**

Do you want to display format:

1 short
2 medium
3 long
ENTER–**1**

Do you want to:

1 look at the items in sequential order
2 examine single items
ENTER–**1**

Please type P (next Page), D (Display next items) or X (eXit reading)

     DISPLAY 1
C88059316   INSPEC Journal Paper Issue 8821 88201631
  OAKDEC, a program for studying the effects on users of a procedural
expert system for database searching
     DISPLAY 2
C88053312   INSPEC Conference Paper Issue 8819 88187447
  Architecture problems in the construction of expert systems for
document retrieval
     DISPLAY 3
C88053310   INSPEC Journal Paper Issue 8819 68180582
  DIALOG aiming at an expert system
     DISPLAY 4
C86035499   INSPEC Journal Paper Issue 8613 86127263
  Document retrieval using a fuzzy knowledge-based system
     DISPLAY 5
C84035963   INSPEC Journal Paper Issue 8409 84134413
  A 'front-end' system: an expert system as an online search intermediary
ENTER–**P**
     DISPLAY 6
C88014488   INSPEC Conference Paper Issue 8805 88045942
  Expert front ends in the environment of multiple information sources
     DISPLAY 7
C88009062   INSPEC Conference Paper Issue 8803 88027873
  Applications of AI in addressing the shortcomings of current gateways
and front ends
     DISPLAY 8
C87042796   INSPEC Journal Paper Issue 8715 87135800
  Artificial intelligence and information retrieval
     DISPLAY 9

C87018162   INSPEC Conference Proceedings Issue 8707 87057938
Online '86 Conference Proceedings
   DISPLAY 10
C85051334   INSPEC Journal Paper Issue 8512 85194344
Why front-end systems?

Search Example 13.1   *Questquorum search from the INSPEC database on ESA-IRS*

appropriate database in the normal manner – the INSPEC file in this case. The special search facility is then invoked by the command RUNQUESTQUORUM.

Query terms are entered in any order without boolean operators – in this case the terms are EXPERT SYSTEM FRONT END INFORMATION RETRIEVAL. QUESTQUORUM automatically applies the boolean AND, starting with all of the terms entered. Thus Search Example 13.1 shows that set 7 results from ANDing sets 1 to 6, and in this case matches with five items. Notice that the computer ANDs the sets in order of increasing postings for greater speed, and shows what it has done using the * as the abbreviation for AND. This result is marked as level 6 as this is the result of ANDing all six terms.

Next the quorum function automatically relaxes this tight search by going down one level and matching every possible combination of five terms. Terms are dropped singly starting with the term with the highest postings; thus the first combination tried is set 1 and 6 and 3 and 4 and 5, and this produces five new documents. The next set tried produces no new items but the remaining three sets do. Each combination tried is restricted to items not previously matched by an automatic use of the boolean NOT, abbreviated to –. Level five contains six boolean statements, and altogether retrieves a further 85 items as Search Example 13.1 shows. The search stops after the first two productive levels are reached, although it does so after the first level if more than 50 items are retrieved.

When the items retrieved are displayed, the highest matching level is presented first, so the hope is that the most relevant items will be seen first. As many, or as few, items as desired may be displayed in three pre-specified formats. ESA's questquorum is menu-driven as can be seen in Search Example 13.1. Further terms can be entered and a list of possible terms can be obtained – this uses the ZOOM command described in Chapter 5. Term truncation is not automatic but requires the user to know the correct symbol '?'. The OR operator should not really be needed with quorum logic but if the user does decide to employ it to take account of synonyms it can be introduced by placing pairs of words in brackets, such as (EXPERT INTELLIGENT) meaning EXPERT OR INTELLIGENT. Prefixes and term proximity can also be used by an expert searcher but the necessary symbols have to be placed within quotation marks.

To summarize: simplicity for the searcher is achieved by hiding the use of boolean; output is in blocks in order of decreasing match with the query; and the use of the levels means that there is virtually always some output to inspect, and either the system or the searcher can stop after the desired amount has been reached. The result is claimed to be good for searches requiring high precision (Muhlhauser, 1985), but because many term combinations may be processed by the system the search time may be lengthy – the example shown took nearly four minutes.

Ranked retrieval

In order to present search output in a more refined ranking than the quorum function it is necessary to employ the technique of term weighting. In conventional boolean systems terms are either present or absent. For example, the sample bibliographic record in Chapter 3 Figure 3.6 on 'Market planning in the software industry' is indexed by 10 single-word terms taken from the title, abstract and descriptor fields. Since the words in the title occur in some of the other fields as well, and the word stem 'market' is repeated several times (six in this record), weights could be assigned to each term stem to reflect this. Figure 13.1 illustrates how this might be done. Against the 10 terms, it shows a term frequency value, a numerical weight reflecting the number of times they occur in the record. This is presumed to reflect the importance or value of each term as an access point for this record. These weights would have to be stored in the inverted index of the retrieval system, thus requiring additional storage space and an altered file structure compared with conventional unweighted systems.

The purpose of such weights is to enable queries to be matched with document records automatically by calculating a mathematical match value. Figure 13.1 illustrates this. It gives a typical query

Sample document

Stem	Term frequency	Postings frequency
Force	1	103
Forecast	1	21
France	1	48
French	1	56
Industr	3	1288
Market	6	1221
Plan	2	487
Profitab	1	108
Software	3	388
Stud	1	155

Sample query

"Marketing software in France"

Examples of three query/document matching equations

(1) Term frequency summation $= 6 + 3 + 1 = 10$

(2) Proportion term frequency $= \dfrac{6 + 3 + 1}{\text{sum of term frequencies}}$

$$= \frac{10}{20} = 0.5$$

(3) Term frequency and postings frequency:
[Term weight = Term frequency × Inverse postings frequency]

$$= \left(6 \times \frac{1}{1221}\right) + \left(3 \times \frac{1}{388}\right) + \left(1 \times \frac{1}{48}\right)$$
$$= (6 \times .00082) + (3 \times .00258) + (1 \times .02083)$$
$$= .00492 + .00774 + .02083$$
$$= .03349$$

Figure 13.1 *An illustration of document term weighting methods and query/document matching equations*

with the terms 'marketing', 'software' and 'france'. Word stems would replace these terms where appropriate, such as 'market'. The simplest matching equation is illustrated in number (1). The document weights for the three search terms are 6, 3 and 1, so summing these given a match value of 10. In a working retrieval system all the other documents containing one or more of the search terms would also have their match values calculated. For example, there might be a record indexed by 'market' and 'software' with a weight total of 15; or another with a value of 5, and so on. The end result of such a matching operation would be a rank ordered list of records with the highest match value at the top. A quite refined rank ordering would be achieved by this method and the searcher could inspect the records one by one until they appeared to be getting less appropriate to the topic of the search.

Figure 13.1 illustrates a second matching equation which expresses the match as a proportion. In the document record the 10 terms have a total weight score of 20 so a proportional query/ document match score for the example query could be 10 out of 20, or 50 per cent. This might well give a better result in the final ranked output in that long documents with a few matching terms would be ranked lower than shorter documents with roughly the same number of weighted term matches. Researchers have devised many other matching equations and compared this performance in small experimental tests.

Another technique of weighting the matching terms is also illustrated in Figure 13.1. Against each term in the document record is recorded the frequency of use of that term in the whole document collection or database. This postings frequency figure is high for 'industr' (1288) but lower for 'software' (388). A high frequency term is regarded as a poor discriminator, whereas a low frequency term is a good discriminator. This factor can be used on its own as the means of weighting the terms in a query/document matching equation, but in Figure 13.1 it is used together with record term frequency in a combined equation.

Equation (3) gives each matching term the weight value equal to the term frequency multiplied by the reciprocal of the postings frequency. (The reciprocal is one divided by the frequency, and is described by researchers as the inverse postings frequency.) So the term 'france', with low postings, will have a higher reciprocal (0.02083) than the term 'software' with a reciprocal of 0.00258; equation (3) therefore gives this query/document match a value of 0.03349, and when all matching collection documents were processed similarly a ranked search output would again be obtained. This mathematical mixture of term frequency and postings frequency is believed by many researchers to give the best result in promoting relevant records to the top of the ranked output list. The pioneering research work on weighting and ranking has been done with an experimental retrieval system known as SMART, developed by Gerard Salton and his associates at Cornell University (Salton and McGill, 1983). A system which compares boolean searching with ranked output for instructional purposes has been developed at Sheffield University (Hendry, Willett and Wood, 1986).

One way in which the results of a ranked output search are presented to the user is given in Search Example 13.2. The well-established text retrieval package, STATUS, now offers an 'Intelligent Query' version called STATUS/IQ (Pape and Jones, 1988). Search Example 13.2 shows an abridged version of a search on a database of Australian law reports for 'Cases involving the Administrative Law Act 1978, natural justice and the duty to act fairly'. The system receives this enquiry and analyses it automatically to identify four search terms. Term weighting factors are used to produce a ranked output. The factors include the density and clustering of the terms in the documents, the length of the documents, and the postings frequency of the terms. The query document matching equation gives a percentage score. Search Example 13.2 shows that two articles have matches of more than 75 per cent, two between 50 per cent and 75 per cent, and so on. The output display then gives a report on the top seven articles showing which they are, how many of the four query terms match, and the percentage match itself, followed by a display of the top eight titles. STATUS/IQ also offers a conventional boolean mode of searching and even allows a boolean start to a search and ranking to conclude it.

STATUS – Version 80, Release 4 – Incorporating IQ with NLQ
SELECT, CREATE or ENLARGE database:

≫ **select VICREP**

VICTORIAN REPORTS 1980–1984

> **iq**
Enter your Natural Language IQ Query
(terminate your query with '?' on a new Line):

Cases involving the Administrative Law Act 1978, natural justice and the duty to act fairly.
?

CURRENT NATURAL LANGUAGE QUERY

IQ–> Cases involving the Administrative Law Act 1978, natural justice and the duty to act fairly.

CURRENT SEARCH LIST

Q1 Administrative Law 1978
Q2 natural justice
Q3 duty
Q4 act//fairly

228 articles have been ranked.
  6 articles contain all 4 significant terms.

    Articles 1–2 have scores equal to or exceeding 75%.
    Articles 3–4 have scores between 50% and 75%.
    Articles 5–15 have scores between 25% and 49%.
    Articles 16–228 have scores less than 25%.

— RETRIEVED ARTICLES REPORT —

Rank	Article	Terms	Score%
1.	449	4	100
2.	505	4	98
3.	831	4	62
4.	277	4	56
5.	716	4	45
6.	409	4	38
7.	353	3	38

More ? Reply YES, No or QUIT:
x
> **titles 1–8**
* 1. KELLER v DRAINAGE TRIBUNAL AND MONTAGUE 1980 VR 449
  2. FOOTSCRAY FOOTBALL CLUB LTD v COMMISSIONERS OF PAY-ROLL TAX
    HAYES v COMMISSIONER OF PAY-ROLL TAX 1983 1 VR 505
  3. CHARLTON v MEMBERS OF THE TEACHERS TRIBUNAL 1981 VR 831
  4. O'ROURKE v MILLER 1984 VR 277
  5. TREVOR BOILER ENGINEERING CO PTY LED v MORLEY 1983 1 VR 716
  6. R v LIQUOR CONTROL COMMISSION EX PARTE SIMS SUPERMARKETS PTY LTD 1983 1 VR 409
  7. NICOL v ATTORNEY-GENERAL FOR THE STATE OF VICTORIA 1982 VR 353
  8. BORENSTEIN v COMMISSIONERS OF BUSINESS FRANCHISES 1983 1 VR 634

Search Example 13.2 *STATUS/IQ search sample (taken from Pape and Jones, 1988)*

Some Online Public Access Catalogues are now appearing with a limited form of term weighting and ranked output. One of the first was an experimental system known as OKAPI (Walker, 1987), and some of the results of this research have been incorporated into the Libertas system from SLS. An operating example is a system called Muscat, in the Scott Polar Research Institute in Cambridge (UK) which also offers conventional boolean retrieval. It indexes a fast growing collection which is searchable by assigned keywords and Universal Decimal Classification numbers (Porter and Galpin, 1988).

Relevance feedback

Searchers of conventional online systems regularly make use of clues spotted in citations retrieved in order to extend a search, clues from both relevant and irrelevant terms. Statistical counting aids are increasingly provided, and are available in most of the systems described which offer ranked output. The pioneering work on the SMART system aimed to make this process entirely

---

Search query
What information is available for dynamic response of airplanes to gusts or blasts in subsonic regime?

Initial search terms
airplane available blast dynamic gust information regime response subsonic

Selection of index terms of a highly ranked relevant document
gust (4) lift (4) oscillating penetration response (2) subsonic sudden

Search terms modified by relevance feedback
airplane available blast dynamic gust (5) information lift (4) oscillating penetration regime response (3) subsonic (2) sudden

A relevant document with rank improved from 14 to 7
gust (2) lift (6) penetration sudden

A relevant document with rank improved from 137 to 6
lift (7) oscillating sudden

Terms are all weighted one unless indicated in parentheses

Table 13.1 *An illustration of automatic relevance feedback from the SMART project (taken from Salton and McGill, 1983)*

automatic. Given the searcher's judgments of retrieved items as either relevant or irrelevant, the system could then be asked to perform another search modified automatically by relevance feedback to provide a new ranked output list. This is thought to improve the rank position of hitherto uninspected relevant items and demote the position of irrelevant ones (Salton and McGill, 1983).

The mechanism for automatic feedback would be the index terms: for example, it is possible to expand a set of query terms by adding new ones and re-weighting existing ones by means of the indexing contained in the relevant items. Table 13.1 illustrates automatic relevance feedback. Three of the nine initial search terms drawn from the query match a highly ranked document which the user marks as relevant (the terms are 'gust', 'response', 'subsonic'). Implementing relevance feedback increases the weights given to these three query terms so that 'gust' is weight 5, 'response' weight 3 and 'subsonic' weight 2. In addition, other terms present in the relevant document are added to the query: the four terms are 'lift', 'oscillating', 'penetration' and 'sudden'. A second or feedback search then takes place. This greatly improves the rank position of two other relevant documents because of the increased weights and added terms. Feedback could be repeated again, but on average little improvement is seen after the first attempt. The tests on the SMART experimental system do not always give such large performance improvements but the technique shows considerable promise.

Query processing and expert systems

Techniques of automating query processing include accepting queries in natural language, automatically creating stems from query words, displaying suggested additional search terms and identifying spelling errors. For example, an enquiry posed as 'the use of biofeedback and relaxation in the treatment of stress headache' is perfectly acceptable to the US National Library of Medicine catalogue CITE (Current Information Transfer in English). A list of some 600 stopwords (including the, use, of, and, in) identifies for processing the five keywords, in this example biofeedback, relaxation, treatment, stress and headache. The system also tries to identify spelling errors. In response to the above query example, CITE offered 13 search terms of various types: text words, medical subject headings, and subheadings, listed in frequency order. The system provides ranked output and relevance feedback (Doszkocs, 1983). STATUS/IQ has a natural language query interface. As Search Example 13.2 shows, the query in sentence form has various stop words removed and phrases recognized. The phrase 'duty to act fairly' is split into two concepts: 'duty' and 'act//fairly', where the '//' indicates that these two words are to occur in the same paragraph.

In OKAPI (Walker, 1987), experiments with automatic stemming have given results as good as the explicit truncation normally practised by skilled searchers. However, its indiscriminate use can produce some bad results, especially with single word queries, such as the topic 'communism' which retrieves everything on 'communication' as well. Automatic presentation of related words in an OPAC, with its normally wide subject coverage, is a severe problem: special lists of synonymous phrases will have to be developed, especially to deal with acronyms. Possible spelling mistakes and mis-keyed words are again not easy to detect automatically and to correct, so current OKAPI practice is to say *Can't find* to mis-spelt words such as SOCIALOGY or PSYCOLOGY. For name searching, where no matches occur, the system presents a list of names which sound similar.

Expert systems as search aids were discussed in Chapter 8, including CANSEARCH, based on hierarchies of menus offering access to specialized medical vocabulary. Another expert system, PLEXUS (Vickery and Brooks, 1987), is a prototype system containing a knowledge base on gardening, storing not only literature references but names of organizations and people, and details of other relevant databases. Input can be in natural question form such as 'Can you prune rose stems in spring?' Knowledge about the user is elicited by question and answer, and the meaning of the query can be elicited in the same way. To do this, more than 1000 rules are stored in the system. The intention is to provide the kind of interaction between user and system that might occur between user and reference librarian. A descendant of PLEXUS is Tome Searcher which is described in Chapter 8. Direct question-answering, then, is yet to come, but expert systems are moving towards this goal.

User–System Interaction

Will the online searcher have to continue to contend with boolean searching in the foreseeable future? Well, the possibility of a change in the external search services is unlikely given the effort and economics involved. It can be argued convincingly that present alternatives are not sufficiently better to justify change, that they have not been tested on a large enough scale, and that they could not give as good a response time as current systems. However, the CD-ROM environment may well provide a suitable smaller-scale situation in which several kinds of new user–system interaction can be offered. Acceptance in this realm would pave the way for changes in the larger systems.

Turning to Cleverdon's final requirement, the really user-congenial system has yet to be invented. Work continues on new ideas for the interface to retrieval systems, on what kinds of data can be offered within a system, and on understanding better the user's needs and problems.

Firstly, in the interface area, touch screens are used in some online systems (e.g. CANSEARCH) and some OPACs. Here the display of a menu or a vocabulary list can be controlled by the pointing finger, although clearly keyboarding is still needed in some circumstances. The use of voice is proposed for both input and output in searching (Philip, Smith and Crookes, 1988). Input would be by speech recognizer as well as keyboard, and output would come via a speech synthesizer as well as screen, probably using a telephone headset. It is suggested that this system would be more natural and convenient for users and that it could speed up the search process. It would certainly be of value to the visually handicapped.

Secondly, the database environment available to searchers can be broadened by means of linkages to citations, text, personal files, graphics, video, and so on. The idea is that associative trails offered by a system would allow new ways of querying and easier browsing in order to find related materials. Navigation would be by maps of various kinds, but such screen presentations are currently often difficult to follow even on a powerful personal workstation offering colour and graphics. The current term for these developments is *Hypertext* (Smith, 1988).

Thirdly, researchers are trying to design retrieval systems to respond to a user's information problem more helpfully. One proposed theory is that problems arise from an inadequacy in that person's extent of knowledge. So, if the structures of personal knowledge and problem areas can be better understood then appropriate retrieval mechanisms can be selected. New methods of dialogue with the user will be needed as well as better representation of content in databases by a choice of text structure to fit a given need. Only then, it is claimed, will users be truly satisfied with their online searches.

References

Cleverdon, C. (1984) Optimizing convenient online access to bibliographic databases. *Information Services and Use*, 4 (1–2), 37–47

Doszkocs, T. E. (1983) CITE NLM: natural-language searching in an online catalog. *Information Technology and Libraries*, 2 (4), 364–380

Hendry, I. G., Willett, P. and Wood, F. E. (1986) INSTRUCT: a teaching package for experimental methods in information retrieval: Part 1 The user's view. *Program*, 20 (3), 245–263

Muhlhauser, G. (1985) Dawn of next generation information retrieval. *Proceedings of the 9th International Online Information Meeting, London, December 1985*, 365–371. Oxford: Learned Information

Pape, D. L. and Jones, R. L. (1988) STATUS with IQ: escaping from the boolean straitjacket. *Program*, 22 (1), 32–43

Philip, G., Smith, F. J. and Crookes, D. (1988) Voice input/output interface for online searching: some design and human factor considerations. *Journal of Information Science*, 14 (2), 93–98

Porter, M. and Galpin, V. (1988) Relevance feedback in a public access catalogue for a research library: Muscat at the Scott Polar Research Institute. *Program*, 22 (1), 1–20

Salton, G. and McGill, M. J. (1983) *Introduction to Modern Information Retrieval*. New York: McGraw-Hill

Smith, K. E. (1988) Hypertext: linking to the future. *Online*, 12 (2), 32–40

van Rijsbergen, C. J. (1979) *Information Retrieval*, 2nd edn. London: Butterworths

Vickery, A. and Brooks, H. M. (1987) PLEXUS: the expert system for referral. *Information Processing and Management*, 23 (2), 99–117

Walker, S. (1987) OKAPI: evaluating and enhancing an experimental online catalog. *Library Trends*, 35 (4), 631–645

Appendix:
Case Studies

BDO Binder Hamlyn

BDO Binder Hamlyn is one of the 10 largest accountancy firms in the world with offices in around 50 countries. It offers a full range of services – accountancy, auditing, management consultancy and financial services. Its operations in Britain are distributed throughout 34 offices employing about 2500 partners and staff. The office in the City of London is the largest, with around 900 employees.

Information services for the entire BDO Binder Hamlyn organization within the United Kingdom are based in the London office, although some of the other offices do have extensive collections of books (these collections are not designated as libraries and their organization is rudimentary). Information Services, as the unit is called, is headed by an Information Manager, and is located within the External Microcomputer Consultancy Service of BDO Binder Hamlyn. The Information Manager, who also acts as a company consultant for a range of outside clients, is assisted by four other full-time staff, three of whom are qualified information professionals. This complement of six is frequently augmented by several accountancy students on attachment to Information Services. The London office also houses an Information Technology Research Centre which has one full-time information professional. The provision of specialized information is seen as an important part of the company's activities and currently some £400 000 is spent annually throughout the United Kingdom on information sources and services.

Much of the work undertaken by Information Services is of the enquiry type, typical examples of which would be share prices, exchange rates, or names and addresses of individuals and organizations. This work is done by the non-professionals. Library operations as such – ordering and cataloguing books, checking in periodical parts, etc. – are kept to a minimum and simplified as far as possible. One job which cannot be neglected in a financial service is the constant updating of loose-leaf books, a common form of publication in this rapidly changing area. Professional staff time is largely confined to information research – finding the answers to requests for information. This often involves not only complex searches through information sources but also processing the raw data in order to provide a specific answer to the query rather than a list of bibliographic references. The Information Manager also spends considerable time in explaining to users how the available information sources can best be exploited.

A financial organization such as BDO Binder Hamlyn requires accurate and above all current information. In order to provide an efficient and up-to-the-minute service, Information Services are very technologically-oriented and online searches form an important part of their work. In fact, the annual online budget is larger than the book budget; it currently stands at £70 000 and is growing at a rate of 50 per cent per annum.

Online searching began in 1983 with the appointment of the current Information Manager. There was an initial need to justify the provision of this new service and an effort was made to demonstrate how effectively online searching could answer a range of important information needs. From the outset there was a heavy reliance on non-bibliographic databases, and especially those supplying business and financial data, but a wide range of databases and online search services have always been used. The first services to be introduced were Reuter Textline and PRESTEL, both of which could provide relevant information without much difficulty. Reuter Textline, with its menu-driven approach, was especially popular with end-users as well as information staff and provided a good public relations image for online searching in particular and Information Services in general.

Many other databases and hosts have subsequently been added, including JORDANWATCH (PFDS); DUN & BRAD-STREET CREDIT RATING REPORTS (Dun & Bradstreet); MANAGEMENT AND MARKETING ABSTRACTS (Profile); MARKETING SURVEYS INDEX (Profile); and the STRATH-CLYDE DATABASE OF INCENTIVES. Reuter Textline also continues to be heavily used. The public services on PRESTEL (but not any closed user groups) are used for such things as news bulletins, information on local traffic congestion and weather forecasts. Access is also available to Telecom Gold but it is only employed very occasionally.

A measure of the important role occupied by online searching at BDO Binder Hamlyn is provided by the number of connect hours in a typical week: 28 hours' searching was being carried out at the end of 1988 on online search services (excluding PRESTEL). Much less use is made of PRESTEL: only about 15 minutes in a typical week.

The hardware used for online searching at BDO Binder Hamlyn is fairly standard. Most searches are done at an IBM PC XT (equipped with Breakout and Chitchat communications packages and a viewdata card). This is supplemented by an Amstrad 1512 HD20 and a Compaq 386, a Dataview Spark and a Finsbury Data Services dedicated terminal. Seven modems are available in Information Services and connection to remote hosts is made via the local PSS node.

An interesting feature of the Information Services department at BDO Binder Hamlyn is that end-users are actively encouraged to conduct their own online searches. This gives the information staff more time to generate new ideas and actively involves them with other departments by running training and updating courses in the use of online systems. Many end-users are taking advantage of this opportunity, some of whom are now regular online searchers. The most popular service amongst end-users is Textline, largely because of its provision of menu-driven searching which users find quite straightforward. A second advantage offered by Textline is that BDO Binder Hamlyn pays an annual subscription (£13 500) rather than paying by connect time. Such a method of charging should be more attractive to the relatively inexperienced and infrequent searcher who is not penalized financially for mistakes and slowness (other than incurring somewhat higher telecommunications costs). End-users are encouraged to search on command-driven services where charging is by connect time, and response generally has been enthusiastic.

Staff from the Information Services Department produce a monthly newsletter on new online developments, operate an internal help desk and assist with the more complicated searches as well as running in-house training courses.

Online search costs are charged to individual departments within BDO Binder Hamlyn. Online searches included in commissioned work for external clients are billed as a part of the total fee.

Online searching is carried out by all members of Information Services – professionals and non-professionals – but at present only the former use the command-driven systems. This is not so much because it is thought necessary to exclude non-professionals from the more complex systems but rather because there is sufficient work to keep the non-professionals busy elsewhere and none of them have expressed a particular desire to try these systems out. Staff from Information Services do take database training courses from time to time.

In-house computerized information retrieval systems are only now being introduced into Information Services. It is intended to use Micro-CAIRS for catalogue and journal subscription records throughout all the BDO Binder Hamlyn offices in the United Kingdom. Word-processing packages (Wordstar, Word Perfect), Supercalc and Dbase III are also available.

Information Services at BDO Binder Hamlyn, then, provide a wide range of services in the specialized business and financial fields. Overall, Information Services have the task of ensuring that both internal and external information systems are exploited rationally and efficiently. They are heavily involved in managing the total information resource for the company.

Birmingham Public Libraries

Birmingham Public Libraries (BPL) is a large metropolitan library system serving just over one million people living over a wide area. The Central Library has several reference departments (for example, Science and Technology, Business Information, and Social Sciences) as well as a lending library. In addition there are 45 branch libraries, one mobile library and 23 community libraries. The total budget for staff, books, binding, periodicals and so on is just over twelve million pounds.

The Science and Technology Department (STD) of BPL first became involved with online searching in 1978 when it joined with other public libraries (Lancashire, Cheshire, Hertfordshire, Leicestershire and Liverpool) in the first phase of a British Library Research and Development Department (BLR&DD) funded project (Siddall, 1980). This funding covered the provision of equipment (a Mellordata VDU, a keyboard and a printer, and the rental of a modem from the Post Office), training of staff and the costs of carrying out online searches. During the period of the project (November 1978 to March 1980) some 119 online searches were carried out at BPL; 55 of these were real-life searches for customers, 42 were for in-house library purposes and 22 were demonstrations to outside audiences. The search services used were BLAISE, Dialog, ESA-IRS and the original InfoLine.

STD has a very strong reference collection comprising over 380 000 volumes, over six million patents, subscriptions to about 800 periodicals and 80 indexing and abstracting publications (including *Chemical Abstracts, Engineering Index* and *Index Medicus*) and a good collection of UK and foreign standards and circuit diagrams. The 10 professional staff in the department handle some 330 enquiries each day; most of these enquiries can adequately be answered by means other than an online search.

In 1984 BPL acquired two Userlink integrated terminals which were capable of working at 1200 baud. One of these was placed in STD and the other in the Business Information Department (BID). The original Mellordata terminal is now in a Humanities Department where it is used for searching databases such as ARTQUEST.

STD uses a variety of search services including Dialog, ORBIT, ESA-IRS and Data-Star. Patent searching forms a large part of searching undertaken at STD and World Patents Index (WPI), as well as other patent databases are highly used. Searching is always carried out by one or other of the 10 professional staff, each of whom has been trained in at least two search services. This training has sometimes been carried by the host services but training databases such as the ONTAP series on Dialog are also used and some in-house training is undertaken. To assist in the problems of keeping staff up to date in online developments the head of STD was instrumental in setting up the local online user group (Weslink Online User Group) which holds monthly meetings on online matters for employees of the 60 or so organizations that are members. As would be expected in a public library the range of search topics is wide. Requests that had been answered recently by an online search by STD staff included:

> Information on AIDS in Lesotho (for a film producer).
>
> Is my idea for a windscreen washer mechanism that won't freeze novel?

The number of searches carried out by STD staff has remained at about 180 per year for the past three years.

The question of whether or not public libraries should charge for online searches is a major one. During the initial BLR&DD funded project a charge of £1.00 per minute plus the cost of online prints was made. Over the years this method of charging has remained, with the rate increasing to £2.00 per minute being applied at STD for bibliographic databases and £3.00 per minute for patent and business databases. However, as the charging algorithms are altered by the host services BPL may reflect these changes by charging for the actual cost incurred and perhaps a surcharge for the enquiry.

The BID at BPL began using online search services in 1984 and since then its use has grown rapidly. BID aims to provide information on business subjects and has a collection of some 18 540 books and subscribes to about 550 periodicals. In addition special publications, such as the *Companies Registration Office Directory*, the cards produced by the Extel Statistical Services detailing financial information on over 4000 public and 2500 unquoted companies and the McCarthy Cards Service (giving press coverage of companies and industries) are received. BID answers some 700 enquiries each day.

Initially the PREDICASTS range of databases on Dialog was used to assist in solving users' queries. By 1987 the most used service was Pergamon InfoLine (now known as PFDS) with databases such as KBE (Key British Enterprises), DUN AND BRADSTREET, ICC, JORDANWATCH, INDUSTRIAL MARKET LOCATIONS and so on. The whole area of business information online has developed greatly in recent years and looks likely to continue doing so. This poses problems for staff at BID who are so busy doing searches for customers that they find it difficult to find time to keep up with developments. Many of BID's customers are regulars and know specifically which databases they wish to be used.

A form (as seen in Figure A1) is filled in for each search undertaken. The actual charging of customers for online searches is carried out by the Administration Department. Estimates are given by BID staff to customers prior to a search; a general rule is that individual company accounts will cost between £6.00 and £12.00 each whilst lists of company addresses will cost between 6p and 30p per company. Search results may be mailed to customers or they may also be transmitted by fax. BPL took part in another BLR&DD project, this time experimenting with the use of fax machines in libraries, and has been using fax since 1984 (Tedd, 1987). BID currently carries out about 300 online searches a year, the average cost of which is £38.43. Between April 1988 and the end of January 1989 BID had spent £9221 on online searching and had received £5964 in income. These figures are less than for the comparable period in the previous year as many heavy users have now acquired their own terminals and passwords. The current rate of charging for BID searches is higher than that for STD searches and is currently £3.00 per minute plus the cost of prints. About five

BIRMINGHAM
Public Libraries

ONLINE INFORMATION RETRIEVAL SERVICE

SEARCH REQUEST

Name _____   Date _____

Tel. No. _____   Date/Time by which information

Organisation _____   required

Address for Results   Address for Invoices (if different
                                                              from results

DETAILS OF ENQUIRY
Title of Search

Details Statement of Search Topic (including
Keywords describing subject if possible)

Limits to Search e.g. Date range, Language etc.

Maximum charge prepared to incur (if appropriate)

Databases appropriate (if known)

Figure A1   *Search request form at Birmingham Public Libraries*

staff at BID carry out searching; all of these use PFDS and ICC;
there is no searching by end-users. Typical searches include:

> Details of the accounts of company X (ICC used).
>
> All companies in Herefordshire and Worcestershire involved
> in list of standard industrial classification codes (KBE used).

More complicated searches would request companies involved
with specific industries, with a specific turnover, a specific number
of employees and in a specific location. Such searches might

LIABILITY

WHILE REASONABLE CARE TO ENSURE ACCURACY AND COMPLETE-
NESS OF INFORMATION GIVEN IN RESPONSE TO ENQUIRIES IS TAKEN,
BIRMINGHAM PUBLIC LIBRARIES ACCEPTS NO RESPONSIBILITY
OR LIABILITY FOR ANY LOSS SUFFERED BY THE USER OF THE
ONLINE INFORMATION RETRIEVAL SERVICE OR ANY OTHER PERSON,
WHETHER ARISING FROM NEGLIGENCE OR OTHERWISE, ARISING AS
A DIRECT OR INDIRECT RESULT OF USE OF THE ONLINE INFORMATION
RETRIEVAL SERVICE.

N.B. Some charges are subject to fluctuation in rates of exchange.
V.A.T. is added to all charges.

Signature ....

FOR OFFICIAL USE ONLY

Date of Search _____   Search Strategy Used

Enquiry No. _____

Date Results sent to
Reader/Collected _____

Invoice/Receipt No. _____

Estimated Cost _____

Actual Cost (Ex VAT) _____

Exchange Rate Used _____

Charge to Reader _____

Searcher _____

Authn. _____

Please Return to :-

Figure A1(cont.) *Search request form at Birmingham Public Libraries*

involve a member of BID staff for 20–30 minutes; this includes the
search preparation, time spent online and resulting paper work.
Some online services such as PFDS and McCarthy's have run
training courses onsite at BPL for BID staff. The BID also
provides the viewdata services of PRESTEL, CEEFAX and
ORACLE for use (freely on demand) by customers. Such services
are used for up-to-the-minute share prices, commodity prices,
exchange rates and weather information. CCN is used through

PRESTEL to obtain credit ratings on companies and information on liquidations and so on; charges are made for these searches.

Staff in the Social Sciences Department at BPL also make some use of online search services using databases such as ABI/INFORM, FOREIGN TRADE AND ECONOMICS ABSTRACTS, MANAGEMENT CONTENTS, ACOMPLINE and the House of Commons database POLIS.

During 1988 BPL increased its number of terminals for online searching to five by acquiring two Apricot computers for use at STD and BID.

References

Siddall, P. M. (1980) *The On-line Information Retrieval Service at Birmingham Public Libraries*. London: British Library (BLR&DD Report No 5555)
Tedd, L. A. (1987) *Facsimile in Libraries Project*. London: British Library. (Library and Information Research Report 57)

Bronglais General Hospital

Since 1973 this library in a new purpose-built study centre has been providing library and information services to health care and administrative staff in Aberystwyth's general hospital (Bronglais), to medical and para-medical workers in the community, that is, general practitioners (GPs), health visitors, school nurses and so on, and to staff in the peripheral hospitals (Tregaron and Aberaeron) in the district. This results in a potential user population of just under a thousand. The library has a collection of about 2000 books and subscribes to 180 current periodicals. Bronglais Hospital is not a teaching hospital but has a postgraduate medical centre and junior staff coming (many from overseas) for attachment in various specialities. There are also medical students from the University of Wales' College of Medicine (UWCM) placed in the hospital for practical work and nurses (training to be Registered General Nurses) doing their practical work in the hospital, all of whom need to use the library for projects, case studies and so on.

Initially the library was staffed by one professional librarian; however since 1986 this post has been job-shared with each librarian working for 2½ days and having a 1½ hour overlap on Wednesdays to sort out various matters. The job-sharing has proved to be extremely effective and it ensures that a professional service is provided during holiday times and the inevitable sick leave. Also working as a one-person band can be demoralizing, especially during the current times of retrenchment, but sharing the job has proved to be a morale booster for both librarians. A volunteer based in the library also provides a service to hospital patients including the children's, old people's and psychiatric wards.

Until early 1982 literature searches were either carried out manually by the librarian using *Index Medicus* or something similar, or were sent to UWCM, which offered a free online search service to health librarians in Wales. However there were various problems in using such a remote service; the requester was not present during the search and so relevant references might not be retrieved; there was a time delay of about two weeks and so on. With an increase in the number of users requiring a literature search and some money left over at the end of a financial year it was decided that equipment should be bought to carry out online searches at the library. A Digital Equipment Decwriter dumb terminal was bought and a password acquired from Dialog. One reason for using Dialog was that the librarian was familiar with Dialog from library school days and had recently attended an 'Introduction to Online Searching' course at which Dialog was used. Other reasons given for using Dialog were "lots of free time for new users" and "useful ONTAP files". Becoming an efficient online searcher is not easy in a one-person library; attending training courses by database producer or online search service is difficult and there is no one on hand with whom to discuss results of searches. At that time (1982) MEDLINE was available on other host services apart from Dialog. Initially it was intended that a password be also acquired for BLAISE, which then had the MEDLINE databases available on its computer in Britain. However, in 1982 it was announced that access to the MEDLINE databases would be available via the BLAISE-LINK service to the National Library of Medicine in Washington (at an increased rate) and so this service was never used.

In 1984 Data-Star ran a free training course at UCWM for health care librarians in Wales and this was attended by the librarian at Bronglais. This, combined with favourable rates for health care librarians, resulted in Data-Star being now used for most of the searches. MEDLINE is the most used database; others include EMBASE (drugs), BMA PRESS CUTTINGS, DHSS DATA

(administrative and management information) and NURSING
AND ALLIED HEALTH (NAHL).

The current budget for the library is about £22000 and this
covers salaries, books, periodical subscriptions and online searching.
The average monthly bill from Data-Star is about 110 Swiss francs
(or roughly £500 per year). The annual number of searches has
grown from 158 in 1983 to 300 in 1988.

Requests for searches are received by telephone, letter or by
personal visit. The librarians tend to know their users well and can
assess the type of search required hence the reference interview is
fairly informal. Often, especially for clinical queries, the user stays
with the librarian whilst the search is in progress and will often use
the references retrieved to modify the original search request. The
two librarians tend not to share their searches, that is, a request
for information to one librarian is satisfied by that librarian; this
works well to everybody's satisfaction. One effect of being a one-
person band is that interruptions from the telephone (internally or
from the switchboard), from library users and so on whilst being
online are not uncommon; in such cases the librarian has to finish
that stage of the search, save it, log off and answer the query.

Some examples of recent searches undertaken include:

> Can you tell me more about Bandit – a smokeless tobacco
> that is highly addictive and is sold in this country to children?

This request came from a health visitor who wanted to satisfy a
mother's not unreasonable fears of this product. A search of
MEDLINE retrieved some relevant references, six of which were
located locally and the original articles given to the health visitor.

> Have there been any papers on the effects of using rifanpicin
> on contacts of a patient with meningo-coccal meningitis?

This request came from a GP who needed to decide whether this
antibiotic (rifanpicin) was suitable/effective for giving to colleagues
of a local student who had recently contacted meningitis. A search
of MEDLINE, with the GP in attendance, retrieved some relevant
references. Three of these were located in the library and were
immediately consulted by the GP who then decided on the
appropriate course of treatment. This search was carried out
immediately by the librarian.

> Post viral fatigue syndrome.

The consultant paediatrician in the hospital was holding a
seminar for parents, doctors and others related to children with

this debilitating syndrome. He asked for a search to be carried out to check on whether any papers on the topic had been published recently. A search of MEDLINE and the linked current-awareness file PREMED, which contains references from key medical journals pre-dating their appearance in MEDLINE by four to 12 weeks, revealed no new papers. In fact two of the main researchers of this syndrome in Britain were due to address the seminar.

Community hospitals in Wales.

The DHSS-DATA database, a database produced by the Department of Health and Social Security library in London and which is based on the library's abstracting and current awareness bulletins, was used for this search for a consultant sitting on a working party looking at this.

Violence to hospital staff.

This search came from a senior nursing manager in the hospital. Three databases were used in the search on Data-Star: DHSS, NAHL and MEDLINE. The *DHSS-Data Thesaurus* was consulted to help choose suitable search terms for the DHSS database and the MESH (Medical Subject Headings) thesaurus was used for the MEDLINE search.

There is no charge made for searches undertaken at Bronglais. All searching is done by the librarians; no users have yet suggested that they carry out the search themselves, and it is not envisaged that this will happen. So far the costs involved from the inevitable increase in requests for interlibrary loans as a result of an online search have not been too great. Sometimes the abstract has provided sufficient information. If the full text is not in the library's collection then the union list of holdings of Welsh health librarians is consulted and this free interlending service is used; otherwise the library of the British Medical Association (BMA) is used and finally the British Library Document Supply Centre.

In 1984 Bronglais was the only library in a district general hospital in Wales offering an online service and so the librarian was asked to talk to gatherings, such as the hospital consultants who organize the postgraduate training programme. Further talks have been given to local doctors and postgraduates in their clinical lunchtime meetings. One of these talks was aimed at promoting Data-Star's CLINICAL NOTES ONLINE database which was a compilation of case notes submitted by clinicians in hospital, general or other practices of concise accounts of notable cases; this database was discontinued in late 1987. Also, with a rapid turnover of some categories of staff, 'introduction to the library' talks are given each month and the online service explained to the new potential users. Staff from the library were also involved in the annual study conference of the Medical, Health and Welfare Librarians group of the British Library Association which, in 1987, was held in Aberystwyth; a paper by the volunteer resulted in the publication of *Miffy and others in hospital: library service in a children's ward* describing the work done at Bronglais in this area.

In March 1987 an OPUS II (IBM-PC compatible) microcomputer was acquired. This is currently located in a lockable room away from the library because of the problem of securing it effectively with the library being open 24 hours a day. The OPUS is used for word-processing lists of journals, volunteer rotas and so on. During 1988 it was decided that a package for building and searching in-house databases be acquired. For reasons such as versatility, cheapness and positive experiences in a local institution the CARDBOX-PLUS (version 4.0) package was chosen and acquired for £350. In a one-person library it is difficult to find time to develop and implement any new system. At Bronglais a person on the Employment Training Scheme has been allotted to the library for three days a week to assist in this work. He is developing the use of CARDBOX-PLUS for in-house cataloguing of books and controlling loans. The use of CD-ROM databases has not yet been investigated although it is thought likely that one might be acquired in the not too distant future.

Plymouth Polytechnic (now Polytechnic South West)

Plymouth Polytechnic is a higher education institution in the south west of Britain offering courses at first degree, higher degree and sub-degree levels to more than 5,000 students and conducting a high level of research. In both teaching and research, there is a heavy emphasis on science, technology and business studies. The Polytechnic is organized into five faculties: Science, Social Science, Technology, the Plymouth Business School and the Institute of Marine Studies. These faculties are further divided into 19 departments. The work of the faculties is supported by central academic services provided by Computer Services, Library Services (formerly the Learning Resources Centre or LRC) and Student Services under the direction of an Assistant Polytechnic Director of Academic Services. Several smaller colleges at other locations in Devon are to become a part of the polytechnic and to reflect this the name is to be changed to Polytechnic South West in 1989.

The Learning Resources Centre (LRC) provides library services, media production services and educational advisory services to the Polytechnic. In 1987–88, the total budget of the Centre was approximately £1 200 000 of which £441 000 is for the purchase of library materials (books, journals, audiovisuals, etc.) and services (for example, online searching and library automation). The library has approximately 170 000 volumes and subscribes to about 2000 periodicals. The library is staffed by 41.5 full-time equivalent staff of whom 15 are professionally qualified librarians. The library has a central services unit which provides acquisitions, cataloguing and circulation services. Services to library readers are organized through four subject teams: science, technology, social sciences and business studies. These subject teams are responsible for the provision of library services including online searching and guidance on the effective use of the library and its information sources to staff and students within their subject areas.

Online searching was introduced to the LRC in April 1980 with a view to extending the range of sources which were available for use with both retrospective searching and current awareness activities. It was also envisaged that online searching would enable the library staff to provide an effective information service to a greater number of its clientele. The first equipment used was a Teletype 43 teletype terminal and an Anderson Jacobson acoustic coupler. In addition, a large screen television with appropriate adaptor was rented to provide access to the teletext systems, CEEFAX and ORACLE, and to the videotex system, PRESTEL. In 1984, the Teletype was replaced by a BBC microcomputer with an Epson FX80 printer, and the acoustic coupler was replaced by a Minor Miracles WS2000 modem. The modem provides communications at both v21 and v23 standards. The microcomputer was fitted with the COMMSTAR communications chip, which enables access to conventional online search services and to public videotex services such as PRESTEL. A dedicated LEXIS terminal was acquired in collaboration with the Business School in 1987. In 1988 the BBC microcomputer was replaced by an IBM PC-AT compatible with an internal modem and the communications software, Mirrorsoft, is used.

The television set is housed in the library quick reference collection facing the entrance. Teletext is heavily used by students to check share prices, election results, budget news and other transitory information. PRESTEL is used occasionally for checking commodity prices but generally it has not been heavily used because the library staff found that it did not have adequate depth to its information. The LEXIS terminal is housed in a small room on the business and social studies floor of the library. The microcomputer which is used for the bulk of the online searching is housed in a similar small room on the technology floor of the library; both these terminals then are well away from public view.

In the 1987–88 budget, £12 000 was allocated for online searching. The Polytechnic has recently entered into a contract for use of LEXIS at the rates charged to law schools (in 1988, approximately 100 hours of searching was obtained for a subscription fee of about £1500, shared between the LRC and the Business School). Advance payment arrangements have not been entered into with any other search service. Online searching is available to all library users without any charge. However, most of the searches are performed for academic staff and research assistants. Searches are only undertaken for students when the appropriate subject librarian takes the view that in the circumstances this is the most appropriate action. This usually means that the student must demonstrate that print resources in the library have already been exhausted.

An analysis of use for the period September 1986 to August 1987 but excluding use of teletext services and LEXIS revealed that Dialog was by far the most heavily used of the search services with approximately 50 per cent of all searches carried out on this service. About 25 per cent of searches were performed on ESA-IRS and the remainder were spread over ORBIT Search Service, Pergamon InfoLine, Data-Star, World Reporter and BLAISE. The most heavily used databases are the large general bibliographic databases with approximately 40 per cent of all searches carried out on just four: BIOSIS, CA SEARCH, COMPENDEX and INSPEC. A further 10 per cent of searches were carried out on three more databases namely INFORM, MANAGEMENT CONTENTS and PSYCINFO. The remaining 50 per cent of searches were spread across 82 other databases, covering a wide spectrum of bibliographic and factual sources but none accounted for more than 2 per cent of searches. This kind of information is easily obtained from the simple record sheets which have been devised to note search details for accounting purposes, as seen in Figure A2.

The library takes the view that any professional member of the subject teams can be an online searcher, that is, that online searching is seen simply as a part of information and reference services. However, it is clear that most of the searching is undertaken by perhaps four people, reflecting a combination of

ONLINE SEARCH RECORDS
=================

(Please use a separate form for a different host/session)

HOST SYSTEM:
(tick one)   ____ Dialog (L)   ____ BMT Abstracts (BMT)
             ____ ESA Dialtech (ESA)   ____ World Reporter (WR)
             ____ InfoLine (I)   ____ Prestel (P)
             ____ SDC Orbit (SDC)   ____ Blaise (B)
             ____ Datastar (DS)   ____ Other (specify) ____

Date of search   Line failures?

DATABASES ACCESSED:

Please use standard name (see comparative cost chart)
(if dialnet used, include below, on a separate line)

Name	Cost	Time online	Online refs	Offline prints

ENQUIRER (DEPARTMENT & NAME) _____
STATUS: ACademic/RESearch/ADMin/PG student/UnderGrad/LRC/____)
LRC SEARCHER: _____   TEAM: B / S / T / Z / None

Figure A2 *Search request sheet at Plymouth Polytechnic*

the variations in bibliographic control in different subject areas and the preferences and skills of the various staff concerned. In addition to the two professional staff in the Business Studies subject team, LEXIS is also searched by three members of the

LEXIS SEARCH REQUEST FORM
===================

Name: Course:

Date and time of search (if arranged)
Date search required by (if not yet arranged)

Subject of Search:

Search terms to be used:

Concept 1	and	Concept 2	and	Concept 3
or		or		or
or		or		or
or		or		or

Files to be searched:

UK cases   UK statutes   Tax files

UK statutory instruments   European law

Index to legal periodicals / Legal resource index

Maritime law   USA law

Others (please specify)

Please fill in this form before beginning each search on LEXIS, whether LRC staff are doing the search with you or if you are doing the search yourself. You need to know how you intend to do the search before switching on the LEXIS terminal. Please ask for help if you need it.

Figure A3 *LEXIS search request sheet at Plymouth*

staff of Plymouth Business School and by an increasing number of students from that school. There is a number of students, for example in Computing and Informatics, for whom online searching has been incorporated into the course. Additionally, the use of online search services is being steadily introduced to the student population through the extensive library user education programme. A search request form as seen in Figure A3 has been introduced for LEXIS searches and it is hoped that this can be extended for use with all online searches in the near future.

A public access CD-ROM facility was introduced early in 1989. This provides access to three bibliographic and two source databases on the science floor of the library. The response from students has been very enthusiastic and it is intended to provide further players on the other two floors of the library as soon as possible. The impact of this development on the use of online search services cannot yet be determined. However, some of the bibliographic databases on CD-ROM have been bought at the same time as their print equivalents have been cancelled (for example, AQUATIC SCIENCES AND FISHERIES ABSTRACTS).

Unilever Research Port Sunlight Laboratory

Unilever is an Anglo-Dutch company formed in 1930 by the merging of the British firm of Lever Brothers and the Dutch Margarine Union. It is the parent company of many subsidiaries throughout the world covering diverse products such as:

1. Edible fats and dairy produce (for example, margarine and yoghurts).
2. Frozen foods and ice-cream.
3. Food and drinks (for example, Lipton's tea and canned fish).
4. Detergents.
5. Personal products (hair shampoo, toothpaste, soap).
6. Speciality chemicals.
7. Agribusiness.
8. Paperboard and packaging materials.

Unilever companies operate in more than 75 countries with 60 per cent of the sales being in Europe and around 20 per cent in North America.

The research laboratory at Port Sunlight (URPSL) is one of the three main large multi-disciplinary research laboratories within

Unilever's Research and Engineering Division. The other main research laboratories are at Colworth, Bedfordshire in Britain and at Vlaardingen near Rotterdam in the Netherlands; there are smaller research laboratories in India and in the United States. The aim of these research laboratories generally is to improve existing products and processes, to provide products which are safe, reliable and good value for money and to identify and develop new opportunities arising from advances in science and technology.

At URPSL the staff in the information centre are part of the information technology section of 80 people. This section also comprises the centralized computer services, office technology, communications, micro-electronics, the photographic unit and development. The aims of the information centre are to:

1. Respond to enquiries or specific requests for information.
2. Keep clients/users aware of developments in particular areas of interest.
3. Help clients use the laboratory's information services to manage their own information.
4. Provide facilities of a traditional library service.

These services are provided to the 600–700 professional scientists at URPSL by 20 information centre staff of whom about half have scientific degrees.

URPSL has used external online services for searching the published literature since late 1976. Early systems used were Dialog, SDC, BLAISE and the New York Times (Tedd, 1979). By 1988 URPSL was using about 15 host services with the most used ones being Data-Star, Dialog, ORBIT (for patent searching) and PFDS. Other systems used for specific searches include:

1. ESA-IRS as it is sometimes cheaper than Dialog, it has some unique databases and it has a gateway to Textline.
2. Télésystèmes-QUESTEL for some patent searching and for the Markush-DARC system for searching chemical structures generically.
3. STN for chemical substructure searching of CA SEARCH.
4. BLAISE for toxicity databases and book details.
5. CIS for specialist ecotoxicology data.
6. Dialcom for some business/commercial queries.
7. ECHO for the EURIDICATOM database for translation purposes.

8. Datacentralen for ECDIN, the CEC's chemical/environmental database.

A wide number of databases are used on the main host services with the most frequently used ones being:

1. CA SEARCH.
2. WPI.
3. MEDLINE.
4. BIOSIS.
5. EMBASE.
6. PREDICASTS PROMT.
7. SCISEARCH.
8. COMPENDEX.
9. INSPEC.

Each month one of the information specialists draws up a comparison chart of the connect hour, online print and offline print charges in £s of these databases on Dialog, ESA-IRS and Data-Star to assist the searchers to decide which host service to use for a particular search. Other factors which affect the searcher's choice of service include:

1. Command language features. Information centre staff feel that Dialog's proximity operators are more powerful than those on ESA-IRS.
2. Loading of database. For example, INSPEC is loaded as one file on Data-Star.
3. Range of databases available. Many of URPSL's queries need to be searched on various databases, for instance dental queries are usually searched on MEDLINE, BIOSIS and CA SEARCH and so OneSearch on Dialog would be used.

The technical searches are mainly carried out by one of the four information specialists each of whom is linked to specific sections within the laboratory. Requests for information normally come by personal visit or telephone call and following a discussion on the nature of the request a form is filled in as shown in Figure A4. The form includes details for the costing of the job as well as search details. If an online search is thought to be the appropriate way to solve the query the searcher decides on the database(s), system(s) and the search strategy. (The only printed abstract and indexing publication received in the library is *Chemical Abstracts*.) Clients are able to sit-in on a search and new employees at the

INFORMATION CENTRE: REQUEST FOR INFORMATION

Enquirer:	Name:
Group: Division: Section:	
Task No:	Date received:
Cost Location:	Date completed:
Telephone ext:	Time Taken:

Description of enquiry:

****

Enquirer's Comments

Figure A4 *Search request form at Unilever*

laboratory are particularly encouraged to do so. A search takes on average about 2.5 hours; this includes the pre-search interview, search strategy formulation, time spent online and post search work. The actual time spent online per search is about 30 minutes; this may not be all at once as some searches may require the use of different hosts. The client is given details of the search strategy and the retrieved references.

IBM PC look-alike microcomputers, with hard discs, are used for searching. Each of the four information specialists has one of these. A local area network links the PCs to the centralized VAX mainframe computer in the building and this has a CASE modem capable of linking to PDN. Search results may be downloaded for later printing or printed online. A laser printer attached to the centralized mainframe is used for all printing. The information centre at URPSL moved away from having individual printers linked to the PCs for reasons of faster printing, less noise and better quality output. The communications software used on the

PCs is AUTOSEARCH, supplied by Cowie of Stirling University. This is an enhanced version, for IBM PCs, of an original software package developed by Cowie and Petrie (Cowie and Petrie, 1982) for use on Cifer microcomputers in the early 1980s. It performs functions such as:

1. Being able to store search statements before going online.
2. Automatically logging on to various hosts.
3. Uploading the search statements one at a time with each one being executed as it is input.
4. Downloading retrieved references to the local hard disc.

Most of the technical queries are of the type:

What work has been done on X?

What are the properties of chemical X?

What patents are there related to X?

Usually these queries need a fairly exhaustive search of the published literature to ensure that scientists do not spend time in the research laboratory re-inventing the wheel or producing potentially harmful products. Because of this need for detailed searches there has not been a pressing demand for end-user searching. However, following a request from its management, during 1987 the information centre ran an experiment to train about 14 clients to do their own searching. It was decided that they be trained to search one database on one host service. CA SEARCH was chosen as the database as they were all chemists and familiar with the printed version of *Chemical Abstracts*. Data-Star was chosen as the host as it provided assistance in training end-users and its billing system enabled separate passwords to be given to end-users. However, it was found that the Data-Star command language was not particularly helpful to naïve users. For instance a search statement of the form CARBON MONOXIDE actually translates into CARBON OR MONOXIDE and so retrieves many irrelevant references. A 1½ day course was organized by Data-Star and held at URPSL. Information Centre staff were insistent that a chemist actually train the end-users and so a consultant chemist and experienced searcher was brought in by Data-Star to run the course. During the months following the course participants were able to carry out their own searches and were then assessed. The full analysis of these results was in progress at the time of the visit.

Business and commercial queries are carried out by the librarian in the information centre; these queries are of the type:

What is the market for product X in country Y?
(Predicasts PROMT might be used)

What is the financial state of company X?
(Disclosure or ICC might be used).

Current-awareness services are provided in two ways. Some 30 biology or chemistry related profiles are stored at the United Kingdom Chemical Information Service (UKCIS), which offers a card-based alerting service of new references. Also about 15 profiles (some of which may be confidential and so might present problems in being run on an external service) are stored on a variety of host services which offer SDI commands. URPSL stopped producing an information bulletin in the early 1980s.

The total budget for online searching of external host services in URPSL is about £60 000; this compares with the total budget for the information centre (which includes salaries, etc.) of £450 000. The online searching budget covers training, development, end-user education and training as well as the actual costs incurred in carrying out the searches. During the calendar year 1987, £16 000 was spent on Data-Star, £11 000 on Dialog and about £3000 on ORBIT. In order to take advantage of discount rates offered by the host services and to have separate passwords for individual groups within URPSL (to ease potential billing problems) the information centre has joined up with similar information centres at other Unilever laboratories and with headquarters.

Text retrieval software developed within Unilever is used at URPSL for retrieving information on internal reports, the patents catalogue, the library catalogue and so on. The system is used by scientists within URPSL and a menu-based approach was incorporated into the software to assist the naïve user (Henry, 1984). In addition a prototype system (PS) was developed in the mid-1980s to convert commands from the in-house system into suitable commands for an external host service. The aim of this experiment (Teskey, Henry and Christopher, 1987) was to provide end-users with the chance to search the external services using similar commands to those they would use for searching in-house databases.

Requests for the full-text of retrieved items from online searches are currently satisfied either from the 450 or so journals subscribed to by the library or by request, via ARTtel, to the British Library

Document Supply Centre (BLDSC) at Boston Spa. The information centre plans to acquire the TINlib software (*Vine*, 1987) in the library to assist with the management of BLDSC requests and loans and subsequently with serials control generally.

The information centre at URPSL has used PRESTEL but decided in 1987 that this service should be discontinued as it did not include relevant information. A password has been acquired for Easynet; however, the information specialists do not, at present, find this method of accessing the host services very useful. There are no CD-ROM databases used at URPSL at present although the information specialists are keeping aware of developments in this area.

In the future the communications facilities will be upgraded thus enabling more end-users to carry out searches. It was thought likely that more training of end-users would be undertaken, possibly using Dialog's Medical Connection service, which provides a menu-based approach to several databases such as CA SEARCH, MEDLINE and BIOSIS and which is aimed at end-users. There was a strong feeling that end-users should be well supported by the information centre after their initial training. In the longer term the development department within the information technology section is looking at free-text searching linked to interactive videodiscs.

References

Tedd, L. A. (1979) *Case Studies in Computer-Based Bibliographic Information Services* BLR&DD Report No. 5463. London: British Library

Cowie, J. and Petrie, H. (1982) A microcomputer-based terminal for assisting online information retrieval. *Journal of Information Science*, **4** (1), 61–64.

Henry, W. M. (1984) Viewdata-type searching, a free-text (DECO) system: modifications that make searching easier for inexperienced searchers. *Program*, **18** (4), 308–320

Teskey, N., Henry, M. and Christopher, S. (1987) A user interface for multiple retrieval systems. *Online Review*, **11** (5), 283–296

Vine (1987) TINlib from Information Made Easy. *Vine*, **69**, 31–39

Index